il faut **V**ISITER

l'exposition

SUR_rÉALISTE

7 AU 18 JUIN

à la

GAL**ERIE** PIE**r**RE Colle

29, rue Cambacerès

de 10 h. à 12 h.
et de 2 h. à 6 h.

Marcel Duchamp : *The Bride Stripped Bare by her Bachelors, Even.* 1915-1923.

Mourir pour la Patrie. Twenty four drawings and a preface; captions, by André Jean.   Cahiers d'Art, Paris 1935.

Pêche pour le sommeil jeté.   Poems.   Sagesse, Paris 1937.

Mnésiques.   Hungaria, Budapest 1942.

Sites.   Collection of Etchings.   Privately printed.   Paris 1953.

In collaboration with Arpad Mezei:

Maldoror.   A study of the life and work of Lautréamont.   Le Pavois, Paris 1947.

Genèse de la Pensée moderne: Sade, Lautréamont, Rimbaud, Mallarmé, Jarry, Apollinaire, Roussel. Corrêa, Paris 1950.

THE HISTORY
OF SURREALIST
PAINTING

BY MARCEL JEAN

WITH THE COLLABORATION OF ARPAD MEZEI

TRANSLATED FROM THE FRENCH BY
SIMON WATSON TAYLOR

Grove Press, Inc. New York

'He lived there in two rooms which he had covered from ceiling to floor with most strange and troubling designs that made certain distinguished critics repeat for the thousandth time:

IT IS NOTHING BUT LITERATURE.'

G. de Chirico, *Le Fils de l'ingénieur*.

I would like to acknowledge my indebtedness to all those who have offered me their help during the course of the long elaboration of this *History of Surrealist Painting*.

On the theoretical level, my friend and collaborator Arpad Mezei has made an invaluable contribution, especially in the studies concerning Chirico, Max Ernst, Miró, Magritte, Tanguy, Dali and Dominguez, and in several other parts of this book.

In the documentation of events, I have received a mass of information, about themselves or about happenings in which they participated or of which they were witnesses, from Suzanne Duchamp, Kay Sage, Dorothea Tanning, Isabelle Waldberg; Jean Arp, Hans Bellmer, William Copley, Joseph Cornell, Jean Crotti, Enrico Donati, Marcel Duchamp, Max Ernst, Wilhelm Freddie, Wifredo Lam, Gherasim Luca, E.L.T. Mesens, Man Ray, Hans Richter, Clovis Trouille, Raoul Ubac, Jacques Villon; Mlle Marguerite Hagenbach and Mme Simone Collinet; Adolphe Acker, Marcel Duhamel, Robert Lebel, Pierre de Massot, Walter Pach, Henri Pastoureau, Jacques Prévert, Henri Roché, Suzuki, Robert Valançay, Patrick Waldberg, Simon Watson Taylor. I have thus been able to complete or rectify my information or my personal recollection. I express my particular thanks, in this respect and in many others, to Kay Sage, Jean Arp, Marcel Duchamp.

The generosity of the Noma and William Copley Foundation enabled me to arrange a voyage to the United States which helped to complete my documentation.

I obtained useful clarifications on important points, and was able to consult numerous documents, through Steen Colding of Copenhagen, Pierre Courthion and Poupard-Lieussou of Paris, Giovanni Scheiwiller of Milan, Julien Levy and James Thrall Soby of New York, Barnet Hodes of Chicago, the Jacques Doucet Fund of the Bibliothèque Sainte-Geneviève of Paris, the Library of the Museum of Modern Art of New York.

Francis Picabia, before his death in 1952, provided me with many details about his career; Mme Olga Picabia, his widow, and Mme Gabrielle Buffet-Picabia also made documents available to me. My personal memories of my departed friends, Yves Tanguy and Oscar Dominguez, have, of course, found their place in this *History*.

PART ONE
SURREALIST PAINTING BEFORE SURREALISM

Georges Seurat : *The Circus*. 1890-1891.

CHAPTER ONE
WHICH DEALS WITH THE ARTISTIC AND ANTI-ARTISTIC REVOLUTIONS FROM 1870 TO 1914

Impressionism, making its first appearance in about 1870, originally involved a deliberate restriction of the art of painting to the basic facts of *sight:* the impressionist painter made it a rule to represent only what was strictly optical, since he considered that his particular means of expression did not permit any greater extension of the field of representation; the artist seemed to envisage nothing beyond making the best of this inevitable limitation. As a result the picture became extremely homogeneous, but, at the same time, contained almost nothing except the immediate visual sensation.

These conclusions are valid in regard to those painters of the new school who abided by their own precepts. But Impressionism could not define itself simply by restrictive notions: even the art of 'pure' impressionists like Monet tends to evoke philosophic theories, such as the mysticism of light of Plotinus and the neo-Platonists. Plotinus said that sight sees everything except itself; that consequently one must find the means of swimming against the visual current so as to succeed to some extent in 'seeing sight'. It would seem that Impressionism provoked a movement of just this sort, which in a sense was the very opposite of its initial proposition, and that its extreme specialization ultimately provided the means for the development of painting in a new direction.

Since all true art is a representation of the world, it should apprehend equally the world's external and ephemeral aspects and its structural and time-space values. The art of painting can become truly representational only if it is able to elucidate the deepest meanings of an ever-evolving reality. But, in this respect, Impressionism had placed the

Henri de Toulouse-Lautrec: *Jeanne Avril.* c. 1892.

11

painter in a paradoxical situation: the very term Impressionism implies the idea of a fleeting, momentary image. How was one to obtain a true representation of the world solely through optical sensations which are essentially fugitive by nature?

Those who have been christened the *Post-Impressionists*, and above all Georges Seurat, sought the solution to this problem from 1880 onwards. Seurat's 'system of contrasts' relied chiefly on the play of the laws of symmetry and asymmetry in the composition of a picture. This is still unnoticeable in *Sunday Afternoon on the*

Paul Cézanne: *House Among Trees.* 1890-1900.

Island of La Grande Jatte (1886), which describes a moment that is calm and peaceful, and seemingly prolonged in time; but, in contrast, asymmetry reigns supreme in *Le Chahut* (1890) where the clash of diagonals and of dark and light surfaces expresses the simultaneity of sensations, gestures, and sounds, the explosion of an instinctual joy. Seurat's composition was always in strict relationship with structural and temporal notions: an object that was equilibrated or regular by nature engendered a symmetrical, regular image; an asymmetrical form would express an 'eccentric' object.

At the same time, the divisionist or *pointillist* technique created a trembling atmosphere, but one that was precise and sharp—bevelled, so to speak: an iridescent light surrounds the branches of trees, the edges of roofs, the contours of a figure. This complex interplay of refractive mirrors seems to

be the transposition of the 'luminous breakings' in Mallarmé's mysterious *Igitur*, and its 'moving limitations' that give rise to an effect mirror-reflection; Seurat's paintings appear like screens revealing the oscillating wave-system in the Room of Midnight, where the form of Time resembles the face of a guest 'with vacant eyes like a mirror'.[1] The image becomes an *elevation* of reality, all the colours of the prism playing around a dominant which is usually blue; this aspect of Seurat's work, which makes it analogous to a blue-print, also places it beyond painting, in an atmosphere trembling with the vibrations of a new, terribly concrete world: the world of Machines.

Standing aloof from all the schools, Toulouse-Lautrec in his turn developed quite spontaneously the psychological meanings of formal relationships, and developed the resources of asymmetrical composition with complete mastery. Figures in extravagant postures, or even cut off by the edge of the picture, and other similar effects correspond organically to the inner disequilibrium of the beings represented: girls, alcoholics, clowns, marginal heroes who even occupy the margin of the picture, people in revolt driven by an infernal volition but still infinitely human. Here asymmetry expresses psychic and social instabilities; it is the mark of a transitional era.

Impressionism originally attempted to give the most instantaneous image of reality, but its vision was enriched by its successors, and in the end it contained something of Zeno's paradoxical instant, the 'confluent' instant which transforms itself into the future and still contains the past. It is possible to find in the developments of Impressionism everything which should, originally, have been eliminated: the art that had intended to restrict itself to the instant came finally to contain duration.

The effect of mirror-light reappears with Cézanne, especially in the water-colours which he executed towards the end of his life, prismatic universes crossed by jagged rainbows. But the work of the painter of Aix contains also what André Breton calls 'subjects with *halos*'[2] such as *The Murder* of 1870, the *Young Man with a Skull*

1. The strange and yet almost scientific problems of Mallarmé's *Igitur* are studied at length by Arpad Mezei and myself in our *Genèse de la Pensée Moderne*, Chs. 17-18 (Corrêa, Paris, 1950).

2. Cf. A. Breton: *L'Amour Fou* (N.R.F., Paris, 1937), pp. 154-157.

(1894-96), and *The Hanged Man's House*;[1] one could add *Skull and Kettle* of 1865-66, *The Autopsy* of 1867-69, and several still-lives with death's heads painted between 1895 and 1904—the halo in question has always been radiant around the figure of Death.

Subjects with a halo and subjects with a mirror-reflection are the two constants which intensify Cézanne's Harlequins (and, later, those of Picasso): the *Pierrot and Harlequin* (1881, Moscow Museum), and the numerous Harlequins, paintings or drawings, dated from 1888 to 1890. Harlequin is a spectral figure—the luminous spectrum clothing the human form. The coloured flashes, the torn material of his costume would indicate, from a psychiatric point of view, the epileptoid nature of the figure, the quintessence of this aspect being the crime of passion. But Harlequin is also a musician; he knows how to cure his own obsessions thanks to the harmony created by his art.

To move up-stream against the current of knowledge, to explore the geography of the mind, was the general tendency of intellectual activity from the close of the nineteenth century. The technical and commercial world also began to have access to 'inner' values through the specialist activities of its scientists and research-workers, and their discoveries of the phenomena of wave-movement (wireless, radioactivity, X-rays) and of micro-organisms (microbiology); these happenings all occurred around the year 1890, which was also the birth-date of psychoanalysis. Occultism and esoteric researches won a renewed popularity at that time. In poetry it was the era of Symbolism, and simultaneously, allegory began to exercise a remarkable fascination in painting. An artist such as Puvis de Chavannes was appreciated not only by officialdom (Puvis covered the walls of a good many public buildings in Paris, Amiens, Lyons, etc., with his frescoes) but also by the most advanced spirits of the time. 'Bare your head before the *Poor Fisherman*,' Jarry orders the reader of *Faustroll*; Félix Fénéon, a subtle critic and one of the most effective defenders of modern painting, did not stint his praises of an artist whom, for his part,

---

1. According to Breton, this picture translates 'the necessity to express the relationship which cannot fail to exist between the sudden fall of a human body, a cord passed round its neck, and the very spot where the fall takes place.'

Gauguin admired greatly. The great allegory by the master of Pont-Aven, *Where Did We Come from? What Are We? Where Are We Going?*, with its landscape painted in dull yet warm colours, populated with Japanese-style figures, resigned and decorative, fulfills effectively the painter's intention of making, according to his own expression, 'a coloured Puvis mingled with Japan'. Even the art of Van Gogh—who has been called '*uniquement peintre*', a painter and nothing but a painter—made concessions to literary preoccupations, even to moral or rather moralizing ones; but it was through the choice and play of colours that Van Gogh tried to evoke (in his *Café de Nuit*, for instance, according to a celebrated letter) 'the Powers of Darkness' in an 'Assommoir,' tinted by 'Japanese gaiety' and 'the good fellowship of *Tartarin*.'

In England, more than anywhere else, Symbolism in art was pre-eminent from the middle of the century onwards in the work of the Pre-Raphaelites. Madox Brown, Rossetti, Millais, Hunt, Burne-Jones and Watts illustrated mystical legends and scenes, where beautiful young women languished in antique or medieval settings, or in the bosom of a luxuriant pasture. The technique of these anachronistic Renaissance painters is diametrically opposed to that of the modern movement in art; its only relevance to our time lies in the extraordinary minuteness of detail which apparently wanted already to emulate photography. It is told of Millais that, in attempting to achieve a greater exactitude for his *Ophelia*, he made his model pose for hours on end, fully clothed, stretched out in a bath full of cold water (the poor girl became consumptive under this regime); while W. Holman Hunt, travelling in Asia Minor and wishing to paint a 'Scapegoat', had a goat tied up on the deserted shores of the Dead Sea, planted his easel opposite the animal and started work, with a rifle slung across his back to defend himself, if necessary, against marauding Arabs.

This delirious academicism lends a sort of strangeness to scenes which usually conform to the dullest of anecdotes. Among the Pre-Raphaelites an occasionally moving intention is visible in paintings of utter banality. The vulgarity of Hunt's *The Hireling Shepherd* disappears when one discovers a Death's-Head sphinx-moth, minuscule and minutely painted, in the half-closed hand which the shepherd is extending towards his shepherdess. The tragic, devastated appearance of a bird's nest, fallen down to the foot of a rock and still containing

Paul Cézanne: *The Harlequin.*

Gustave Moreau: Drawing for *Oedipus and the Sphinx.* 1864.

unbroken eggs, is reproduced by Hunt with an insensate precision which removes this subject far from the Easter card it recalls at first sight. And it must be said that Rossetti attained the

Gustave Moreau: *Galatea*. 1880.

expressive intensity of an ecstatic dream in his *Beata Beatrix*.

The art of Gustave Moreau, the greatest painter of myths of the last century, is connected, in this sense, with that of the Pre-Raphaelites; but although Moreau was a member of the Institut and a professor at the Ecole des Beaux-Arts, one can certainly not class him among the academicians. Even in 1864, when one of his first works, *Oedipus and the Sphinx*, was shown at the Salon, the critic Jean Rousseau wrote that 'his muted harmonies, his biting accents, his passionate conception have nothing in common with the ordinary, elegant art of the Institut. *Oedipus and the Sphinx* constitutes a fantastic vision haunted by the ardent soul and the feverish dreams of Delacroix, M. Gustave Moreau's first teacher'.

One must visit the astonishing museum, rue de La Rochefoucauld, in Paris, where almost all Moreau's work is gathered, and linger in the curiously faked rooms (built from plans left by the artist himself on his death) whose furniture and even walls can be opened up and leafed through like immense albums crammed with sketches and projects, to grasp the importance of the man who, at the Ecole des Beaux-Arts, was the understanding and respected master of many artists who became famous later on (Matisse, Rouault, Marquet, etc.). Many of the technical procedures of the Fauves—and some others—are foreshadowed here, in the huge preliminary drafts as well as in the countless drawings, watercolours and small paintings. Most of the works are, in fact, unfinished, and were, it seems, left so voluntarily. Moreau had a liking for forms which interpenetrated, for figures modelled with precision contrasting with others left indefinite and ghost-like—and, here and there, the splash of virgin colours. To speak of these projects which are always situated in the heart of the marvellous is, in one sense, to recite dreams. Very ancient memories, yet still only outlines: this bond between the past and the future gives a mediumistic quality to Moreau's compositions. Even the 'finished' paintings remain apparitions. In *Jupiter and Semele*, the colour, finely detailed and worked in thick surfaces, is alive with wings, rays of light, faces of Medusas. The delicate, translucent body of his *Galatea* throws into shadow a strange forest of corals and women-flowers, where the mask of Cyclops glows sombrely.

But the thought which creates these visions is never rudimentary: symbols and myths are always expressed in their most exact and profound sense. A large sketch for a *Prometheus* suggests the connection between the pagan legend and the Christian myth by showing the thief of heavenly fire in the attitude and with the classic features of the Crucified; the hero of antiquity is moreover crowned with a very Christian aureole. His *Leda* in no way recalls the well-known erotic subjects; the latent content of this mythological adventure—the descent of the spirit into matter—can be interpreted in the gesture of the swan placing his beak chastely on the top of the nymph's head. A genuinely initiatory approach may be discerned in the manner in which the artist has treated *The Triumph of Helen, The Suitors, The Chimeras...* He himself described in the following terms his *Triumph of Alexander* which shows transparent architectures towering above mists teeming with elephants and warriors: 'The young conquering king dominates this whole mass of people, captive, defeated and grovelling at his feet, overcome by fear and admiration. The little Indian valley where the huge throne stands contains all of India, the temples with fantastic faiths, the terrible idols, the underground passages full of mysteries and terrors, this whole unknown and disturbing civilization.—And Greece, the soul of Greece shining and superb, triumphs far beyond in the unexplored regions of dream and mystery.'

During the same period, another painter was exploring dream and mystery and had recourse, also, to legends and myths, peopling his pictures with centaurs, sirens, dragons and phantoms. The Swiss Arnold Böcklin, like the English Pre-

Arnold Böcklin: *Island of the Dead.* 1880.

Raphaelites, used supremely conventional pictorial processes. But it seems that he wished thus to invest the imaginary with the power of reality, an attempt which presupposes a very special kind of humour that was doubtless not always involuntary.

Mythological beasts, in the *Battle of the Centaurs*, are shown in theatrical combat, like the cuirassiers on rearing steeds in the Cavalry Charges of

and this pot-bellied triton are most certainly beer drinkers. Elsewhere, some idlers contemplate an ancient centaur with wrinkled crupper and grey hair, standing on the threshold of a smithy and pointing out one of his shoes to the smith, with a finger. In *Diana's Hunt*, however, this bizarre irony has disappeared. Here three women dressed in Greek fashion are running towards a stag being attacked by dogs; this commonplace image is not redeemed by its gigantic format, but it does give a sensation of sudden illumination, of flashing sunlight. *The Storm* is a dark version of *Diana's Hunt*, the picture representing a landscape seen this time in the glare of lightning; in the harsh and momentary light the furious movement of trees twisted in torment seems solidified. But the celebrated *Island of the Dead* is the most extreme example of this premeditated confusion of the concept of time. The scene takes place beyond time and beyond the very idea of the Beyond. The boat which is landing at the sinister island, where cypresses stand guard over a cliff pierced by hypogea, while a storm hovers menacingly over a silent black sea, is not transporting a mortal remnant but a soul, whose whitish phantom stands upright at the prow, a soul which is going to be placed in a tomb. The deep anguish emanating from *Island of the Dead* results from the fact that this painting materializes a negative instant, a duration of time which has stepped over the threshold of death and is prolonging itself into nothingness.

With Odilon Redon—influenced by the legendary aspects of Moreau and Böcklin, by that ancestor of pictorial Romanticism, William Blake, and also by the arts of the Far East—everything is apparition; even the bouquets of field-flowers seem to be emerging from mist-filled craters. Time is measured with mythological clocks: solar quadrigæ, of which two chargers are rearing straight up into the sky, one other is moving horizontally, while the fourth is plunging towards the earth through iridescent vapours and flashes of light. Redon was one of the first to affirm explicitly the importance of the part played by the unconscious in the process of artistic creation: 'Nothing is achieved in art by the will alone,' he said, 'everything is achieved by docile submission to the advent of the unconscious.'

so many academic hacks. Here, on a rock against which waves are breaking, nereids frolic like so many *Mädchen* on holiday; this fat, red-faced siren

About 1900, industrial technology offered certain achievements to the public at large which had, more or less directly, decisive consequences for

Chronograms by E. J. Marey.

Running long jump.

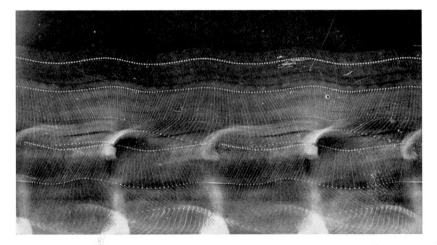

Man marching.

High jump without run.

Long jump without run.

painting: I refer to the popularization of photographic procedures. Practical and cheap cameras made it possible for anyone to obtain perfect reproductions of the exterior world. In terms of exactitude, photography brought a total and guaranteed success. Even if it lacked (temporarily) colour, the photographic eye could still surpass that of the painter by perceiving a world existing beyond appearance: the precision of the plates as well as the unexpected results of the pose or the snapshot (discoveries which the cinema later elevated to their ultimate importance) revealed forms that were invisible previously; a fourth dimension was made perceptible, the chronological dimension, which had a quite special importance for human beings.

As Eddington has effectively put it, in a formula which also possesses an element of humour: 'An individual is a four-dimensional object of greatly elongated form; in ordinary language we say that he has considerable extension in time and insignificant extension in space.'[1] This definition can be applied to the physiologist Marey's famous photographs, to his *chronograms*[2] which reunite in one single plate, that can 'extend itself' indefinitely, the successive postures of a creature in movement (man, bird, etc.). Marey had also constructed some astonishing sculpture-chronograms reproducing, for example, the flight of a pigeon: four-dimensional objects, in truth, whose 'extension' represents the chronological dimension.[3]

In Eddington's formula, quoted above, and in Marey's photos and objects, temporal extension is still distinct from spatial dimensions, on to which time adds itself, in a manner of speaking. But if one refers to a more complete presentation, that of the English logician Whitehead, who sees the object as a dimensional synthesis where time and the measurements of space are intimately bound up, then the object becomes a true *event*.

Sculptures coming from Africa and Oceania were revealed to western artists at the very moment when the problem of the representation of appearances was being posed, as a result of photography, in absolutely new terms. It is said that James Ensor became acquainted with primitive objects in 1900, the expressionist Kirchner in Dresden in 1904,

and tradition credits one of the Fauves, Vlaminck, with their discovery in France in about 1905. It is entirely wrong to speak of 'Negro art' in connection with these works, which were conceived by their creators neither as objects of art, nor even as object-individuals (that is to say, as spatial complexes on to which, according to Eddington's formula, duration of time would be added). In every sense of the term, they were *object-events*, expressing the relationship between man and the elements, the seasons, the vital functions; between man and fire, summer, night, storm, hunt, maternity—creation. Classical time, with its double profile turned towards the two infinites, past and future, lost all significance faced with these hieratic beings whose structure constituted a periodic function of the event which they incarnated, and which contained within themselves the universal cycles.

African mask (Itumba region).

1. Eddington: *Space, Time and Gravitation* (Cambridge University Press, London, 1920).

2. This is the name that I gave to these images in an article in the revue *Minotaure* (No. 1, June, 1933).

3. See, for instance, fig. 104 in E. J. Marey: *Le vol des Oiseaux; physiologie du mouvement* (Masson, Paris, 1890).

Pablo Picasso: *The Acrobat's Wife*. 1904.

Guillaume Apollinaire, in *The Cubist Painters*,[1] speaks rather mysteriously of Picasso's discovery of African and Oceanian statuettes: 'One of his friends brought him one day to the border of a mystical country whose inhabitants were at once so simple and so grotesque that one could easily remake them.' Not so simple, as we have seen, nor merely grotesque, these 'inferior Christs of obscure beliefs', as Apollinaire calls them with greater depth and lyricism in his poem *Zone*. Negro objects appeared charged with veiled significances, with hitherto unknown lessons, to the young painters who were beginning to preoccupy themselves with the *fourth dimension*.

Pablo Picasso, arriving in Paris at the dawn of the twentieth century, had, from the very first, been the centre of special attention, because of his exceptional gifts as a painter, and because of an extraordinary fecundity founded, it would seem, on a sort of mimetic faculty which allowed him to use the enormous resources of a past still very near or else very distant as a documentary repertoire of forms and procedures. We read in *La Revue Blanche* of July 15, 1901, in reference to Picasso's first exhibition in Paris, an enthusiastic if somewhat astonished article by Félicien Fagus, under the title: 'The Spanish Invasion—Picasso.' 'Just as,' writes the critic, 'for Picasso any subject can be a work of art, so every means of translation is acceptable to him, even slang, or Gongorism—that other slang, even his fellow artists' vocabulary. One can easily distinguish, apart from the great precursors, many probable influences, Delacroix, Manet, Monet, Van Gogh, Pissarro, Toulouse-Lautrec, Degas, Forain, Rops, perhaps... Each one transitory, each one no sooner captured than set free again: his personality lies in this capacity to be carried away, this juvenile impetuous spontaneity (it is said that he is not yet twenty, and that he paints up to three canvases a day)...'

If Picasso used the methods of others with remarkable freedom, at the same time he deepened and extended them. At first, he copied the forms, the technique, the subjects of Lautrec almost without alteration *(The Supper Eaters)*. In *The Absinthe Drinker*, asymmetry becomes an organic component of the woman represented, who appears hunch-backed as if to give outward expression to her inner blemishes. Deformation goes beyond physical affliction and identifies itself with the condition of mankind in the double figures (one might say, duplicated figures) of the 'blue epoch': cripples, one-eyed or pregnant women. Then, later, his allegories transform Puvis de Chavannes' resigned and superficial optimism into something internal and tragic. 'They greet danger with secret smiles', wrote Apollinaire about the women that his friend painted during the blue period.

But one day Picasso, following the example of primitive craftsmen, began to paint truly real beings, human in their essence and not just in their appearance. Many of his paintings of about 1906, especially in the design of the heads, seem to have been 'remade' after primitive African models. No doubt his use of the almost unknown evidence which Negro sculpture embodied at that time included, once again, an element of disrespect and playfulness, but on this occasion the enterprise had considerable repercussions. It imposed upon appearances the rites and rhythms of images which contained the invisible dimensions of reality. 'If we were alert, all the gods would awaken.'[1] One can witness the awakening of the savage gods reincarnated in the famous painting *Les Demoiselles d'Avignon*[2] (1906-1907), conceived at the end of the 'rose period', in which the figure on the left still recalls his previous styles while on the right side the picture is already almost a cubist composition.

After the discovery of primitive objects, it was clear that henceforth painting would concern itself with something quite different from the 'loud and colourful cries' which Apollinaire had ascribed to Fauvism in his *The Cubist Painters*. The author continues: 'When that barbarous but not savage city, given over to luxury and violent orgies, was deserted by the Barbarians, when the Fauves had ceased to roar, nobody remained except peaceful bureaucrats who, feature for feature, resembled the officials of the rue Bonaparte, in Paris. And the kingdom of the Fauves, whose civilization had seemed so powerful, so new, so astounding, suddenly took the aspect of a deserted village.' Basically, Fauvism (and this applies equally to the movement in Germany which was its contemporary if not its exact counterpart: Expressionism),[3] remained attached to a concept of the

1. Published in a translation by Lionel Abel (Wittenborn, Schultz, New York, 1944).

1. Apollinaire, beginning of the section on Picasso in *The Cubist Painters*.

2. The original title of this composition is *The Avignon Brothel*.

3. The tendencies of Expressionism were also extrapictorial; its painters wanted to *express* emotions, sensations, and even a social message. Georges Braque emerged from Fauvism, and Max Ernst and Paul Klee from Expressionism.

object, and of reality in general, which had already become out of date in 1905, and which could no longer lead to any decisive discoveries. The management of events was soon to escape it. Braque left the Fauves in about 1907. Derain, although one of the first to grasp the importance of the impact of primitive objects, never abandoned the aesthetic of appearances and developed fairly quickly a sort of Cézannism moderated by French Classicism. And Matisse's master remained Gauguin rather than Gustave Moreau, whose sense of myth seems only to have touched him during one period, that of his allegorical compositions. However it is perhaps the title of one of his early allegories: *Le Luxe*, which symbolizes best the true nature of his dazzling art.

Much has been written and even more has been argued about the birth of *Cubism*. It seems established by now that the first pictures to carry the label 'cubist' were created in 1908 by Picasso and Braque, working in close collaboration and accompanied in their researches by the painters and poets grouped around Guillaume Apollinaire. One might say schematically that Cubism conjugated the Negro influence through Picasso and the Cézannian influence through Braque; the latter seems to have predominated, in the sense that the first cubist pictures systematized the mirror-light effect of Cézanne's water-colours and projected reality on intersecting planes, as in a broken mirror. Indeed, it was only after the appearance of these first pictures that theories began to be elaborated around them; Braque first of all, then Pierre Reverdy and others, presented these works as being guided by 'the rule which corrects emotion', or by 'the quest for the eternal in the object (for instance: in a glass, the round shape)', etc. Certainly none of the other schools which smashed the mirror of appearances at the start of the new century was anterior to Cubism, but it remains true that the first cubist paintings provided a *signal* rather than a lesson to be learnt. A signal hoisted at random: but by then a revolution of the arts was ready to be launched. The first deliberate, explicit call for the exploration and conquest of fresh territory dates from the beginning of 1909: the *Futurist Manifesto*.[1]

1. Published in France in the newspaper *Le Figaro* in February 1909.

The futurists made a violent and unequivocal challenge: they wanted to rid Europe and especially Italy 'of its gangrene of professors, archaeologists, cicerones and antiquarians'—an Italy that had indeed been turned into a museum-nation exhibiting catalogued attractions, Davids in marble

Pablo Picasso: *Les Demoiselles d'Avignon.* 1907.

looking more like lard, cathedrals in sugar and pistachio, pseudo-oriental palaces built by the merchants of past centuries, and on the museum walls the endless wearisome procession of madonnas and crucifixions! And yet, in no other country were machines roaring into life with a greater frenzy: industrial suburbs encircled the old cities, and the noise of motors reverberated through the medieval lanes. 'A motor-car driven at full speed is more beautiful than the Victory of Samothrace,' claimed the author of the *Futurist Manifesto*, the poet Marinetti: more beautiful than marbles and bronzes and more beautiful also, no doubt, than

Umberto Boccioni: *Unique Form of Continuity in Space.* 1913.

With Futurism, he proposed a combination of 'the analysis of colour (the divisionism of Seurat, Signac, and Cross), and the analysis of form (the divisionism of Picasso and Braque).' *(Manifesto of Futurist Painting,* 1910.) From this sprang the syntheses of colour and movement attempted by other futurists, such as Severini's *Dynamic Hieroglyph of the Bal Tabarin, Pan-Pan at the Monico,* etc. which interpret the lessons of Seurat's *Chahut* and of the disintegrations achieved by Cézanne and the cubists. The futurist picture also exceeded the traditional limits of painting by attempting to express extraplastic phenomena, such as noise: *Automobile e Rumore* (Balla), and, more especially, an emotional and intellectual dynamism: *The Forces of a Street* (Boccioni). The concept of painting was enlarged, became theatre and music, and Boccioni gave expression to these researches in three-dimensional plastic works: his *Unique Form of Continuity in Space* concerns itself with the movement of a human being in the act of walking and has affinity with the chronograms of Marey.[2]

As several commentators have already pointed out fairly clearly, Futurism and Cubism presented two different conceptions of time. Picasso's landscape: *The Factory, Horta del Ebro* (1909), transforms a cylindrical chimney into a pattern of dark and light parallelograms (one of these surfaces even represents the interior of the flue, its upper internal section), and the whole effect, in this and other pictures of the same period, is of a projection by the artist onto a single plane of the various facets of the object. It is evident that such a representation presupposes a journey by the observer—at least in imagination—around the immobile object, so that the image gives the possibility of seizing with one single glance the successive views obtained during this movement.[3]

In a world which increasingly resembled a madly whirling roundabout, the cubists, remaining at the outer edge of the whirlwind, and swept along by it, placed the object at the centre of this gyratory system: the fascinating object around which they turned became for them the sole stable point of the universe, in any case the one point upon which they could fix their attention, and whose successive aspects they attempted to record in their paintings—rather like someone trying to arrange on a page of a family album several different

still-lives—even cubist still-lives. Marinetti was the front man of those Italian artists who grouped themselves under the sign of Futurism, but 'the prince of Futurism was Boccioni, who conceived the most convincing manifestos at a time when the world was thirsty for new art expressions'.[1] Umberto Boccioni had been influenced by Post-Impressionism since the beginning of the century.

1. Marcel Duchamp, in: *Collection of the Société Anonyme: Museum of Modern Art 1920,* the catalogue of the Katherine Dreier collection, edited by Yale University Art Gallery, 1950.

2. Rather than with Rodin's *Man Marching.*

3. It may be noted that the method of 'perspective of development' existed in the East in Hindu painting.

photographs of the same person at different ages. But the futurists, on the contrary, placed themselves at the centre and saw objects revolving around them which had become semi-transparent as a result of their rapid motion, like the meteors one can see whizzing past on a motor-racing track; and it was this whirlwind that they tried to express —the vitrified universe of speed.

The cubist method of giving a chronological structure to form was thus different from the futurist intention: the former situated movement in the spectator, the latter in the object. During this same period, the idea of movement as a factor in the relationship between the object and the observer constituted the basic principle of a scientific theory which was to become famous: the theory of relativity (1905). At that time, too, an identical situation was developing in psychology: Rorschach's psychodiagnosis first made itself known in 1912, and certainly no other scientific experiment has ever made use of psychic mechanisms so directly bound to artistic creative activity as the famous *Rorschach test*.

In *A Rebours*, Huysmans had sketched out a theory which his hero Des Esseintes 'claimed to be almost mathematically precise: to wit, that a harmony exists between the sensual nature of a truly artistic individual and the colour which his eyes see with particular strength and clarity'.

But it is generally agreed that an inner relationship exists between free perception of tones and forms and the character of the person seeing them. The human eye is capable of discovering many different images in what Rorschach has called 'chance pictures' *(Zufallsbilder)*. Projected shadows, crystallizations, clouds, damp stains, all sorts of natural formations attract one's attention by the evocative richness of their contours and textures. Famous artists and anonymous artisans have found inspiration in this fact. Pliny the Elder relates that Protogenes of Rhodes, annoyed at being unable to render the lather round a horse's mouth, hurled a sponge at his picture: 'The sponge deposited the colours with which it was charged in the very manner which he had sought in vain, and thus chance constructed nature in a painting.' One must also quote the advice of Leonardo da Vinci in his note entitled 'A way of developing and arousing the mind to various inventions': 'I shall not fail to include among these precepts a new discovery, an aid to reflection, which, although it seems a small thing and almost laughable, nevertheless is very useful in stimulating the mind to various discoveries. This is: look at walls splashed with a number of stains or stones of various mixed colours. If you have to invent some scene, you can see there resemblances to a number of landscapes, adorned in various ways with mountains, rivers, rocks, trees, great plains, valleys and hills. Moreover, you can see great battles, and rapid actions of figures, strange expressions on faces, costumes, and an infinite number of things, which you can reduce to good, integrated form. This happens thus on walls and varicoloured stones, as in the sound of bells, in whose pealing you can find every name and word you can imagine... I have seen clouds and stains on walls, which have given rise to beautiful inventions of different things; although these stains were completely lacking in the perfection of any part, yet they did not lack perfection in their movements or other actions.'[1] We know, too, that certain German Romantics, as well as Victor Hugo and others, used ink-stains, crushed between two sheets of paper to compose endless fantastic scenes from the shapes thus obtained: just as the caprices of some cabinet-makers of previous eras led them to inlay the surfaces of their furniture with slivers of curiously veined wood or agate, to suggest miniature landscapes.

Pablo Picasso: *Factory, Horta del Ebro*. 1907.

1. Da Vinci: *Treatise on Painting*, transl. by A. Philip McMahon (Princeton University Press, Princeton, 1956).

But the Swiss doctor Rorschach had the idea of exploring the various aspects of this interpretative faculty which all individuals possess to a greater or lesser degree. The material of his test consists, as is well-known, in a series of ten plates reproducing figures obtained by folding, pressing and then unfolding a sheet of paper stained with fresh ink, black or coloured. The six plates are shown successively to the subject who is asked what he sees in these shapes. In this experiment, the interpretative work is undertaken in an atmosphere of extreme freedom, because of the absence of any intrinsic significance in the images—of their neutrality, so to speak, since they obviously represent nothing, apart from the mechanical means which contributed to their formation. The subject's replies can, in consequence, indicate with a maximum of authenticity the essential components of his way of *seeing*, and, thus, of his psychic structure.

The clinical applications of the Rorschach method are not the concern of this present study, but it is apposite to stress the fact that this test reveals, among other things, the aptitude of the subject in imagining either static or kinetic representations. Two general interpretative groups are distinguished in the main divisions of character which Rorschach established after a considerable number of experiments: the first group is formed of individuals who see mostly stable, coloured forms in the test plates, the second is formed of those who prefer to interpret the stains as objects in movement and notice the colours to a much lesser degree. Rorschach designates these two groups in terms of Jung's division of human types into *extroverts* and *introverts*, the former turned towards the external world, the world of problems to solve, a domain of determination subordinated to the principle of reality; the latter turned towards themselves, towards the inner personality, a domain of liberty controlled by the pleasure principle. The extrovert, extremely mobile, changing his point of view continually, compensates his tendency to dispersion by seeing exterior objects as fixed elements; the introvert, on the contrary, finds it necessary to counteract his own possible immobilization by seeking manifestations of movement in the world exterior to himself. And the relationship between colour and fixity and between grisaille and movement derives from the physics of visual perception: for instance, a coloured disc, when rotated quickly enough, appears to be grey.

The two classes of character defined by Rorschach obviously include an infinite number of variations

(the study of which is the field of psycho-diagnostics), but it is an established fact that these two types have always been distinguished under various labels over the years: thus, the poet Schiller speaks of 'naïve' and 'sentimental' characters.[1] Two important functions correspond to these categories, on the one hand that of the conscious, of reasoning intelligence (extroverted character, fixed and coloured forms), and on the other hand that of the unconscious (introverted character, movement, grey blurred forms).

The complex relationships between vision and personality and the manifold interplay between these two psychic constants are apparent in all works of art and in the evolution of schools of art as well as individual creations. To some extent the interpretative process is reversible: the changing personality of the artist is expressed in the different phases of his work, the latter being, of course, a 'projection' of himself; but it goes without saying that we cannot expect to categorize all the shades of a particular temperament (or, indeed, of a collective movement) within the framework of a psychological theory, however malleable, or to make any claim to *define* consequently certain works or certain relationships between different works. All we can do is *situate* them. With this reservation, it is possible, if one studies for example the evolution of Seurat's painting, to recognize that the gradual change in the work of this 'theoretician' from a fairly flat and openly coloured technique (*La Baignade* of 1884) to a vibrant pointillism with a monochromatic effect (*The Circus* of 1891), indicates the ever-increasing importance of unconscious signs: that is to say, a growing interiorization of his thought. With Van Gogh, on the contrary, one can see the conflict between will-power and the urges of the unconscious grow inexorably in dramatic violence: the cypresses turn into flames and the stars into vast whirlwinds, while an ever-heavier outline attempts to retain a form of ever-decreasing stability. The immensely variegated production of Picasso is revealed as being an alternation of these two attitudes. The recurrent monochromatic compositions correspond mainly to phases of profound self study: blue period, Negro period, the first sepia-toned cubist paintings, the 'Scaffoldings' in grisaille of 1912 (the entire first period of Cubism is in grey, dull tints). On the other hand, the brilliant 'Lautrec' period around 1900, the so-called 'rose'

1. Cf. his study: *Über Naive und Sentimentale Dichtung.*

(in fact brightly-coloured) period of 1905-06, are, rather, periods of preparation and, in a certain sense, repose; from 1914 onwards one can observe the forms standing out sharply like silhouettes, and the colour become colouring. His surrealist period, and that of the pen-drawings and grey and black pictures of the *Metamorphoses*, about 1930, denote a fresh phase of deep introspection.[1] The works of the futurists, on the other hand, which are essentially animated and unstable, producing a grisaille from even the most brilliant colours in juxtaposition, and often ignoring the laws of composition, frequently show indications of being typical products of the unconscious. The futurists were concerned to translate not only movement but 'states of the soul'. *Those who Go, Those who Stay*, by Boccioni, are grey visions peopled by ghosts, as indistinct as the being without form or colour met by Ibsen's hero, Peer Gynt, who, on being asked his name, replied: 'My name is myself.'

The polemic which was inevitably engaged between cubists and futurists had something of the nature of a quarrel between extroverts and introverts. Apollinaire declared in 1912: 'The futurists want to paint states of the soul: this is the most dangerous kind of painting imaginable.' Boccioni and his friends replied that the cubists 'stubbornly paint the immobile, the frozen and all the static aspects of nature; they worship the traditionalism of Poussin, Ingres and Corot, ageing and petrifying their art with an attachment to the past which seems absolutely incomprehensible to our eyes'.

Meanwhile the futurists' dynamism did not fail to influence the opposing tendency. The technique of *papier collé*, and more generally the use in a work of art of new substances—a procedure inaugurated brilliantly by Braque towards the end of 1912—had been proposed, in its most developed forms, in April of the same year, by Boccioni in the *Manifesto of the Futurist Sculptors:* 'It is necessary to destroy the supposed nobility, utterly literary and conventional, of marble and bronze and to deny point-blank that one should make use exclusively of one single material for a general pictorial effect. The sculptor can make use of twenty or more different materials in one single work: glass, wood, cardboard, concrete, horsehair,

leather, fabric, mirrors, electric light, etc...' Picasso and Braque made use of some of these procedures with an astonishing plastic sense—a sense which was rather frequently absent, and with good cause, from the futurists' productions—in what were called derisively 'panoplies' at the time.

Apollinaire himself, so enamoured of invention and novelty, could not fail to be attracted by the

Pablo Picasso: *Man with Violin*. 1911-1912.

1. See Part II, pp. 187-188.

futurists' attitudes. His poetry remained profoundly influenced by futurist inventions, and these ideas took on a humorous accent with him which presaged Dada. 'On June 25, 1913, the day of the Grand Prix, 200 feet above the Boulevard St-Germain,' the author of *The Cubist Painters* wrote *The Futurist Antitradition*, a 'manifesto-synthesis' which, by its mystificatory references, its violent tone and also its poetic felicities, is a precursor of the proclamations of the Dada movement. Apollinaire says SHIT (musically) to all rehashed values—to critics and pedagogues, to Venice and Versailles, Bayreuth and Montmartre, 'the Siamese twins D'Annunzio and Rostand', Montaigne, Wagner, Edgar Alan Poe, Walt Whitman and Baudelaire, etc.! To this list of outcasts he opposes that of his friends, the modern painters, making a joyful mixture of all the different tendencies: Marinetti and Braque, Boccioni and Derain, Picasso, Picabia, Matisse, Marcel Duchamp... He takes up the futurist slogans: 'art of noises, machinism, words at liberty, simultaneity', adding to these the 'art of voyages' and 'analogies and puns lyrical springboard and only science of language'.

But anti-tradition could not group itself under one label. New schools proliferated and individual artists also launched themselves on isolated voyages of discovery. There was the *Suprematism* of Malevitch and the *Rayonism* of Larionov in Russia (1913), the *Neo-Plasticism* of the Dutch painter Mondrian (1914), the *Vorticism* of Wyndham Lewis in England (1913), the *Synchromism* of MacDonald Wright and Morgan Russel in America (1913)—tendencies deriving either from cubist immobilism or futurist dynamism. In Munich, Kandinsky's landscapes turned into 'Improvisations', and in 1910 the artist painted his first abstract picture: the voice of reality was interpreted by Kandinsky both as the echoes of a normal vision and as the expression of new beings created from the confrontation of these very echoes and endowed with an astonishing power of suggestion. From 1911 onwards, Chagall created strange compositions which resemble pictures cut into separate pieces; the artist appears to have cut his own paintings into different fragments and then reassembled the pieces into hallucinatory compositions whose scenes evoke the atmosphere of dreams, childhood stories and folklore. The Rumanian Brancusi, about 1908-10, had begun to sculpt symbolic forms in which an entirely unadorned plasticism expresses an intellectualism driven to its very limits. The Swiss Paul Klee, who was to be made known in France by the first surrealist publications, began, in about 1914, after a voyage to Tunisia (Kairouan), to create a world of graphic symbols bound up with living beings, architectures and landscapes.

In France, Apollinaire classified as *orphists* a group of painters who had in fact very disparate means and temperaments, who in no way formed a closely-knit team but whose work at that time derived more or less from cubist geometrizations and from the futurist analyses of movement. This word Orphism (which was originally applied to a particular period of Picabia's painting) needs to be defined. It had nothing to do with music, and concerned itself solely with movement: the orphists were chiefly intrigued by those new beings, so mobile and so precise, *machines*, the modern sisters of Erichthonius, 'child born without mother' according to Ovid in his *Metamorphoses;* this particular son of Vulcan sprang, in fact, from the ground.

'It seems incomprehensible to the present generation,' wrote Mme Gabrielle Buffet-Picabia,[1] 'that the machines which populate the visual world with surprising and spectacular forms, hitherto unknown, could for a long time have remained the victims of a frenzied ostracism in the official world of the arts, and that they could have been looked upon as essentially anti-plastic, both in substance and in function. I remember a time when their rapid proliferation passed as a calamity, when every artist thought he owed it to himself to turn his back on the Eiffel Tower, as a protest against the architectural blasphemy with which it filled the sky. The discovery and rehabilitation of these strange personages of iron and steel, which radically distinguished themselves from the familiar aspects of nature, both by their construction and by the dynamism inherent in the automatic movements they engendered, was in itself a bold, revolutionary act; but one which, if it had not gone beyond descriptive representation, would have remained very close to the landscape and the still life...'

It was in this atmosphere that Fernand Léger painted the smoke from factories and a metallicized nature in dull shades; then he was to produce,

1. This and following quotations from Mme Buffet-Picabia are taken from articles originally published in 1937 and since included in a volume entitled *Aires Abstraites* (Pierre Cailler, Geneva, 1958). See also the contributions by Mme Buffet-Picabia to the important collection of documents edited by Robert Motherwell, *The Dada Painters and Poets* (Wittenborn, Schultz, New York, 1952).

Pablo Picasso: *Violin, Bottle and Glass*. 1913.

J.E. Millais: *Ophelia*. 1852.

Gustave Moreau: *Temptation of Saint Anthony*.

'in series', crudely-coloured pictures (red, blue, yellow, with green sometimes added), all of which were variations on the theme of gear-wheels and pipe-lines. ('His private pipe-line certainly gets him results,' said the critic Roger Allard). For his part, Robert Delaunay glorified the Eiffel Tower in all its different guises; his 'simultaneous colour' shimmers with the tremulous fixity of a rainbow. For an exhibition of paintings by Delaunay in 1912 which were portholes opened onto a world revolutionized by the machine, Apollinaire wrote a conversation-poem, *Windows*:

Vancouver
Where the train white with snow and fires of the night
O Paris   [*flees the winter*
The yellow fades from red to green
Paris Vancouver Hyères Maintenon New York and
The window opens like an orange   [*the Antilles*
Lovely fruit of light.

These two painters, particularly Léger, represent the cubist-inclined branch of Orphism: in Léger's still-lives, the wrench and cog-wheel replace the packet of tobacco and the bottle. Much nearer to Futurism was Marcel Duchamp, who, developing a deeply meditated work, established in about 1912 the preparatory designs of the most astounding machine of our time, *The Bride Stripped Bare by her Bachelors, Even*. At the same time, Francis Picabia, while inventing abstract art and a few other original formulas on his own, was about to inaugurate his 'mechanist period.'

By 1910, Picabia and Duchamp had developed a close relationship which lasted many years. In the words of Mme Gabrielle Buffet-Picabia, 'they emulated one another in their extraordinary adherence to paradoxical, destructive principles'. Apollinaire, whom Duchamp first met at Picabia's home in 1911, occasionally abandoned his role of 'high pontiff of Cubism', according to Mme Buffet, and 'often took part in these forays of demoralization, which were also forays of witticism and clowning. Better than by any rational method,' she continues, 'they thus pursued the disintegration of the concept of art, substituting a personal dynamism, individual forces of suggestion and projection, for the codified values of formal Beauty.'

Picabia, ostentatious and brilliant, throwing out ideas carelessly, and Duchamp, in whom intuition and reflection were engaged in an infinitely subtle interplay, are two men of absolutely opposite temperaments and yet, each in his own manner, lords of the human spirit. Neither of them was ever to range himself among those whom Robert Lebel calls ironically 'producers': 'men with a profession, persevering workers', thanks to whom, from the twenties onwards, the picture 'will lose its quality of manifestation to become just one more object easily handled and sold over any counter'.[1] The higher the tide of paintings rose, the more Duchamp demonstrated his essential reticence—for him a single exemplary gesture was worth a thousand times more than the thousand repetitions of a single example—and finally he abstained almost entirely from any kind of intervention. Picabia continued to gather windfalls throughout his career, adapting every possible style to his own purposes on the way and making a point of spoiling the game for the art-dealers and their suppliers: an extraordinarily gifted painter and the anti-artist *par excellence*. It must have been Picabia, virtuoso driver of the most powerful and luxurious cars of his time and indefatigable discoverer of new poetic perspectives, whom Apollinaire had in mind in these verses from his poem, *Hills*:

The driver grips the steering wheel
And every time along the road
He blows the horn rounding a curve
There appears on the horizon's rim
A universe as yet unknown.

Francis Picabia was born in Paris on January 22, 1879, in the house at 82, rue des Petits-Champs (now 26, rue Danielle-Casanova) belonging at the time to his maternal grandfather, Davanne, a well-known photographer who was the friend of Daguerre and Nadar. It is in this same house that he died in 1953. His father, of Cuban nationality and the descendant of an old Spanish family (an ancestor had been a privateer in the service of the King of Spain and his statue can still be seen in the port of Corunna), fulfilled the role of attaché at the Cuban Legation in Paris. The young man attended the Ecole des Beaux-Arts (Cormon's studio) and the Ecole des Arts Décoratifs; at the age of seventeen he exhibited at the Salon des

82, rue des Petits-Champs.

1. Cf. 'Picabia et Duchamp ou le pour et le contre', by R. Lebel (review *Paru*, no. 55, Paris, November 1949).

Artistes Français. He painted impressionist pictures which met with great success and gained him a most advantageous contract with the Galerie Georges Petit. However, he was already thinking about a different kind of painting. From 1905 onwards, his *Snow Scenes* and *Farmyards* began to alternate with graphic sketches tending towards abstraction.

Picabia's precocity was also exercised against art. While still a child, in order to procure funds

Francis Picabia: *Edtaonisl*. 1913.

for his stamp-collection, he got the idea of copying the pictures of the 'masters' which decorated his grandfather's apartments and selling the originals, after replacing them in their frames by his own copies. This went on until all the 'masters' were liquidated and the young boy finally confessed his hoax to his grandfather. The latter was not in the least put out, having never concealed from his grandson his own doubts concerning the destiny of traditional painting: as a photographer he was

able to judge severely those painters who were bound by the reproduction of appearances. These opinions of his grandfather's became a sort of challenge for Picabia which he finally took up. From 1907, his painting shows an increasing detachment as regards appearances: in his *Paysage de la Creuse*, Picabia was the first to paint the sky red and the ground blue.

He then developed his 'orphic' period, with paintings such as *Tarantella*, *Danses à la Source* and the famous *Procession in Seville* (1912), in which the spectacle of the world appears to him like a kaleidoscope—and he changes the apparatus as soon as the patterns repeat themselves too often. The picture titles end by having nothing whatsoever to do with the 'subjects'. Instead of being a sort of tautology (a sunset is usually entitled *Sunset*, a still-life with pitcher *Still-life with Pitcher*) the title goes beyond the appearance of the painting and extends it or reveals another aspect of it. In 1916, Picabia explained this procedure, which he had evolved during his mechanist period, and which constitutes a direct intervention by *metaphor* in the pictorial field: 'In my work the subjective expression is the title, the painting is the object. But this object is nevertheless somewhat subjective, because it is the pantomime—the appearance of the title; it furnishes to a certain point the means of comprehending the potentiality—the very heart of man.'[1]

In *The Cubist Painters*, Picabia's Orphism is presented by Apollinaire as a sort of 'musical painting', a transformation of plastic values into chronological elements, the latter manifesting themselves in the picture like the notes in a musical score (one may remark that if that were so Kandinsky and his followers would have been the true orphists; in fact, they entitled their paintings *Improvisation*, *Fugue*, *Counterpoint*, etc.). But Apollinaire added also that 'this art had as much in common with music as any art could have which is its exact opposite'.

New compositions of enormous size demonstrated the insufficiency of this exegesis: *Catch as Catch Can*, *Udnie Jeune Fille Américaine*, *Edtaonisl*. If the first title may be considered descriptive (the picture was inspired by a session of Japanese wrestling which Picabia had attended with Apollinaire), and if the second is a humorous explanation of a non-representative image, with *Edtaonisl*—a completely meaningless word—the trap closes

1. In *291*, no. 12, edited by Alfred Stieglitz, New York, February 1916—the final issue of this review.

again, giving an incomprehensible solution to the rebus.

Picabia and his wife went to the United States in 1913, to attend the opening of the great exhibition of modern art known as the Armory Show which took place in New York, in the huge Sixty-ninth Regiment Armory. The Armory Show presented all the most sensational experiments which had been accomplished in Europe during the previous ten years, and summarized the exhibitions which had first revealed them: the Salon des Indépendants, the Salon d'Automne, the Blaue Reiter, the futurist exhibitions, the exhibition of the Section d'Or. Since 1886, the year in which Durand-Ruel had mounted his first exhibition of impressionists in New York, the American public had remained almost entirely ignorant of the new painters and still regarded the impressionists as the only innovators. In 1913, *sixteen hundred* modern works were assembled at the Armory Show: Archipenko, Friesz, Cézanne, Marcel Duchamp, Toulouse-Lautrec, Derain, Münch, Segonzac, Delaunay, Odilon Redon, Dufy, Maillol, Picasso, Léger, Henri Rousseau, Marie Laurencin, Signac, Matisse, Picabia, Van Gogh, Jacques Villon, Seurat, Vuillard, Marquet, Duchamp-Villon, Brancusi, Rodin, and many others; without counting representative works of the period from Ingres to the end of Impressionism. One can say that modern art sprang to life in America with the Armory Show (which was transferred later to Chicago and Boston). And its success was not simply to be judged in terms of attendance: three hundred and fifty of the works on show were acquired by American collectors.[1]

The 'hit' of the Armory Show, the picture most frequently discussed and the one which became immediately the most celebrated in America, was the *Nude Descending a Staircase*, by Marcel Duchamp.

Marcel Duchamp belongs to a family of artists, a quite unusual circumstance in our time, as Mr Walter Pach remarked in 'A family of artists', his preface to the catalogue of the exhibition *Duchamp Frères & Sœur, Œuvres d'Art*.[2] Gaston, the eldest of six children of M. Eugène Duchamp, a notary in the Rouen region, studied law but soon gave in to his penchant for the fine arts and began, about 1900, under the pseudonym Jacques Villon, to publish illustrations and drawings in various newspapers and reviews. Then he joined the cubist-futurist movement, bringing an important contribution to Orphism. His studio at Puteaux was the meeting-place for some of the most brilliant representatives of modern ideas in art. Villon revealed himself, over a period of time, to be a painter and engraver with an extraordinary mastery of his media. His brother Raymond abandoned medicine to devote himself to sculpture; dying prematurely in 1919 of an illness contracted in the army during the first World War, Raymond Duchamp-Villon left a comparatively small body of work, but one that places him as the first in date and one of the greatest of all cubist sculptors; his model of the Cubist House, partly constructed to scale, created a sensation at the Salon d'Automne in 1912. Marcel Duchamp, born in Blainville (Seine-Maritime) in 1887, became a painter in his turn. Lastly, one of the three sisters, Suzanne, also devoted herself to painting and took part in the avant-garde exhibitions preceding the Dada movement, in whose activities she participated with the painter Jean Crotti, whom she married in 1919. This artistic vocation in the Duchamps can be traced back to their maternal ancestry; their mother was an accomplished painter and their grandfather, Emile Nicolle, was a talented engraver who recorded many features of the old town of Rouen.[3]

Marcel Duchamp came to study painting in Paris, attended the Académie Julian, and published occasional drawings in those newspapers to which his brother was contributing; he was also, for a time, a librarian in the Bibliothèque Sainte-Geneviève. Those of his first paintings which remain (he destroyed a great many of them) are landscapes, in bold brush-strokes and restrained colours. In 1910 he was painting compositions and portraits, including a large picture, *The Chess Players*, showing the members of the Duchamp family gathered together in the garden of Jacques Villon's studio, and the authoritative portrait, *The Artist's Father*. But already certain of his paintings were showing a Cézannian mirror-effect; broken shading-

1. I am indebted to the late Walter Pach, who was one of the organizers of the Armory Show, for the above information.

2. Rose Fried Gallery, New York, February-March 1952.

3. Conserved in the department of prints at the Musée du Louvre, these plates have become precious historical documents as a result of the destructions during the last war.

off tones slash the contours of the objects: *Draught on the Japanese Apple-tree, Young Man and Girl in Spring*.[1]

Concerning Young Sister (1911) is a silhouette treated in grey, white and brown prisms; *Yvonne and Madeleine in Tatters* is a picture of apparitions, in which the profiles of the artist's sisters are multiplied and superimposed, mingled with heavy masses of hair. The *Coffee Mill* is already a preliminary sketch of the great mechanisms which were to appear later on the Glass of *The Bride Stripped Bare by her Bachelors, Even*.

In December 1911, with *The Sad Young Man in a Train* and a study for the famous *Nude Descending a Staircase*, Duchamp abandoned what realism remained from the foregoing period, and the field of his investigations became considerably wider.

The exterior of an object, its actual state, is

The garden of Jacques Villon's studio in Puteaux.

like the envelope of previous states which have become interiorized with time. A cross-section of this object can thus reveal the existence of forms accumulated in a definite sequence, like the concentric circles in the cross-section of a tree-trunk. In the inorganic world, the stratifications of the earth's crust have a similar significance: the different rock-strata are arranged—or disarranged—chronologically. The fact of stratification is bound up with the problem of space-time.

According to one of the experimental data of the Rorschach test, 'introversive-contemplative' subjects have a tendency to interpret images as geological *stratifications*. The 'wise man' who sees a stratified structure in a 'chance picture' will reproduce a similar vision on his canvas, if he is a painter. Thus, in ancient times, Chinese artists, who were also Taoist sages, painted human figures as though they were enclosed in the folds of a landscape, similar to the fossil creatures which are discovered embedded among the crystals and stones of a rock-stratum.[2] And, as we know, Leonardo da Vinci was intensely interested in geology and in the study of the stratifications of rock-formations.

One finds a curious variant of this problem in the paintings of Picasso and Braque known as 'Scaffoldings', which correspond to what is certainly the most esoteric phase of their researches. Inspired, it appears, by the traces left on the surfaces of buildings in the course of being demolished—the black smears left by vanished chimneys, fragments of wall-paper still clinging to the walls, the mosaic of bricks and stones, etc.—these pictures can be called geological cross-sections of a dead house, the fossil of dispersed or vanished existences.

Futurist art used stratification more as a secondary result of movement, the latter determining its serial elements (cf. Balla's amusing *Dog on a Leash*). With *The Sad Young Man in a Train*, which shows Duchamp clearly influenced by Futurism, the stratification becomes the main theme of the picture: a sort of rhythmic melancholy emerges from the composition's play of broken surfaces, with successive planes withdrawing jerkily into a deep shadow, evoking the very idea of travel. The colour-scheme includes all the shades of brown, and this fact confronts us with one of Duchamp's 'Chinese' characteristics: in many of his works, the colour is predominantly yellow, or yellow-brown, and some of his paintings seem to be *lacquered* with a bright varnish (an impression scrupulously reproduced in the facsimiles collected by the artist himself in his *Boîte en Valise*);[3] indeed, was not *The Bride Stripped Bare...* conceived originally as *a world in yellow*?

In January 1912, Duchamp painted the definitive version of *Nude Descending a Staircase*. The effect of stratification creates an almost unfathomable

---

1. The first of these paintings, reproduced in the *Almanach Surréaliste du Demi-siècle* (La Nef, Paris, 1950) represents a corner of the garden of the Puteaux studio. Under the blue and rose of the sky and the apple-trees, a thick figure is squatting, a sort of female Buddha: this is a model who used to pose for the Duchamps and whom they called 'The Japanese'. The other picture, executed in yellow-beige tones, belongs to Mme Suzanne Duchamp.

2. Cf., for example, plate 29 in W. Cohn: *Chinese Painting*, (Phaidon Press, London, 1950), reproducing a ninth century work after Kouan Hsieou.

3. See pp. 34-35.

NU DESCENDANT UN ESCALIER

Marcel Duchamp: *Nude Descending a Staircase.* 1912.

depth, while the composition accentuates a lightning-like movement which was already perceptible in the *Young Man*. But the picture suggests a lewd intention, a desecration of the most hidden

Francis Picabia: *The Cacodylatic Eye*. 1921.

unable to explain objectively the reason for their disquiet—began to worry about the possible scandal if the picture was hung at the Salon des Indépendants of 1912, where Duchamp intended to show it to the public for the first time. For a nude to be posed standing, lying down or by the edge of a lake, remained entirely permissible; but that a nude, transformed into flashes of glacial lightning, should begin to descend a staircase... If even the picture were entitled 'Composition' or 'Figure': but the only too explanatory title was written on the canvas itself![1] Marcel Duchamp agreed finally to keep his work back for the Section d'Or exhibition[2] which Albert Gleizes was organizing during that same year, 1912, a display which was to include Archipenko, Duchamp, Jacques Villon, Picabia, Duchamp-Villon, Juan Gris, La Fresnaye, Léger, Lhote, Marcoussis, Metzinger, Suzanne Duchamp and several others.

The studies on the theme of the king and queen in chess also date from 1912: paintings the colour of varnished wood, in which the reverie of nudes flashes across the surface like pale rockets. Finally, during the summer of this year, while staying in Munich, the artist began to elaborate the first practical projects for *The Bride Stripped Bare by her Bachelors, Even*, a work to which a special chapter will be devoted.

The beginning of 1914 witnessed the birth of what one might call the 'anti-art object': the *readymade*, invented by Marcel Duchamp.

A calendar picture—a vague colour-print representing some completely vapid clearing in the woods—with two small splashes of colour added, one green, one red, became *Pharmacy* in January, 1914; a little later, and without even modifying it, Duchamp *signed* a bottle-rack in galvanized iron of the 'tiara' type. These were the first examples of a whole series of objects—about twenty in all— 'designated' (rather than created) from 1914 to 1925, all of which are reproduced in the *Boîte en Valise* (1940): the *Boîte* itself is a sort of *ready-*

human impulses: it is impossible to avoid, here, the psychoanalytical interpretation of the dream of walking down a staircase as symbolizing the act of love. Confronted with this painting crammed with meaning and yet indecipherable enough at first sight, even the artist's own friends—although

1. Apollinaire, in *The Cubist Painters*, emphasized the importance of this new procedure, which Picabia was to take up and develop when he covered his 'mechanist' compositions with ironic phrases and even produced a picture— *The Cacodylatic Eye*—composed entirely of inscriptions: the signatures of his friends.

2. The title of this exhibition was chosen by Jacques Villon, who was at that time studying the famous mathematical formula of the Golden Rule.

made, a suit-case designed by Duchamp and containing facsimiles or miniature copies of most of his pictures and objects.

Outside painting and the long-established truths of art—plasticity, harmony, craft, matter—but at the heart of reality, of poetry and of humour; disarming syntheses of chance discovery and everyday objects; creations-destructions; definitive and fragile objects which appear to derive from unknown psychological categories; 'simple, assist-

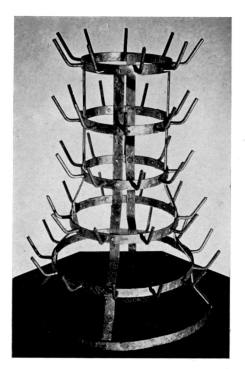

ed, rectified' readymades, 'unhappy' readymade, 'assisted' readymade 'with hidden noise': many of these objects belong to the cycle of research concerning *The Bride Stripped Bare...*, and most of them were elaborated by Duchamp during his stays in New York.

A project also exists of a 'reciprocal readymade', but one still awaits the art-lover or dealer capable of realizing it: it would simply involve 'using a Rembrandt as an ironing-board'.

As can be seen, the author's presence is unnecessary at the birth of these objects: the *Unhappy Readymade* was constructed by Suzanne Duchamp, in Paris, according to the instructions sent from

America by her brother, who advised her to suspend an *Introduction to Geometry* from her balcony and leave it exposed to the elements—like a 'geometry in space'.

'Specify readymades,' Duchamp has noted,[1] 'by planning for a moment to come (on such a day, such a date, such a moment), "to *inscribe* a readymade". The readymade can later be looked for (with all kinds of delays). The important thing then is just this matter of timing, this snapshot effect, like a speech delivered on no matter what occasion but *at such and such an hour*. It is a kind of rendezvous.—Inscribe this date, hour, minute on the readymade, of course, as *information*'.

'Also the exemplary significance of readymades,' the note adds. *Readymade*: this expression is opposed sartorially, of course, to the expression 'bespoke' or 'to measure,' the symbol of the smart personality. Duchamp's readymade is a far from banal development of the *principle of banality*; in these disconcerting objects, the personality bases itself upon a vaster generality, the collective fact becomes the one exemplar—the example.[2] We are concerned here with a very similar approach, basically, to that of the *Poésies* of Lautréamont, which we have analyzed elsewhere.[3] To designate a typewriter cover as a *Traveller's Folding Item*; a coat-rack nailed to the ground as a *Trap*; to give the title *In Advance of the Broken Arm* to a snow-shovel; to place 'panes' of waxed black leather in a window which is thereby transformed into a *Fresh Widow*,[4] etc., etc., all this amounts to saying: 'Whenever a thought presents itself to us as a commonly accepted truth, and we take the trouble to develop it, we will find that it is a discovery'[5] —instead of: 'Whenever a thought presents itself to us as a profound discovery, and we take the trouble to develop it, we will find that it is a commonly accepted truth.'[6]

Marcel Duchamp
Readymade. 1914.

1. In the papers, plans and notes concerning *The Bride...* (see Chapter 4).

2. 'Limit the number of readymades yearly', in the words of Duchamp.

3. See *Genèse de la Pensée moderne*, chap. 12 et seq. Though Duchamp was well acquainted with the *Chants de Maldoror*, he had probably not yet read the *Poésies* when he first concerned himself with readymades.

4. *Fresh widow*: a play on 'French window.' The object in question is, in fact, a French window as opposed to sash-window (which in French is a 'fenêtre à guillotine': the guillotine's slang name in French is *La veuve*, 'the widow').

5. Lautréamont: *Poésies* (Cf. *Œuvres complètes*, G. L. M., Paris, 1938).

6. Vauvenargues: *Maxims*.

For Marcel Duchamp, as for the Lautréamont of *Poésies*, banality is the point of departure for a series of complex developments; and, with Duchamp in particular, it constitutes a sort of mathematics of signs and significations, of which one of the most curious examples is the *Assisted Readymade with Hidden Noise*, constructed in 1916, on Easter day, in New York. The object consists of a ball of

Marcel Duchamp :
Assisted Readymade with Hidden Noise. 1916.

string pressed between two brass plates by means of four metal rods; W. Arensberg, art-collector and friend of Duchamp, put into the hollow centre of the ball of string an object which makes a sound when it strikes the brass plates. Only Arensberg knew the nature of the object which makes the noise. On the lower plate is inscribed:

.IR.	.CAR.É	LONGSEA
F.NE,	HEA.,	.O.SQUE
TE.U	S.ARP	BAR.AIN

On the upper plate is inscribed:

P.G.	.ECIDES	DÉBARASSE.
LE.	D.SERT.	F.URNIS.SENT
.AS	HOW.V.R	COR.ESPONDS

Several of the abbreviated words can be recognized (both English and French), though it is impossible to glean any general sense from the inscription, despite the promising ending *However corresponds*.

But the author himself is responsible for the simplest and clearest commentary concerning readymades. The organizers of the first Salon des Indépendants in New York, in 1917, refused to exhibit a *Fountain*, which was in fact simply a urinal, sent in by Duchamp and signed R. Mutt.[1] Upon which, Duchamp withdrew from the organizing committee of the Salon and had the following text published in *The Blind Man*,[2] a fine example of '*ironism of affirmation*: differences from negative ironism dependent solely on Laughter'.

THE RICHARD MUTT CASE

They say any artist paying six dollars may exhibit. Mr Richard Mutt sent in a fountain. Without discussion this article disappeared and never was exhibited.

What were the grounds for refusing Mr Mutt's fountain:—

1 Some contended it was immoral, vulgar.

2 Others, it was plagiarism, a plain piece of plumbing.

Now Mr Mutt's fountain is not immoral, that is absurd, no more than a bath tub is immoral. It is a fixture that you see every day in plumbers' show windows.

Whether Mr Mutt with his own hands made the fountain or not has no importance. He CHOSE *it. He took an ordinary article of life, placed it so that its useful significance disappeared under the new title and point of view—created a new thought for that object.*

As for plumbing, that is absurd. The only works of art America has given are her plumbing and her bridges.

1. The name of a New York manufacturer of sanitary hardware.

2. A little review edited by Duchamp and his friends, which consisted of only two numbers (April, May, 1917). There was also *Rong-Wrong* (June, 1917), whose title is due to a typographical error (the review was originally supposed to be called *Wrong-Wrong*).

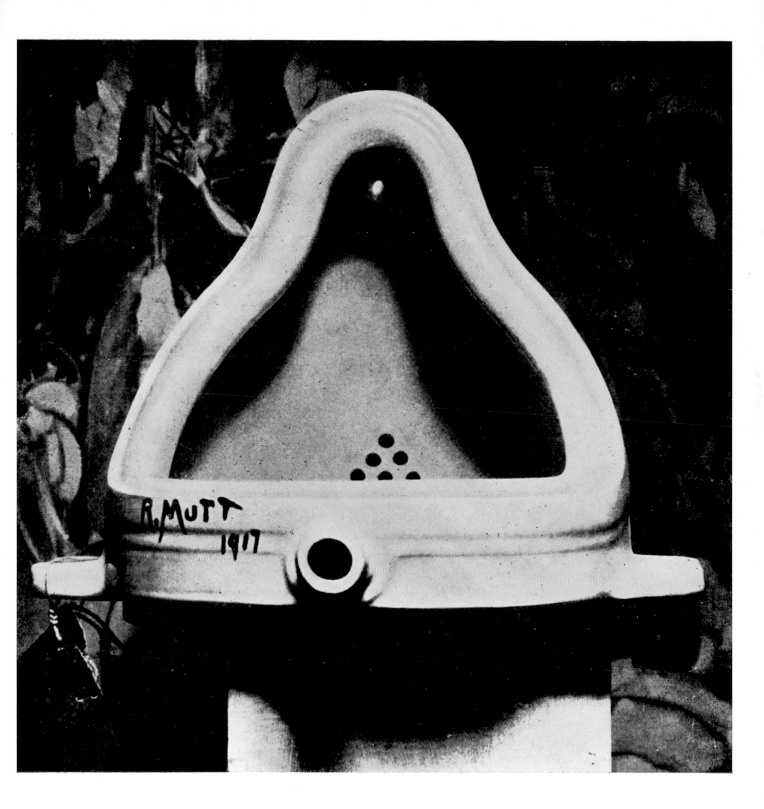

Richard Mutt: *Fountain.* 1917.

Henri Rousseau: *The Merry Jesters*. 1906.

CHAPTER II

CONCERNING THE GREAT HOTHOUSES OF THE CITY OF PARIS AND THE ISLAND OF HALLUCINATIONS

The process of recognition of inner values should not be considered as resulting simply from the precise and logical opposition of the concepts of conscious and unconscious. Things are much more complicated. Conscious and unconscious are essentially antagonistic *forces*, the first tending towards concentration and a state of rest, the second towards expansion and unlimited acceleration. The conscious plays the part of a brake in respect of the impulses which form the unconscious, controls them and tends to immobilize them. In this way a dynamic equilibrium establishes itself in the human being's 'normal' psyche, resulting from a sort of alternating current, a 'pulsation' of conscious (centripetal) and unconscious (centrifugal) forces.[1]

When the equilibrium is broken, that is to say when a 'scission' is produced in the human soul —that *schizis* so often discussed since Bleuler— the elements of *both* forces are liberated and attain a sort of autonomy; they become 'individualized', and consequently appear (conscious or unconscious) to be strange and unrecognizable. It can happen, then—for instance in an epileptic crisis—that the unconscious takes entire possession of the psyche; but, more frequently, a new pair forms itself, composed of individualized elements, *alongside* the original conscious-unconscious pair, which survives more or less precariously. A complex drama has taken shape: the normal dynamic pair is weakened, and the individual can no longer pursue his social activities, while certain conscious elements appear to become reinforced and exaggerated as if to regain control of an unfettered unconscious. The symptoms of catatonic schizophrenia are very characteristic in this respect. This condition is considered to be a typical manifestation of the unconscious, but it seems more probable that the muscular stasis, the 'solidifications of movement' which characterize this curious state, in which the patient is capable of retaining the most extravagant postures, sometimes over a long period of time, express a *controlling* element denoting repression. In addition, the catatonic retains the memory of his actions, while the epileptic crisis is a complete extinction of the conscious.

Some disequilibriums, therefore, resolve themselves into a new equilibrium which is established at a different level and, in particular, according to an entirely different *tension*. As the Rorschach experiments demonstrate, immobility and stationary forms remain in any case the distinctive signs of those elements deriving from the conscious; and asymmetry and movement those of the unconscious elements. The strange drawings of schizophrenics sometimes show brilliant colours; more often still one can notice precise, solidified, geometric shapes, and an assertive composition (sometimes going as far as symmetry) which combine to give to some of these spontaneous designs the status of genuine works of art.

Thus, because a certain element seems strange, it does not mean necessarily that it emanates from the unconscious; the strangeness derives initially from the removal of this element from its usual surroundings, and from the ruptured equilibrium which has liberated it and allowed it to show itself in its original, individual form.

1. Arpad Mezei and I have dealt with the thesis of *psychic pulsation* in connection with Lautréamont, in whom this pulsation is particularly vigorous, in our preceding works: *Maldoror* (Editions du Pavois, Paris, 1947—see the Chapter 'L'Alternance') and *Genèse de la Pensée Moderne*.

Pathological cases such as schizophrenia are by no means the only ones to reveal individualized elements. In dreams, for instance, or during childhood—that is to say each time the conscious brake is not working at full power, or when the usual state of conscious-unconscious tension is modified—these elements surge forward with their bizarre and unusual features. In the world of the child, the antagonistic forces are present in a practically pure state; fresh and natural, they express themselves in drawings which are simultaneously slipshod and conscientious, colourful and full of movement, almost always remarkable in composition, brimming over with that graphic imagination which is so typical of childhood. We know that this inspiration falters and then disappears fairly quickly. Except, indeed, with those who have been labelled the *naïves*.

Arpad Mezei and I have discussed naïvety elsewhere, in connection with the Hungarian Csontvary, an East European Douanier Rousseau. He was contemporary with Rousseau but his destiny was tragic; Csontvary never knew the friendship of fellow-artists and poets and died unknown and in frightful misery, leaving behind him an uneven body of work which nevertheless included the series of 'Cedar' paintings *(Pilgrimage to the Cedar, The Solitary Cedar)* which add a genuinely esoteric note to the splendours of pictorial ingenuousness. The naïve, we suggested in an article devoted to Csontvary[1] is someone who, after reaching adulthood, retains intact the childish feeling of absolute power, the conviction that *desire and reality are synonymous*. Naïvety is based on wish-fulfilment and includes a very important conscious element; not just the realization of desire in the manner of a dream but the 'realization of the real', the real embodying in this sense dream and the waking state.

Henri Rousseau, called the Douanier, submitted himself to reality with—one might say—passion. When he painted a portrait, he measured his model with a ruler and copied the dimensions onto the canvas. For his outdoors themes, he painted the picture in his studio from rough sketches of the subject drawn on the spot, brilliant outlines which had the fault in his eyes, nevertheless, of not being 'finished'. Direct observation always remains contingent, and Rousseau wanted to go further. On being shown paintings by Matisse he exclaimed: 'Why does this painter not finish his pictures?'

The finished paintings of Rousseau reveal an important contribution which is his style itself, and the *naïve style* in general: a conscious and 'conscientious' intervention, controlling, specifying, immobilizing forms. When he finally copied his sketch in his studio, a subtle and pure colour, sharply contrasted, adorned a world of precise objects and freshly created appearances.

Perhaps the marvellous virgin forests which he painted towards the end of his life were reminiscences of far-off countries: Rousseau is supposed to have taken part in Napoleon III's Mexican campaign—although this is more than doubtful. But as Roch Grey has very justly remarked,[2] the vegetation of these luxuriant 'forests' resembles the greenhouses of a botanical garden rather than a real virgin forest: greenhouses in which an *inner* jungle grows, tier upon tier of reeds, foliations and palms. Equally, the Douanier's fauna belongs in a zoo, as do his lions, tigers, antelopes and parrots; his monkeys are Merry Jesters who amuse the Sunday visitors. And no doubt his savages and his Arabs came straight out of the pages of travel memoirs and popular publications. In fact there are no rare words in Rousseau's poetry: his exotic visions can all have been observed in Paris. And yet there is often an unexpected juxtaposition between objects which are in themselves banal: in the middle of the carefully arranged tangle of these great unglazed greenhouses a lady is stretched out, naked, on a Louis-Philippe couch. The conscientious transposition of reality attains a truly poetic synthesis: a bouquet of flowers, a path through a park, the rosy-pink flamingos of the Botanical Garden contain the voyage, the memory and the dream, and reveal poetic reality connected directly with concrete reality.

Henri Rousseau died in 1910, and in that same year a painter appeared who seemed also to be isolated in his own epoch and unaffected by any of the artistic movements around him. The art of Giorgio de Chirico is authentically naïve: it never abandons the world of appearances, and describes this world with the conscience and scrupulosity of a child-painter. But these so faithfully reproduced appearances are in reality profoundly disturbed. Something seems to menace the marvellous equilibrium; a mysterious disquiet spreads through the tranquil and sunlit landscapes of consciousness.

1. In the review *Cahiers d'Art*, No. 1, Paris, 1949.

2. *Henri Rousseau*, by Roch Grey (Valori Plastici, Rome, 1922).

Giorgio de Chirico's first years were spent in Greece. He was born of Italian parents on July 10, 1880 in Volo, Thessaly, where his father was supervising the construction of a railway line. Twenty-five years later, that obsessive reminiscence, an old-fashioned locomotive puffing smoke, could be seen again and again drawing its length along the 'vast, immortality-echoing horizon' of Chirico's pictures. The same memory occurs in the artist's writings; a text published in 1926 is significantly entitled *The Engineer's Son*; *Hebdomeros* especially, an astonishing book, half-dream, half-novel, which appeared in 1929, contains numerous allusions to engineers 'employed to extend a railway track'; whole pages of this work are devoted to the memory of the author's father, his tastes, his habits, his ideas; and the hero himself, Hebdomeros, says that the goddess Immortality 'has the eyes of his father' (which explains a curious symbol described at the beginning of the book: 'an old-fashioned locomotive surrounded by a snake biting its own tail'). The artist's mother was a domineering woman, controlling her household with absolute authority. Giorgio also had a sister, who died very young, and a brother, Andrea, whose activities, under the pseudonym of Savinio, became multifarious later in the fields of music, painting and literature.[1]

Giorgio de Chirico showed a lively inclination for painting early in life; while still a child, he took lessons from a certain Mavroudis, 'a Greek from Trieste who spoke a little Italian with a Venetian accent',[2] who apparently taught him the first rules of perspective, the way to draw shadows, and so on. In Athens, where his family lived from 1899 onwards, a Swiss painter, Gilleron (who specialized in pictures of ancient ruins) gave him lessons before he entered the School of Fine Arts of the Greek capital: here, he was a fairly dull pupil, neither outstandingly successful nor unsuccessful. It is said that he painted lugubrious landscapes and seascapes at the time, inspired by Caspar David Friedrich and Karl Blechen.

His father died in 1905 and Chirico returned to Italy with his mother and brother. After brief stays in Venice and Milan they left for Bavaria; Giorgio spent two years studying at the Royal Academy of Munich, while Savinio studied music. The young painter seems to have become increasingly interested by the work of Arnold Böcklin (by that of Max Klinger, too; and perhaps, in James Thrall Soby's opinion, by other 'literary' painters such as Franz Stuck and Alfred Kubin). He went through a 'Böcklin period' after his return to Italy in 1909. His *Battle between the Hoplites and the Centaurs* is a replica of Böcklin's *Battle of the Centaurs*, and a *Seascape* shares something of the oppressive atmosphere of *The Island of the Dead*. At the same time, Chirico got to know the works of Nietzsche while he was in Munich. (Mr. Soby has mentioned some passages from *The Birth of Tragedy* and from *Human, Too Human*, on 'symbolical dream-pictures', dealing with the importance for an artist of the dream-world, which correspond to certain preoccupations that are to be found in Chirico's artistic development). In other respects, Schopenhauer and his famous *Essay on Apparitions*, and the writings of the Austrian philosopher Otto Weininger, were also revelatory for Chirico. From 1909 to 1911 he was to be found in Turin, Milan and Florence—always accompanied by his mother. He had almost no contact with other artists and it seems that he was hardly aware of Cubism, Futurism or any other development in contemporary art.

Up to that time he had never shown (or sold) a single picture. In July, 1911 the family moved to Paris, and it was 'in a dreary studio in the rue Campagne-Première' that Giorgio de Chirico—as he said later—began to discern 'the first ghosts of a more complete, more profound and more complicated art, an art which was—in one word—*more metaphysical*... The huge glove in painted zinc, with its terrible golden finger-nails, swinging over the shop door in the sad wind blowing on city afternoons, revealed to me, with its index finger pointing down at the flagstones of the pavement, the hidden signs of a new melancholy...'

At first they were landscapes in which the ice-clear reflection of green skies enveloping rigid architecture is perhaps a reminiscence of the 'Athens of the North'. But the squares and the arcaded streets which provide the theme for Chirico's first pictures are more reminiscent of Italian cities: Florence, perhaps, with the delicate arcades of the Piazza della SS. Annunziata, and its anachronistic street-car swaying along the shady side of the square like a ghost rattling its chains.

1. I wish to thank here M. Giovanni Scheiwiller, of Milan, and M. Pierre Courthion, for much information about Chirico as well as for some important documents. I also found many useful references in the works of Mr James Thrall Soby: *The Early Chirico*, and its entirely revised new edition, *Giorgio de Chirico* (The Museum of Modern Art, New York, 1955).

2. G. de Chirico: *Memorie della mia vita* (Astrolabio, Rome, 1945).

Giorgio de Chirico: *Self Portrait*. 1913.

But, above all, Turin, one of the most 'urbanized' cities in Italy—'Turin, the one living-place that reason suggests to me', said Nietzsche in *Ecce Homo*—with the regular chequer-work of its streets becoming mysteriously labyrinthine by virtue of the arcades whose ceaseless cavalcade keeps pace with the avenues and squares. Turin, with its statues of melancholy gentlemen in frock-coats carrying stone books in their hands; its façades with clocks; the trains which run through the suburbs in cuttings; the red brick Roman towers of the Palatine Gate; and the incredible Mole Antonelliana, the prototype of so many of Chirico's towers, an enormous, crazy synagogue, rearing up for nearly seven hundred feet of colonnades, façades and roof placed upon roof—and then, more peristyles, more roofs and porticos, from which at last is thrust a vertiginous spire with columns and foot-bridges, ending only with the star on its topmost pinnacle! When Chirico wrote, in *Hebdomeros*, 'Lyphontius the philosopher lived in a modest apartment above the portico which framed the town's main square. From his window he could see the back of the statue of his father, which was set up on a low plinth in the centre of the square', it was almost the literal truth; the statue exists, in Turin, in a square with arcades, and does indeed immortalize that railway engineer who possessed the remarkable surname of Paleocapa.

The Period of Arcades is in fact an Italian town seen 'with closed eyes'—with the eyes of remembrance. *Hebdomeros* also conveys to us the atmosphere and scenery of this quiet, mysterious city, recreated in the silence of memory, where each building has the appearance 'of a huge plaything finally placed in position after several efforts'. Everything is still, even the oriflammes displayed above the towers like medieval illuminated scrolls, and everything seems silent. On the palace frontages, the clock-hands have stopped: it is always afternoon in Chirico's pictures, a late summer afternoon, an hour impregnated with 'the quite special *stimmung* which emanates when, going out into the streets at sunset, at the end of a hot summer's day, after having slept through the afternoon, one smells the odour of those freshly-watered streets'. And, in the background, stretch 'those distant horizons heavy with adventures, which Hebdomeros had always loved since his days of sad childhood'.

In the deserted town, one can see 'a few transient demigods, their faces inscrutable, their robes dignified': silhouettes which evoke the crepuscular

Giorgio de Chirico: *The Enigma of the Hour.* 1912.

Giorgio de Chirico:
The Anxious Voyage.
1913.

Giorgio de Chirico:
The Fête Day. 1914.

Giorgio de Chirico:
Portrait of Guillaume Apollinaire. 1918.

Giorgio de Chirico: *The Uncertainty of the Poet.* 1913.

Giorgio de Chirico:
Nostalgia of the Infinite. 1913-1914.

figure of Ulysses in Böcklin's *Ulysses and Calypso*, 'much more interesting and complicated ghosts than those who usually appear about midnight'. The hard shadows of the objects attract more attention than the objects themselves, for the shadows seem to possess more reality than the objects whose shadows they are. And sometimes the shadow is the object: the equestrian statue of *Departure of the Poet*, the little girl with the hoop in *Mystery and Melancholy of a Street* stand out in black silhouettes although the scenes' lighting does not justify such an unusual effect. The presence of human beings is asserted in an indirect manner; everything is elaborated, manufactured: objects are grouped following a clearly premeditated order, turning towards us as if they had something to say, a message to transmit. One calls to mind ghost-ships, mysteries that have become famous in the annals of navigation like the *Marie-Céleste*, the ship discovered, during the last century, in the middle of the Atlantic, its sails billowing beneath the sun, the tea still warm on the captain's table, and not one soul on board.

Not long after his arrival in Paris, and thanks to the support of the painter Laprade to whom a friend had given him an introduction, Chirico exhibited a few paintings at the Salon d'Automne; he also sent some to the Salon des Indépendants. Apollinaire soon discovered his existence and proceeded to hail him as 'the most astonishing painter of the younger generation', comparing him, in an article in *Soirées de Paris*, with the Douanier Rousseau. At that time Chirico attended the meetings which took place every Saturday at Apollinaire's house, and the relationship between the painter and the poet became close enough for the latter to add occasionally a new dimension to the melancholic enigmas contained in his friend's images by baptizing them with evocative titles. It seems, too, that the dealer Paul Guillaume, one of Chirico's first buyers, invented some of the titles. (Later on, the surrealists in their turn rechristened certain of his paintings.) From this era dates the well-known prophetic portrait of Apollinaire by Chirico, in which the poet's profile is shown as a black silhouette, and a circular white line marks the spot where the author of *Poète Assassiné* was to undergo a trepanation in 1916. After the event, Apollinaire used to show the picture—which he had already referred to, before he was wounded, as 'my portrait *as human target*'—with the remark that the scar of the operation seemed to be on the left side (and not on the right as in reality) 'because

this is not my head, but its cast shadow'.

From 1911 to 1914, Chirico painted mostly urban landscapes, less often unexpected arrangements of objects such as the *Self-portrait* of 1913 in which two sculpted feet detached from some statue, an egg, and something like a roll of paper are to be seen in front of a wall on which an immense X is traced. Human beings hardly ever appear: in *I'll Be There... the Glass Dog* (1913) the man's torso is merely an anatomical simulacrum, opened by a shutter showing the heart; as for the ironic, sly, pot-bellied figure with lowered eyes of the *Child's Brain*, everything points to it being a phantom: the picture was originally called *The Ghost*, and the apparition—according to Chirico himself—evoked at the same time his own father and Napoleon III.

From 1914-15 onwards, assemblages of objects become the centre of interest: gloves, hands from anatomical models, eye-glasses, cigar boxes, etc., an incongruous medley including also some incomprehensible geometrical objects; compositions resembling still-lives in the open air—or rather in the centre of town, for the arcades, towers and chimneys are always present in the middle ground. And, about 1915, the *Mannequins* appear. Alone, or in couples, these beings with smooth, egg-shaped heads lacking sense-organs but bearing sometimes the mathematical sign of infinity in place of their absent eyes, pose on floors whose planks recede in perspective towards the distant arcades; they adopt the meditative, disquieting poses of those articulated figurines which serve as models for physical attitudes in art studios.

Italy's entry into the war in 1915 had forced the Chirico family to return to their own country. The artist was mobilized into the 27th Infantry Regiment at Ferrara, in Emilia, a countryside which has actually been created by the hand of man: what had always been swamp-land transformed into a flourishing landscape divided neatly by the rectilinear lines of canals and roads. It was in Ferrara, in a military hospital where he was spending a few weeks recuperating from an illness, that he met Carlo Carrà who was beginning to detach himself from Futurism, of which he had been one of the first adherents. The two friends obtained permission to work together in a private room, and it has been said that the army doctors were so disturbed by their pictorial productions that they thought it best to send them both on extended sick-leave! However that may be, it is certain that the paintings of this period are part of Italy, in shops selling technical equipment—elaborate stacks of carpenters' rules, T-squares, frames and set-squares. Easels hold pictures (these pictures within the picture sometimes represent his earlier landscapes: a factory, an arcaded palace), anatomical charts lean against the wainscoting, and geographical maps showing the contours of unknown continents festooned with the conventional dotted lines of navigational itineraries. Sometimes the centre of the composition is occupied by a kind of panoply formed by rows of biscuits, resembling the window-displays in the Jewish bakeries of Ferrara which had also fascinated the artist.

The Castello Estense in Ferrara.

Carrà's paintings were no less strange, borrowing many elements from Chirico's repertoire, but transposing them into a personal, less tragic style: *The Enchanted Room, Solitude, The Oval of Apparitions.* (A little later, Carrà, with Giorgio Morandi, founded a short-lived *Scuola Metafisica.*)

Chirico prolonged the period of his *Metaphysical Interiors* until 1918, with the Mannequins making occasional reappearances: *The Troubadour, Hector and Andromache,* and the celebrated *Disquieting Muses* who, from an elevated platform, dominate the town of Ferrara, with the Estense Castle glowing red in the background.

As I have already remarked, it is difficult, at first sight, to detect any connection between Chirico's painting and that of the contemporary movements in art. The most that can be said is that the stable forms of Cubism influenced him slightly, but extraneously and belatedly: the tangles of woodwork in his *Metaphysical Interiors* of 1916-17 seem to materialize Picasso's transparent *Scaffoldings* of 1911-12. But Chirico represents, in fact, a further stage of evolution. He expresses the

Giorgio de Chirico: *The Disquieting Muses.* 1917.

among the strangest which either of these artists ever produced. Chirico's urban landscapes had given way to *Metaphysical Interiors*; one can still just glimpse these landscapes occasionally from the windows or, rather, the portholes of rooms where extraordinary trophies reach from the floor to the ceiling: trophies such as can be seen, in this specific values of the 'civilized' psyche: with him, modern intelligence takes on an hallucinatory quality.

By making an effort to resist coldly the suggestions emanating from these taciturn paintings, we can detect certain relationships which regulate their inner existence. The man who was capable of carving out these geometric minerals and constructing these rigid monuments was equally capable of fabricating their disquieting arrangements. He was capable of subduing nature, subjugating it and practically excluding it from his universe. Nature only shows itself to this civilized human being in the form of foodstuffs: fruits, vegetables, and most often manufactured foodstuffs: biscuits, sweets. The universe is made of works created by the hand of man, architectures, statues, scientific-magical objects. When, in a text published in 1920 in the review *Il Convegno* (no. 4), Chirico emphasizes the masterful treatment by Böcklin 'of the tragic aspects of statuary',[1] he is clearly referring to his own preoccupations, to his mannequins absorbed in the contemplation of an incomprehensible problem drawn on a blackboard (*The Seer* of 1915) by an 'engineer' of whom one can glimpse only the shadow thrown along one corner of the picture. His prophetic work is sonorous, too, with echoes of ancient times, of the memory of an era of builders, sculptors and realistic painters: Roman civilization. It is the reverie of an idler in an ancient town where certain aspects of latter-day civilization are as surprising as ghosts.

Chirico, in his writings, has more than once shown himself intrigued by the adventure of the 'father of civilizations', Prometheus, the creator of the first moving statue: man himself. He situates this myth in relation to that of Christ, but in a rather sarcastic manner: in *Hebdomeros* he describes to his readers a certain picture entitled *Caucasus and Golgotha*, painted by a Negro artist and representing Hebdomeros himself meditating in front of the panorama of an industrial town, while on a nearby mountain the scenes of the Crucifixion are enacted; this painting, he adds, 'had won a silver medal for its balanced composition'. In *The Engineer's Son* he uses a Nietzschian expression in ascribing to Prometheus and Jesus the quality of *superior beings*; and, without abandoning his ironic tone, he describes the rescue of Prometheus: 'Mercury, being an efficient god, and never at a loss, held the wounded man with a hand under his knees, like those figures shown in paintings of the *Entombment*.'

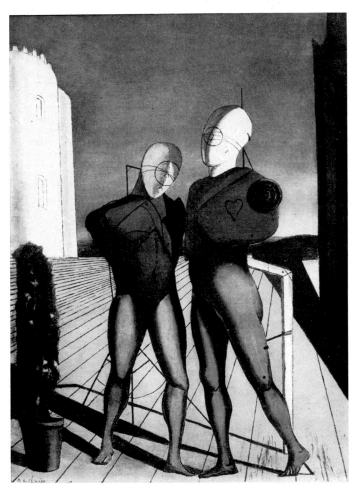

As myths of civilization, the story of Christ and that of Prometheus are closely connected (as Gustave Moreau had already shown in his *Prometheus*). The crucifixion of Jesus and the spear wound recall the binding-down of Prometheus and the vulture's snapping beak, and the two heroes appear as two kinds of *scapegoat*: one is tortured by the gods from whom he has stolen that basic ingredient of civilization, fire, the other offers himself as a holocaust to expiate the original sin which had revealed knowledge to an innocent

Giorgio de Chirico: *The Duo*, 1915.

1. Chirico has also mentioned the impression made on him by Versailles, with its palace and its grandiose, absurd park, where each tree has been formed and deformed by man, and where baroque statues confront one with their frozen gestures around the curves of every path.

49

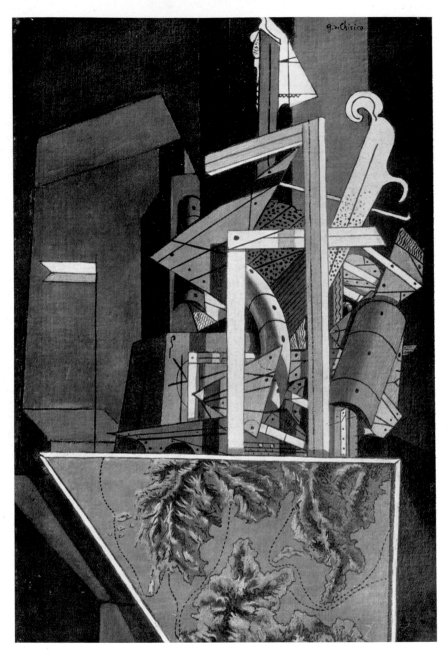

Giorgio de Chirico: *The Melancholy of Departure.* 1916.

scapegoat, which, in different forms is common to all religions (Frazer). It is clear, however, that Chirico's painting includes no element whatsoever borrowed from Promethean or Christian imagery, except, perhaps, for the *Sacred Fishes* of 1919 which are, in any case, red herrings! The painter himself has written that 'there are many more enigmas in the shadow of a man who walks in the sun than in all the religions of the past, present and future'.

If André Breton is right in thinking that the juxtaposition of towers and arcades expresses the relationship between the male and female sexes, 'the first justifying titles relating to *nostalgia*, the second inspiring titles which emphasize the *enigma*',[2] one can probably attribute a more specifically *maternal* value to the arcades: *The Sailors' Barracks, The Amusements of a Young Girl, The Playthings of the Prince*, etc., are all paintings which give the impression that their author, the painter-child, has just fled, abandoning his ultracivilized playthings at the foot of the menacing arcades. The perpetual sensation of being *at fault*, not towards Mother Nature but towards his own mother (the despotism with which Mme de Chirico reigned over her children has already been mentioned), a sort of panic before the maternal sphinx, was certainly a major obsession with Chirico. His painting abounds in veiled representations of terrors and desires, despite his own declaration of the need 'to rid art of all that has been its familiar content until now; all subject, all idea, all thought, all symbol must be put aside'; but the context shows that he was in fact attacking classic allegorization. His own symbols derive from modern psychological analysis, and reveal much more than an individual maladjustment. The enigma contained in his pictures is that of man at the threshold of the twentieth century, still living in the past, despite the fact that he has elaborated a new intellectualism divorced from the traditional systems and can feel stirring within him an unconscious liberated from age-old interpretations. Chirico's haunted, prophetic work is the meeting-place for forces which are extremely disquieting for humanity in our civilization.

'Above all a great sensitivity is needed. One must picture everything in the world as an enigma, not only the great questions one has always asked oneself—why was the world created, why we are

and 'natural' being. It is, in fact, upon the notion of culpability and the idea that each fault must ineluctably be paid for that the whole concept of the *sacred*[1] is founded, as, indeed, is the rite of the

1. According to Quatrefages de Bréau, quoted by H. Baruk in his *Précis de Psychiatrie* (Masson, Paris, 1949).

2. A. Breton, article on Savinio in *Anthologie de l'Humour Noir* (Sagittaire, Paris, 1950).

Giorgio de Chirico: *The Jewish Angel*, or *The Two Sisters*. 1915.

Giorgio de Chirico: *The Rose Tower*. 1913.

born, live and die, for after all, perhaps there is no reason in all of this. But rather to understand the enigma of things generally considered insignificant. To perceive the mystery of certain phenomena of feeling, of the character of a people, even to arrive at the point where one can picture the creative geniuses of the past as things, very strange things that we examine from all sides.'

Chirico speaks, too, of 'the invisible ties that join a people to its creations. Why for instance are the houses in France built in a certain style and not in another? There is no use citing history and the causes of this and of that; this describes, but it explains nothing for the eternal reason that there is nothing to explain, and yet the enigma always remains. The dormer windows on the roofs of the houses in Paris always fascinate me; I believe there is an unknown force which has driven the architects to make these *dormers*, to *feel* them'.

The feeling that the unconscious had at last appeared on the scene is certainly at the origin of the influence exercised over Chirico by Courbet, in whom Apollinaire saw 'the father of the new painters' and of whom Marcel Duchamp said that he represented the first intervention of the 'subconscious hand' in painting.[1] In his monograph on Courbet,[2] Chirico writes: 'Every work of art embraces the sense of reality, and the deeper that sense is, the more poetic, the more romantic will it be. Mysterious laws of perspective and equally mysterious reasons govern this verity. Who can deny the existence of a perplexing connection between perspective and metaphysics?'

The mystery begins to take shape, with him, in what has been called 'disturbances of perspective'—it would be more accurate to speak of new, split, multiple perspectives. There is almost an excess of perspective in his painting: the contours of objects 'recede' in absolute strictness, but towards a point situated well above the vanishing line, as in *Lassitude of the Infinite*; or again, the existence of several vanishing points placed on different vanishing lines produces a strangely labyrinthine effect, with a sort of overlapping of the arcades, as in *Anxious Journey*. In these images which are not superhuman but *superhumanized* the laws of art are forced rather than perverted, and certainly not ignored.

The maternal memory emanating from the multiple and magnetic gaze of the arcades is compounded with another which seems to have played a dynamic and creative role in his work: the nostalgic paternal memory. The symbolic presence of the engineer from Thessaly can be divined in the innumerable objects of a scientific nature that Chirico groups in his paintings, and in certain leitmotifs concerning travel, the famous locomotives for instance, and clocks like the ones in stations. These aspects even influence the maternal symbols: the arcades have a tendency to give Chirico's buildings the appearance of railway stations. Picasso once called him 'the painter of stations', and his picture *Melancholy of Departure* was, in fact, inspired directly by the Gare Montparnasse in Paris.

Anguish of Departure, Departure of the Poet, Anxious Journey, Endless Voyage: whether invented by himself or by Apollinaire or, later, by the surrealists, at all events these titles show the degree to which Chirico was attracted by the atmosphere of voyage and adventure.

A strange and motionless voyage. One never sees the sea in Chirico's pictures, yet one feels it to be very close. 'Where is the sea?' was the first question posed, in 1933, during the course of experimental researches[3] carried out by the surrealist group 'on the irrational possibilities of penetration and orientation in a picture', the example chosen being Giorgio de Chirico's *Enigma of a Day* (this huge canvas hung at that time in Breton's studio). Two replies seem to have played unconsciously upon the alliteration *mer-mère* (sea-mother). Where is the sea? Eluard: 'Inside the arcades.' Breton: 'Behind the statue.'[4]

'One must never forget,' wrote the artist in a text dating from his first stay in Paris in 1911-15,[5] 'that a picture must always be the reflection of a profound sensation, and that profound means strange, and strange means uncommon or altogether unknown... To be really immortal a work of art must go completely beyond the limits of the human... In this way it will come close to the dream state, and also to the mentality of children.' Beyond

1. In the *Catalogue of the Collection of the Société Anonyme*, notice on Sophie Taeuber-Arp.

2. G. de Chirico: *Gustave Courbet*, reprinted in English translation in M. Evans: *The Painter's Object* (Howe, London, 1937).

3. Cf. the review: *Le Surréalisme au Service de la Révolution* no. 5-6, May, 1933.

4. Which can be taken to represent the *father* of the artist.

5. This manuscript which belonged to Paul Eluard, as well as another in Jean Paulhan's collection, were published for the first time (in English translation) in James Thrall Soby's *Giorgio de Chirico*. The quotations on pp. 50 and 54 are also from this manuscript.

the limits of the human: the reference is to the limits within which the *adult* mentality is enclosed, for the dream and the mentality of children do not really contain anything superhuman.

Yet Nietzsche's philosophy can be detected behind these comments of Chirico's: Nietzsche may be called a 'naïve' among philosophers,

Giorgio de Chirico: *Joy*. 1913.

who wanted to transfer to those of adult age the a-religion, a-morality and will to power which are some of the most characteristic manifestations of the infantile mentality. Nietzsche's themes suggest a new tension between the conscious and the unconscious: 'The distance, and as it were the space around man, grows with the strength of his intellectual vision and insight: his world becomes profounder; new stars, new enigmas, and notions are ever coming into view. Perhaps everything on which the intellectual eye has exercised its acuteness and profundity has just been an occasion for its exercise, something of a game, something for children and childish minds. Perhaps the most solemn conceptions that have caused the most fighting and suffering, the conceptions "God" and "sin," will one day seem to us of no more importance than a child's plaything or a child's pain seems to an old man;—and perhaps another plaything and another pain will then be necessary once more for "the old man"—always childish enough, an eternal child!'[1]

Chirico claimed to have found in Nietzsche the first example of inspiration-revelation. The following passage from *Ecce Homo* anticipates

effectively the surrealists' theses on *automatism*:[2] 'The involuntary nature of inspiration is strangest in the case of image and metaphor; one no longer knows which is symbol, parallel or comparison. The image presents itself to you as the most accurate, simple and direct expression.' And the author adds, with an authentic and proud naïvety: 'I am convinced that one would have to go back thousands of years in the past to find someone who had the right to say: That experience is mine also.' In fact, observations of this nature on unconscious thought-processes had been published since the early years of Romanticism, in France and elsewhere, and some psychologists were beginning to realize that it was a question here of an experience common to all mankind. But the French 'psychologists' whom Nietzsche admired were 'Messrs Paul Bourget, Pierre Loti, Gyp, Meilhac, Anatole France, Jules Lemaître' *(Ecce Homo)*; it is true that the Douanier Rousseau's favourite painter was Bouguereau!

Chirico's reflections on music, however, are far from Nietzschian; he was doubtless more influenced, in this matter, by Apollinaire's circle, in which music, as later with the surrealists, was held in lowly esteem: '*No music*,' says the painter of *The Silent Statue*. 'Music cannot express the essence of sensation. One never knows what music is about, and after all, having heard any piece of music, whether by Beethoven, Wagner, Rossini, or Monsieur Saint-Saëns, every listener has the right to say, and can say, *what does this mean?* In a profound painting, on the contrary, this is impossible; one must fall silent when one has penetrated it in all its profundity, when one turns the corner of all its walls, and not of its walls alone. Then, light and shade, lines and angles begin to talk, and music too begins to be heard, that hidden music that one does not hear. What I listen to is worthless: there is only what I see with my eyes open—and even better closed. There is no mystery in music; that is precisely why it is the art people enjoy most, for they always find in it more *sensations*.'

'What one must do is *discover*,' says Hebdomeros. The town of Chirico's birth, Volo in Thessaly, is the ancient port of Pagases, whence the Argonauts left in their quest of the Golden Fleece. And the artist was to give a fresh reality to that legendary adventure: the *floors* of the mannequin period are astonishingly like the *deck* of a ship. 'In the *Iliad* heroes and gods alike always maintain

1. *Beyond Good and Evil*, I, 57.

2. See Part Two, chapter 5.

a robust reality... Throughout Ulysses' wanderings in the *Odyssey*, he can always feel his feet firmly planted on the four tarred planks of his good ship.'[1]

Thus, the chief mechanism of strangeness in Chirico's work is *disorientation*, with all the obscure menaces that this notion implies. Disorientation is as much the 'sense of prehistory' as it is the sign of enigma or of prophecy, and is equally the network of meanings which is woven between these two. Disorientation in time and space: the strangeness of Chirico's minutely realistic technique at a time when the new schools of painting had rejected verisimilitude, the disorientation of Italian towns painted and shown for the first time in Paris, the anachronism of scientific objects in antique surroundings, a coexistence between incomprehensible realities and commonplace realities, or instead, the clash of two realities commonplace in themselves but temporally out of balance (the furniture van abandoned alongside an arcaded palace)... Chirico's problem is basically the same as that of the Italian futurists, but expressed with totally different means: it derives from the disorientation of modern civilized man grappling with the reality of his own memories. But whereas Chirico expresses the *anguish* of man in this 'twofold civilization', the futurists express his *revolt*.

Chirico's journey is the exploration of its own maze: the inner labyrinth of twentieth century man. A journey during which marvellous spoils accumulate, gradually invading what was once an almost empty scene. The *Metaphysical Interiors* show the end of the adventure. The town is always there, a few cables'-lengths away; one can just distinguish it through the portholes of these capernaums piled high with ultra-civilized fetishes, portolanos of unknown coast-lines, sextants and theodolites for new dimensions. In this vessel returning from mysterious islands, the perspectives appear deformed, as in a ship's bunkers where the slanting bulkheads and sloping deck take the shape of the hull's external lines. And the cargo—as if to withstand what siege?—includes ship's stores, of course. More exactly: biscuits.

1. G. de Chirico: *Gustave Courbet*.

Giorgio de Chirico: *Metaphysical Interior*. 1917.

Was ist **dada**?

Eine Kunst? Eine Philosophie? eine Politik?
Eine Feuerversicherung?

Oder: Staatsreligion?

ist **dada** wirkliche Energie?

oder ist es ☞ Garnichts, d. h.
alles?

What is Dada? (Der Dada, no. 2, Berlin, 1919).

CHAPTER III
HOW, PREPARED IN NEW YORK,
THE DADA BOMB EXPLODED IN SWITZERLAND,
SET FIRE TO GERMANY
AND FIZZLED OUT IN PARIS

One of the first results of the declaration of war in 1914 was the sudden difficulty, if not impossibility, of retaining contact between the most active centres of modern art and poetry: France, Italy, Germany, New York, Russia... With varying degrees of willingness many poets and artists transformed themselves into warriors; others took measures to participate as little as possible in the imminent slaughter. Francis Picabia had to don French uniform, and became chauffeur to a general. The civilian costume which Marcel Duchamp was able to retain as a person judged medically unfit had certain disadvantages in the jingoistic atmosphere which soon began to reign in France. Duchamp decided to leave for the United States, and arrived there on June 15, 1915. Picabia soon joined him : he had got himself sent on an official mission to purchase molasses in Cuba, but once disembarked in New York he immediately forgot the object of his journey, fell ill and was declared medically unfit on the spot by a French military commission.

At that time there existed in New York an extremely vigorous avant-garde circle, inspired by Arthur Stieglitz, the great pioneer of photography. Stieglitz preserved the momentum generated by the Armory Show: his review *Camera Work* had reproduced the first cubist paintings as well as *Nude Descending a Staircase* and *Danses à la Source*; he himself had exhibited pictures by Braque and Picasso and orphist water-colours by Picabia in his apartment at 291 Fifth Avenue, where some rooms were set aside for exhibitions by young painters. The number '291' had become a sort of symbol of modern ideas and *Camera Work* finally appeared, in March, 1915, under the new title *291*. On the threshold of a new adventure, this ironic imp of photography made a point of suggesting to artists the limits which they should exceed rather than

respect. Marius de Zayas, one of the contributors to *291*, wrote in 1915, in no. 7-8, a commentary on a photo by Stieglitz, *The Steerage*, in which he said: 'Stieglitz has surpassed "Art", that idiotic word which for centuries has dominated everything, and which in reality has only expressed a mental state, a state of unconsciousness. "Art" had become an esoteric God who had for his sole prophet "Conventional Beauty". "Art" and "Conventional Beauty" together have exercised a tyranny. It is surely due in great part to photography, that we have finally freed ourselves from that spell.'

One may perhaps discern in this anti-artistic diatribe an echo of the ideas of Marcel Duchamp, already surrounded in New York 'by the halo of popularity resulting from the astonishing success of his *Nude* and from a sympathetic atmosphere which in no way compromised his role of smiling demoralizer'. Mme Gabrielle Buffet-Picabia relates, too, how she and Picabia were 'assimilated from the moment of their arrival into an incongruous international group which turned night into day and was the rallying point of conscientious objectors of all categories and all nationalities, expressing themselves in a fantastic outburst of sexual activity, jazz and alcohol'. In the centre of this chaos, 'a small number of artists, mostly from Europe, whose stars were undoubtedly Duchamp and Picabia, associated themselves with Alfred Stieglitz and his gallery at 291 Fifth Avenue, as well as with Walter and Lou Arensberg, far-sighted and generous art-lovers and art-patrons,[1] at whose home one was always sure to find at any hour of the day or night sandwiches, first-class chess players

Francis Picabia: *Francis par Picabia*. 1920.

1. The Arensberg collection (now in the Philadelphia Museum) includes the greater part of the works of Marcel Duchamp among its other artistic splendours.

and an atmosphere entirely free from traditional and social prejudices'.

Carrying on the activity of *Camera Work*, *291* published, apart from the work of contemporary American painters and poets, a calligram by Apollinaire *(The Little Car)*, drawings by Braque and Picasso, an orphist drawing by Picabia and, in no. 4 (June, 1915), one of this painter's first *mechanist* arrangements: *Girl Born without Mother*. No. 5-6 (July-August, 1915) is absolutely different in appearance: it is an immense folding album, devoted entirely to Picabia and his machine-drawings. *Portrait of a Young American Girl in a State of Nudity* represents an enormous spark-plug bearing the inscription FOR EVER; *The Saint of Saints—It's Me this Portrait Is About* reproduces a hooter; *This is Stieglitz, Faith and Love* is a very strange piece of photographic equipment; etc. Picabia's 'machine period', an inexhaustible series of pictures and drawings inaugurated before 1914 with paintings such as *The Discs*, proposes curiously realistic but improbable diagrams, emphasized by joking inscriptions; both forms and inscriptions appear to demand some impossible psychomechanical explanation.

After a few months stay in New York, Picabia and his wife left for Central America, then crossed the Atlantic again and reached Barcelona where they discovered other Parisians: Marie Laurencin, Albert Gleizes and Juliette Roche, and Arthur Cravan who was soon to leave for New York in his turn. In Barcelona, Picabia changed *291* into *391*, on January 15, 1917 with Stieglitz's approval. Thus was born the famous review which was to appear intermittently until 1924, without programme or method, but unflaggingly animated by the graphic and typographic inventions, the poems and the ironic aphorisms of Picabia; all the members of the Dada movement contributed to it. The first four numbers appeared in Barcelona, and numbers 5, 6 and 7 in New York where Picabia had returned in July, 1917. While in Barcelona he had painted a series of 'Spanish women', faces sketched with a maliciously academic stroke, eyes like black diamonds, great combs and mantillas—a complete contrast with the pictures and machine-drawings which he continued to invent and reproductions of which decorated the covers of *391*: *The Saint of Saints*, *Comb*, *Flamenco*, *American Woman*, *Mechanical Ballet*...

In New York, Marcel Duchamp, who had begun to build up the great Glass: *The Bride Stripped Bare by her Bachelors, Even*, continued his series of readymades: *In Advance of the Broken Arm* (1915); *Rendez-vous of Sunday 6 February 1916 at 1 h. 3/4 p.m.* (addressed to Mr. and Mrs. Walter Arensberg); the rusty metal comb with the inscription: '*3 or 4 Drops of Loftiness*[1] *have Nothing to Do with Savagery*' (1916); the *Bicycle Wheel 1916 Model*; the *Assisted Readymade with Hidden Noise* (1916); *Apolinère Enameled* (1916-17); the *Trap* (1917); the *Fountain* signed Richard Mutt (1917); the *Traveller's Folding Item* (1917). Other objects were conceived, too, in Buenos Aires, where Duchamp stayed briefly in 1918, and again in New York, after the war; it would be impossible to describe them all at length here. Emanating from a particular constellation of occurrences, the readymades emerge as a result of special decisions or intuitions, each one of which would require a separate study.

Marcel Duchamp: *Tu m'*. 1918.

1. *3 ou 4 gouttes de hauteur* can also mean '3 or 4 drops from a height'.

In 1918, Duchamp painted a picture of great complexity, entitled simply: *Tu m'*.[1] About ten feet in length, and sixteen inches high, this picture, according to Duchamp, is 'a dictionary of the principal ideas preceding 1918: readymades, standard-stoppages, rent, bottle-brush, cast shadows, perspective'. I would personally be inclined to view this work as a recapitulation of pictorial conventions, dealt with here once and for all. *Colour:* this would be all the colour-samples on countless quadrangular forms constituting a sort of horizontal pyramid at the top of the picture that comes into perspective from greyish distances and ends in yellow. *Proportions:* These would be the 'standard-stoppages,' new units of length obtained in 1913-14 by plotting the twisting of thread one meter in length falling from a height of one meter three times in succession; the three 'traced projections' resulting from this procedure can be seen at the bottom left of the picture, while four double lines representing the standard-stoppages start from the four corners of a white square on the right-hand side of the picture. *Feeling* and *matter* do not seem to have been forgotten either: a bottle-brush is fastened to a rent in the canvas, but the rent, painted in *trompe-l'œil*, is an imitation, closed nevertheless by means of three *real* safety-pins. Finally, may we not consider that the title of the painting indicates, not too discreetly, the feelings that Duchamp might have had at that time towards classical codes and methods and towards painting processes—and, indeed, towards painting in general: 'Tu m'?' *Movement* remains to be considered: a hand (painted by a sign-painter who signed it in tiny letters on the painting) in the centre of the composition points its index finger in the direction of the white square, from which emanate—together with the standard-stoppages—a complicated network of geometric outlines suggesting the idea of a displacement of the square towards the right-hand side of the picture. Then, there are the readymades: drawn by lead-pencil rubbing, their shadows are projected ghost-like over the whole image.

At all events, *Tu m'* was to be Duchamp's last painting.

Man Ray was born in Philadelphia in 1890. His first picture, painted at the age of seven, was copied

1. *Tu m'* implies '*Tu m'ennuies*' ('you bore me').

from newspaper photographs and reproduced with a wealth of detail the American cruiser *Maine* which had just blown up in Havana harbour. In New York, where his family came to live in 1897, he studied architecture and engineering and took painting lessons in the evenings. Then he worked as an advertising illustrator and became familiar with numerous graphic processes. In 1911, he composed an abstract picture with the aid of rectangular fragments of cloth taken from a fabric sample-book. In 1912 he was painting oneiric images *(Dream)*. He married a Frenchwoman, Adon Lacroix, in 1913; his wife's library included

Man Ray: *Dream.*1912.

authors who were completely unknown in America at that time, and some who were still little known in France; Man Ray did not know French and his wife translated for him passages from Baudelaire, Rimbaud, Lautréamont and Barbey d'Aurevilly. The young artist exhibited for the first time at the Ferrer Centre, a group with anarchist tendencies frequented by painters, poets and sculptors. Towards 1914 he got to know the American artists

59

Man Ray: *Revolving Doors*. 1916-1917. One of the ten plates.

VIII

Man Ray in New York, 1918.

portions of space which they cover together, whence a modification of colours but not of forms. It is nevertheless possible to see the common zones as distinct objects; just as in the other scenes the lines constitute only a rather vague border of the design.'

The artist took part in 1916 in the exhibition at the Galerie Montross with Duchamp, Crotti, Gleizes, etc., and in 1917 in the big exhibition of contemporary painting at the Galerie Bourgeois (Duchamp's readymades: *In Advance of the Broken Arm, Traveller's Folding Item*, were exhibited in the umbrella-stand at the entrance to the hall).

Man Ray had been on friendly terms with Duchamp since the latter's first arrival in America in 1915, and collaborated in his friend's projects, notably, in 1920, in the *Rotary Glass Plates*, a machine in which the whirling plates created a great transparent rosette of dark and light circles (Man Ray was nearly killed when the motor of the rotatory mechanism got out of control and broke one of the plates while it was revolving at full speed). When Katherine Dreier and Marcel Duchamp founded the first Museum of Modern Art in New York in 1920, it was Man Ray who suggested the title: Société Anonyme, Incorporated.

In the group which surrounded Duchamp and Picabia in New York, mechanist painting, preferably on glass, was in great favour, as was the construction of objects. At that time Jean Crotti created transparent object-pictures (*The Clown*, 1916) and, with the collaboration of the model, an astonishing object-portrait of Marcel Duchamp made out of iron wire, lead and lead wire.[3] Meanwhile Man Ray brought fresh life to mechanist painting by making use of machines for applying the paint: his *air-brush paintings* (1918-20) bring to a picture for the first time the subtle hues of this graphic process. He used an air-brush to paint on glass a machine-picture bearing an inscription which can read either DANGER or DANCER, and also a curious composition in which the subject is hardly indicated but the idea clearly so: *Admiration of the Orchestrelle for the Cinematograph*.

'Man Ray has always dreamt of killing plasticity ...a love murder. But to allow his pleasure to last longer, he has never ceased to remake a virginity for it', wrote Ribemont-Dessaignes in a monograph published in 1924.[4] Conceived as anti-artistic

Joseph Stella and Louis Bouché. That year he painted a picture which at first sight appeared post-Cézannian and cubist, indeed abstract, but was in fact already dadaist: the picture contains, as the sole elements of composition, the name and date: 'Man Ray 1914.'[1] In a picture, is it not above all the signature that counts?

In 1915 the Galerie Daniel showed twelve of his pictures—brightly coloured sketches with a 'fauve' air—which were all bought by Jerome Eddy (the first owner of Marcel Duchamp's *King and Queen Surrounded by Swift Nudes*). In 1916-17 his compositions came very close to abstraction, but the play of forms is intellectual as much as plastic. Man Ray made this commentary on 'The Meeting,' one of the ten panels of the graphic series entitled *Revolving Doors*,[2] using a *collage* of coloured papers: 'Three beings meeting on a plane are contrasted: a yellow concave, a red convex and a blue spiral. The colours affect each other mutually in those

1. This painting was reproduced in the review *Minotaure*, no. 10, 1937—but upside down.
2. Published in Paris in 1926.

3. Reproduced in *Jean Crotti*, by Waldemar George (Editions Graphis, Paris, 1930). Crotti invented later a process for making stained-glass windows which he called *Gemmeaux*.
4. 'Peintres nouveaux' series (N.R.F., Paris).

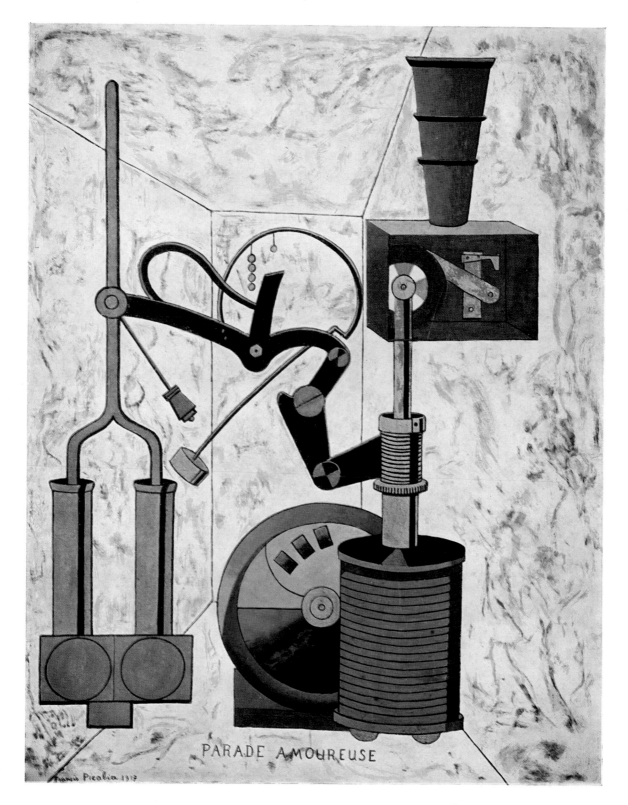

PARADE AMOUREUSE

Francis Picabia: *Amorous Procession.* 1917.

L'ANTITRADITION FUTURISTE

Manifeste-synthèse

ABAS LEP*ominir* A *liminé* SS *korsusu*
otalo EIS *cramir* ME *nigme*

ce moteur à toutes tendances impressionnisme fauvisme cubisme expressionnisme pathétisme dramatisme orphisme paroxysme DYNAMISME PLASTIQUE MOTS EN LIBERTÉ INVENTION DE MOTS

DESTRUCTION

Suppression de la douleur poétique
des exotismes snobs
de la copie en art
des syntaxes *déjà condamnées par l'usage dans toutes les langues*
de l'adjectif
de la ponctuation
de l'harmonie typographique
des temps et personnes des verbes
de l'orchestre
de la forme théatrale
du sublime artiste
du vers et de la strophe
des maisons
de la critique et de la satire
de l'intrigue dans les récits
de l'ennui

Pas de regrets

SUPPRESSION DE L'HISTOIRE

INFINITIF

The ancestor of the Dada manifestoes: First page of *L'Antitradition Futuriste*, by Guillaume Apollinaire, 1913.

LE 14 AVRIL 1921
OUVERTURE
DE LA
GRANDE SAISON
DADA
VISITES · SALON DADA · CONGRÈS ·
COMMÉMORATIONS · OPÉRAS ·
PLÉBICISTES · RÉQUISITIONS ·
MISES EN ACCUSATION ET JUGEMENTS

Se faire inscrire au SANS PAREIL

les dames sont priées d'apporter tous leurs bijoux

AU SANS PAREIL
37, AVENUE KLÉBER
PARIS 16°

VOUS N'ÊTES QUE DES ENFANTS

du 3 mai au 3 juin
EXPOSITION DADA
MAX ERNST
dessins mécanoplastiques plasto-plastiques peinto-peintures anaplastiques anatomiques antizymiques aérographiques antiphonaires arrosables et républicains

ENTRÉE LIBRE *SORTIE FACILE*
mains dans les poches tableau sous le bras

AU-DELA DE LA PEINTURE

Prospectus (recto and verso) for the Opening of the Grand Dada Season, 1921.

APOLINÈRE ENAMELED

[from] MARCEL DUCHAMP 1916 1917

ANY ACT RED BY
HER TEN OR EPERGNE NEW YORK. U.S.A.

Marcel Duchamp, *Apolinère Enameled*, 1916-1917.

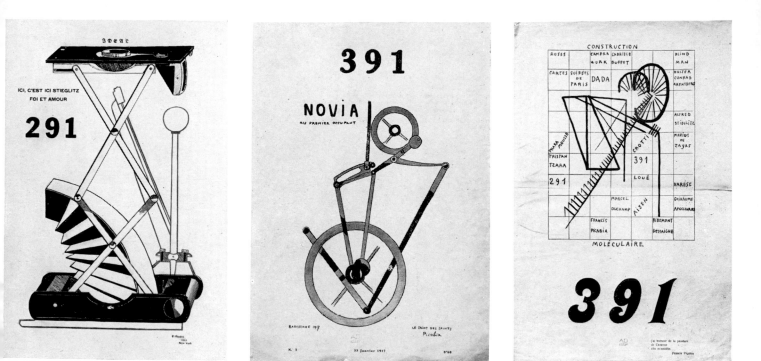

291, no. 5-6. Cover by Francis Picabia, New York, 1915.

391, no. 1. Cover by Francis Picabia, Barcelona, 1917.

391, no. 8. Cover by Francis Picabia, Zurich, 1918.

At Weimar, 1922. From left to right: Hans Richter, Tristan Tzara, Jean Arp.

Man Ray: *Seguidilla*.
1919.

Man Ray: *Lampshade*.
1919.

invented the 'unupsettable' chess set: a board made of iron, with magnetic pieces.

Finally he began to interest himself in photography, initially to make sure of good reproductions of his own works. His objects, especially, raised delicate questions of atmosphere and angles of vision. Although less evident, these same difficulties exist in photographing a picture; they are essentially the problem of the photographic portrait. Photography, which, in the hands of Stieglitz and other pioneers, had gone beyond traditional painting, was destined in this era to cease being simply a descriptive technique, a perfected *trompe-l'œil*, to which it had been condemned by the new painting that had outstripped it in its turn. Photography was about to embark on paths where even the modern painters themselves could no longer follow, leaving behind once and for all 'the horror of *artistic photographs*, opaque, dirty maroon, confused and idiotic... showing us only the everyday, pallid, boring aspect of people and things'.[2]

In America, photography and the cinema used light directly, so to speak, a lighting which became increasingly a human creation. 'These are towns! This is an entire people for whom these Alleghenies and these Lebanons of dream have ascended!' Rather than to the London of 1870, Rimbaud's invocation seems to address itself across time and space to the great modern cities of the United States 'where savage gentlemen chase their news in the light man has created'. Back-lighting, spot-lighting glittering above the throngs deep in New York's canyons, at night the sudden dawn-like reflection of lamps and illuminated signs on faces: only the photographic eye could perceive the shades of movement in the infinite palette of greys, all the nuances and brilliancy, all those violent or tender effects which were more attenuated, less noticeable in those days in the low-built towns of the Old World.

Man Ray was one of the first of his era to *see* beings and things with the dramatic appearance conferred on them by the lights of civilization.

manifestations, and close, in this respect, to Duchamp's readymades, the *objects* of Man Ray nevertheless possess an emotional-plastic content which can act directly thanks to the surroundings, the visual angle and the lighting. Plasticity, denied and mocked, reappears, renewed, with an unexpected value. *Décollage* (1917) was destroyed by a mother outraged that her daughter should have purchased that type of work of art and brought it into their home; *Lampshade* (1919) has a white spiral surface made from an unrolled lampshade; another abstract marvel is a parcel wrapped in sackcloth and tied with string—but the object wrapped up is a sewing machine: this is called *The Enigma of Isidore Ducasse* (1920); *Export Commodity* (1920) is a jar containing steel balls instead of olives;[1] *Inquiétude* (1920) consists of the mechanism of an alarm-clock placed in a glass case filled with tobacco smoke; and there are many other unusual discoveries, like *Cadeau* which is an iron whose surface bristles with a row of nails. Man Ray also began to design chessmen, transforming the classic shapes of the pieces into geometric figures; he

Meanwhile, in the centre of a Europe torn by war, some men, who had kept clear of the battlefields, either through particular circumstances or personal choice, met together in Zurich, Switzerland. At the beginning of 1915 a German conscien-

1. This object, as well as the preceding one, was reproduced in the review *La Révolution Surréaliste*, no. 1, December 1924.

2. G. de Chirico, in his text on *Courbet*.

tious objector, Hugo Ball, with his friend Emmy Hennings, took over a café in Spiegelgasse in the old section of Zurich, the cabaret Voltaire, for soirées where poems were recited, painters presented and commented on their work, and dancing entertainments were produced. The Alsatian Jean Arp soon joined Ball, as did Tristan Tzara and Marcel Janco who had just arrived from their native Rumania, and, some time later, the German poet Richard Huelsenbeck. The origin of these soirées is related by Ball in an introductory notice to an artistic and literary publication, *Cabaret Voltaire*, that appeared in 1916 (with a cover drawn by Arp) with the collaboration of the chief participants in the Zurich café. Ball concluded his introduction to *Cabaret Voltaire* with these words: 'The aim of this publication is to remind people that there are still some men, outside of war and country, who live by different ideals.'

The word *Dada* appeared for the first time in this preface, and at the beginning of a Franco-German poem by Tzara and Huelsenbeck which was also published in *Cabaret Voltaire:* 'Dialogue between a coachman and a lark.' Ball and Huelsenbeck, who were trying to hit on a surname for one of their cabaret singers, had the idea of opening a Franco-German dictionary at random, as others open the Bible to find a rule of conduct therein. The first word to strike their eyes was *Dada*, and Dada became the name of a movement in the process of birth rather than the pseudonym of an individual.

The performances at the Cabaret Voltaire were sometimes fairly noisy, the poetry recitals being conducted if necessary by vigorous shouting. With considerable support from the bass drum, the organizers initiated the Zurich public into a certain 'Negro' music, while Tzara and Huelsenbeck took part in a ponderous dance entitled 'noir cacadou'. Sometimes, too, the programme was more serious or more ambitious, and on those occasions, the group transported itself to the Dada Gallery, or to the Zurich theatre stages, such as Kaufleuten or Waag. In 1917, for instance, an evening performance took place at the Waag Theatre where Arp read passages from the 1450 *Chronicle of Duke Ernst* and extracts from Jacob Böhme, Tzara read pages from Nostradamus, and Janco gave a lecture on the principles of ancient architecture.

'In Zurich,' Arp wrote later, 'uninterested in the blood-baths of the World War, we devoted ourselves to the fine arts. While cannon rumbled in the distance and gun-batteries thundered, we made *collages*, recited, versified and sang with all our heart.'[1]

One of his biographies presents Jean Arp as having been 'trilingual from the age of one': he was born on September 16, 1887 in Strasbourg—then still a German town—where he attended the Ecole des Arts et Métiers around 1903. In his native city he spoke the Alsatian dialect, German at school and during a course of instruction at Weimar in 1905-06, and French in his family circle and during several visits to Paris before 1914.

He had started drawing at an early age; in fact, Arp recalls that he executed his first drawings during a childhood illness, a scarlet fever contracted at the age of seven.

His parents were the owners of a cigar and cigarette factory in Alsace. Nevertheless, when the time for military service was approaching for the boys (Jean has a younger brother), the family preferred to go and live in Switzerland, at Weggis, in 1907, and Jean Arp showed his paintings for the first time at the *Modern Bund* of Lucerne in company with Lüthy, Helbig and others (1911). He was invited to participate in the *Blaue Reiter* exhibitions in Munich; in 1913 he met Max Ernst in Cologne; they each sent pictures to the first German Salon d'Automne, organized in Berlin by Walden's *Der Sturm* Gallery.

In July, 1914 Arp was at Strasbourg. Being far from anxious to participate as a soldier of the Kaiser in the events that were then unfolding, he left for France just a few hours before the frontiers were closed. Arriving in Paris, he took lodgings in Montmartre, rue Gabrielle. But the German armies were closing in; one September morning the concierge ran up to Arp scared out of her wits: 'They've been sighted, you know!' 'Who?' 'The uhlans, of course!' 'Where?' 'In the bois de Vincennes!' At that very moment a fearful cannonade broke out: it was the aerial defence batteries thundering against a *Taube* flying over Paris. Provided with a French passport, as a citizen of Alsace-Lorraine, Arp lived for some time in this heroic atmosphere. In the rue Gabrielle he was

The Spiegelgasse in Zurich. The entrance to the Cabaret Voltaire was on the right, in this photograph.

1. The premises of the Cabaret Voltaire, or rather of the 'Meierei,' still exist in the ancient and picturesque Spiegelgasse in Zurich—but the decor and interior fittings have been completely altered, and nobody in this place nowadays seems to be aware of its past.

the neighbour of Max Jacob, who introduced him to Picasso; at the canteen which Marie Wassilief had opened in the avenue du Maine for the benefit of artists he met Arthur Cravan, and Modigliani, who drew his portrait.[1] He often saw Robert Delaunay, with whom he had struck up a friendship in 1914.

The war pursued him once more, this time in the shape of a medical board which he was summoned to attend; but the French military authorities exempted him from warlike activities.

Sophie Taeuber and Jean Arp, Zurich, 1918.

In July, 1915 he reached Switzerland. The German authorities immediately began to investigate the presence in a neutral country of someone whom they considered to be under their jurisdiction, and old enough to don the uniform of the Landwehr. In order, one might say, to have peace, Arp let it be known that he was suffering from mental illness, upon which the German consulate instructed him to present himself for medical examination. 'Well!' said the psychiatrists to him, 'do you not want to defend your country?' 'Which country?' replied the Alsace-Lorrainian, with a little too much

logic perhaps for someone who was suspected of being normal. He was then asked for his age, and Arp took a piece of paper and wrote the date of his birth again and again in a column which he proceeded to add up. The doctors gave up.

The exhibition at the Tanner Gallery in Zurich, in November 1915, in which Arp, Otto Van Rees and A.C. Van Rees-Dutilh participated, was to be 'the most important event in my life,' as Arp wrote later in Jalons.[2] It was there he met for the first time Sophie Taeuber, who became his companion and collaborator, and whom he married in 1921. In 1915, Sophie was teaching at the School of Decorative Arts in Zurich; she was a painter, and also danced in the Laban-Wigmann troupe which presented curious choreographic experiments during the course of the dada performances; she took part in these dance programmes several times, but under a pseudonym and with her face hidden by a mask, having been threatened with dismissal by the School. Arp, meanwhile, had reached the stage of a non-figurative painting in which cubist-futurist influences could still be distinguished. In the introduction he had written for the Galerie Tanner exhibition he had come out 'against illusion, fame, artifice, copy or plagiarism', declaring himself 'for reality, the precision of the indefinable, rigorous precision'. 'But the essential feature of this exhibition,' he says in Jalons, 'was that the artists were disgusted with oil painting and were searching for new materials.' He himself was composing 'embroideries' and 'carpets' which were, in fact, pictures executed with swatches of different fabrics.

Arp was struck by some of Sophie's work, constructed on vertical and horizontal axes. 'The limpid calm which emerged from these vertical and horizontal compositions influenced the irregular shapes of my abstract configurations.' Thus the painter was led to break finally with all previous influences. 'Sophie Taeuber and I,' continues Arp in Jalons, 'had decided to renounce completely the use of oil-colours in our compositions. We wanted to avoid any reminder of the paintings which seemed to us to be characteristic of a pretentious, self-satisfied world. In 1916 we began to work together on large compositions in fabric and paper', that of 1916, for example, in which the equilibrium of dark and light rectangles is varied 'according to the laws of chance'.

But these assemblages of new materials provoked

1. Reproduced in *Cabaret Voltaire*.

2. *Jalons*, privately printed, Paris, 1951.

some disquieting phenomena: the pictures *changed* over a period of time, the papers in particular deteriorated, became unstuck in places, their colours faded. Despite repeated repairs these accidents continued to occur. Very slowly, almost unconsciously—so Arp himself has told me—the necessity appeared of integrating into a work the idea of destruction and death; of including the concept of duration in it in some way. On the shores of lakes, on the Italian frontier, Arp gathered brushwood, stones, flotsam; he made drawings of their worn, polished shapes. 'Finally I simplified these forms and united their essential natures in moving ovals, symbols of metamorphosis and the future of human bodies.'[1] Some of his wood engravings which preceded this period were composed symmetrically, like primitive fetishes containing the rhythms of time; and the grain of the wood traced white creases on the black silhouettes, so that the history of the tree itself was set down and the vicissitudes of the seasons:[2] a phenomenon of stratification was integrated into the work.

'Up till 1920 we had no idea of the importance that should have been attributed to the experiments that Sophie Taeuber and I had carried out. When, at the war's end, the first international publications started arriving, we were not a little surprised in reading them to realize that identical attempts had been made in other parts of the world... But that anyone should go into raptures over having drawn a square amused us considerably. Nevertheless we determined to register our own squares at the patent office. But our static researches had emanated from essentially different intentions than those which animated most of the "constructivists". We envisaged pictures of meditation, mandalas, landmarks. Our landmarks of light were to mark the paths towards space, depth, the infinite.'[3]

In about 1916, Arp created his first *Reliefs*. Curves, the sensitive waves of a natural element brought to a state of eternity, cycles made supple by patient or mocking wilfulness: these superimposed surfaces, at first painted in bright colours, then in grey—or black—and white, then entirely white, or else in natural wood, have the appearance of pieces from a jigsaw puzzle turned over, as if the artist had cut his paintings into arabesques and presented the fragments back to front. We may recall this reflection of Arp's concerning Vermeer de Delft: 'What can one discover in this painter's canvases? There is nothing behind them.' What is there *behind* these enigmatic Reliefs, the very antithesis of a maniacal reproduction of appearances? What would the invisible image of these games of patience and humour represent, if reconstituted?

The written work of the poet-sculptor may give the key; Arp started writing poetry while still very young, though he only began publishing it in 1920 (in German): *Der Vogel Selbdritt*, *Die Wolkenpumpe*, etc. A florescence of images, pictures, picture titles which could also be the titles of the Reliefs: 'The flinty sky swarms around the spongy larks', 'the claws grasp glass dumb-bells', 'the kings dress their forests' hair, brandishing their drunken birds', 'he lays his zig-zag eggs in windmills of moustaches', 'the fleece of snow covers itself with

Jean Arp: Wood engraving. 1916.

1. See for example 'Catalogue of Insects' in the review *Dada III* (Dec., 1918), as well as the illustrations to *Vingt-cinq Poèmes* (Zurich, 1918) and *Cinéma Calendrier du Cœur Abstrait Maisons* (Paris, 1920) by T. Tzara.

2. Illustrations for *Phantastische Gebete*, by Huelsenbeck (Collection Dada, Zurich, 1916).

3. *Jalons*.

67

Jean Arp: *According to the Laws of Chance.* 1917.

Jean Arp: Illustration for Tristan Tzara's *Cinéma Calendrier du Cœur Abstrait Maisons.* 1920.

graphite'.[1] Here we can see objects meet each other as though chance were a rendez-vous. The most naked, the simplest words designate eternally renewed figures: an astonished and amused acknowledgement of the evidence of irrational relations, a childish and subtle gaiety at the discovery that the world is both absurd and poetic. 'Laughable but superb world,' said Lautréamont.

The table and the chair
the chair and the table
the chair on fire
the table on fire
. . .
the tables are waiting until they start growing chairs
the chairs are waiting until they start growing tables
. . .
the chair climbs on to the table
the fire climbs on to the chair
the voice climbs on to the fire
what is under nature grows and climbs on to nature
and speaks of chairs and of tables on fire.[2]

The objects in the Reliefs overlap and hide each other from view, revolving like the constellations in the great transparent globe of the heavens.

But this hidden humour ('*humour sous roche*', André Breton has called it) explodes occasionally in some unusual invention. Arp suggested a series of game-objects, describing them in these terms: '*Egg board*, a game for families of the Establishment, to be played either in the drawing-room or open air. The participants leave the field, covered from head to foot with egg yolks. *Navel bottle*, a monstrous household article in which bicycles, sea-serpents, brassière and Pernod spoon couple. *The glove*, which can be worn in place of the now obsolete head, was intended to make the bourgeois feel the unreality of his world, the futility of his efforts and even the inanity of the patriotic real estate business. This was of course a naïve enterprise on our part, since the bourgeois has less imagination than the earth-worm and in place of a heart has an over-life-size corn which twitches in times of approaching storm—on the stock exchange.'[3]

1. 'Clair de rêve,' 1915. (In *Le Siège de l'Air*, Vrille, Paris, 1946).
2. 'La chaise, la table', 1917. (*Le Siège de l'Air*).
3. Cf. Arp: *On My Way, poetry and essays 1912-1947*, compiled by R. Motherwell (Wittenborn, Schultz, New York, 1948).

Since its beginnings in Switzerland, there existed side by side in the Dada movement constructive realization and humorous anti-conventionalism. Their first publication, *Cabaret Voltaire*, followed, in 1917, by the reviews *Dada I* and *Dada II*, were open to every avant-garde opinion. They sometimes contained violent and scandalous declarations, like the article by Alberto Savinio against music, 'a mad and immoral art, the perfect example of bourgeois perversity, more odious and slimy than pity'. They also presented poetic and typographical researches: poems by the simultaneist Pierre Albert-Birot and the Italian futurists. Apollinaire, Marinetti, Cendrars and Van Hoddis, Picasso, Modigliani, Delaunay, Kandinsky, Eggeling, Prampolini and Chirico are featured in the pages of these publications by the side of the directors of the cabaret in the street of Mirrors. Tristan Tzara writes in *Dada 1* ('Note 18 on art'): 'I open my heart that men may be better... artists are carrying on tradition, the past...' and in *Dada II* ('Note 2 on art', speaking of Arp): 'The artist makes man better. Tend the garden of your intentions, set it in order... The purity of a principle makes me happy... Belief gathered clearly in simple bodies—Wisdom knowledge.' But elsewhere (in the preface to the *Première Aventure Céleste de M. Antipyrine*, 1916) he had said: 'Dada is art without bedroom-slippers or parallels; is for and against unity and definitely against the future... Severe necessity without discipline or morals and let's spit on humanity.'

In February, 1918 Picabia found himself in Switzerland, and published in Lausanne his *Poèmes et Dessins de la Fille Née sans Mère*; and in Zurich he met the Dadas. Then, in December, 1918, *Dada III* appeared, marking a complete transformation in the tone, manner and whole spirit of the review. In contrast with the clarity and neatness of the first two numbers, *Dada III* was a kind of immense prospectus crazily printed, with a quite fantastic page lay-out, and a cover barred diagonally with the sentence 'I do not even wish to know if there were men before me (Descartes)', while Tristan Tzara proclaimed in the violent *Manifeste Dada 1918*, published by the review:

'I write a manifesto and I want nothing, yet I say certain things, and in principle I am against principles, as I am also against manifestoes... We are a furious wind, tearing the dirty linen of clouds and prayers, preparing the great spectacle of disaster, fire, decomposition... If I cry out:

Ideal, Ideal, Ideal,
Knowledge, Knowledge, Knowledge,
Boomboom, boomboom, boomboom,

I have given a pretty faithful version of progress, law, morality and all other fine qualities that various highly intelligent men have discussed in so many books.' The author then explains rapidly the two

Jean Arp: *Tears of Enak.* 1917.

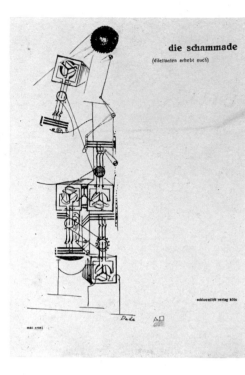

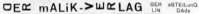

Max Ernst: Cover for
Die Schammade, or *Da-
dameter.* Cologne,
1920.

John Heartfield: Cover
for *Der Dada,* no. 3.
Berlin, 1920.

Raoul Haussmann :
Tatlin at Home. Ber-
lin, 1920.

Francis Picabia : *The
Holy Virgin (391, no.
12.* Paris, March, 1920).

Francis Picabia: *Portrait of Louis Vauxcelles*. 1917.

Page from *New York Dada*, April, 1921.

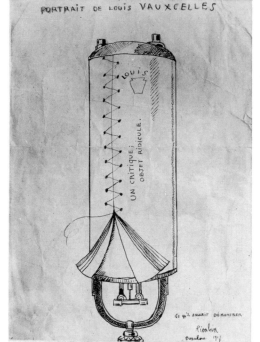

Francis Picabia: *Natures Mortes (Cannibale*, no. 1. Paris, March, 1920).

Man Ray: Cover for *Littérature* new series, no. 3. Paris, May, 1922.

LEGEND

Man Ray: *Legend*. 1916.

Max Ernst: *The Hat Makes the Man (the Tailor is the Style)*. 1920.

Jean Arp: *Torso with Flower Head.* 1924.

methods of vision, cubist and futurist, but emphasizes: 'We have had enough of the cubist and futurist academies.' He gives short shrift to psychological interpretations: 'Psychoanalysis is a dangerous disease, it puts to sleep the anti-objective impulses of man and systematizes the bourgeoisie.' Conclusion: 'Freedom: *Dada dada dada*, a roaring of tense colours, and interlacing of opposites and of all contradictions, grotesques, inconsistencies: LIFE.'

The meeting between Tzara and Picabia had ignited the fuse. 'Long live Picabia, the anti-painter arrived from New York' shouted *Dada III*. The author of the *Very Rare Picture upon Earth* had indeed brought from New York the spirit of destruction and invention that he had put into practice since the war with Marcel Duchamp. Another text by Tzara (again in *Dada III*) is dedicated to Picabia 'for the annihilation of traditional beauty,' and Picabia in his turn published a short poem in the review, *Salive Américaine*: 'Taste is as tedious as good company.'

No 8 of *391* appeared in Zurich, on bright pink paper. Cover by Picabia, *Molecular Construction*, a chess-board half covered by a mechanist drawing; some squares contain names: Stieglitz, Crotti, de Zayas, Tzara, Gabrielle Buffet, M. Duchamp, Apollinaire, Picabia; titles of reviews: *Camera Work*, *The Blind Man*, *Soirées de Paris*, *Dada*, *291*, *391*. As an epigraph: 'I have a horror of Cézanne's painting, it bores me stiff.'

A dismembered alarm-clock was used to provide the cover for *Dada IV* (February, 1919, also entitled *Anthologie Dada*). 'Arp, Tzara, Picabia and myself,' writes Mme Gabrielle Buffet 'collaborated in the execution of this illustration. The medium was an old alarm clock which we bought for a few centimes and took apart. The detached pieces were bathed in ink and then imprinted at random on paper. All of us watched over the execution of this automatic masterpiece.' The *Anthologie Dada* was no less typographically eccentric than *Dada III* or *391*; but it continued to give some kind of account of the modern movement. New collaborators appeared: Aragon, Breton, Cocteau, Radiguet sent poems from Paris, Soupault sent a text about the re-edition of the *Bestiaire* by Guillaume Apollinaire, who had just died (*Dada III* had published tributes by Tzara and Picabia to the author of *Calligrammes*: 'His death still seems impossible to me,' wrote Picabia; 'Guillaume Apollinaire is one of the rare people who have followed the entire evolution of modern art and understood it completely'). Woodcuts by Arp and Raoul Haussmann

and drawings by Picabia illustrate these pages, and there are reproductions of Kandinsky, Paul Klee, Hans Richter, Van Rees.

The war was over, contact had been re-established between the various countries—and Dada was all set to conquer Europe.

While still a child, Max Ernst dreamt of becoming a railway-crossing gate-keeper. 'Maybe he was seduced by the nostalgia provoked by passing trains and the great mystery of telegraph wires which move up and down when you look at them from a moving train and stand still, when you stand still.[1]

'To scrutinize the mystery of the telegraph wires (and also to flee from the father's tyranny) five-year-old Max escaped from his parents' house. Blue-eyed, blond-curly-haired, dressed in a red night shirt, carrying a whip in the left hand, he walked in the middle of a pilgrims' procession. Enchanted by this charming child and believing it was the vision of an angel or even the infant of the virgin, the pilgrims proclaimed "Look, little Jesus Christ." After a mile or so little Jesus Christ escaped from the procession, directed himself to the station and had a long and delightful walk beside the railway line and the telegraph wires. To appease father's fury, when the next day a policeman brought him home, little Max proclaimed that he was sure he was little Jesus Christ.' Upon which, M. Ernst made a portrait of his son as a little Jesus-child, and 'little Max, slightly flattered by this image, had however some difficulty in throwing off the suspicion that daddy took secret pleasure in the idea of being God-the-Father, and that the hidden reason of this picture was a blasphemous pretension. Maybe,' adds Max Ernst, 'my picture *Souvenir de Dieu* (1923) has a direct connection with the remembrance of this fact.'

Max Ernst's family was deeply religious; the father was a Sunday painter and, during the week, a professor in a deaf and dumb institute, remaining deaf himself to anything except the teachings of the Catholic, Apostolic and Roman Church. Max passed 'the most boring hours of his childhood' at the convent-school of the little town where he was born in 1891: Bruhl, near Cologne,

1. 'Some Data on the Youth of Max Ernst, as told by himself'; in *Max Ernst: Beyond Painting*, compiled by Robert Motherwell (Wittenborn, Schultz, New York, 1948).

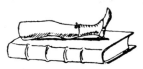

where 'eleven thousand virgins gave up their lives rather than give up chastity. Their gracious skulls and bones embellish the walls of the convent-church, and maybe their company was helpful to the child'. The painting of M. Ernst senior reflected his exacting convictions. He composed an allegory in imitation of Raphael's *Disputa* in which his friends figured, on the right hand of God, surrounded by the Church's most famous Scholars and Saints, while on the side of the outcasts were to be seen the great heretics, as well as the little town's most notorious libertines and his own personal enemies. As a reply to his father's picture, Max Ernst painted a *Rendez-vous des Amis* in 1923 which grouped (around Raphael) his poet friends, he himself being depicted sitting on Dostoievsky's knees and pulling his beard.

In 1897, during an attack of measles, the child experienced fever-visions 'which were provoked by the suggestive designs on an imitation-mahogany panel opposite his bed... he later delivered himself voluntarily to provoke hallucinations of the same kind in looking obstinately at wood-panels, clouds, wallpapers, unplastered walls and so on to let his "imagination" go.' When someone would ask him: 'What is your favourite occupation?' he regularly answered, 'Looking.' In 1898, 'he saw his father make a painting *d'après nature* in the garden and finish it in his studio. Father suppressed a tree in his picture, because it disturbed the "composition". Then he suppressed the same tree in the garden so that there was no longer any difference between nature and art. The child felt a revolt growing in his heart against candid realism and decided to direct himself towards a more equitable conception of the relationship between the subjective and the objective world.' One day during 1906, he found his cockatoo, of which he was very fond, dead, and at the same moment his father announced the birth of his sister Loni—'the *perturbation* of the youth was so enormous that he fainted... A series of mystical crises, fits of hysteria, exaltations and depressions followed', accompanied by a confusion between humans and birds.

Max Ernst commenced very early his 'excursions in the world of marvels, chimeras, phantoms, poets, monsters, philosophers, birds, women, lunatics, magi, trees, eroticism, stones, insects, mountains, poisons, mathematics and so on'. In 1914 he was painting pictures in the expressionist style, such as *Promenade*, in which strange dreaming figures seem to be caught in a net of shapes and colours. But he 'died the 1st of August 1914' and 'resuscitated the 11th of November 1918 as a young man aspiring to become a magician and to find the myth of his time'.[1]

After his resurrection, Max Ernst rallied to the Dada cause and became, with his friend Baargeld (the pseudonym adopted by the son of a Cologne banker),[2] the chief animator of the movement in the Rhineland. In 1919 appeared his *Fiat Modes*, 'Mondändada Max Ernst (pereat ars)'—eight lithographs published by A.B.K., Cologne. Only a few copies of this album have survived (the author destroyed almost the whole edition); its images, signed 'dadamax ernst', introduced Chirico's methods into the dadaist proceedings for the first time (Ernst had just had his first glimpse of this painter's arcades and locomotives through reproductions in the Italian review *Valori Plastici*). *Fiat Modes* installs Dada inside a metaphysical interior and describes a universe of machines and automats, cog-wheels and mannequins, mocking inscriptions ('Dada NoBis valuTamTam') and cast shadows. Ironic pieces of apparatus sit enthroned on floors drawn in perspective, the show-cases of the mechanized palaces come to life, the fashion parade starts, with this inscription written in 'mirror-writing': *Zurneuenkunst? DD.*

The municipality of Cologne, which at this period was showing a certain solicitude for the arts (several painters had received subsidies to publish albums of their works), financed—on trust—the edition of *Fiat Modes;* but the town-councillors had a real shock when they finally inspected the production which had been made possible by their munificence. And when the author presented himself to request a few copies he was received with indignation: 'Clear all this out of our way at once!' he was enjoined; 'go on! take it all away!' And Max Ernst left Cologne Town Hall laden with his own work.

Max Ernst invents collage.—The first *collages* contained no element genuinely glued (*collé*); but Max Ernst has declared that he was not responsible for the term *collage;* and, in addition, 'if it is the plumes that make the plumage, it is not the glue (*colle*) that makes the *collage*'.[3] It is far more the poet's vision, disrupting and reconstructing engravings, photos and everyday images.

1. All these quotations are taken from texts by Max Ernst in R. Motherwell's compilation.

2. *Baargeld*, in English: 'spot cash'.

3. Max Ernst: 'Au-delà de la Peinture,' originally published in the French review *Cahiers d'Art*, no. 6-7, Paris, 1936, and included, under the title of 'Beyond Painting,' in Robert Motherwell's compilation (*op. cit.*).

It would be incorrect to associate the process of *collage* with that of the *papier collé* as practised by the cubists. The two approaches are essentially different. 'The *papiers collés* of Braque and Picasso,' writes E.L.T. Mesens,[1] 'are simple plastic solutions in which the cut-out elements imitating a real material (wood, marble, newspaper) play the part of counterpoint to the lines or shapes which the artist has invented or interpreted. In his *collages*, on the contrary, Max Ernst is far from being principally concerned with plastic construction. With a single stroke he plunges us into the drama by making the elements of our known world confront each other in an irritating manner, thus violating the accepted canons of thought, logic and morality... What was only a revolution in plastic art became, thanks to Max Ernst, mental subversion.'[2]

Max Ernst has, indeed, explained himself most precisely in this matter:[3] 'One rainy day in 1919, finding myself in a village on the Rhine, I was struck by the obsession which held under my gaze the pages of an illustrated catalogue showing objects designed for anthropologic, microscopic, psychologic, mineralogic, and paleontologic demonstration.' In these extremely logical data, Ernst found brought together 'elements of figuration so remote that the sheer absurdity of that collection provoked a sudden intensification of the visionary faculties in me and brought forth an hallucinatory succession of contradictory signs... These visions themselves called for new planes, for their meeting in a new unknown... It was enough then to add to these catalogue pages, in painting or drawing, and thereby obediently reproducing only *that which was to be seen within me*, a colour, a pencil mark, a landscape foreign to the represented objects, the desert, a tempest, a geological cross-section, a floor, a single straight line signifying the horizon, to obtain a faithful fixed image of my hallucination...' Soon Max Ernst was to reduce these interventions and simply cut out and reassemble various elements according to his personal vision, with a minimum of manual additions.

1. Preface to the catalogue of the Max Ernst exhibition at Knocke-le-Zoute, Belgium, 1953.

2. Mesens, in the same text, points out the difference between 'collage' and *photo-montage*,' and remarks that 'ex-votos going back to the eighteenth century, English 'valentines,' raised calendars and the post-card picturing a postman whose sack, when opened, disgorges a strip showing a dozen views of some town are already *collages* from a technical point of view'.

3. In *Beyond Painting*.

4. J. Cocteau, *Le Mystère Laïc*, in *Œuvres Complètes*, Vol. 10 (Marguerat, Geneva, 1946).

However menacing the rise of unconscious forces seems in the work of Giorgio de Chirico, it can be interpreted in an even more disturbing light in that of Max Ernst. For if the empty spaces in Chirico's paintings are simply haunted by an apparition, Ernst's *collages* go one step further in this respect: the spirits appear in person.

M. Jean Cocteau has claimed[4] that Chirico's enigmas result essentially from combinations of scenery and light. If he were right, it would be just a matter of conjuring technique (and M. Cocteau's as well), the conjuror's tricks appearing mysterious only because the public does not know the secrets even though it has been invited to inspect

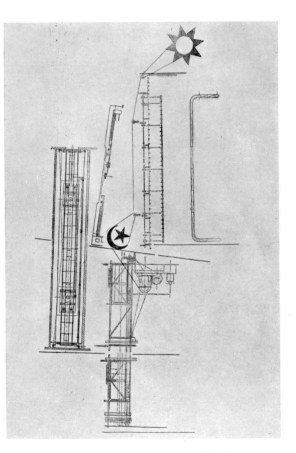

Max Ernst: *Hypertrophied Trophy*. 1919.

allways the best man wins
soda liten schneeberger drückethäler rosinen und mandeln schlagen die eingeborenen mitteleuropas

max ernst/1920

zu meerschaum und eilen nach stattgehabter denudation den ereignissen in bester absicht voraus.

Max Ernst: *The Enigma of Central Europe.* 1920.

the miraculous boxes and top-hats to satisfy itself that they are perfectly empty. None of the gullible spectators who marvelled at Baron von Kempelen's automatic chess-player saw the operator hidden in the machine; yet he was there, though in an extremely uncomfortable position. But Chirico himself has squashed this illusionist theory in advance by constantly reiterating, at the time of his early painting, his belief in the authenticity of the phantoms contained in his pictures. The professional illusionist of Cocteau's type makes use of a pseudo-machinery, a bric-à-brac of accessories to dissimulate his real role of string-puller, while with Chirico there is no mystification but only *enigma* extending behind the scenery, beyond the painting processes. If he can discover and understand the 'mechanism', the spectator of one of Chirico's paintings will not turn away disillusioned: he will, on the contrary, have made a step in the direction of a most unusual and disturbing initiation.

Such an initiation was undergone by Max Ernst,

as later on by other surrealist painters who derived part of their original inspiration from Chirico: Tanguy, Magritte. Perhaps the idea of *collage* presented itself to Ernst more or less consciously under the influence of those pictures in which the famous biscuits, painted in *trompe-l'œil*, seem literally glued to the canvas. He, too, could have reproduced his visions meticulously by the classic methods of art; but he chose a shorter and less respectful path, making use of other people's handiwork as a prefabricated material: *trompe-l'œil*, academic drawing, perspective—Ernst found them all in the catalogues. His point of departure is, literally, a *cliché*.

But it is exactly in seeming to wish to remove any ambiguity that, on the contrary, he adds a new dimension to the magic enigma. He gives the ordinary man full liberty to take his accessories to pieces, even to break them into fragments, instead of just allowing him to open up a few cupboard-drawers. Everyone can see what a

78

collage is made of, can recognize its elements, can ascertain that they are borrowed from some old book or well-known manual. And yet the hallucinatory element, far from disappearing, becomes still more intense.

At the moment—1919—when Chirico abandoned the labyrinth he had discovered and let his inspiration lead him on an entirely different course, Max Ernst appeared, prepared to carry on the exploration. Floors in perspective, in the distance the taut skyline: one can recognize the bridge of the ship *Argo* laden with new cargo, strange and absurd objects turning into legitimate beings.

The Hat Makes the Man (the Tailor is the Style) is the title of one of his first and most curious *collages*, with hats and suits arranged in a bizarre relationship. Max Ernst claims that, in a restaurant in Cologne one day, he saw the hats and overcoats leave the rack where they were hanging and move away to another rack; Chirico, equally, was used to meeting ghosts in cafés. *The Hat Makes the Man...* appears to reconstruct one of these enigmatic adventures. The spectator can inspect and verify the enchanted top-hats and magic capes at his leisure. Ernst is fully aware that if the experience can be repeated it will only be in terms of its original significance, since its success does not depend on the accessories but on the magical power of the spectators themselves: an hallucinatory consciousness is expressed in his work with a humour that is perfectly sure of its means. In *The Hat Makes the Man...* the human figures, rendered palpable by the artist, have become visible and one might say that it is the clothes that have disappeared. Despite all this, there are certainly people who can see nothing in this picture except hats hanging on coat-racks.

The *titles* are very important indeed, always extremely brilliant, an indispensable frame to the image, setting off the humour of the process while at the same time enhancing its poetic possibilities: *Bone Mill for Peaceful Hairdressers*; *The Little Tear Gland that Says Tic-tac*; *The Stamens of Arp*; *...The Transfiguration of the Chameleon on Mount Tabor Takes Place in an Elegant Limousine while the Angels and Halcyons Fly from the Houses of Man and while the Very Holy Costume of Our Lord Exclaims de profundis Three Times before Whipping the Exhibitionists' Flesh*; *Somnambulistic Escalator*; *Dada in Usum Delphini*; *Dada Degas*; *Dada Gauguin*; *Above the Clouds Midnight is Walking, above Midnight the Day's Invisible Bird is Soaring, a Little Higher than the Bird the Ether is Growing,*

and the Walls and Roofs are Floating; *Ingres Gasometric*; etc., etc.

Such titles, according to Ernst, are sometimes *verbal collages*. For instance, the *Phallustrade*, 'alchemical compound of "autostrade", "balustrade" and a certain quantity of phallus'; or *Fatagaga*: 'FAbrication de TAbleaux GArantis GAzométriques' which designates *collages* made collectively (Max Ernst, Baargeld and Arp).

This new method of composition, a short circuit between vision and realization, seemed clearly scandalous to the dedicated craftsmen of art —quite a few 'moderns' could already be classed in this group. In Paris, the Section d'Or exhibition of 1920, in which a certain number of these newly respectable artists were included, refused a *collage* (or rather a stencil) sent in by Max Ernst, on the pretext that 'it was not made by hand'!

In 1920 the Dada exhibition of Cologne took place, organized by Ernst and Baargeld with the

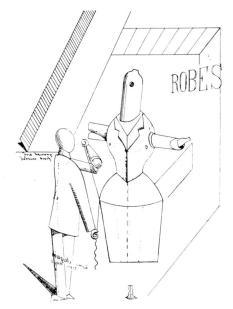

Max Ernst:
Fiat Modes. 1919.
One of the eight plates.

participation of Arp and Picabia. It was held in a room behind a café, which could only be reached through a public urinal. In one corner of the premises the exhibitors showed works to be taken away *free:* drawings, lithographs and so on, which even at this price found no takers. Baargeld exhibited the *Fluidoskeptryk*, an aquarium filled with red water with an alarm-clock at the bottom, a head of woman's hair floating on top, and a wooden arm protruding from the water. Ernst had chained an axe to one of his objects so that it could be more easily destroyed. The exhibition was inaugurated by a young girl in her first communion dress reciting poems by Jacob van Hoddis which were immediately denounced as obscene by those present; someone proceeded to smash the *Fluidoskeptryk*, and its imitation blood swirled around the feet of the indignant spectators. The scandal was such that the police ordered the exhibition closed (on a warrant issued by Max Ernst's own uncle, the Cologne public prosecutor). However the gallery was allowed to reopen when it was noticed that the picture that had been considered most shocking of all was Dürer's etching *Adam and Eve!*

At the same time a catalogue-review was published called *Dadameter (Die Schammade)*, 'cryptogram of the love life of dada flora and fauna',[1] to which most of the German and Parisian members of the Dada movement contributed, and which carried as an epigraph the slightly modified Marxist slogan: *Dilettanten erhebt euch!* Dilettantes arise!

No contemporary document, as far as I know, indicates any political standpoint of the Dada movement or of its individual participants in America, Switzerland or Paris concerning, for instance, such an event as the Russian revolution of 1917. Much later on, there was talk of an 'Association of revolutionary artists' which Hans Richter allegedly founded in Zurich in 1919 and which most of the dadaists were said to have joined; but Richter himself has told me that this supposed group never existed. In Germany, however, things were different.

In Cologne, Baargeld had been one of the founders of the Communist Party in the Rhineland; in 1919 he had directed an extreme left-wing newspaper *Der Ventilator* (that sometimes printed as many as 20,000 copies), in which Max Ernst published articles and poems, but the publication was hastily suppressed by the British occupation authorities. In Berlin, the two Hertzfelde brothers (one of them under the pseudonym of John Heartfield), Raoul Haussmann the 'Dadosopher', Baader, a mystic who proclaimed himself 'Superdada', Huelsenbeck, who had just returned from Switzerland and was named Commissar of Fine Arts during the brief Berlin insurrection of 1918, and others, combined to give Dadaism a revolutionary complexion.[2] The review *Der Dada*, published during 1919-20 and directed by Haussmann, proclaimed the most subversive slogans. During the course of a meeting of the Weimar constituent assembly, Baader handed out leaflets signed by the Dada Central Committee of the World Revolution! Dada humour became a violent and direct satire; the caricaturist George Grosz contributed to the Dada publications in Berlin and made a series of anti-bourgeois, anti-religious, anti-patriotic drawings for a re-edition of Huelsenbeck's *Phantastische Gebete* (Berlin, 1920). At the great Dada exhibition in Berlin (June, 1920), the main attraction was a tailor's dummy with a pig's head, wearing a German officer's uniform and hanging from the ceiling.

In central Europe, the public attending the lectures given by Haussmann and Huelsenbeck at the beginning of 1920 in Germany and Bohemia sometimes reacted hysterically: the petty bourgeoisie vented all its hatred of modern poetry and its terror of social revolution on the movement. It must be remembered that its most distinguished representative, Adolf Hitler, reserved a few imprecations for Dada in *Mein Kampf.*

'Art is dead,' proclaimed one of the posters for the Berlin exhibition, 'long live the machine art of Tatlin.' The Russian constructivist Tatlin was at that moment showing in Petrograd a scale-model in wood of a spiral-shaped super-Eiffel Tower which was to reach a height of over 1,300 ft., a monument to the Third International—which was never built.

But signs soon appeared (for the first but not the last time) of the impossibility of collaboration between the poetic revolution and the social revolution—at least in the form in which the latter developed. The new Russian regime began gradually to discourage the efforts not only of Dada

---

1. According to *391* (no. 12), '*Une Nuit d'Echecs Gras*', a page of 'advertisements' for Dada publications, put together by Tristan Tzara. (Reproduced on p. 342 of *The Dada Poets and Painters, op. cit.*).

2. Huelsenbeck has given an historical summing-up of this activity in a brilliant pamphlet published in 1920, *En Avant Dada: A History of Dadaism* (published in English translation in *The Dada Poets and Painters*). The recently published book by Raoul Haussmann, *Courrier Dada* (Editions du Terrain Vague, Paris, 1958), gives a wealth of detail about the period.

but also of all modern artists in general; the avant-garde studios of Petrograd and Moscow were forced to close their doors one after another; even in such a sphere as theatre production, in which the Russians had been pioneers since the beginning of the century, the most traditional æsthetic principles gained the upper hand.

It must be stated that the fact of considering modern poetry and art as a stupidity, an aberration or a sin—if not, indeed, an actual crime—was by no means the sole prerogative of the new Russian regime: fascism, and, even more systematically, Hitlerism, followed the same path. Basically, the old terror of the unconscious is still alive. In some parts of the world an effort had been made to suppress—to 'liquidate'—this disturbing element with a view to 'safeguarding' the conscious ego: dialectically a not entirely justifiable procedure, which has necessitated the elaboration of a system of police repression on a vast scale—vast because such a system requires supervision of each single individual. In other parts of the world, where particular manifestations in art have conquered a wide public, the opposition to new art-forms continues, more or less confusedly, in many circles.[1]

In Germany, during 1921, the Dada manifestos and the theses of extreme-left politics could only meet in opposition to the old social order; outside that sphere, the perspectives divided sharply. Those of the dadaists who had conducted a political activity were forced to abandon it, or, like Heartfield, they submitted themselves to politics.

While it was invading Germany, Dada was engaged in the conquest of Paris. There, during the war, in 1917, performances such as the 'surrealist drama' by Guillaume Apollinaire, *Les Mamelles de Tirésias*, and the ballet *Parade* (music by Erik Satie, decor and costumes by Picasso, based on a scenario by Jean Cocteau) had already excited avant-garde circles. Among the new reviews, *Sic*, founded by Pierre Albert-Birot, was inspired by Futurism, and Reverdy's *Nord-Sud* had cubist leanings; though Reverdy himself, Apollinaire and others contributed to *Sic* as well as to *Nord-Sud*. Ozenfant's luxurious publication *L'Elan*, full of anti-'boche' drawings, represented patriotic modernism.

Most of the initiators of the Dada movement joined each other in France in 1919 (except Arp who went on living in Switzerland until 1926). Marcel Duchamp and Picabia arrived in Paris about the middle of the year, Tzara in December. In November the ninth issue of *391* appeared: 'If you go to the Grand-Palais,' wrote G. Ribemont-Dessaignes in an article on the Salon d'Automne, 'don't go near the shadow enveloping the foot of the staircase. It seems that a living creature has been chained up there'. The reference was to Francis Picabia's mechanist paintings which were drawing huge crowds despite their relegation to the darkest corners of the building. The artist heard one visitor exclaim in front of one of his works: 'If I got hold of the man who painted that I'd really deal with him.' Some of the officials showed themselves equally excitable, all the more so because Picabia had been a full member of the Salon since the distant era of his impressionist painting and could thus exhibit without approval by the jury. Desvallières, a painter of religious subjects and member of the jury, apostrophized the author of the *Saint of Saints* thus: 'And, in any case, what did you do during the war?' 'I got bored as hell,' replied Picabia.

The work which Picabia produced during this time included pictures which used simultaneously the techniques of *collage* and *papiers collés*, but their chief characteristic is the painter's dazzling, startling imagination: landscapes in which the trees are steel pens; portraits with combs in place of hair and matchsticks replacing the outlines of the face; fireworks made from spirals of fuse-wires glued to a background of black 'Ripolin' paint—one would need pages to describe so many incredible inventions, each one of which constitutes an autonomous and scandalous being.

The Holy Virgin is the title of one of Picabia's pictures; it shows a huge ink-stain—a true 'drop of intellectual blood'—and was reproduced in no. 12 of *391*, (March, 1920). Profane art was also featured in this number; the cover depicts a 'Dada picture' by Marcel Duchamp: the *Gioconda* adorned

1. Cf. for example *L'Homme Révolté* by M. Albert Camus, (N.R.F., Paris, 1952) translated as *The Rebel* (Knopf, New York, 1954). Like the American senator who discovered the premonitory symptoms of communism in Stravinsky's *Rites of Spring*, M. Camus has seen in Sade the precursor of the concentration camps ('a modest precursor,' concedes M. Camus, doubtless because Sade only spent twenty-five years in prison and died in prison); while Lautréamont is charged with heralding 'the taste for intellectual subservience which is spreading in our world.' M. Camus was greatly astonished, at the time his book was published, that a living person, André Breton, should have assumed the defence of these vanished poets and should, in his turn, have taken issue with him violently. He would have been even more astonished to hear what Sade and Lautréamont would have said to him in reply, had they been alive.

with a set of moustaches, with the title: *L.H.O.O.Q.*[1] This 'assisted readymade' incorporates several different features: infantile desire—to virilize a beardless face by endowing it with hair; *humour noir*—the most famous and beautiful picture in the world treated like any vulgar mass-produced reproduction, and casually disfigured; lastly, the irony of affirmation, if Robert Lebel is right in suggesting that 'among all contemporary artists it is Marcel Duchamp who evokes Leonardo most irresistibly, even in his refusal to be simply a great painter'.[2]

Picabia, on the other hand, continued to stud the pages of *391* with his light-hearted, mocking or poetic thoughts. Some day, perhaps, someone will realize that the scoffing maxims of *391*, added to his unpublished texts and those that appeared in other publications[3] would provide the material for an incomparable collection of *Aphorisms*: 'Human beings win diplomas and lose their instincts.—The more one pleases, the more one displeases.—The only way to have followers is to run faster than the others.—Spinoza is the only person who never read Spinoza.—It is easier to scratch one's arse than one's heart (Saint Augustin). —The unknown is an exception, the known a deception.—Vegetables are more serious than men and more sensitive to frost.—A favourable wind has blue feathers.—Teeth spring to the eyes like tears.—To be seasick in a transport of joy.—The wisest, most perfect picture grazes in my garden. —Desire vanishes if you possess: possess nothing. —The tables turn, thanks to the spirit; pictures and other works of art might be called safe-deposit-tables: the spirit is inside and becomes increasingly inspired as the auction-room prices mount.' And these appreciations of the 'young reviews':

'*Sic* should change its tires and take the silencer off its exhaust pipe.—*L'Elan* has lost its hair if it ever had any.—*Nord-Sud* lacks ventilation especially when it breaks down under the Seine.'[4]

In Paris, Dada soirées began to be organized on the pattern of those in Zurich, but with the intention of being even more provocative. Like the Dada reviews which were now proliferating, the demonstrations organized by the movement in Paris became more and more frequent and varied, and there can be no question of giving a complete account of them. A few examples will suffice. The 'First Friday meeting of *Littérature*' at the Palais de Fêtes, on January 23, 1920, displayed a picture of Picabia's (also entitled *L.H.O.O.Q.*) while Tzara read out a newspaper article announced as poetry, his voice being drowned by bells and rattles manipulated behind the scenes. At the Théâtre de l'Œuvre, on March 24, 1920, André Breton read out the *Cannibal Manifesto in Darkness*[5] written by Francis Picabia. It was the acme of Dada provocation. 'You are all defendants, rise. The author can only speak to you if you are standing up. Stand up as if for the *Marseillaise*, stand up as if for the Russian anthem, stand up as if for *God Save the King*, stand up as if facing the national flag, finally stand up before DADA, which represents life and which accuses you of liking everything from snobbism, just as long as it's expensive... What are you doing, parked there like serious oysters—for you *are* serious, aren't you? Serious, serious, serious till death. Death is a serious thing, eh? People die heroes, or idiots, it's the same thing. The one word that's not ephemeral is the word death. You like death for other people... It's only money which doesn't die, it just takes a trip. It's God, somebody everyone respects, the serious person—money family respect... Hoot, laugh, beat me up, and then? and then? I'll still tell you that you're all idiots: in three months my friends and I will sell you our pictures for a few francs.' One of these pictures was on show in the theatre entrance: a plush monkey (Picabia had tried vainly to obtain a live monkey for the occasion) attached to the centre of a canvas and surrounded by inscriptions: 'Portrait de Cézanne—Portrait de Rembrandt—Portrait de Renoir—Natures mortes.'

1. In reality Duchamp's *Gioconda* also wears a small pointed beard. Duchamp having returned to New York in December, 1919, Picabia reconstructed *L.H.O.O.Q.* for *391*, with Duchamp's authorization, but forgot the beard. Many years later, in a bookshop, Jean Arp, by the merest chance, came across the photograph of the *Gioconda* modified by Picabia. Soon thereafter he had the opportunity to show this version to Duchamp, who immediately completed it by drawing in the missing ornament and writing at the foot of the picture: 'Moustaches by Picabia, beard by Marcel Duchamp.' This story, related at the time in various circles, was heard by a small boy who, on being asked a little later by his school teacher: 'Who painted the *Gioconda*?' asked quite naturally in return: 'With or without beard, sir?' (L.H.O.O.Q.: in French, these letters are pronounced phonetically 'Elle a chaud au cul' i.e. 'She's got hot pants'.)

2. Robert Lebel: *Léonard de Vinci* (Presses du Livre Français, Paris, 1952).

3. The reviews *Littérature*, *Proverbe*, etc.; *Francis Picabia*, by Marie de la Hire (Galerie La Cible, Paris, 1920); *De Mallarmé à 391*, by Pierre de Massot (Au Bel Exemplaire, St. Raphael, 1922). See also *491* (Galerie Drouin, Paris, 1949).

4. *Nord-Sud*: also the name of an independent underground railway company in Paris at the time.

5. Reproduced at the time in *Cannibal*, a review of Picabia's and in *Der Dada* (Berlin, no. 3).

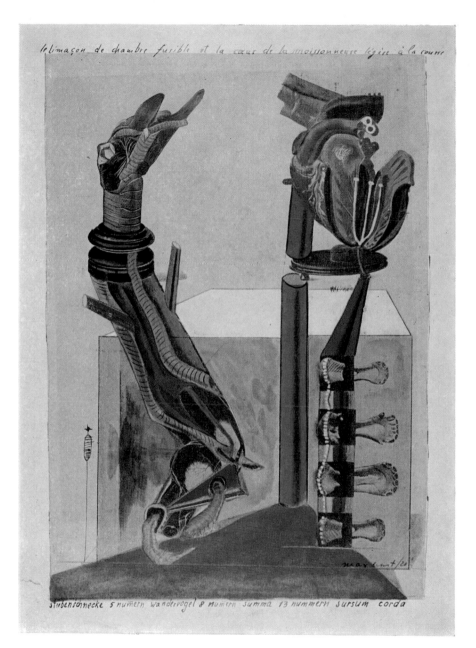

Max Ernst: *The Fusible Room Snail and the Heart of the Light Harvester-woman Racing.* 1921.

Man Ray: Rayogram. 1921.

The review *Littérature* announced in its nineteenth issue (May, 1921) 'the placing under whisky-marine' *(mise sous whisky marin)*[1] which took place at the Galerie Sans-Pareil in honour of the author of *Fiat Modes* from May 3 to June 3, 1921,[2] as part of the Great Dada Season. 'Free entry, hands in the pockets—easy exit, picture under the arm,' said the invitations. Fifty-six *collages* (with or without glue) were on show: 'mechanoplastic plastoplastic pictoplastic anaplastic anatomic antizymic aerographic antiphonary sprayable and republican drawings. BEYOND PAINTING.' Max Ernst was not present, having been unable to obtain a visa to leave Germany in time to attend his own opening; but André Breton was there chewing matchsticks, Benjamin Péret and Louis Aragon shook hands every second, and Ribemont-Dessaignes kept shouting: 'It's raining on a skull!' In his preface to the catalogue, Breton reassumed his habitual seriousness in order to note the influence of photography on the recent evolution of the arts, and to observe that 'the belief in an absolute time and space seems ready to vanish' (and that, consequently, 'Dada does not claim to be modern'); he 'has a deep presentiment as to the real nature of this localized time that we are hearing about... Who knows,' he adds, 'if, in that way, we are not preparing ourselves to escape one day from the principle of identity?' He sees the images in the Max Ernst exhibition unfold like a moving film of the inner life. At a time when Einstein's theories were just becoming known in France to the public at large, this was probably the first occasion that an attempt had been made to link the problem of time considered from a relativist point of view with a poetic-pictorial expression.

In Cologne, during 1921, Max Ernst had painted compositions resembling magnified *collages*, such as *Œdipus Rex* and *Celebes*, known as *The Elephant of Celebes*—an indescribable cauldron with huge legs, sprouting a pipe terminated by the horns of a bull; in the foreground a headless woman makes a melancholy gesture, of appeal or farewell; high in the sky fishes are floating.

In 1921, also, Duchamp in New York published *New York Dada*, a review prepared in close collaboration with Man Ray. The cover reproduced a new readymade: a scent-bottle whose label carried Duchamp's photograph (made-up and wearing a female wig—rather like Pearl White in *The Perils of Pauline*) and the title 'Belle Haleine—Eau de Voilette—R.S.'[3] R.S. is Rrose Sélavy,

3. Man Ray took the photo and drew the letters on the label. *Belle Haleine-Eau de Voilette*: 'Sweet Breath-Veil Water.'

Max Ernst: *The Elephant of Celebes*. 1921.

1. Max Ernst explained later in a footnote to the English translation of his essay *Beyond Painting*: 'Whisky-Marine—like aquamarine. A distortion, humorous and very serious at the same time.' Cf. Motherwell's *Max Ernst, Beyond Painting*, p. 12.

2. This is the one exhibition of paintings mentioned by *Littérature* throughout the twenty numbers of the first series. On this occasion the review broke precedent by reproducing an *hors-texte* by Max Ernst, *Relief Tricoté*.—The first issue of *Littérature*, founded in March, 1919 by André Breton and Philippe Soupault, seemed to be following in the footsteps of Reverdy's *Nord-Sud*. Then the review introduced Isidore Ducasse's *Poésies*, printed various unpublished texts of Mallarmé, Rimbaud, etc., the work of young poets, notes on other reviews, music criticism; but *Littérature* was rapidly invaded by the dadaist spirit.

Francis Picabia: *M'amenez-y.* 1918.

the pseudonym with which Duchamp signed some of his productions from then on.[1] Rrose Sélavy concerned himself especially with language: 'If what you want is a grammatical rule: the verb agrees with the subject *in consonance.* For instance: *le nègre aigrit, les négresses s'aigrissent ou maigrissent.*'[2] One associates Rrose Sélavy in particular with scabrous puns and practical advice, true

verbal *readymades* (sometimes constructed as spoonerisms):[3] '*Des bas en soie—la chose aussi.*' '*Question d'hygiène intime: faut-il mettre la moelle de l'épée dans le poil de l'aimée?*' 'Among our articles of lazy hardware we recommend a faucet which stops dripping when one isn't listening.' '*Daily lady cherche démêlés avec Daily Mail.*' '*Ovaire toute la nuit.*' 'Rrose Sélavy's dye-works: specializes in oblong gowns for people suffering from hiccups.'   And the imperative '*M'amenez-y*'.[4] One may perhaps mention finally the unambiguous pun in English that appeared originally in *391* no. 17 (June, 1924): 'Oh! do shit again!   Oh! douche it again!'

However the dadaist demonstrations in Paris were by now maintaining their agitated rhythm only in an increasingly artificial manner. Later, Gabrielle Buffet-Picabia wrote of this period: 'The spirit which had blown so hard and ardently degenerated in the post-war climate of Paris into a battle of clans, or even of individuals.'   The atmosphere in the French capital was basically different from that of Zurich, Cologne or Berlin: those who attended the Dada festivals in Paris were mostly initiates who were much more disposed to have fun than be indignant, and created an uproar chiefly in order to add excitement to programmes that they were sometimes justified in finding inadequate; doubtless the memory of the scandal of *Les Mamelles de Tirésias*, if not of *Ubu Roi*, was hovering nostalgically over these demonstrations.   At the beginning of 1921 Picabia quit Dada, and in June refused to exhibit at the Salon Dada, claiming it to be an enterprise incompatible with the 'anti-art' character which the movement had assumed. Crotti and Suzanne Duchamp also broke away. Duchamp, featured in the catalogue, cabled from America the three words: '*Peau de balle*' ('nothing doing'); the organizers tried to save face by pinning the telegram to the section of the wall reserv-

1. This name appears for the first time on the signature-picture *The Cacodylatic Eye* (see p. 34, note 1) where Duchamp wrote 'en 6 qu'habilla rrose Sélavy' ([Fr]ancis [Pi]cabia [a]rrose, c'est la vie) thus creating a double-initialled first name Rrose.   On a portrait of Duchamp in 1923, Man Ray wrote *Cela vit*, and entitled one of his Rayograms: *Sel à vie.*

2. Cf. *Le Philhaou-Thibaou*, supplement to *391* (July, 1921).

3. Published in *Littérature* (no. 5, new series, October, 1922), in *391* (no. 18, 1924), and on the front inside cover of Pierre de Massot's *The Wonderful Book* (1924).   Most of these phrases are collected in the *Boîte en Valise*, handwritten on music paper.   During 1922–23 Robert Desnos composed a large number of such puns and spoonerisms in the manner of Duchamp: 'Rrose Sélavy,' said Desnos, '*connaît bien le marchand du sel*' (*marchand du sel* is a spoonerism of 'Marcel Duchamp').

4. '*M'amenez-y*' (bring me there'): a 'grammatical' substitution for the incorrect '*Amenez-moi-z-y.*' But it is also a play on the word '*amnésie.*' This phrase figures also in one of Picabia's paintings, and as the title of a Dada review edited by Céline Arnault.

ed for Duchamp's contributions. At this time, Jean Crotti declared himself to be no longer Dada but *Tabu*. A *Tabu* exhibition (Jean Crotti and Suzanne Duchamp) took place in 1921 at the Galerie Montaigne.

Published in the autumn of 1921, in Switzerland, far from Parisian intrigues, *Dada Intirol Augrandair Dersängerkrieg*, dated September 16, 1886,[1] was the last to evoke the old spirit. Tzara, Arp, Fraenkel, Ribemont-Dessaignes, Baargeld, Eluard and Ernst collaborated; Ernst's *The Preparation of Glue from Bones*, reproduced in the review, was the first *collage* entirely constructed of cuttings from old zinc-engraved illustrations. *Dada au Grand Air*, as it is usually called, also published 'Fatagaga' poems, written by Ernst and Arp together.

Max Ernst: *The Preparation of Glue from Bones*. 1921.

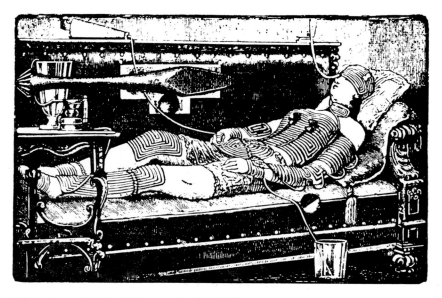

In June, 1921, Duchamp introduced Man Ray to the Dada group, which was meeting at that time at the Café Certa, passage de l'Opéra. Man Ray's first Paris exhibition was held in December, 1921 at the Librairie Six, avenue Lowendal, comprising thirty-five works dating from 1914 to 1921, and a catalogue which included texts by Arp, Eluard, Ernst, Man Ray, Ribemont-Dessaignes, Soupault, Tzara. 'No flowers, no crowns,' announced the invitation, 'no umbrellas, no sacraments, no cathedrals, no carpets, no folding screens, no metric system, no Spaniards, no calendar, no rose, no bar, no conflagration, no bonbons.'

At the Hôtel des Ecoles, rue Delambre, where he was living in 1921, Man Ray saw his first *Rayograms* develop. On sheets of photographic paper left inadvertently in the light, abandoned objects—a key, a ball of cotton-wool, a length of thread—traced extraordinary silhouettes in white shadows on a black background. Chance, revealing to Man Ray the shadow's dimension, produced the same effect that he had previously sought by means of an air-brush, where, by directing the jet of coloured vapour towards an object placed on a sheet of white paper, then withdrawing the object, its imprint and shadow became perceptible.[2] The Rayograms *developed* this process: artistic sensibility, the laws of composition and plasticity found themselves once more destroyed and recreated. Original visions and knowledge of the real, neither photography nor painting, a semi-mechanical technique for the

fabrication of inimitable works (each Rayogram was of necessity unique): the cleverest *trompe-l'œil* or instinctive painting paled in comparison with these radiant black and white prints. Rayogram: the handwriting of light, of the creator of images. *Champs Délicieux* was the title of the album in which Man Ray put together the first results of his invention in 1922; Tristan Tzara wrote in the preface: 'The negotiator of luminous values takes up the wager proposed by the stable boys. The ration of hay that he allows each evening and morning to the horses of modern art could never impede the thrilling progress of his game of suns and chess.'

At the same time Man Ray was continuing his graphic activities; at the beginning of 1922 he drew a new cover for *Littérature*, the review founded by André Breton in March, 1919. In parting from Dada whose official organ it had meanwhile become, *Littérature* also abandoned the yellow cover and the attractive romantic format which it had preserved against all Dada's stormwinds and tidal waves, and its new dress was rather dadaist: the word 'littérature', superbly calligraphed and completed by a blot of ink, emerges—like a rabbit—

1. That is to say, one year exactly before the birth of Arp.
2. *First Object*, 1918, for example.

from a top-hat marked with the conjuror's name. After three 'top-hat' issues, the review appeared with other covers, all different and all drawn by Picabia.

Picabia was now inaugurating the series of his *optical pictures*, globes, circles, targets, already foreshadowed in 1919 by *Volucelle*. *Spanish Night* (1920) is a large canvas, half black and half white, with two contrasting figures, white and black, perforated by small holes, like figure-targets in a shooting gallery. In *Optophone*, shown in 1922 at the Picabia exhibition in Barcelona, a female figure floats nonchalantly above concentric black and white circles. The exhibition catalogue was prefaced by André Breton: 'There are some of us who, every morning on awakening, would wish to consult Picabia like a marvellous barometer on the atmospheric changes recorded during the night... The man who changes Picabia's climate is above all Picabia himself.'

In 1922 *collages* by Max Ernst illustrated collections of poems by Paul Eluard: *Répétitions*, *Les*

Max Ernst: Collage for *Répétitions*, by Paul Eluard. 1922.

Malheurs des Immortels (in the second book Ernst also collaborated in the text). His *collages* had become technically perfected and gave a remarkable impression of unity of composition. Ernst was now using mostly wood or zinc engravings from catalogues and old books. This method of reproduction had by then been supplanted by new techniques; the engraved pictures which Max Ernst transformed into visual poems were already childhood memories for people of his generation, possessing a picturesque quality that is both derisive and very engaging, and which becomes

enhanced, revivified in a sense, by the very humour of the *collage*.

Picabia had made much fun of Picasso's 'Ingres period',[1] and imitated him lightheartedly in drawings illustrating the new covers of *Littérature*, though in all of them an extra- or anti-plastic intention intervened, a 'literary' idea, a metaphor or a pun; sometimes a cheeky blasphemy, such as, in no. 4 (September, 1922), the magnificent flaming heart encircled by thorns and topped by a cross, the whole being surmounted by the word 'Littérature'; or a satirical allegory: in no. 9, a monocled figure wearing shorts is lifting at arm's length an enormous dish in which a female angel is kneeling; another drawing reproduces an alliteration by Rrose Sélavy: *Lits et ratures* ('beds and erasures') and accompanies it with suggestive designs; for no. 8, a rose-bush planted in a flower-bed composed of the word 'Littérature' bears as flowers the faces of the contributors; no. 8 shows bodies of naked women inscribed with the title of the review; and so on.

As one can see, the Dada spirit was not dead —with Picabia it never died—but the movement dissolved in a confusion of quarrels, accusations, erroneous actions and occasional free fights. At the end of it all, André Breton proved to be the rallying-point for a new circle composed almost exclusively of ex-Dadas, most of whom were included among the first surrealists. *Le Rendez-vous des Amis* painted by Max Ernst in 1922 shows Crevel, Max Ernst, Fraenkel, Paulhan, Péret, Baargeld, Soupault, Arp, Ribemont-Dessaignes, Eluard and his wife Gala, Aragon, Breton, with two newcomers: Max Morise and Robert Desnos. Chirico, transformed into a statue, also figures in the group.

Marcel Duchamp, half Parisian, half New Yorker, and Arp, still a Zuricher, remained outside the conflagrations that marked the end of Dada. *Littérature* died in 1924 after a last 'demoralizing number,' while *391* reappeared and featured a series of caricatures in which Picabia treats the future leader of Surrealism most severely. Rrose Sélavy and Man Ray contributed to these sheets which were also to be the last of Picabia's review. In the final no. 19 of *391* appear the names of E.L.T. Mesens and René Magritte, who were to become the protagonists of the Belgian surrealist group.[2] Also in this number is to be found an

1. Particularly in one of the Barcelona issues of *391*
2. See Chapter 7.

announcement of the entertainment that Picabia was about to have performed by the Swedish Ballet company: *Relâche*.

About 1910, the oriental, barbaric splendour of Serge de Diaghilev's first Ballets Russes had introduced Fauvism into the theatre and then into the decorative arts. In 1917, Diaghilev enlisted some futurist and cubist painters: in Rome, Balla and Depero designed the decor and costumes for Stravinsky's *Feu d'Artifice* and *Chant du Rossignol*, Picasso those of Erik Satie's and Jean Cocteau's *Parade*. A framework was imposed upon the music and dancing that eliminated the decorative arabesque and orgies of colour typical of the Russian company, as also the precise realism of traditional decor; the new tendency was towards plastic symbolism and a metaphorical exposition of the characters and action. The futurist ballets were performed in Italy, and *Parade*, shown in Paris, created a scandal. But with the acrobats' white and blue striped trunks, evoking aerial arabesques, the 'managers' like wobbly skyscrapers, and the splendid Chinese in his asymmetrical robe on which a golden sun glittered, Picasso set the fashion for a complete renovation in theatre production and costume which today's designers still follow.

The Ballets Russes proceeded to commission other modern artists, as, a little later, did Rolf de Maré's Swedish Ballet. In 1924, a company patronized by the Comte de Beaumont and directed by the great dancer of the Ballets Russes, Léonide Massine, presented a season at the Théâtre de la Cigale consisting of a series of creations by Tzara, Braque, Jean Cocteau, Jean Hugo, Derain and Picasso: the latter dressed and decorated *Mercure*, 'plastic poses' accompanied by music by Erik Satie.

Picasso had by this time abandoned theoretical Cubism and its still-born offspring (such as Ozenfant and Jeanneret's Purism) to his followers. He had held aloof from the anti-Art enterprises of Dada, but his penchant for playfulness led him naturally to occasional manifestations of a rather dadaist flavour: *Littérature* (new series, no. 10) reproduced his *Married Couple*, a cubist painting signed in huge letters with Manet's name. During this period the artist coaxed objects of superb plasticity from a combination of most unlikely materials; he painted huge earthy-fleshed women against bright blue skies, idols of some cyclopean

Francis Picabia: Cover for *Littérature*, new series, no. 4. Paris, September, 1922.

Francis Picabia : Cover for *Littérature*, new series, no. 10. Paris, May, 1923.

Pompeii, for this was his period of 'giants'; he was fashioning countless variations in his graphic methods; everything within sight became plastic matter to be used with the most complete virtuosity. He continued his 'Ingres-type' drawings, and painted perfect portraits of his wife and his

Pablo Picasso: *The Married Couple.*

son. For *Mercure*, he invented both charming and funny costumes, and the scenery consisted of silhouettes in wire fastened onto frameworks which invisible scene-shifters changed from time to time during the course of the action; on the whole the decor was more animated than the dancers (rather as with *Parade*).

Mercure was greeted with 'general restlessness'. The public's hostile reaction was due in part to Erik Satie's score; his music had already provoked hoots and jeers at the time of *Parade*. Satie, a native of Honfleur as was Alphonse Allais (French humorist and author of countless short stories that he listed among his 'anthumous' works), had long exasperated musical officialdom by the seeming frivolity with which he treated his art (even before 1900, he had shown a predilection for comical titles: *Pièces Froides—Airs à Faire Fuir—Danses de Travers* (1887); later: *Morceaux en Forme*

de Poire (1903); *Trois Préludes Flasques (pour un Chien).*[1] But he was a composer of rare originality and technical accomplishment; he had been the friend, and sometimes counsellor, of Claude Debussy, and a few brilliant young musicians had gathered around him and formed the 'groupe des Six'.—Some of them were to disown him as a result of *Mercure*.

The score of *Parade* had united very subtly a futurist 'art of noise' with classically inspired developments and popular melodies. 'Fair-ground music', declared the critics almost unanimously: a judgment repeated for *Mercure* which, in fact, staged dances inspired by circus acts rather than by mythology.

Marcel Duchamp and Man Ray regularly attended the performances of the *Soirées de Paris*, whose ballets constituted an excellent back-cloth for their activities; these centred upon the bar of the Théâtre de la Cigale, a most attractive spot both on account of the quality of its drinks and the charm of the sophisticated girls who frequented it, quite unconcerned by the excitements of stage and audience. Duchamp, Man Ray and Picabia were all on close terms of friendship with Satie. Shortly after the performances of *Mercure*, Picabia offered a libretto of his own to Satie for a ballet which he wanted to call *Relâche* ('Theatre closed'). The title alone was eloquent: though the intention was not, perhaps, to do away with 'art' entertainments altogether, at least it was hoped to point out their limitations—even in this hitherto privileged domain.

Rolf de Maré's company presented this 'ballet', whose score the critics, faithful to themselves, promptly described as 'low dance-hall music'. The first performance had been set for November, 27, 1924, but on that day the doors of the Théâtre des Champs-Elysées remained closed: the *premier danseur*, Jean Borlin, had fallen ill and now *Relâche* really did mean 'theatre closed'! The curtain eventually rose three days later.

The overwhelming impression was of light and movement. The first act decor was literally dazzling: scenery festooned with innumerable spotlights so blinded the public that they could barely make out, on the stage, a fireman pouring water interminably from one bucket into another while chain-smoking cigarettes. In the background, vague dancers revolved in a darkness where occa-

1. *Cold Pieces—Airs to Run Away From—Dances Askew —Fragments in the Shape of a Pear—Three Limp Preludes (For a Dog).*

90

sional beams of light revealed, briefly, the *tableau vivant* of a couple stark naked representing Cranach's *Adam and Eve*. A man sitting on a chair at the edge of the stage in an attitude of total idleness got up from time to time and paced up and down.[1]

During the interval the now famous *Entr'acte* was shown, a film conceived and carried out by Picabia (the young René Clair was cameraman and technical assistant), with a musical accompaniment by Satie. This was the first time the cinema had been used in a theatrical performance, and the

first time also a musical score had been especially composed for a film. The years have not blunted its sheer force of comedy, power of surprise, and astonishing rhythm: the dancer in a tutu (Jean Borlin in female costume) seen from below as in the 'mystery wells' at fun-fairs, dancing on a transparent glass floor; the open-air chess game on the roof of the Théâtre des Champs-Elysées between Marcel Duchamp and Man Ray, watched by Erik Satie; the indescribable funeral cortège crossing Luna Park with the mourners filmed in slow motion, the hearse decorated with advertising posters, the gentlemen of the family sobbing while eating the bread-rolls tied to the catafalque; and then, the whole procession's mad flight and the cortège and dead man finally vanishing. It may be noted, incidentally, that film libraries and film clubs persist today in presenting *Entr'acte* as 'a film by René Clair', without even mentioning the name of the author and director: Francis Picabia.

The decor of the second act of *Relâche* carried enormous inscriptions: 'Erik Satie is the greatest

1. This role was interpreted by Man Ray.

musician in the world'—'If you are not satisfied you can buy whistles at the box-office for a few farthings'. However, after the 'entr'acte', Borlin's ponderously dull dances ended up by boring those present rather than scandalizing them as Picabia would have wished. The audience only revived in order to boo the authors loudly when they appeared on the stage to take their bows in a little five-horsepower Citroën.

'*Relâche* is life,' wrote Picabia in the programme's introduction. 'Life as I like it, all for today, nothing for yesterday, nothing for tomorrow.' This work, so ironically detached at first glance, was in fact crammed with a redoubtable measure of 'black' humour; the Swedish Ballet could not survive it and it was their final interpretation. It was also Erik Satie's last ballet, for he died the following year; he might perhaps have wished for a burial like that in *Entr'acte*, with the 'Groupe des Six' as pall-bearers chasing after his runaway hearse.

The funeral in Luna Park, a scene from Francis Picabia's film *Entr'acte*, 1924.

Dada activities ceased in Germany about the end of 1921, when Max Ernst left Cologne for Paris and the Berlin group broke up. But Dada continued to exist in Hanover in the person of Kurt Schwitters, who had already contributed to the publications of the Swiss group (*Der Zeltweg*, 1919). Schwitters wrote poems and stories,[2] and had invented with Raoul Haussman an onomatopoeic musical language, a true 'bird language' with which he greeted his visitors, perched in a tree in his garden.[3] From 1919 onwards he made *montages* with the aid of all sorts of discarded objects, torn and dirtied newspapers, bus tickets, old rags. *Montage*, which Haussman had already developed in 1919, was made use of by Dada very freely: the German reviews reproduced *montages* executed in collaboration, sometimes by as many as ten participants. Schwitters, assembling pieces of scrap and rubbish, succeeded in obtaining subtle colour harmonies, rich and delicate works of art.

Merz was the name he gave to his productions from 1920 onwards (this title was found on a scrap of newspaper which bore only the remains of the word *kommerz*). The *Merz* enterprises ranged from a children's picture-book *(Merz 3)* to

2. See *La Loterie du Jardin Zoologique*, published in French with other texts, accompanied by the drawings from *Fiat Modes* by Max Ernst (trans. Robert Valançay, 'L'Age d'Or' collection, Editions Fontaine, Paris, 1952).

3. Cf. in the above publication the poem 'Scherzo' (the third part of a 'pre-syllabic sonata').

The Villa des Arts in Montmartre, Paris, where Picabia lived during the early twenties.

91

a revue of functional architecture *(Merz 2)*, from abstract art *(Merz 8-9*, an issue drawn up by the esthetician Lissitzky), to *Merz 4* which enjoyed the collaboration of Tzara and Arp and reproduced a Picasso, *Le Violon*, with the title: 'Sacipos—Le Lonvoi', and *Merz 6* which also carried the title *Arp I* (Tatlin, Sophie Taeuber, Mondrian, Arp).

There were dozens of *Merzes*, books, catalogues, poems, pictures; certainly the most remarkable of them all was Schwitter's own house, and he devoted years to its decoration. Each room was entirely 'merzized', with labyrinths of angles, stepped faces, boxed surfaces, geometrical stalactites; the architectural jumble spread from floor to floor, and even the roof sprouted prismatic columns and pyramids.

This building no longer exists in Hanover. Strategic air bombardments during the last war completely razed it.

Born in several countries at the same time, developing in two continents, Dada had as much right as any other movement to be called international (there were Dada or dadaistic reviews in Italy, Holland, Austria, Poland, Japan, etc., and there were pseudo-dadaist reviews in Germany, published by vague humorists on the look-out for notoriety). Though Duchamp played the role of initiator, while Picabia incarnated most effectively the dadaist spirit, and Tzara was a tireless organizer and propagandist, still no one was really the 'head' of Dada. 'All the Dadas are Presidents,' said one manifesto.

Nevertheless, one reaction was constantly affirmed within this fluid 'group', varying according to the tendencies and means of expression of the participants: a reaction against the tragically comical spectacle of a world destroying itself during the endless conflict of the first World War. Nothing is more certain than that Dada was never a 'serious' movement, and nothing too is farther from removing its significance. On the contrary: Marcel Duchamp's extremely complex ironic method; Picabia's mordant fantasy; Man Ray's anti-plastic plasticity; the boisterousness of the cabaret Voltaire; Arp's candid precision; Max Ernst's *vulgär-dilettantismus* in Cologne; the Berlin group's violent satires; the provocative Parisian festivals; the deliberate confusion of *Merz*—such aspects are clearly insufficient in themselves to embrace fully either the personalities or the work of the participants. They are nonetheless the variants of a *humorous reality* which stamped its imprint on all of Dada's multiform activities. The success of the word itself is a humorous fact of considerable importance: a vocable signifying nothing, or anything,[1] became a rallying cry and a symbol of their state of mind for the most gifted young poets of that era.

This humorous reality appeared also to be a result of the upheavals that had been experienced in art and thought in general, and an aspect of that 'dual civilization' composed of hostile elements whose struggle might well lead to annihilation and devastation or to a new affirmation of life. Dada was, in a sense, the 'unnatural son' of the pre-1914 schools: it exterminated its parents in a most Oedipean manner. 'Futurism has died. Of what? Of DADA,' claimed *Dada Soulève Tout*, on January 12, 1921. Expressionism and Cubism were no better treated. *Da-da*, double affirmation, and double negation; a mechanism which disorganized consciousness and dream like an alarm-clock, that disastrous instrument in which Man Ray, Picabia, and also Jacques Vaché (though he never knew Dada) saw the perfect symbol of humour.

---

1. In French: 'hobby, pet subject'—or 'horse' in baby-talk; in German: a slang phrase for 'good-bye'; in Russian and Rumanian: 'yes-yes'; and according to Tzara (*Dada Manifesto* 1918), 'the Krou Negroes call the tail of a sacred cow: DADA'.

Kurt Schwitters: The interior of his *Merzbau* in Hanover.

Man Ray: *Portrait of Rrose Sélavy.* 1923.

In many respects the work of Marcel Duchamp offers a more complete lyrical-scientific synthesis than anything envisaged by other creative spirits before him. In his *Méditations Esthétiques*, Guillaume Apollinaire concludes his notice on Marcel Duchamp with these lines: 'Just as Cimabué's pictures were paraded through the streets, our century has seen the airplane of Blériot, laden with humanity, with the efforts of thousands of years, with necessary art, escorted in glory to the museum of Art and Industry. It is perhaps reserved for an artist so detached from esthetic preoccupations, so preoccupied with energy as Marcel Duchamp, to reconcile Art and the People.' And André Breton has said that in studying the Glass of *The Bride Stripped Bare...*, 'one very soon abandons oneself to the charm of a great modern legend where everything is unified by lyricism'.[1]

We have seen this legend take shape in the preceding pages, a theme that is sometimes hardly perceptible and at other times is compellingly present in the foreground, but which penetrates and supports the revolution in the arts and the whole forward thrust of our civilization. The epic of mechanics resembles those film serials in which every week a fresh mystery opens up exciting and anguishing perspectives which develop unexpectedly during successive instalments, without the enigma ever being solved. One could almost say that the adventure unfolds in a geometric progression, sucking people into an ever-expanding whirlwind.

The *machine myth* can be traced to the very dawn of modern times, with the researches of Paolo Uccello, of da Vinci, artist and engineer, and in

1. A. Breton: 'Lighthouse of the Bride', reprinted in R. Lebel's *Marcel Duchamp* (Trianon Press, London, and Grove Press, New York, 1959).

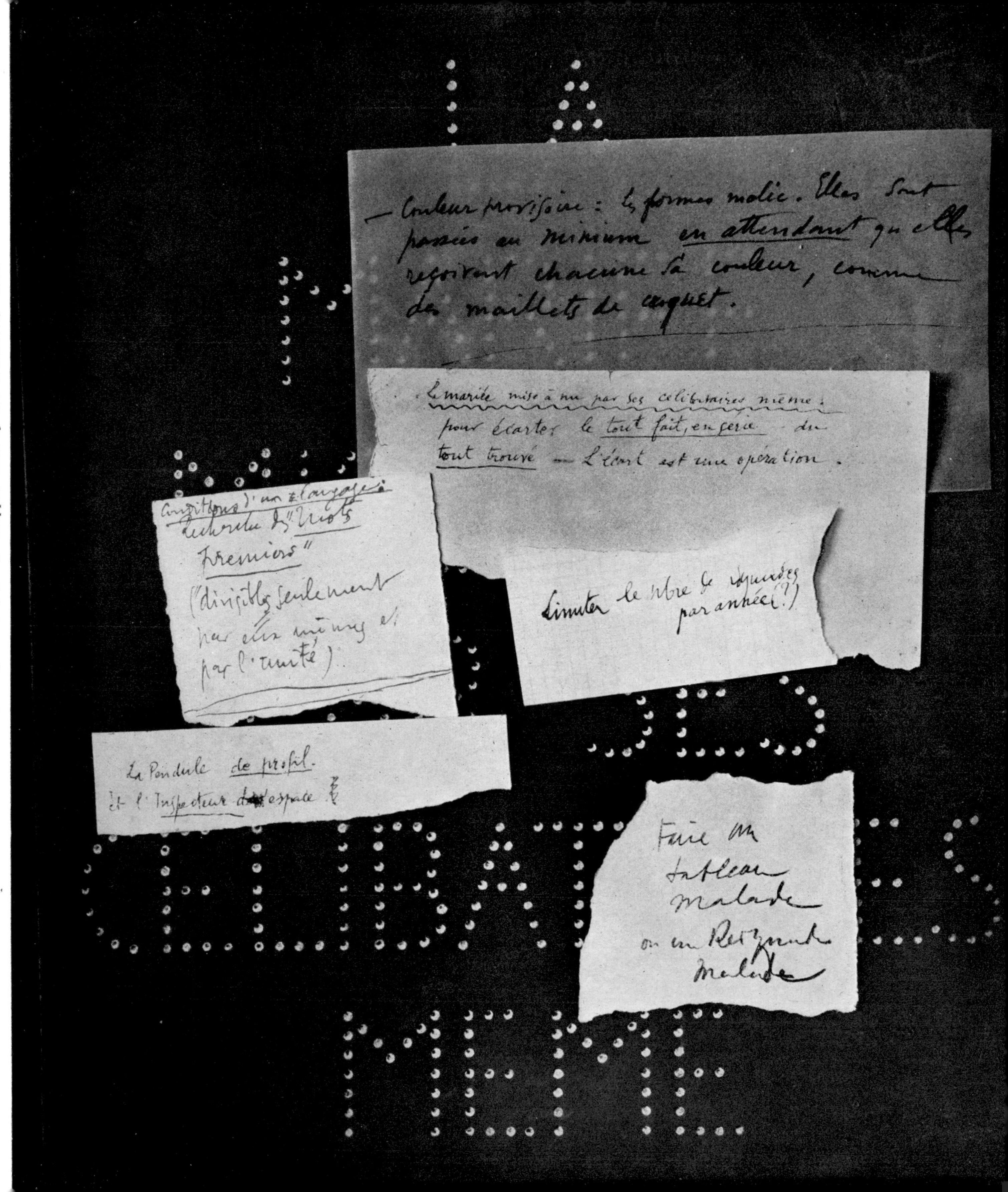
— Couleur provisoire : les formes mâlic. Elles sont passées au minium en attendant qu'elles reçoivent chacune sa couleur, comme des maillets de croquet.
La mariée mise à nu par ses célibataires même :
pour écarter le tout fait, en série du tout trouvé — L'écart est une opération.
Conditions d'un langage : recherche des "mots premiers" ("divisibles seulement par eux-mêmes et par l'unité")
Limiter le nbre de readymades par année (?)
La Pendule de profil.
et l'Inspecteur de l'espace
Faire un tableau malade ou un Readymade malade

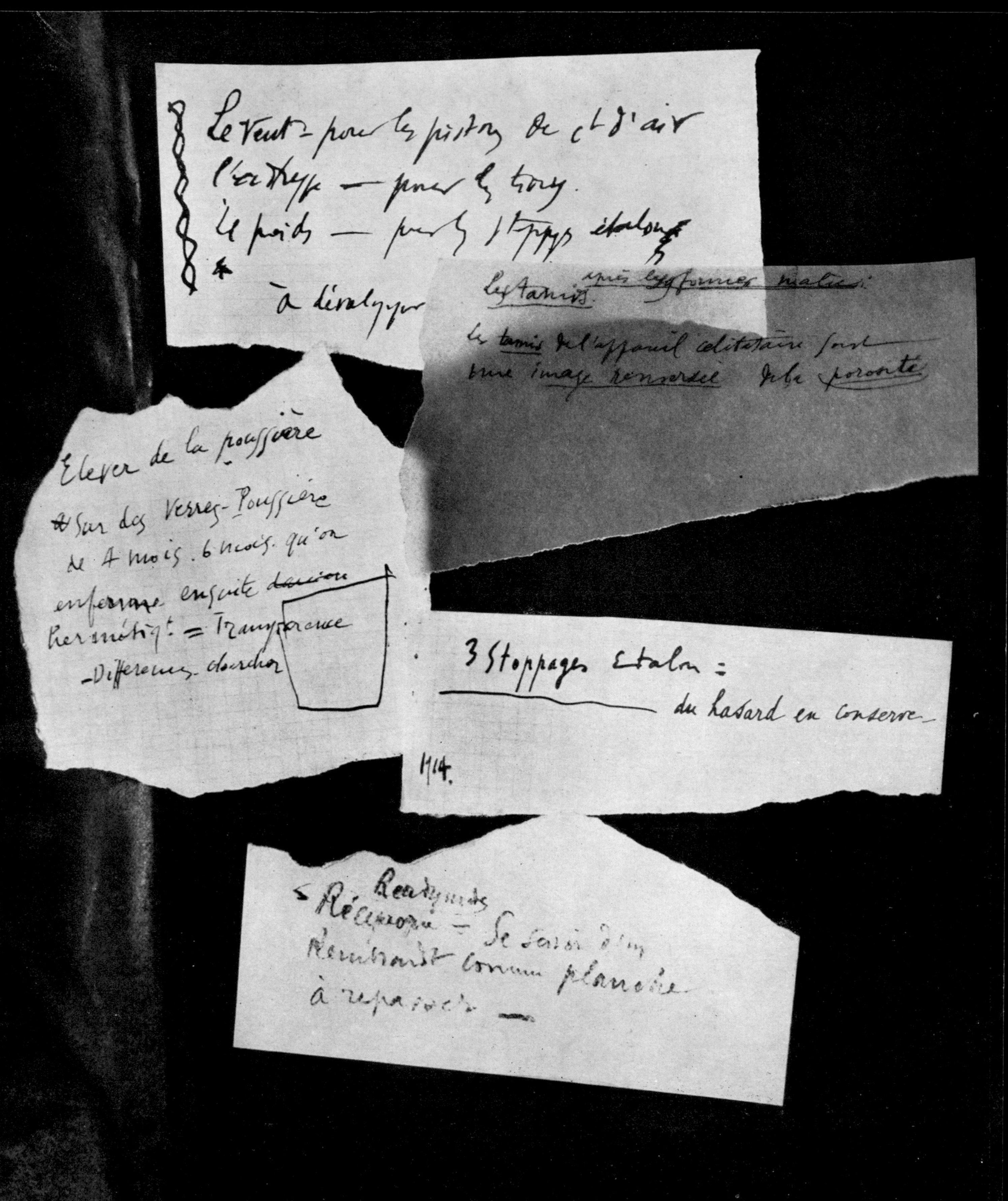
Le vent – pour les pistons de c^t d'air
l'adresse – pour les trous.
Le poids – pour les 3 stoppages étalons
à développer

Les tamis après les formes malic.
Les tamis de l'appareil célibataire sont une image renversée de la porosité

Elever de la poussière
sur des Verres – Poussière
de 4 mois. 6 mois. qu'on
enferme ensuite
hermétiqt. = Transparence
– Différences. chercher

3 Stoppages Étalon =
du hasard en conserve –
1914.

Readymades
Réciproque = Se servir d'un
Rembrandt comme planche
à repasser –

the experimental work of numerous adepts, creators of utopias, imaginary voyagers, constructors of impossible but realistic machines. It gained strength towards the middle of the eighteenth century, enriched by episodes which we cannot even begin to mention here; but we all know the interest that automatons and living statues aroused during that era.

During the epoch of Romanticism and the industrial revolution, the machine began to assert itself as the great mythical reality. But the romantic poet tended to reject this new reality and prefer to it a past without railways or steam-boats. He viewed scholars (who returned the compliment) rather as creatures from another planet. Victor Hugo, in *Le Rhin*, wrote that a scholar in love was 'a problem' for him, and continued, in mock-scientific language: 'Can you imagine Romeo with his eye glued to the microscope, counting the seventeen thousand facets of a fly's eye; Don Juan, in a serge apron, analyzing paratartrate of antimony and paratartrovinate of potassium, and Othello peering through a magnifying-glass, looking for gallinules and gomphonemes in Chinese fossilized flour?' But the contrast between sail and steam navigation on the great European waterway showed him 'with an exceptional degree of clarity the dual nature of our epoch: the daughter of a religious past who fancies herself the mother of an industrial future'. Events have shown that this future was not just a fanciful belief: *industrialization* is today the one credo shared by all the nations of the earth.

Those whom Arpad Mezei and I have named elsewhere 'the seven sages of dual civilization': Sade, Lautréamont, Rimbaud, Mallarmé, Jarry, Apollinaire, Roussel,[1] were all synthetist poets and able to overcome the dualism of their time. Sade studied the psychological and physiological problems of the human being as an impassioned experimentalist; Lautréamont and Rimbaud were without doubt the first to amalgamate the visions of other eras with the appearances of civilized 'supernature': although Rimbaud's *Illuminations* are the children of Aloysius Bertrand's medieval prose-works, they would certainly not have shown such a power to renew written poetry if they had not also been the songs of a new humanity for whom coal-smoke is 'the shadow of woods' and 'the summer night'; and Lautréamont's famous comparisons most often bring into play scientific objects, mechanisms, scientific observations: 'Beautiful as

the fleshy wattle—conical in shape, furrowed by deep transverse lines—which rises up at the base of the turkey's upper beak... beautiful as a corvette armed with gun-turrets... beautiful as the chance meeting on an operating table of a sewing-machine and an umbrella!'

Apollinaire, who knew the ancient myths and tales of chivalry so well, himself finished by being 'weary of this ancient world'—according to his poem 'Zone'—and, like the futurists, found he had had 'enough of living in Greek and Roman antiquity'. At the beginning of his important poem 'Hills' *(Calligrammes)*, he places the past and the future, and poetry's future discoveries, under the sign of the new beings of the industrial era:

> *High over Paris roofs one day*
> *Two airplanes struggled in the sky*
> *The one was red the other black*
> *While at the zenith timelessly*
> *The airplane-sun flamed in its track*

The myth of mechanics has the power to restore the old legends and polarize most of the ancient beliefs. Charles Cros, in 'Le Grand Canal Royal des Deux-Mers', a poem devoted to what we have called 'the modern myth of great technical achievements',[2] had already seen the new techniques follow the paths laid down thousands of years ago. And, in our own time, electricity centres are rising up in predestined places haunted by the guardian spirits of water and the sun, such as, in France, Génissiat and Mondragon; while it is planned to build a hydro-electric generating plant on one of the sites most charged with ancient traditions—the bay of Mont Saint-Michel and Tombelaine, rocks consecrated since time immemorial to the god of Light. The ancient legends were able to reincarnate themselves in the mechanic adventure and, in fact, they reappear in contemporary science-fiction: Daedalus, the first engineer of the western world, the first bird-man and the constructor of the Cretan Labyrinth, the quest for the Golden Fleece, the Great Work, the old dreams of super-man and artificial man, imaginary voyages, Paradise and Hell, and the Golden Age which technical knowledge is always promising us for some date that is always in the future.

But the machine has its own gods and demons: Black gold, white coal, the fairy of Electricity, queens of the sky, the atom.... It is no longer

1. Cf. our *Genèse de la Pensée Moderne (op. cit.)*.

2. *Genèse de la Pensée Moderne*, ch. 7.

calvaries that are set up at crossroads but metallic fetishes attracting other mechanisms around them. The machine has even revived the hallucinations and miracles of Fatima, with its stories of flying saucers.

Different writers have described 'the sexual frenzy of factories', obsessive rhythms, exhalations, cries, panting sounds, shining dart-pointed instruments, articulated rods dripping with sweat, simulacra of inexhaustible loves. Could not man himself become a machine in his amorous activity and make love indefinitely, like a machine? Alfred Jarry's 'modern novel' *Le Surmâle* shows the human being transformed into a machine for making love, and even into a machine for inspiring love. Eros remains the supreme god in the world of machines, as one can again see in Apollinaire's erotic-scientific story *Le Roi-Lune*.

When, in the best vein of anticlerical humour, Jarry united science, sport and Christianity in *The Passion Considered as a Hill Climb Bicycle Race*, transforming the Cross of Calvary into a special type of bicycle on which Our Lord pedalled lying flat on his back, did he perhaps want to show us the Machine and the Champion as new objects of passion gradually replacing the Divine Bridegroom? According to Jarry, the cyclist Jesus 'completed the Calvary circuit as an aviator'; but Apollinaire, like a good heresiarch, wrote: 'Jesus climbs into the sky better than an aviator.' Kafka's torture machine in *The Penal Colony* is of a more sombre humour. It is a commentary rather than an interpretation to say that this machine is a crucifixion that breaks down, a sacrificial ceremony which shatters into separate pieces when given the order: 'Be just!'

The marriage between the machine and poetry is celebrated at the altar of humour. (One of the principal charms of science-fiction is a comic aspect which is most often involuntary.) In addition, many of the episodes in the scientific quest could serve to emphasize the common etymology of the words 'myth' and 'mystification'. The learned researches of Leonardo da Vinci sometimes had a rather ambiguous side; take, for instance, the 'alarm clock to be used by those who grudge the wasting of time... furnished with a device which at the required time jerks violently upwards the feet of the sleeper, who is thus awakened and goes to his work'.[1] The great humorists have been curious about scientific prob-

lems. Lichtenberg as well as Swift proposed utopian and comical mechanisms of very considerable ingenuity. The remarkable mathematical puzzles composed by Lewis Carroll to amuse the little girls who were his favourite companions are well known, as is Charles Cros' ironic text, *La Science de l'Amour*. Jarry, too, was well acquainted with what he called 'Science with a big *Scie* [bore]': in *Faustroll* the series of equations by which he proves that God is the tangential point between zero and infinity are developed with an impeccable algebraic strictness; and he is also the inventor of the Debraining Machine *(machine à décerveler)*....

This relationship between the comic and the mechanical (which Bergson was one of the first to point out in his study on laughter) can be sensed in painting: in the work of Seurat, for example, when he showed the women in *La Grande Jatte* literally 'machine-turned' like dolls; his *Woman Powdering Herself* (at the Tate Gallery in London) is really a puppet-show,[2] the spectators in the picture *The Circus* are mere jumping-jacks; one can certainly not accuse so marvellous a draughtsman as Seurat of clumsiness in these instances. We have seen that Chirico also has treated the theme of the scientific object with a mysterious and disquieting irony. Picabia mocks the machine as much as he exalts it in his mechanical paintings—while Marcel Duchamp considers his *Bride Stripped Bare...* as an 'hilarious picture'.[3] In fact, Dada had treated the mechanical motif with the humour it deserved. With Surrealism we shall see this humour occasionally reappear with undertones of sadism, in Max Ernst's *Garden Airplane Traps*, in certain 'surrealist objects' by Oscar Dominguez, in Matta's immense paintings whose vitrified personages twist and stretch themselves, and finally, in the germination of a whole host of beings with metallic or transparent flesh in Yves Tanguy's last works.

After the 1914-18 war, which had revealed their aggressive and destructive possibilities, the machines began to integrate themselves into men's lives. Fabre d'Olivet claimed at the dawn of the nineteenth century that our civilization was that

1. Da Vinci: *Notebooks*, Cape, London, 1938, Vol. II, Chapter on inventions.

2. This painting, half colour-print, half naïve painting, provides in addition an ideal subject for Pointillism: a cloud of multicoloured powder appears to cover the whole picture. Seurat seems to be mocking both his subject and his technique here.

3. Picabia also made fun of the artists who, about 1920, rushed to buy small cars with the advances from their first contracts. No. 14 of *391* contains a list of painters who had bought Citroëns—with comments such as : 'Braque has just bought a Citroën to continue turning out art. Recently he returned home with the gear inside his trousers'.

of the 'hominoid reign'. In fact, accompanied by Futurism, by Orphism, by the machine art of the Russian constructivists, by the mechanical painting that had become a sort of style for Dada, and by the surrealist procedures baptized with the significant name of *automatism*, it is the *mechanical kingdom* which seems to be gradually extending its sway over the whole planet.

In the *Catalogue of the Collection of the Société Anonyme*,[1] Katherine Dreier sums up the conversations she had with Marcel Duchamp in 1949-50 on the subject of *Nude Descending a Staircase*, in the following terms. When asked whether he called it a painting, he replied: 'No, it is an organization of kinetic elements, an expression of time and space through the abstract presentation of motion. A painting is, of necessity, a juxtaposition of two or more colours on a surface. I purposely restricted the *Nude* to wood colouring so that the question of painting *per se* might not be raised. There are, I admit, many patterns by which this idea could be expressed... But remember, when we consider the motion of form through space in a given time, we enter the realm of geometry and mathematics, just as we do when we build a machine for that purpose. Now if I show the ascent of an airplane, I try to show what it does. I do not make a still-life picture of it. When the vision of the *Nude* flashed upon me, I knew that it would break forever the enslaving chains of Naturalism.'

Marcel Duchamp had just completed *The King and Queen Surrounded by Swift Nudes* when he left for Munich where he stayed during July and August, 1912. Already putting into practice the art of voyages which his friend Apollinaire was to extol in *l'Antitradition Futuriste*, he travelled to Germany third-class by local trains, so that the journey should last longer.... From Munich date two drawings entitled *Virgin*, two paintings: *The Passage from the Virgin to the Bride* and the *Bride*, and another drawing: *The Bride Stripped Bare by the Bachelors*.

The Virgin: broken planes, vibrant structures traversed by what seems a dynamic flow of matter giving one of these two sketches something of the lightning-like movement of the *Nude Descending a Staircase*.—The full title of the third drawing, dated 'Munich, Juli 1912', written at the foot of the picture, is 'First research for: *the bride stripped bare by the bachelors*'; in the centre is the Bride, stretched out between two figures bristling with menacing antennae; at the base of the sketch is this note: 'Mechanism of sexual modesty [*pudeur*], Mechanical sexual modesty.' Composition in *lightning flashes* reappears in the accentuated contrasts of lines and planes of the *Passage from the Virgin to the Bride*; in the centre of the picture, the attention is drawn by a singular detail—a small narrow tube seen lengthwise, a sort of mortice rising out of a conically-shaped mass: this representation cannot fail to suggest the drawings of female sexual organs in anatomical charts.

The Sad Young Man in a Train and the *Nude*, which I have already mentioned, were works in full motion. Then the studies and pictures on the theme of chess showed the King and the Queen penetrated in some way by speed, and by feelings—by that deepest and most instinctual of feelings: *erotism*; the vision of whirling nudities 'traverses' the intellectual thought-process. *The King and Queen Surrounded by Swift Nudes*: rational symbols and sexual images are separate and well defined, while the whirlwind now 'surrounds' the stationary objects. Thus, up to the Munich *Bride*, Duchamp's researches are expressed in representations—illustrations, one might say—of duration: descents, crossings, passages. But a decisive change is apparent with the *Bride*: the dynamic whirlwind seems halted, and one can distinguish the shapes of things and their proper colours. Everything seems to indicate that the function is giving way to the organ, and this realization gives a clue to the real nature of the previous works: Nudes, Kings, Queens, Virgins; these beings are not only natural forms interpreted or recreated, they are above all *machines* in full motion.

The Munich *Bride* is a silent, halted machine that is ready to spring to life again with a human ardour betrayed by the ironically 'excited' flush of some of its mechanism. Perhaps indeed (as we shall see later on, in connection with certain passages of the Large Glass) the image only seems immobile because it is a *snapshot* of a motor in action; the lightning flash of zigzag lines is frozen into a series of complex mechanisms curved in a semi-circle, whose axes are set in relation to the small shining mortice first seen in the *Passage*....

1. *Op. cit.*, Chapter one.

Marcel Duchamp: *The King and Queen Surrounded by Swift Nudes*. 1912.

It is at Munich then that Duchamp began to develop the conceptions for his great picture on glass which, he has told us, 'was only *incompleted* in 1923'. During ten years he slowly built up this work, at leisure, with a sort of negligent persistence. He first established certain parts separately: the 'Chocolate grinder' in 1913, the 'Nine Malic moulds' in 1914, and the 'Glider' between 1913 and 1915. At Buenos Aires, in 1918, he constructed the first version of the 'Oculist witnesses' under the title: *To be Looked at with One Eye, Close To, for Almost an Hour*. The Large Glass itself began to take shape in New York in 1915.

A quantity of notes, plans and drawings having to do with the preparatory period (1911-15) were published in 1934 under the supervision of Duchamp himself, in the form of facsimiles reproducing exactly the handwriting, size and paper of each original document, all arranged in a box covered with green velvet-paper.[1] The genesis of Duchamp's Great Work is enclosed in this box: inspirations scribbled down on the spot or meticulously developed problems, each text, in either case, formulated with the most admirable clarity.

Among the many notes in the Green Box is to be found one dated 1912, redrafted subsequently during the stay in Munich and concerning the project for a picture, *The Jura-Paris Road*; the title had been suggested to Duchamp by a voyage in the Jura in the company of Apollinaire, and Picabia and his wife, at the end of 1912.[2] There is no sketch accompanying this note. However, 'the machine with five hearts' and 'the pure child, of nickel and platinum', which 'should dominate the Jura-Paris road', appear to be a parallel development or a first version of the Bachelor-Bride relationship in *The Bride Stripped Bare...*, or equally a bridge between the period of Nudes and that of the *Bride*: 'On one side the chief of the five nudes will be ahead of the four others *in the direction of* this Jura-Paris road. On the other side, the head-lamp-child[3] will be the conquering instrument of this Jura-Paris road.' The road in question, which was to start off from the chief of the five nudes so as 'to have no end' in the head-lamp-child, which 'could, in pictorial terms, be a comet', seems already to put into concrete form the dynamic influx which, in the Large Glass, ascends from the Bachelor Group towards the heights where the Bride and her 'Milky way' are hovering. Nevertheless, the two principal elements (head-lamp-child and group of nudes) of the *Jura-Paris Road* picture were meant to be juxtaposed (as are the Bride and the Bachelors in the Munich drawing) and not *superimposed*, as they were destined to be in the Glass.

Originally envisaged as a painting on canvas ('Long canvas, in height. Bride on top, Bachelors at the bottom,' according to another document in the Box), *The Bride Stripped Bare...* became the subject of numerous studies concerning the materials to be used in its realization. At first Duchamp described only certain parts as being in glass, others 'in dull metal (pure copper, steel, silver)',

1. Three hundred examples issued by Editions Rrose Sélavy, 18, rue de la Paix, Paris.

2. It was also during this voyage, according to the reminiscences of Mme Gabrielle Buffet-Picabia, that Apollinaire found the title of his poem 'Zone' (published in 1913 in *Alcools*); the four friends had been the guests of Gabrielle Picabia's mother at Etival, a village situated in a region near the Swiss frontier which the local people called 'the zone'.

3. *Enfant-phare*.

others again in nickel and platinum, or in mica, and others 'to be looked at while squinting, like a silvered area in a pane of glass, in which the room's trappings are reflected'.[1] The *Notes for an Hilarious Picture* propose to 'put the whole Bride under a glass dome' (like the orange-blossom crowns preserved by pious families). The artist also considered 'raising dust' (to find a 'transparent pastel') 'on dust-glasses of four months or six months which will then be hermetically sealed';[2] and a metaphysical 'colour raising' allowing one to obtain 'ripe, unputrefiable colours';[3] and an 'interior lighting' by means of matter-colours resembling the enigmatic light of glow worms (glowing glass):[4] 'colours which molecularly have a luminous focus casting no reflections on to the other parts'.

All these researches converged towards the choice of *glass* as a support for the projected representations;[5] these were finally executed according to a variety of procedures, such as those we have just mentioned, but generally (in the lower part of the picture or Bachelor Machine) rather in the manner of a stained-glass window: strips of metal-foil glued behind the transparent wall follow the contours of the objects and sometimes outline the colour.

According to its author, *The Bride*... is intended as a DELAY IN GLASS. 'Employ *delay* instead of picture or painting; picture on glass becomes delay in glass—but delay in glass does not mean picture on glass.—It is simply a way of reaching the point of no longer considering that the thing in question is a picture—make a delay of it as generally as possible, not so much in the different senses in which delay can be taken, but rather in their indecisive reunion *delay*—a delay in glass as one says a poem in prose or a spittoon in silver.'

A support in transparent material could also give maximum efficacy to the *setting into perspective*, the last stage in working drawings. The metaphysical aspect of perspective preoccupied Giorgio de Chirico at that time, as we have seen. In one of Duchamp's notes, the antithetical notions of *certitude* and *futurity* appear at the origin of perspective processes and of pictorial conventions in general, canons, etc.: 'Through perspective, lines, design are *forced*, and lose the approximation of the "always possible"—with in addition the irony of having CHOSEN the original body or object, which *changes inevitably* according to this perspective.' The Bachelor Machine of *The Bride Stripped Bare*... is drawn entirely in perspective (the vanishing line is 54 1/2 inches from the base of the Glass, the vanishing point equidistant from the two sides) and the transparency of the support places the objects in space, adding the third dimension to their plane image.'

With Duchamp the mystery does not lie in an exotic vocabulary, an obscure style or imprecise thought-processes: the notes in the Green Box are, indeed, transparent and one might say that they create an echo, thanks to a play of angles and perspectives, in a labyrinth of mirrors where the possibilities of losing one's way are a function of the sharpness of the reflections. But if we wish to attempt to deal with the strange problem of *The Bride*..., we cannot avoid plunging into the labyrinth—at our own risk.

---

1. Whence the title: *To be Looked at with One Eye, Close to, for Almost an Hour*, for the first version of the *Oculist Witnesses*.

2. Duchamp used this 'raising' for the realization of certain parts of the Glass (the 'Sieves'), spreading a layer of varnish where required to which the dust gradually adhered. *Littérature* (new series, no. 5, October, 1922) published a photograph of the Glass covered in dust, with the title: *View Taken from an Airplane by Man Ray, 1921*, and this commentary: 'Here is the estate of Rrose Sélavy. How arid it is—how fertile it is—how joyous it is—how sad it is!' In the *Notebooks* of Leonardo da Vinci (*op. cit.*), one finds the same humorous idea of the utilization of the fall of dust as a measure of time; Duchamp's procedure is almost identical to that which Leonardo formulated as follows: 'The glass should be varnished or soaped on the inside, so that the dust that falls from the hopper may attach itself to it; and the spot where it strikes will remain marked; and by this means you will see and will be able with certainty to discern the exact height where the dust struck because it will remain sticking there'. One may note finally that the fall of dust is an important theme in Chinese Buddhist (Zen) thought: which is not surprising in view of Buddhism's ultimate objective of mastery over time. But Duchamp seems to have perfected the somewhat mystifying disciplines of the Chinese by introducing his own affirmative irony: he does not rub the dust away from the 'Mirror of the mind', he does not even eliminate it by the idea of Vacuity—he *grows* it.

3. The 'nine malic moulds' were painted with red lead 'while waiting' to receive their final colour.

4. In the French: *vers luisant* (*verre luisant*).

5. For *The Jura-Paris Road* Duchamp had thought of *wood*, 'which appears to me', he writes, 'as the affective translation of powdered flint'; flint is in fact used to pave main roads, while the floors of private houses are made of wood—the idea of 'support' passes here from the collective plane to the individual and affective plane.

6. See also the *Hand Stereoscopy* (Buenos Aires, 1918), consisting of two photographs on each of which a pencil drawing of a pyramid has been added, so that when looked at through the stereoscope the pyramids appear in relief and in correct perspective with the scenic background—like a '*collage* in space'.

I. DOMAIN OF THE BACHELORS (Machine-Group, Laboratory and other apparatus). Displaced slightly to the right of the vertical passing through the vanishing point, at the base of the Glass, stands the *Chocolate Grinder*; this is surmounted by a horizontal disc, the *Cravat*, itself traversed by the prolongation of the Grinder's axis, the *Bayonet*; on the top of this rests the axle of the large *Scissors* whose blades stretch to the right as far as the lateral edge of the Glass, and to the left are attached to the tops of the uprights of the *Slide Containing a Water Mill*. This collection of mobile mechanisms in the foreground partly masks what we shall call the Laboratory of the strange bachelor-factory, a laboratory composed of a series of fixed appliances, situated diagonally from the left background to the right foreground: the *Nine Malic Moulds* joined by 'capillary tubes' to the *Sieves*, from which leads the toboggan of the *Drainage Slopes*, at whose foot the *Splash* is produced.[1]

Chocolate Grinder.

Such is the residence of the Bachelors, permitting a minimum of comfort: that is, water and gas. Water for the Machines, gas for the Laboratory. A 'waterfall' enters (is supposed to enter) in a half circle from behind the Malic Moulds to drop on to the mill-wheel of the *Glider* in the left foreground; as for the lighting gas, it undergoes a series of transformations, which we shall describe later, starting from the reservoirs which contain it (and which are nothing else than the Malic Moulds) and finally exploding as it forms the Splash.

The representation confronting us on the Glass is a sort of *snapshot* (literally and symbolically speaking) of a factory working at full capacity. 'Given 1 — the waterfall, 2 — the lighting gas, we shall determine the conditions for the super-rapid exposure (allegorical reproduction) of several collisions (acts of violence) appearing strictly to succeed one another in accordance with certain laws, *in order to* extract the *sign of relationship* between this super-rapid exposure (capable of all eccentricities) *on the one hand* and the choice of the possibilities available under these laws *on the other.*' Among the 'laws, principles, phenomena' which command the instantaneous allegories, the principal ones are: (a) for the machine group, the '*Adage* of spontaneity: the bachelor grinds his chocolate

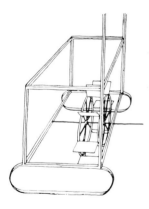

Glider (Containing a Water Mill).

himself'; (b) for the laboratory-group, the '*Phenomenon* of extension within the unity of length'.

(a) The Chocolate Grinder (whose ancestor is the *Coffee Mill* of 1911) functions as a true automat, in an absolutely spontaneous manner, with no intervention from any external force: the bachelor grinds his chocolate himself; it has no contact with the other mechanisms apart from just supporting the axle of the Glider's Watermill on its left side, and the Scissors on its own axis (their opening and closing being dictated by the Glider's to and fro movements). The Grinder grinds beneath its three rotating wheels the chocolate 'coming from no one knows where': as Jean Suquet[2] has perspicaciously commented, it 'is *grinding something black* (chocolate or coffee).[3] During this time, the Glider, moving horizontally to and fro as a result of the Mill's rotation, recites its 'Litanies': 'Slow life. Vicious circle. Onanism. Horizontal. Return trips on the buffer. The trash of life. Cheap construction. Tin, ropes, wire. Eccentric wooden pulleys. Monotonous fly-wheel. Beer professor.' This is the mechanism of a Bachelor's life: solitude, mediocrity, gloomy enjoyments, automatic gestures, habits.[4]

(b) But the 'vegetative life' of the Bachelors is balanced by a sort of 'animal life'—and it is curious to note that the first manifests itself in the mobile mechanisms of the machine-group, the second in the fixed appliances of the Laboratory.... 'By womb of Eros we understand the set of nine hollow uniforms or liveries designed to contain the lighting gas which takes nine malic forms': first comes the priest, then the department store delivery-boy, gendarme, cuirassier, policeman, undertaker's mute, flunkey, page-boy, station-master—the most distant form in the picture's perspective is that of the priest, the nearest that of the undertaker's mute; here is the 'cemetery of uniforms and liveries', with specifically masculine dress (and trades) having no female equivalent.[5] 'At the head

2. Jean Suquet: 'Le Signe du Cancer', *Almanach Surréaliste du Demi-Siècle* (La Nef, Paris, 1950).

3. 'Grinding something black': in the French, *broie du noir*, a phrase for 'has the blues'.

4. Duchamp had thought of a *Hook* (not carried out in the picture—perhaps, in this particular case, because it was not absolutely indispensable to the theoretical sequence of events), 'made from a material of oscillating density (a bottle of Benedictine)', falling between the Grinder and the Glider and pulling the mill-wheel along by a system of pulleys 'in order to economize on the rate of flow of the waterfall'.

5. The Bachelors were originally only eight, like the principle pieces in chess; the ninth (the station-master) was added later. The forms which symbolize them recall the appearance of chessmen.

1. The *Drainage Slopes* and the *Splash* were never into the picture.

(summit) of each Malic Mould three capillary tubes to cut the gas in pieces, to cut the *gas* in long, already stable needles, since before it becomes explosive liquid it assumes the form of a haze of solid spangles of frozen gas, all this through the phenomenon of *extension in the unit of length*.' And what is important here is 'not the unit of length but the phenomenon of *extension* of the gas', taking place in the capillary tubes which have the form of *standard-stoppages*—those new units of length of which I have spoken earlier.[1]

Psychoanalysis would be in its element here were it not for one's feeling that Duchamp is perfectly conscious of the meaning of his symbols. The 'desire-mechanism' is particularly active in the background, in the Laboratory half cut off from view by the moving Grinder and Glider,[2] and it is not difficult to relate the idea of onanism to this 'ameliorization of the lighting gas', this 'journey' made by a fluid first contained in reservoirs, then drawn out in tubes, changed subsequently into a haze which finally splashes, vertically, towards the Bride! 'The mouldings of gas would hear the litanies that the Glider recites, the refrain of the whole bachelor machine, without ever being able to transcend the mask: it is as if they would have been enveloped, along with their regrets, by a mirror reflecting their true complexity to the point of their being hallucinated rather onanistically.' It is possible, too, to detect a castration complex in the Scissors' movements: in closing, they interrupt the Splash.

With the Splash the series of bachelor operations proper come to an end. The liquid jet rockets upwards through the *Oculist Witnesses*, as a ray of light goes through the pupil of an eye. The Witnesses consist of three superimposed elements: a circle with radii, a ring, and a star, all of whose designs obey certain numerical relationships based on the number 12: the star has twelve radiants (each composed of five strokes), the ring is formed of twelve concentric lines, while inside the circle are drawn sixty radii (12×5).

1. See p. 59. Cf. Duchamp's note: 'The *idea of the Construction*:—if a straight horizontal thread one meter in length falls from a height of one meter onto a horizontal plane while twisting *at will* and gives a new form to the unit of length.'

2. The 'desire-mechanism' in reality occupies much more space than appears on the Glass—cf. a dimensioned sketch, in the Green Box papers, showing the Bachelor-machine in scale. In particular, four Malic Moulds even protrude beyond the Glass's frame and are only brought back into the body of the picture thanks to the reducing effect of perspective.

In the region of the Witnesses, and at the moment when the Splash is thrown vertically, a 'combat-marble' sets off a clockwork system by knocking successively against two 'battering-rams' or supports of the Bride's Clothing (which is represented by a triple horizontal line traversing the whole Glass along the centre). The marble's shock 'unhooks' the battering rams—in fact it is rather the Bride who is unhooked: the fall of the supports entails that of the Clothing; after which the cog-wheels 'raise the fallen battering rams again by rack-rail', thus restoring the whole system. This is the *Boxing Match* which starts off at the moment of the Splash and of which it seems to constitute a sort of echo (sport being a substitute for sexual activity). 'The clockwork' of this part of the Glass (elaborated in a diagram dated 1913 but not executed on the picture) puts into concrete form the special nature of Time which governs the monotonous automatism of the Bachelor Machine: 'The stripping bare by the Bachelors expresses the sharp jerk of the minute-hand on electric clocks in railway stations.'

II. BRIDE-MOTOR. *The Clothing of the Bride*, symbolized by three parallel lines dividing the picture into two sections, one on top of the other (this 'clothing' was originally to have been the only part in glass, the 'cooler'—evidently—of the masculine ardours) separates the domain of the Bachelors from the upper domain, that of the Bride. We are now about to enter an entirely different world from that of the Bachelor Machines, in which automatisms, repetitions, serial and foreseeable acts no longer reign; this is a universe of possibilities: the world of the imagination.

The *perspectives* are thus profoundly modified. The change of atmosphere shows itself first of all in the presentation of the objects. A kind of *fourth dimension* has come into play. Duchamp treats the universe here as the shadow of a four-dimensional world, just as the shadow of a three-dimensional object is a two-dimensional form, or the shadow of a plane surface may be just a line, and that of a line, a point.... No definitive description or mensuration can, then, be applied to the beings in the Bride-space, since they are capable of modifying themselves according to the displacement of their four-dimensional bodies, being shadows which nevertheless postulate the concrete reality of their bodies. 'The *principal forms* of the Bachelor Machine are imperfect: rectangles, circle,

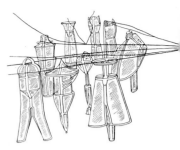

Malic Moulds with their 'capillary tubes'.

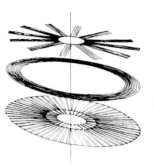

Oculist Witnesses

parallelepiped, symmetrical handle, semi-sphere —that is to say, they are mensurated (relationship of their relative dimensions and relationship of their principal forms to their destination in the Bachelor Machine).—In the Bride, the *principal forms are more or less big or small*, have no longer a mensuration in relation to their destination: a sphere, in the Bride, will be of a certain radius (the given radius for the representation is fictitious and dotted)... parabolas, hyperbolas (or derivative volumes) lose all the qualities of a mensurated situation. The material representation will be only one *example* of each of these *principal free (freed) forms*. (An example without representative value but allowing most or least.)'

The dynamism also changes nature: the bachelor machinery proceeded by precise rotations, regular comings and goings, releasing of clockwork mechanisms; in the Bride-domain appear the swings, jugglings, floatings and movements 'allowing most or least'. Thus, above the Boxing Match, the 'juggler of the centre of gravity' (the 'space inspector', the *Gravit Manager* or *Gravit Caretaker*),[1] 'having his three fulcrums on the Bride's Clothing, dances to the pleasure of the descending battering-rams commanded by the stripping'. Higher still, the Clothing, which is conceived as a sort of prism,[2] has projected the *images* of the Splash drops towards the *Shots*, towards the TARGET which Duchamp defines thus: 'a *correspondence* of the vanishing point', the reflection of perspective.... But the true, absolute target has not been reached; one will see only its *demultiplication*: the traces swarming around this imaginary centre, like arrows on a target, nine points of impact obtained by 'an average skill directed towards the target', represented here by nine holes, at the very top and right of this great transparent surface. End of the journey, ultimate waves of desire of the nine bachelors.[3]

Finally, the Stripping itself has an entirely different aspect in the upper domain. It results

1. Not represented on the Glass.

2. In the manner, says Duchamp, of those 'Wilson-Lincoln system' portraits which, looked at from the right show a portrait of Wilson, and from the left one of Lincoln.

3. Beneath the nine Shots, a scene of *cast shadows* might have taken place, according to a note not reproduced in the Box but published by the review *Instead*, no 5 (New York, 1948), ('on a plane—on a surface with a particular curvature or several transparent surfaces') to 'obtain a hypophysic analysis of the successive transformations of objects (in their contour-shape)'. These 'cast shadows' would have been 'formed by the splashes coming from below just as certain jets of water catch shapes on the hooks of their transparency'.

not so much from an instinctual need as from the Desiring-Bride's *imagination*: if the Bachelor Machine is an instinctual factory, the Bride-motor is an imagining machine.

The Bride, the *Pendu Femelle* (or 'hanging female object', a 'skeleton' of the *Bride* painted in Munich —which is to say that the latter is reduced, on the Glass, to its essential components), is fastened to the upper edge of the Glass and can swing 'according to the four cardinal points', the socket for the swinging motion being none other than the delicately fashioned mortice which we have already discussed. It is 'the form *in ordinary perspective* of a *pendu femelle* for which one could perhaps try to discover the true form'. We will restrict ourselves, here, to an attempt at imagining its methods of functioning.

An erotic machine, as is the Bachelor Machine, but with very different behaviour.... By studying the notes of the Green Box, we are able to conclude that the *Pendu* indulges in a complete stratagem of coquetries; her mechanism palpitates and trembles, at once reticent and cupidinous, in an attitude of provocative refusal: 'The Bride rejects warmly —not chastely—the Bachelors' sudden offer.' The motor's most sensitive organ is the 'sex-cylinder' or 'wasp' (the motor is an internal-combustion type, more advanced and complicated than the bachelor machines). The *Wasp* is endowed with a '*Flair* or sense' which allows it to recognize 'waves of disequilibrium' emanating from the Gravit Manager who is dancing on the other side of the picture: the echoes of male desire. The Wasp possesses a vibrating 'pulse-needle', producing the 'ventilation' which determines 'the balancing of the *Pendu* over her accessories'; it also inhales the motor's fuel, 'the love-essence secreted by the Bride's sexual glands' ('sort of automobiline' coming from the 'life-centre') and projects it, 'by osmosis', as a dew on to the 'matter with filaments' contained in a receptacle held up by the 'type-tree', or 'staff'—this receptacle, fitting onto the swinging mechanism's mortice, performs the function of the vertebral column of the *Pendu*. The Wasp is also in touch with the 'Oscillating bath (hygiene of the Bride)'; finally, it can control differences of atmospheric pressure reacting upon the 'matter with filaments': submitted to this kind of panting, the matter with filaments 'resembles a steady flame, that is to say one with a solid force, in its meteorological protraction. It licks the ball that the Manager is juggling with, and shifts it as it wishes'.

One should point out finally that in the fixed part which surmounts the trembling wasp-waisted motor, two semi-spheres form between them, in a vertical direction, an angle of 35 or 40 degrees: 'this angle expresses the necessary and sufficient corner of the eye'.

We hope devoutly that the reader bold enough to have accompanied us thus far into the labyrinth is not experiencing the horrors of the character in *Modern Times* who tries to set in motion a terrifyingly complicated, huge machine, and is suddenly sucked into the mechanism when it starts up unexpectedly, disappearing among the whirling cogwheels but reappearing from time to time, head first or feet first, without ever being quite released by the monstrous motor. But after one last vanishing trick the engineer reappears, unharmed though somewhat bewildered, sitting on an escalator that rises from the centre of the machine and carries him up towards the ceiling.... Be reassured, then, that we in our turn will emerge from the gear-systems of the Bachelors and the Bride, and reach the upper regions.

III. BLOSSOMING OF THE STRIPPING.

'This cinematic blossoming is the most important part of the picture (in terms of graphic stress). It is, in general, the halo of the Bride, the sum-total of her splendid vibrations: graphically, it is not at all a matter of symbolizing in a lofty composition this goal, the Bride's happy-desire; but a lighter painting in this whole blossoming, elements of the sex-life imagined by the desiring Bride. In this blossoming, the Bride reveals herself in two guises: the first is that of her being stripped by the bachelors, while the second is that of the Bride's own voluntary-imaginative stripping. On the coupling of these two guises of pure virginity, on their collision, the whole blossoming depends, the higher design and crown of the composition.'

The blossoming of the stripping takes the form of a large cloud along the top of the Glass, a 'flesh-coloured milky way', surrounding the three Draught Pistons which are a concrete representation of *wind*. 'Draught pistons, that is to say material accepted and rejected by the draught.' (Duchamp had obtained these three images by registering three successive chance distortions of a square of white material flapping in the wind.) And, just as telegraph wires transmit messages, so the rose-coloured cloud in which the wind's mouldings are cut should serve as a conductor for an *Inscription*, since the 'Elements of the blossoming' are also the elements of the Bride's imaginative and desiring language: 'decisions, orders, commands' that emanate originally from the Wasp, whose ultra-sensitive mechanism reacts constantly to the upper system's basic instability.

This language does not express reasonings but rather the Bride's desiring imagination. It almost recalls the semantics constructed by modern scientists to deal with polyvalent systems of logic, which draw legitimate inferences from paradoxical or contingent ideas and which resemble 'those imaginary geometrics from which we can expect no diagrammatic representations but which physics does not hesitate to make use of'.[1] In the Bride's language 'the whole series of alphabetical units is no longer arranged strictly from left to right'; on the Milky Way the text will read like a sort of alternating current sending and returning messages between the Bride and the Target. In addition, code language is involved. The Draught Pistons alter the Bride's Orders as they pass through, playing the role of 'grilles' which serve to encode confidential messages. To crown all this, these telegrams in code would be in a hieroglyphic writing: Duchamp had thought of representing each 'abstract' word in the dictionary by a schematic sign so as to constitute a sort of alphabet to be used for the Bride's Orders. Were these 'abstract' words that had been transformed into alphabetic signs to have functioned within the Inscription in the same way that concepts of traditional logic are modified when confronted in *relational logic*? 'This alphabet,' Duchamp notes, however, 'is very probably suitable only for this picture's writing.'

As regards the object: *Glider Containing a Water Mill*,[2] constructed from 'neighbouring metals' in 1913, I asked Marcel Duchamp what metals were involved. 'I do not know what these metals are,' he replied, 'but I know that they are *neighbouring*.' An instructive reply, because it drew my attention once again to qualities rather than substan-

---

1. Charles Serrus: *Traité de Logique* (Aubier, Paris, 1945).
2. Model of the apparatus figuring in the Glass.

ces, to the function not the essence, in fact to those enigmatic *relationships* which we have already observed in the readymades. A functional concept governs the mathematics of *The Bride...*, and, through its superposed composition, the picture itself assumes the character of a relationship:

$$\frac{Bride}{Bachelors}$$

a relationship with several equivalences, depending on the point of view from which one considers the relation—from the sexual point of view (that of 'sexual relations' obviously):

$$\frac{female}{males}$$

or from the angle of psychology: $\dfrac{imagination}{instinct}$

physics: $\dfrac{undulation}{stability}$

mechanics: $\dfrac{dynamism}{organism}$

time: $\dfrac{development}{moment}$

or as a representation of the world:

$$\frac{noumena}{phenomena}$$

Still other relationships might be found in terms of other categories. These are, of course, only general and schematic formulas, and we have seen that in reality the equation is far more complex and is constructed upon an infinity of correspondences. Just as, in chess, each piece's potentiality works *at a distance*, in space and in time, upon the game's whole configuration, so, in *The Bride...*, each machine incarnates a *force* which combines with those of the other representations according to their respective positions in the picture.

If, in studying the Glass, one takes into account the result of certain tests[1] relating to the concepts of *right* and *left* in a projective configuration, the

left indicating the past and individual characteristics, the right indicating the future and collective characteristics, it will be noticed that the general direction of the Glass's forces (as also the direction of the network of cracks which now run through it) is *from left to right*; in addition, the uncompleted portions of the picture are all situated on the right hand side—that is to say, in the future. Most of these relationships, then, could be formulated horizontally, with the lower term to the left and the upper term to the right: instinct-imagination; organism-dynamism; moment-development; determination-possibilities. Finally the Large Glass could be interpreted as a *proof by 9*; for example:

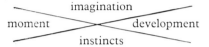

The note quoted previously on the waterfall and the lighting gas is completed by an 'algebraic comparison: the ratio $\dfrac{a}{b}$ is in no way given by a number c $(\dfrac{a}{b} = c)$, but by the sign(-)which separates a and b... sign of agreement or of relationship.' The *sign of agreement* in the $\dfrac{Bride}{Bachelors}$ relationship is symbolized by the *Clothing of the Bride*, the horizontal line that divides the picture into two equal parts. The problem of the Stripping, which the Bachelor Machine and the Bride Motor make incessant attempts to resolve, is evidently centred on the Clothing—and remains eternally posed. Even the final Blossoming of the Stripping, 'without any causal distinction', is not the definitive solution, since it is only 'the final state of this naked Bride before the enjoyment that would cause her fall (will cause her fall)'. And Duchamp says also that 'the Blossoming of the Stripping is unanalyzable by logic'. The solution is not given: the end of this mechanical-erotic problem, the Mate of the Bride by the Bachelors, is unknown. The Large Glass is a proof, not a solution—an example, not an explanation.

The 'solution' of the Game, the agreement between the terms of the relationship, is simply the mechanism of the Glass itself and its motive power: DESIRE.

$$\frac{Bride}{Bachelors} = Desire.$$

---

1. Such as the 'Village test' perfected in France by the late Dr Pierre Mabille, in which the subject is invited to 'design' a village by arranging models of buildings, people, walls, etc, according to his inclination.

One of the precursors of the machine epoch was the writer of whom Giorgio de Chirico said[1] that his books 'are not for children but for grown-ups, *big grown-ups*': Jules Verne. Novels of scientific prediction achieved an extraordinary popularity as a result of his pioneer activity in the field (Wells, etc.), but in terms of poetry Jules Verne's most direct successor is Raymond Roussel, who hailed the author of *Voyage through the Solar System* and *Voyage to the Centre of the Earth*[2] as a man of 'immense genius' and an 'incomparable master'.

The sunlit mystery of Roussel's novels is, indeed, most evocative of Chirico's painting; the description of the Square of Trophies in Roussel's *Impressions d'Afrique* is strangely reminiscent of Chirico's paintings of arcades in the pure light of late afternoon, littered with incomprehensible objects. But Roussel's ideas have an even closer—and, in a sense, organic—connection with those of Duchamp.

In 1911, Duchamp, accompanied by Apollinaire, Picabia and Gabrielle Picabia, attended the performance of *Impressions d'Afrique*, the play which Roussel adapted from one of his novels: "It was more than a flop, it was a riot" wrote Roussel in *Comment j'ai Écrit Certains de mes Livres;* 'the actors were shouted down, coins were thrown on to the stage....' One can well imagine that, despite this hurly-burly, the four friends were deeply impressed by the author's inventive qualities; in any case, certain aspects of the conception and realization of Duchamp's productions are reminiscent of particular passages in Roussel's works. The 'mirroric return' of the Splash, which according to Duchamp constitutes 'a sculpture of drops', recalls the shapes formed in the *aqua-micans* of the great diamond in *Locus Solus* by escaping air-bubbles, or again, the prophetic inscriptions spat out in little drops of blood by the cock Mopsus. The fantastic minuteness with which the mirroring geometry of the Oculist Witnesses was realized (to carry out this part of the Glass, Duchamp silvered the plate, then removed the silvering by scratching so as to leave only a bright filigrane of the lines composing the drawing) brings to mind the work on 'nocturnal wax' of one of Roussel's characters, the sculptor Jerjeck; and the sketch of the

Witnesses, in which the figures appear as white lines on carbon paper recall the 'Gilles in strokes' by the same Jerjeck, which were drawings consisting of white lines scratched out on a black background.[3] Finally the whole *Bride...*, with its complicated machinery designed to give an appearance of depth, surely resembles the singing tarot in *Locus Solus*, the 'Lightning-Struck Tower' which contains a complicated and extraordinarily tenuous musical mechanism inside the infinitesimal thickness of its sheet of cardboard?[4]

Charles Cros, in his *Principes de Mécanique Cérébrale*, deduces an organ functionally, an organ that is different from the human brain but whose functioning produces more or less the same effects. One might say that Cros studies our senses from the point of view of the machine, and reinterprets speech, vision, etc, in mechanical terms and as mechanical objects: a conception which led him to his inventions of the gramophone, the photophone and colour photography. But Cros' apparatus is based on classical physical and chemical laws, whereas Roussel's mechanisms, while perfectly probable and concrete (the author describes them in the style of a letters-patent), require 'exalted' laws in order to function: in other words, Roussel makes use of magnetism, meteorological science, oxygenation of liquids, nerve tension, etc, in their known forms but raised to a superior power, usually by postulating the use of new substances: *bexium, erythritis, resurrectine* and so on.

In the *Bride...* we find at the same time the machine-language invented by Cros—as if a machine-being, a robot, were to undertake the description and reconstitution of a couple in the act of making love in terms of its own 'physiology'—and natural laws modified far more drastically than is the case with Roussel, laws that are expanded rather than exalted. 'Adage of spontaneity, oscillating density, neighbouring metals, ironic causality': such are a few of the axioms, combining the psychic and the physical, which control the operations of the Large Glass. 'Almost the whole of this representation,' says Duchamp, 'is the drawing of a reality which could be made possible by stretching slightly the laws of physics and chemistry.' And an *ironic*

---

1. In *Le Survivant de Navarin.*

2. This work is one of the 'twenty-seven equivalent books' in the library of Dr Faustroll. Cf. Alfred Jarry: *Exploits and Opinions of Doctor Faustroll, Pataphysician.*

3. Jerjeck: a character in Roussel's *Locus Solus*, who made 'copies' of Watteau's picture *Gilles* in this manner.

4. Certain authors (cf. J. Basilide: *Le Profond Mystère du Tarot*) believe that the XVIth arcanum or 'major trump', the *Maison-Dieu*—or Hospital—originally represented the *male and female sexual organs*, transformed in later tarots to a Tower struck by lightning.

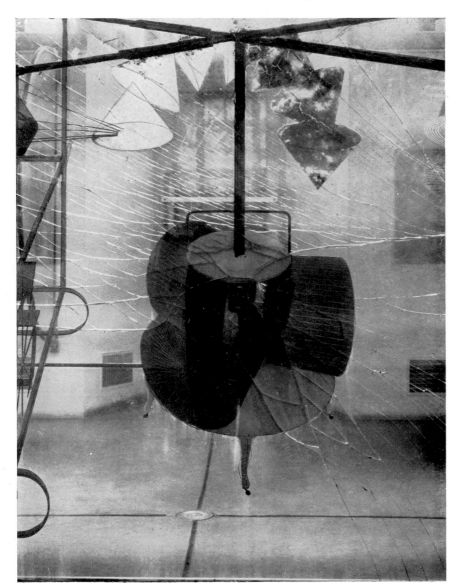

Marcel Duchamp: *Chocolate Grinder*, area of the Large Glass.

force enters into this 'stretching' in which one can recognize the coming into play of CHANCE.

Duchamp's 'science of examples', or *science of exemplary chance* (which has nothing to do with statistical chance in the calculation of probabilities) is no less humorous than Alfred Jarry's 'science of exceptions': *pataphysics*. With Duchamp, humour originates in the association between choice and chance, and this mastery of chance consequently dominates the idea of duration. Chance is the 'grille', the code which enciphers and deciphers the messages. It is also a sort of stage-director who knocks three times with his stick throughout the drama of the Bride—3 being the 'refrain in mathematical duration' of a picture where we can find three standard-stoppages in which *weight* intervenes, nine Shots using *dexterity*, three Air Pistons that put the *wind* into concrete form: three examples of 'canned chance'.

There is no doubt that Duchamp played on the possibilities of the destruction of his Trismegistic anti-picture, and on the spectator's fear of breaking this marvellous window (or his unconscious desire to do so); but he left to Chance the decision which he had imposed upon it to some extent from the beginning. His glass constructions, so productive of abortive actions, have all been accidentally broken (except, so far, the Glider in the Arensberg collection).[1]

Here is Duchamp's account of the events which led to the breaking of the Large Glass: 'After being shown at the Brooklyn Museum in 1926, the two sections of the Glass,[2] placed one on top of the other, flat, in a truck, were returned at full speed to their fold—Katherine Dreier's home at Redding, sixty miles from New York, after being generously shaken up by the vehicle's jolting. The fact that the two parts of the Glass were lying flat, one on top of the other, explains the similarity in the pattern of the principal cracks.'[3]

According to Duchamp, 'the Bride is the apparition of an appearance'—a conception embodied transparently and vitrified. It is surely the most personal and original work that has ever been

1. The 'Nine Malic Moulds' were not broken purposely (as the text on Duchamp states in the volume *De Picasso au Surréalisme* published by Editions A. Skira) but by accident.

2. That is to say, the upper and lower halves, on either side of the Bride's Clothing.

3. The Glass was repaired by Duchamp in 1936; the broken surfaces were kept together by applying fresh panes of glass on both sides. The Glass is now in the Philadelphia Museum.

The Large Glass, upper section. 1: Bride Motor. 2: Gravity Manager. 3: Shots. 4: Draught Pistons.

The Large Glass, lower section. 1: Chocolate Grinder. 2: Cravat. 3: Bayonet. 4: Scissors. 5: Glider. 6: Malic Moulds (a: Priest. b: Department-store Delivery Boy. c: Gendarme. d: Cuirassier. e: Policeman. f: Undertaker's Mute. g: Flunkey. h: Pageboy. i: Station Master). 7: Sieves. 8: Drainage Slopes. 9: Splash. 10: Oculist Witnesses. 11: Boxing Match. 12: Clothing of the Bride.

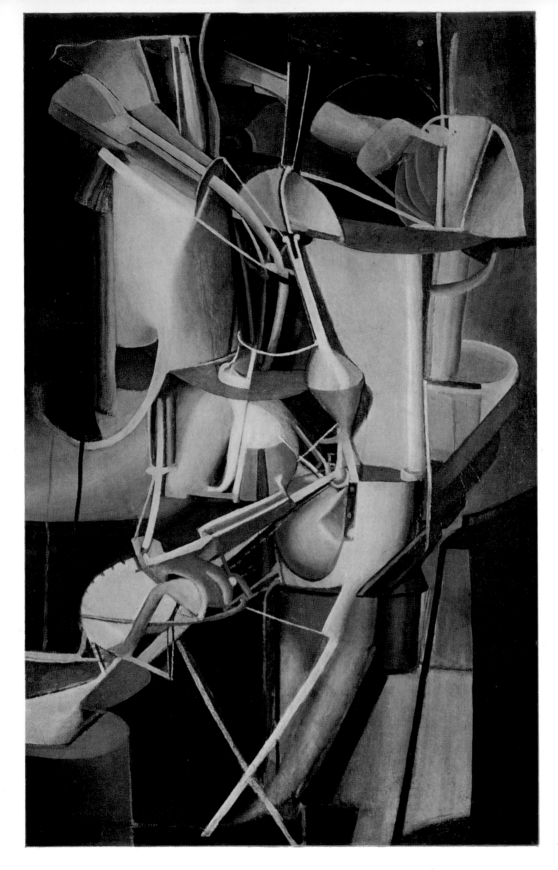

Marcel Duchamp: *Bride*. 1912.

Rear surface of Marcel Duchamp's Large Glass (area of the Grinder and the Sieves) showing the inscription: *The Bride Stripped Bare by her Bachelors, Even—Marcel Duchamp 1915-1923—uncompleted—broken 1931—repaired 1936.*

Marcel Duchamp: *50 cc. of Paris Air.* 1919.

conceived in the field of plastic expression; an anti-picture, or rather 'non-picture', and therefore a masterwork of the Dada spirit; a prism which condenses and displays an infinite variety of meanings; an equation which, in logician's terms, rests on a *non-saturated* concept (Duchamp's object inspired, to a great extent, the surrealist object); the Glass is also the echo and realization of the pictorial revolutions inaugurated fifty years previously by Georges Seurat's *The Circus*: this last painting by Seurat (which, too, remained unfinished) already contains Futurism, Cubism and mechanist painting—a strange 'blue-print' that seems isolated among the masterpieces of Impressionism which surround it at the Orangerie Museum in Paris, a tornado flashing blue and yellow reflections like a machine made of steel and copper in which humour, instinct and the most exact calculations meet face to face.

The Bride Stripped Bare... summarizes and crowns the whole of poetic painting since Georges Seurat, and its *incompletion* marks a boundary whose importance cannot be exaggerated. On the far side of this boundary, Duchamp's exemplary poetry projects itself into the future. People today seem to have become aware of their own ephemeral nature: they like movement and light and they worship machines—machines which age and die in a few years, real only as long as they are useful. But Duchamp's machines, real beyond utility, begin to live on their own account; they are about to make love.

Up to 1925, the series of readymades received a number of additions: the enormous *Check* made out to the *Teeth's Loan and Trust Company*; the *Phial containing 50 cc. of Paris air*; *Why not sneeze*—a birdcage filled with lumps of sugar that are unexpectedly heavy (in fact made out of white marble); *The Brawl at Austerlitz* which we have already mentioned; *Wanted*—a poster promising $2,000 reward 'for information leading to the arrest of George W. Welch, alias Bull, alias Pickens... also known under the name of Rrose Sélavy', with photographs of the criminal, full-face and profile; finally *Monte Carlo Bonds*, published in thirty copies, which were to finance the playing of a martingale which allowed neither gain nor loss.

Duchamp had concerned himself with rotating objects ever since the first sketches of the machines in the *Bride...*, and the *Coffee Mill* of 1911. His film

Marcel Duchamp: *Rotary Demi-sphere.* 1925.

Anemic Cinema, shot by Man Ray in 1924, studies the creation of a third dimension by flat surfaces. Each part of a revolving spiral, for instance, is moving both in time and in space, and depicts that chronological 'extension' of which Eddington speaks; the third dimension thus becomes a result of the chronological dimension: movement creates a sense of illusion, the moving spirals of *Anemic Cinema* appear in relief.

The *Rotary Demi-sphere* (1925), whose centre is a revolving hemispheric spiral, represents another stage of these researches (taken up again in 1934 with the *Rotoreliefs*).[1] A rotary object such as *Anemic Cinema* associates Rrose Sélavy's wordplays with the object's own gyration; the phrase *'Rrose Sélavy et moi esquivons les ecchymoses des esquimaux aux mots exquis'*, engraved around the rim of the copper disc which surrounds the semisphere, whirls around with it, so that the words *make a ring* in time as well as in space and thought.

Then, Marcel Duchamp, who had abandoned oil painting in 1918, and whose Delay in Glass remained unfinished, was even to give up designing readymades. But can it be said that he therefore ceased all activity? Like Lewis Carroll, who discovered a game of chess being played on the other side of the mirror, and like Raymond Roussel, Duchamp is a chess master; since 1925 he has devoted himself throughout the years almost exclusively to chess-playing. There is no hint here of a renunciation of his own work (we shall see later that he has never lost interest in his production) or of a romantic attitude of *poète maudit*: no doubt the creator of the *Bride* is capable of treating even Ennui itself with the same irony of indifference, the *meta-irony* whose secret he guards.

In Europe and America, he has participated in a number of tournaments and championships, either privately or as a member of the French team. Here are the reports of two games played by Duchamp in 1928:[2] two examples of solutions obtained in chess, a millenial and constantly renewed synthesis of intuition and reflection.

1. See pages 253-254.

2. These reports with their commentaries, which appeared originally in newspapers of the time, have been communicated to me by M. Pierre de Massot, together with other documents concerning Marcel Duchamp and Francis Picabia. I take this opportunity of expressing my thanks.

PARIS INTERNATIONAL TOURNAMENT OF 1928
(commented by Gaston Legrain)

White: Tartakower   *Black:* Duchamp

Zukertort Opening

1. Kt-KB3	Kt-KB3	23. R-K2	Kt-Q2
2. P-QKt3	P-Q3 (a)	24. P-QR3	B-KB1 (g)
3. P-Q4	P-Q4 (b)	25. KtxKt	RxKt
4. P-K3	B-KB4	26. R (Q1)-K1	K-B2
5. B-Q3	BxB (c)	27. K-B3 (h)	P-KKt3
6. QxB	P-QB3	28. P-KKt4	PxP
7. QKt-Q2	P-K3	29. KxP	B-KKt2
8. o-o	QKt-Q2 (d)	30. P-Q5	QBPxP (i)
9. P-K4	PxP	31. BxB	KxB
10. KtxP	KtxKt	32. PxP	RxP
11. QxKt	B-K2	33. RxP	RxR
12. P-QB4	o-o	34. RxR (j)	K-B2
13. B-QKt2	B-KB3	35. R-K3	K-B3
14. QR-Q1	R-K1	36. P-KR4	P-KR4ch
15. Kt-K5	Q-QB2	37. K-B3	K-B4
16. P-KB4	QR-Q1	38. P-QKt4	P-QR4
17. KR-K1	Kt-KB1	39. PxP	RxP
18. Kt-KKt4 (e)	B-KR5 (f)	40. R-QKt3	R-QR5
19. P-KKt3	P-KB4	41. R-QKt5ch	K-B3
20. Q-K5	QxQ	42. R-QKt6ch	K-B4
21. KtxQ	B-K2	43. R-QKt5ch	K-B3
22. K-Kt2	B-QKt5	44. R-QKt6ch	K-B4

Draw.

(a) This unusual move is made to provoke P-Q4.— (b) Black has lost a tempo in order to obstruct the long black diagonal.— (c) Against someone of Tartakower's stature it is not disadvantageous to clear the chess-board through exchanges.— (d) 7 White moves as against 4 Black moves. This difference will result in prolonged difficulties for Black.— (e) Hitherto, White has played mechanically. This last move made some careful considera-tion necessary.— (f) By this peculiar move, Black is carrying out his plan: to disengage himself through exchanges.— (g) It would clearly cost a P to return to K2.— (h) To attack Black's backward KP, White has only the K left.— (i) If 30. BxB, White wins the exchange.— (j) A fresh liquidation leading quite clearly to a draw. Our friend Duchamp has been most successful in annihilating his redoubt-able adversary's endeavours.

GAME PLAYED IN JANUARY 1928
AT HYERES
2ND ROUND OF THE PHILIDOR CUP
(commented by G. Renaud)

White: M. Duchamp   *Black:* E.H. Smith

Queen's Pawn

This game is probably the most brilliant of those played this year at the Hyères Congress, and it is likely that it will be awarded the brilliancy prize. White was able to exploit an error by Black with elegant precision.

1.	P-Q4	P-Q4
2.	Kt-KB3	Kt-KB3
3.	P-QB4	P-K3
4.	Kt-QB3	P-QKt3

At this stage of the game, the development of the QB *en fianchetto* is certainly unwise, and the usual moves B-K2, Kt-Q2 or P-QB3 are surely preferable.

5. PxP

A classic move in positions of this kind. Black is forced to retake with the P and, consequently, to close the diagonal in which he wishes to instal the B.

5. ...   KtxP

The capture by the Kt in fact gives White the chance of gaining time by 6. P-K4. But he prefers here to develop his QB.

6. B-Q2   B-QR3

This odd move has the object of preventing P-K4, which would be followed by BxB. White quickly refutes it.

7.	Kt-K5	KtxKt
8.	BxKt	P-KB3 ?

Marcel Duchamp playing on a chess-board designed by Man Ray.

One fault generally leads to another. This move is a grave error, resulting from Black's incorrect development with P-QKt3.

9. P-K3 !

One cannot overemphasize the fact that the combination inaugurated by this move is not the creation of White but that of Black who, playing badly, has placed himself in a bad position. The role of White, in such an occurrence, is to exploit his good position, and to consolidate the potential advantage by discovering the winning combination.

9. ...   PxKt

The other alternative was prettier than the actual text. He could in fact have played: 9. ... BxB; 10. Q-KR5ch, K-K2 (if P-KKt3: KtxP etc... with catastrophic results for Black); 11. Q-KB7ch, K-Q3; 12. B-QKt4ch, P-QB4; 13. PxPch, KxKt; 14. B-QB3ch, K-KB4; 15. Q-KR5ch, P-KKt4; 16. P-K4ch, KxP; 17. Q-KB3 mate!

10.	BxB	KtxB
11.	Q-R4ch	Q-Q2
12.	QxKt	B-K2
13.	PxP	o-o
13.	o-o	P-QB4
15.	QR-Q1	

Possession of the open file. It will soon be followed by the decisive occupation of the advanced square.

15.	...	Q-QB2
16.	Q-QB4	

Putting pressure on the isolated weak P on K3.

16.	...	Q-QB3
17.	P-QR4	QR-Q1
18.	P-KB4	

Threatening RxR followed by P-KB5.

18.	...	RxR
19.	RxR	P-KKt3

To oppose the advance of P-KB5. But the occupation of the advanced square, with the sacrifice of the exchange, opening a diagonal towards the castled position of the Black K and creating an advanced pawn as powerful as a piece, is now decisive.

20. R-Q6 !   BxR

The withdrawal Q-QB1 would have been no better. The game is lost.

21.	QxPch	R-KB2
22.	PxB	Q-Q2
23.	Q-K5	Resigns

The position is hopeless. If, for example, R-KB1; 24. Q-KR8ch, K-KB2; 25. QxPch and the passed pawns are irresistible.

PART TWO

SURREALISM AND SURREALIST PAINTING

Man Ray: *The Enigma of Isidore Ducasse.* 1920.

CHAPTER V
HISTORY OF SATANAS, OF NARCISSUS AND OF SOME OTHER MYTHS

The organs of the senses and the intellect convey a series of images and interpretations to the human being through which he makes contact with reality. In order to share these impressions with his fellow humans, man is compelled to use a universally comprehensible vocabulary, and a subjectively perceived 'presentation' gives place to a 're-presentation' utilizable by others. It is thus that reality tends to transform itself into a collection of factors apparently independent of the individual and stripped of any subjective element.

Nevertheless, the subjective psyche and individual sensation remain inseparable from reality, for they are its living heart and creative brain. To rediscover original sensations and images beneath appearances conventionalized and fixed by habit, to deepen these appearances and give a concrete form to hidden realities is the particular role assigned to those whose sight has become *second-sight*. Such people, artists, inventors, poets, see what is in process of being born, for the faculty of traversing the mirror of appearances, far from remaining passive, helps to bring new phenomena to light.

It may be possible to agree with Apollinaire in his dictum that 'everyone is a poet', at least theoretically, but in actual fact most people's perception is not adapted to any process of inquiry outside conventional truth. The creative gift, rarely used, remains in a latent state, falling asleep after childhood and most often only showing signs of life in what are called the unconscious forms of the psychic structure: the dream, for instance. It is understandable, then, that the new poets and painters should have wished to study and utilize those mental states in which the visionary faculty seemed to express itself most vigorously: even, where necessary, fomenting such states by appropriate means.

From the very beginning of its investigations, *Surrealism* excluded the rational and logical in favour of the irrational, which was itself envisaged originally simply as an aspect of hallucination. From visual sensation, the basic element of Impressionism, we pass with Surrealism to 'hallucinatory sensation', offering new and immense possibilities of development. This point of departure is in fact a point of *condensation* of the real: 'The image,' says Taine, 'like the sensation it repeats, is, in its very nature, *hallucinatory*. Thus the hallucination, which seems a monstrosity, is the very fabric of our mental life.'[1]

This phrase of Taine's sums up the thesis which André Breton's *Surrealist Manifesto* was to put forward when it was published in October, 1925. Indeed, Breton quotes the work of this philosopher in connection with the hallucinatory experience of 'the apparition of the hand',[2] a theme to which he reverts at length in *Le Surréalisme et la Peinture*. The word *automatism*, by which Surrealism defined itself in the *Manifesto*, is also to be found in the first pages of Taine's book: 'We are going to sleep. As the image becomes more intense so it becomes more absorbing and independent.... We seem no longer actors, but spectators; its transformations are spontaneous and *automatic*.'[3] Simi-

1. H. Taine: *On Intelligence* (transl. by T. D. Haye, Reeve & Co, London, 1871; 1 Vol. in 2 Parts). Cf. Part Two, Book I, Chapter I.

2. See *De l'Intelligence* (Hachette, Paris, 1900, 9th ed.) Vol. I, Book IV, Chapter III; note 2 (not in the English edition).

3. *Ibid*, Part One, Book II, Chapter I. The italics are Taine's, who ascribes the paternity of this word to Baillarger *(Des Hallucinations)*. The term is also found in the work of Maury *(Le Sommeil et les Rêves*, frequently quoted by Taine), and has been used subsequently by many other psychologists.

larly, André Breton's personal experience, described in the *Manifesto* and considered by him as the point of departure for Surrealism, repeats Taine's observation: the experience involves the appearance of a succession of absolutely gratuitous auditive images in the subject's mind at the approach of sleep. Exploited systematically by Breton and Philippe Soupault (*Les Champs Magnétiques*, 1920), developed with the collaboration of Robert Desnos and others in regard to spoken language (the so-called 'sleep' period of 1922), these and similar experiments led in 1924 to the definition of Surrealism as 'pure psychic automatism' *(Surrealist Manifesto)*.

The *Manifesto* was based, therefore, upon scientific experiments and theories already well known to specialists. Its originality and positive virtue was to throw a bridge between the work of those authors who had elaborated the new psychological sciences (with chief honours being paid to Freud and his researches on the dream) and the Romantic and post-Romantic works which, in their turn, examined human subjectivity poetically. Maury had posed the problem of 'what becomes of intelligence when it gives a tug at the ceremonial clothing called reason, and a jolt to the rather tiresome façade called conscience'. He nevertheless considered it 'humiliating to see a moment of sleep or drowsiness degrade us to the level of the wailing child or drivelling old man'.[1] Taine had brought to light the universal significance of hallucination; but in fact he shared the opinion of Gustave Flaubert who had written to him: 'Do not assimilate the mental vision of the artist with the state of a man labouring under hallucination. I know both states perfectly; there is a chasm between them. In strict hallucination, there is always fear; you feel your personality escaping you; you think you are about to die. In poetic vision, on the contrary, there is pleasure; it is something which enters into you. It is none the less true that one loses consciousness of where he is.' Often this vision is sudden and 'fugitive, like the hallucinations preceding sleep; ...you must seize it on the spot, greedily'.[2] Flaubert establishes differences rather than hierarchies between the two phenomena, whereas Freud and Maury both share the concept of the 'lowering' of the psychic level during sleep, and consider the unconscious to be an 'inferior' realm (the conscious representing the 'superior' component of the mind). But it is the *poetic* value of hallucination, *including pathological hallucination*, which Breton invokes in the *Manifesto*, quoting the experiences of scientists and psychiatrists as well as those of poets. 'Automatism': the word is borrowed from psychiatry and designates involuntary, unconscious psychic-poetic happenings; but, as we have already seen, this word also contained the passion mixed with anguish of human beings in their relationship with machines that seem always to be on the point of liberating themselves from their creators and leading an autonomous existence. 'Surrealism' was a neologism created by Apollinaire, who intended to convey the idea of poetic invention; the new word had the sort of mysterious, enchanting brilliancy that only a magician like Apollinaire could bestow on the language. The *Manifesto* juxtaposed these two strangely suggestive image-words, one defining the other: and so *Surrealism* was born, a concept endowed with an extraordinary power of expansion, as later events were to prove. In this suit to restore the rights of hallucinatory phenomena, dreams and insanity, Breton was more than eager to pronounce the verdict; he was determined to 'deal drastically with that *hatred of the marvellous* which is rampant in some people.... Let us speak plainly,' he wrote, 'the marvellous is always beautiful, any facet of the marvellous is beautiful, indeed only the marvellous is beautiful'.

The mechanist theme deriving from Futurism and Dada had undergone a new and curious transformation. The Large Glass of *The Bride Stripped Bare by her Bachelors, Even*, an ironic precursor of the robots of science-fiction, presented machines capable of making love, and not only on the physical plane as with Jarry's *Supermale*: Duchamp's *Superfemale* mechanizes both emotions and erotic thought. But, with Surrealism, does it not seem that man is condemned to be a poetry-writing machine, and that the poet must inevitably limit himself to the role of a 'modest recording apparatus'[3] of his inner voices?

'At the end of all the sciences dealing with bodies,' says Taine, 'one will never find anything other than mechanics; so that the various nervous actions which provoke various sensations can only be conceived as being systems of movements.' In the *Manifesto*, 'automatism, recording apparatus, mechanical writing' (which are, of course, themselves images) inevitably suggest, under the cir-

---

1. Alfred Maury: *Le Sommeil et les Rêves* (Didier, Paris, 1861).

2. Quoted in *On Intelligence*, Part Two, Book I, Chapter II.

3. *Surrealist Manifesto*.

Max Ernst: *Relief.* 1927.

Max Ernst: *The Origin of the Clock*. 1925.

cumstances, an interiorization of the machine within the human being. The anonymous photograph, untitled and undated, printed on the first page of the first issue of the review *La Révolution Surréaliste* (December, 1924)—a photograph which can be identified as the object constructed by Man Ray in New York in 1920, called *The Enigma of Isidore Ducasse*[1]—was an effective symbol of this interiorization. Lautréamont's famous comparisons had proposed human equivalents to the scientific and mechanical elements of civilization; in Man Ray's plastic metaphor, the rigid shapes of a sewing-machine, hidden under rough canvas, suggested the supple contours of a living body. A preface signed by Boiffard, Eluard and Vitrac was printed as a kind of frame around the mysterious image: 'Already the automats are multiplying and dreaming. In the cafés they ask eagerly for writing materials, the marble's veins are the graphs of their evasion and their cars go driverless to the Bois de Boulogne.'

The author of the *Manifesto* had no intention, however, of reinvigorating or transforming the mechanist theme: Breton's attitude towards the machine was the thoroughgoing suspicion and even aversion of a nineteenth century Romantic. And, then, how was painting to adapt itself to a 'dictation of anunalterable design' in which retouching was forbidden?

The *Manifesto* was almost entirely uninformative. Surrealism in painting is mentioned accessorily: 'Uccello in former times, and, in the modern era, Seurat, Gustave Moreau, Matisse (in *Music* for instance), Derain, Picasso (far the purest of all), Braque, Duchamp, Picabia, Chirico (admirable for so long), Klee, Man Ray, Max Ernst and—so close to us—André Masson.'[2] Elsewhere, in discussing the possibility of a graphic transcription of hallucinatory images, Breton writes: 'It is not a question of drawing, it is simply a question of *tracing*.'[3]

However, in the first issue of *La Révolution Surréaliste*, Max Morise investigated the problem more closely: 'A painting by a madman or a medium is to *x*' (i.e. to an authentically surrealist painting) 'what a medium's speech is to a surrealist text' (i.e. a text obtained through automatic writing). 'But who will provide us with the marvellous drug that will give us the means of achieving *x*? And what jealousy the painter must feel when he considers the shadows that surrealist writing can conjure up without assistance.... For the real difficulty lies, not in starting, but rather in *forgetting what has just been accomplished*, or even more in *ignoring it*. Closing one's eyes, concealing part of the canvas, concentrating only on one particular section of it—all these means of upsetting normal visual processes are perfectly childish expedients which are bound to miss the mark. It is not a question of mutilating a technique but of rendering it as ineffective as possible.'

In the third issue of the review (April, 1925), Pierre Naville, who apparently found it impossible to adapt the principles of automatic writing to painting, declared categorically that surrealist painting did not exist and could not exist: 'Everyone knows by now that there is no *surrealist painting*. Neither pencil-marks recording chance gestures, nor images representing dream figures, nor imaginary fantasies, of course, can be so qualified.' Nor indeed, one might add, Naville's own pictures, his hobby at the time being painting: he published several reproductions of his own work in the first numbers of *La Révolution Surréaliste*, of which he was then editor. One of them (reproducing, in fact, an idea of Robert Desnos') shows a bottle of wine standing on a table and reflecting the image of the drinker in the act of throwing himself out of the window.[4] Other compositions appearing in the review—such as those of a certain Dédé Sunbeam—also confirmed Naville's reservations suitably. All in all, Morise's humorous drawings were infinitely more surrealist—such as *At the Hairdresser's*,[5] in which the patrons of a hairdressing establishment are seen having their heads cut rather than their hair and then walking headless to the cashier to pay for their 'cuts': clearly an act of pure automatism in which human behaviour is compared with the reflexes of a decapitated insect....

When Breton took over the effective direction of the review (from No 4, July, 1925), and began to publish articles, spread through several issues, not on surrealist painting but on *Surrealism and painting*, he brushed aside all controversy by mentioning in the very beginning the two stars of Apolli-

1. See above, p. 64.
2. *Manifesto*, note, p. 44.
3. *Ibid.*, note, p. 35.

4. *La Révolution Surréaliste*, No. 2.
5. The review *Variétés*, special surrealist issue: June, 1929.

Dédé Sunbeam: Drawing. 1926.

naire's *Cubist Painters*: Picasso and Braque. But it was precisely what could be considered an extra-pictorial, literary or oneiric element in their work which justified this new appraisal at a distance of ten years, so that a *papier collé* was granted the poetic vibration of a *collage*: '...dancers dragging fragments of marble mantelpieces behind them....—Braque is responsible for the fact that the invariable pattern of the paper which covers the walls of our room now resembles for us a tuft of grass on the face of a precipice....'

As far as Braque's more recent work was concern-ed, Breton made all sorts of reservations; but if one was seeking an authentic dream painting, why—here were Picasso's pictures, and here, too, was Breton's reply to Naville (without naming him): 'It has been said that there could be no such thing as surrealist painting. Painting, literature—what are they to us, O Picasso, you who have carried the spirit, no longer of contradiction, but of eva-sion, to its furthest point! From each one of your pictures you have let down a rope-ladder, or rather a ladder made of the sheets of your bed, and we, and probably you with us, desire only to climb up into our sleep and down from it again. And they come and talk to us of painting, they come and remind us of that lamentable expedient which is painting!' The whole surrealist enterprise is placed under the aegis of the inventor of Cubism: 'A single failure of will-power on his part would have been sufficient for everything we are concern-ed with to be at least put back, if not wholly lost.' It even involves the future of the movement: 'If Surrealism ever comes to adopt a line of moral conduct,[1] it has only to accept the discipline that Picasso has accepted and will continue to accept.'

The reproductions illustrating this article are mostly taken from the 'synthetic' period of Cubism. They seem to have been chosen because of the *distance* existing between the titles and the pictures. This disparity is unusual with Picasso, his titles being in general perfectly commonplace (*Still-life, Nude, Figure*, etc.); but in the surrealist review one can find the geometric forms of a *Schoolgirl*, and of a *Student*; *Adam and Eve*, two female nudes of the 'giant' epoch; *Young Girls Dancing in Front of a Window*, triangular monsters which seem closer to the Palotins that Jarry drew than to feminine forms. One can also find reproduced for the first time in

La Révolution Surréaliste the geometric patterns of intercrossing lines accentuated with black spots at each juncture with which Picasso illustrated Balzac's *Le Chef-d'œuvre Inconnu*, dedicated to Uccello; and there, too, is that supreme example of plastic freedom and sureness, the scrap of linen nailed to a board and crossed by stretched strings that represented the latest metamorphosis of the famous Guitars.

Absolutely no mention was made in the original version of *Le Surréalisme et la Peinture* either of the futurist precursors or of Dada. In general, Surrea-lism (and Max Ernst himself, in *Beyond Painting*) behaved in as oedipean a manner towards Dada as Dada itself had behaved towards the movements which had preceded it: the whole series of twelve

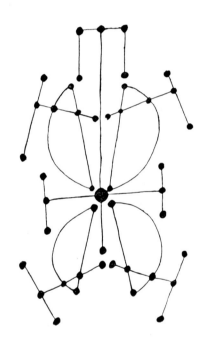

Pablo Picasso: Drawing. 1924.

numbers of *La Révolution Surréaliste* contains hardly any references to Dada. Nevertheless several decisive experiments during this first period of Surrealism were carried out far more in the spirit of the creators of Dada, Picabia and Duchamp—we shall return shortly to the part played by Max Ernst—than of Picasso or Braque. During the period of 'sleeps', Rrose Sélavy spoke through the mouth of Robert Desnos with a surpris-ing authenticity and, in 1922, one could read in *Littérature* the following lines by Breton himself

1. The word 'moral' is suppressed in the 1945 edition of *Le Surréalisme et la Peinture*, published by Brentano's in New York.

on the subject of the hallucinatory image: 'This priceless confidence can be attained repeatedly only by those who are inured to the most complex mental gymnastics. Their names at present are Picabia and Duchamp.' But three years later, Breton was on bad terms with Picabia; although he praises, in *Le Surréalisme et la Peinture*, the artist's disgust for 'the commercial transactions to which every work of art is subject today' and acknowledges that Picabia 'has thwarted such manoeuvres in regard to his own work with the greatest possible energy', he nevertheless deplores 'his complete incomprehension of Surrealism'.

As for Duchamp, his name was never introduced into these essays. In any case, the creator of *The Bride...* was usually in America, worked less and less on his great Glass which was still, in Europe, a kind of legendary object—until, one day, it was learnt that he had left it definitively uncompleted.

Picasso, Braque, Chirico, Max Ernst, Man Ray and Masson are all studied in turn in Breton's notes on painting published in *La Révolution Surréaliste*. With the addition of articles on Miró, Tanguy and Arp, these texts were put together in one volume, published by N.R.F. in 1928 with reproductions of the works of these painters, plus Picabia.

Despite Robert Desnos' statement,[1] *Le Surréalisme et la Peinture* is something more than a 'collector's journal'. At the time of his break with the surrealists, Desnos claimed that the only painters praised in this book were those whose pictures figured in the author's collection. There is no doubt that dealing in pictures was almost a second profession for Breton and other writers in his circle, and that they were able to count on a constant, if variable, source of income from the sale of paintings by artists whom they liked and encouraged. And we know that Breton was for some time—with Louis Aragon—the salaried adviser of the collector Jacques Doucet. A number of Chiricos, some *papiers collés* by Picasso, many works by Max Ernst, Miró, Dali, Magritte, Tanguy and so on, appeared in the collections of Breton, Eluard and others—either as gifts from the artists or by purchase—before ending up in the possession of well-known collectors or on museum walls. For instance: the paint-

ing *The Bride*, given by Duchamp to Picabia in 1912, was exchanged or sold later to Paul Eluard, who exchanged it for a picture belonging to Breton; in 1934 Breton sold *The Bride* to the New York dealer Julien Levy, from whom the collector Arensberg bought it in 1936; today it is in the Philadelphia Museum of Art. But as it was still possible, during the early twenties, to buy Picassos, for instance, at modest prices, it would have been extraordinary if young poets with occasional money to spare had *not* patronized the 1921 Kahnweiler sales.[2] With ironic satisfaction, the review *L'Esprit Nouveau*, which was dedicated to the defence and glorification of Cubism, noted in its ninth issue, in June, 1921, that 'several dadas (MM. Tzara, Aragon, Breton, writers of talent when they feel like it) have bought Picassos for themselves at the Kahnweiler sale.... Well, that really is reassuring'.

It must be appreciated that the attention paid by the poets to the work of the painters was largely responsible for the reception that the painters received. To be represented in these collections, to obtain from the owners a preface for an exhibition, may not have been an absolute guarantee of success (or, in some cases, even of talent), still, it was a by no means negligible method of attracting the attention of a so-called 'aware' public. The author of *Le Surréalisme et la Peinture*, in particular, has performed a constant function of *preface-writer* in the surrealist movement, and the book in question is more than anything else a collection of prefaces in which the theoretical aspect, as much as the moral judgments and historical justifications, are dictated by a sort of strategy designed to support either a present or future policy.

'Fewer manifestoes, more results!' said the critics to the surrealists. But, after all, did not Surrealism think of itself as a constantly renewed Preface? In the eyes of the new poets and painters, real existence lay in the future. Anything already achieved, known, acclaimed, anything that lost the nature of pure, free, malleable and multiform potentiality, and forced this nature to assume a determined, definitive, fixed aspect, automatically forfeited most of its interest for them.

1. 'Third Manifesto of Surrealism,' by Robert Desnos (see *Documents Surréalistes*, Editions du Seuil, Paris, 1948).

2. At the second Kahnweiler sale, many of the sixty works of Picasso listed in the catalogue did not fetch 500 francs (less than £10 or $40 at that time). There were also a number of paintings sold at prices well below those officially fixed: a *Still Life* offered at 300 francs (less than £6 or $25) realized 141 francs (about £2.17s. 6d. or $11).

The past is memory, while the future is based on the capacity for creation. To fight the past it is necessary to fight against memory and its tendency to mould existence into a rigid pattern: a pattern which is, moreover, far from historical. 'It is curious to note,' Marcel Duchamp said to me at a time when I was asking him questions about events in which he had been involved long before, 'to what an extent memory is unfaithful, even for the most important periods of one's life. It is that, indeed,' he added, 'that explains the delightful fantasy of history.'

Memory operates through an identification of roots, bases, foundations of everything that it wishes to retain. Take words, for instance: memory assembles words with a common root, uses this root as a unity, and groups words by identification of their roots. Such is the philological process. Breton's approach to words is very different. He proceeds by what one might call *identification by the edges*, by the fringe, in a sense. Let me anticipate my account by quoting a poem which he dedicated during the forties to the painter Matta:

> ...*what was spacetonia*
> *Becomes muscatelastic*
> *For brand new activity*
> *Here is the glazier on the shutter*
> *In that totemic language Mattattoucantharide*
> *Mattalismanchineel.*[1]

For brand new activity.... From Matta, tattoo, toucan and cantharide, a single word is born whose structure resembles in fact that of a totem, in which the images are superposed and form a long symbolic phrase spelling out an incantation of the future. It is quite possible that Breton does not attach great importance to this poem, and sees in it merely a verbal fantasy which he composed one night while waiting to go to sleep. But this text is of interest to us precisely because it reveals a thought-process closely related to 'dream-work', a process which one can find not only in Breton's texts of automatic writing, in which, according to the explanations in the *Manifesto*, the phrases and words 'are drawn to each other', but also in his more consciously elaborated prose works. Many passages in *Le Surréalisme et la Peinture*

develop, not by the logical application of a root-concept, but by a 'magnetization' of ideas bound together by their 'intellectual fringe'.

'When we were children we had toys that would make us weep with pity and anger today. One day, perhaps, we shall see the toys of our whole life, like those of our childhood, once more. It was Picasso who gave me this idea.... I never received this impression so strongly as on the occasion of the ballet *Mercure*, a few years ago....'[2] What are we to make of this passage? Did Breton include the stage-designs for *Mercure* among those toys which at present would make him weep with pity and anger? But once again it is not a question of logic. Breton's 'serious spirit' encounters Picasso's 'playful spirit' by the 'fringe' idea of greatness, which reveals the sophisticated entertainment in question as a plaything for adults while still raising it to the level of tragedy. 'We grow up until a certain age, it seems, and our playthings grow up with us. Playing a part in the drama whose only theatre is the mind, Picasso, creator of tragic toys for adults, has caused man to grow up and, sometimes under the guise of exasperating him, has put an end to his puerile fidgeting.'[3]

In truth, Breton does not belong to the 'reasoning type' whose appearance Lautréamont called for in his *Poésies*: on the contrary, he is essentially an 'agitational type'—he himself has spoken of his 'liking for agitation'. His most persuasive 'reasonings' draw their power of conviction from their sheer incantatory quality, from a rhetoric closely resembling the long sentences of the *Chants de Maldoror*, and from a syntax which seems designed, curiously enough, to cast a spell over the mind's logical tendencies and to glorify, though surreptitiously, the disorientation of thought-processes. The reader may very well lose his footing in this terrain, but not the author: 'In the domain of poetry, Lautréamont, Rimbaud and Mallarmé were the first to endow the human mind with what it lacked so much: I mean a real *insulation*, thanks to which the mind, on finding itself ideally withdrawn from everything, can begin to occupy itself with its own life, in which the attained and the desired no longer mutually exclude one another, and can thereupon attempt to submit to a permanent and most rigorous censorship whatever has constrained it hitherto. Since the existence of these poets, the idea of what is per-

---

1. *Mot à Mante* ('Mantis Word'), poem published in the catalogue of the Matta exhibition at the Galerie Drouin (Paris, 1946). [...*ce qui était espacétoine | Se fait muscadenas | Pour l'action toute neuve | Voici le vitrier sur le volet | Dans la langue totémique Mattatoucantharide | Mattalismancenillier*].

2. *Le Surréalisme et la Peinture.*
3. *Ibid.*

mitted and what is forbidden has assumed its present elasticity, to such a point that the words family, fatherland, society, for instance, seem to us now to be so many macabre jests. It was they who really caused us to make up our minds to rely for our redemption here below upon ourselves alone, so that we have desperately to pursue their footsteps, animated by that feverish desire for conquest, total conquest, that will never leave us; so that our eyes, our precious eyes, have to reflect that which, while not existing, is yet as intense as that which does exist, and which has once more to consist of real visual images, fully compensating us for what we have left behind.'[1] Once one has accomplished the logical analysis of this phrase, the context throws additional light on the author's intentions: once more, Picasso is the theme, and, according to Breton, his pictures reveal that other country which the precursors of Surrealism had already described in literature.

It is clear today that Picasso never in fact played the role of Guide in Surrealism, and that in 1924 he was neither at the head nor the tail of the movement, merely elsewhere, with his huge Pompeian women, his Ingres-style drawings and his synthetic still-lives.[2] But it was no gamble by then to acknowledge the 'exceptional predestination'—in the words of *Le Surréalisme et la Peinture*—of an artist whose glory had continued to increase for twenty years. There was no one left but the official art-school professors, most of the critics and, of course, the general public, to treat the inventor of Cubism as a 'fraud'; but the avant-garde recognized his dominant position, and even a few art-dealers were able by then to see which way the land lay. So it was safe enough to pay homage to a man whose sheer mastery of his medium justified his discoveries—or his rediscoveries. If Picasso were to become a surrealist—though Breton spared him this label, as indeed the label of cubist—there would be no danger of Surrealism lacking masterpieces.

In the prefaces collected in *Le Surréalisme et la Peinture*, it is not so much the painters that we

can study and get to know as Breton himself with his peremptory moral contradictions, masked and abetted in some degree by a seductive power which he makes use of consummately and deliberately. In the final analysis, his mental attitudes seem both syncretic and sectarian, and thus possess an affinity with those of the ancient Chinese schools.[3] It must be admitted, though, that a sense of humour is entirely lacking from the pages of this book, that true humour which always contains some element of self-punishment.[4] But the *tone* is remarkably successful. Just as Picasso's superbly irreverent plastic sense justifies all his themes, so Breton's sometimes audacious but always infallible syntax transfigures the ideas it discusses. Everywhere doors open and roads appear. A turn of phrase, a single word suffice to transform the lighting. One cannot even say that there is an embarrassingly large choice of different roads, for the development of the author's views imposes successive and sometimes contradictory choices on the reader. Writing of cubist *papiers collés*, Breton evokes in admiration 'all that remains hanging from that immemorial newspaper LE JOUR...';[5] further on, commenting on Max Ernst's *collages*, he returns to this newspaper to say disdainfully that it was 'not even tomorrow's'; one cannot help being seduced and won over each time, in seeing that Braque and Picasso did in fact confer immortality on the ephemeral with their *papiers collés*, while still understanding that it was Max Ernst (and Dada) who had transformed a successful plastic experiment into an invention charged with future significance.

Automatic writing is certainly not the secret of poetry, if indeed such a secret could ever be revealed or taught. In the beginning, Breton no doubt saw in it the secret of writing poems, a problem which, according to the *Manifesto*, had long preoccupied him. If it was a solution as far as he personally was concerned, many surrealist poets never made use of the process, and others soon got tired

André Breton, c. 1925.

1. *Ibid.*

2. A later text by Breton claimed that Picasso 'joined up with' the surrealists in 1926. Cf. *Genesis and Perspective of Surrealism*, one of three essays (others by Mondrian and Arp) written as Introductions to *Art of this Century*, a compilation edited by Peggy Guggenheim, New York, 1942 'as a catalogue to the permanent collection exhibited at Art of this Century'. The essay was later republished in French in the Brentano edition of *Le Surréalisme et la Peinture* (New York, 1945).

3. Cf. Marcel Granet: *La Pensée Chinoise*, in the series 'L'Evolution de l'Humanité' (Albin Michel, Paris, 1934).

4. The only humour apparent in Breton's work is in the *Manifesto*, still close to Dada, in which the author occasionally treats his own arguments lightheartedly. On the other hand, Breton has often practised *irony*, which is an attack against others rather than against oneself.

5. 'Le *Jour*...' : in some cubist *papiers collés*, the incomplete title of Le *Journal*, a former Paris newspaper.

of it. Texts of automatic writing (and *uncommentated* dream recitals) very quickly disappeared from the surrealist reviews. André Breton went so far as to say, in 'The Automatic message'[2] that 'the history of automatic writing in Surrealism has turned out to be a constant misfortune'; it is true that he puts the blame, not on the method, but on the negligence or preoccupation with the picturesque shown by most of those who had practised it. It should be noted that there is no mention of automatism in the first edition of *Le Surréalisme et la Peinture*, which by no means implies, however, that the emphasis placed on this approach by the *Manifesto* was mistaken. It may be appropriate to suggest here, in the light of past experience, some answers to this still controversial issue.

'Pure' automatism might be compared to the photographer-seaweed in Raymond Roussel's novel *Impressions d'Afrique*—an aquatic plant which is a kind of living magic-lantern and whose functioning might symbolize the return to consciousness of first memories. The extraordinary vegetable described by Roussel carries a membrane sensitive to light, a sort of screen comparable to a photographic plate capable of recording images, but only during a very brief period—the few moments of its submarine florescence. And on this marvellous screen the plant can, thanks to subtle variations in its constituent molecules, thereafter project throughout its entire existence, and in an eternally renewed cycle, the scenes recorded during the course of its brief period of receptive blooming.

But the beings and things emanating from the ocean of the unconscious are not all amphibious by nature, like Roussel's seaweed whose screen functioned as effectively in the air as in the sea. Living flowers fade and wither away, beach pebbles, so attractive when gathered during the holidays, soon turn into sad little stones—the brilliance of the scenes and speeches perceived in dreams often evaporates in the light of day. In addition, their unconscious origin in no way frees these representations from the grip of habit which is inevitably bound up with any automatic operation (as Marcel Duchamp has clearly indicated with the 'Litanies of the Glider' of the Bachelor Machine). In Roussel's novel, the spectators are fascinated at the beginning by the performance of the screen-plant, but in the end their attention wanders: the same cycle of images repeats itself indefinitely. Habit

tends to make a conscious action nothing less than automatic and monotonous; inversely, it introduces a factor of monotony, of real stereotype, into any too prolonged or too often repeated unconscious experience. 'Anything can become a bore, even the planet Mars,' declared the psychologist Flournoy in reference to the initially thrilling but ultimately tedious séances, during which the medium Helen Smith described her supposed adventures on another planet.[2] And the surrealists themselves ended up by having enough of Desnos' interminable speeches during the course of his 'sleeps'.

Monotony and disillusionment are, then, the two hazards of automatic activity. Confronted, by the very nature of their means of expression, with a quite different technical problem to that of writing, the surrealist painters were obliged to work out their own methods to express their visions.

As far as Max Ernst is concerned, this painter has consistently made use of a combination of two contradictory factors whose importance we have already noted in the work of Marcel Duchamp: chance and choice. A picture by Max Ernst, instead of being a 'window' or a simple 'projection screen', resembles a complex, living machine. It can first of all be compared to the chance-images of the Rohrschach test. That is to say, the 'screen' is not a blank page on to which the inner image is to be projected unmodified. On the contrary, the image is suggested, and led to define itself, by the nature of the screens themselves: screens for which Ernst finds infinite variations, either in the external world—as in the case of the *collages*—or making them according to many techniques, such as *frottage* (rubbing), and *grattage* (scraping). The use of these mechanical (rather than automatic) means permits the hatching of an initial 'plot' of meanings which can serve as a point of departure and a basis for poetic hallucination. The texture of Max Ernst's screens is, in fact, essentially designed to stimulate the imaginative faculties. At a later date, the artist was to say that these processes were *means of forcing inspiration*[3] and not only of forcing it but of creating it as well. The mechanist aspect of so many of the

---

1. Published in the review *Minotaure*, No. 3-4, 1933, and reprinted in *Point du Jour* (N.R.F., Paris, 1934).

2. Th. Flournoy: *Des Indes à la Planète Mars* (Alcan, Paris, 1900).

3. Max Ernst: 'Inspiration to Order', in *Le Surréalisme au Service de la Révolution*, No. 6 (May, 1933), published in English translation in Robert Motherwell's compilation *Max Ernst: Beyond Painting (op. cit.)*.
Text quoted below, p. 230.

imposed, one upon the other, with the persistence and rapidity characteristic of amorous memories.' Subsequently, Ernst began 'to experiment indifferently and to question, utilizing the same means, all sorts of material to be found in the visual field: leaves and their veins, the ragged edges of a bit of linen, the brushstrokes of a "modern" painting, the unwound thread from a spool, etc.'[1]

Thus, at the moment when ghosts are materializing themselves, when the machine is springing from the physics text-book, and the forgotten heroes of old adventure stories return to life, when the deck of the trusty ship Argo reverts to its original forest state, and Leonardo da Vinci's wall becomes a landscape, Max Ernst confers their own existence upon these marvels. An existence which is that of *disorientation*. '*Surreality will be the function of our will to absolute disorientation*', writes Breton in his 'Advice to the reader' at the beginning of Max Ernst's album of *collages*, La Femme 100 Têtes; and that is certainly one of the best of all the definitions of Surrealism that Breton or others have proposed. In the concept of disorientation can be recognized Rimbaud's 'je *est un autre*,' the idea of *surprise*—'the great new incentive' according to Apollinaire, as well as Minotaur's *hubris* (to which I shall return in a later chapter); and, of course, *contradiction*.

Never having passed through the mill of the official art schools, Max Ernst had no need to throw off the burden of conventional teaching in order to reach the sources of the unconscious. It is as if someone other than himself had created his artistic production, the real creator being that 'someone' who directs the work and who dictates to the conscious what it should achieve and, literally, *project*. But even though Ernst has always sought to restrict his share of participation in a picture, his conscious mind (in a certain form) nevertheless remains in contact with this 'someone' and plays the part of a 'fixing agent': conscious signs—bright colours or fixed shapes— are evident in Max Ernst's work.

In terms solely of a 'psycho-technical' interpretation of his works, it is the blending, flexible

collages derives from the science text-book engravings which served for their construction. Cross-grained wooden planks, during the period of *frottages*, or the veins of the *grattages* obtained with the aid of combs such as craftsmen use to produce an imitation-wood surface, often provided the basis of the Forests; the stony appearance of the 'decalcomanias-without-object' created rock-filled landscapes....

'On the 10th of August 1925, finding myself one rainy evening in a seaside inn, I was struck by the obsession that showed to my excited gaze the floor-boards upon which a thousand scrubbings had deepened the grooves. I decided then to investigate the symbolism of this obsession and, in order to aid my meditative and hallucinatory faculties, I made from the boards a series of drawings by placing on them, at random, sheets of paper which I undertook to rub with black lead. In gazing attentively at the drawings thus obtained, the dark passages and those of a gently lighted penumbra, I was surprised by the sudden identification of my visionary capacities and by the hallucinatory succession of contradictory images super-

---

1. Duchamp notes, in the *Catalogue of the Collection of the Société Anonyme*, that Max Ernst's procedure duplicates an ancient Chinese technique. One may also notice that the motivating idea of the *frottage*—to conjure up the shadow or ghost of an anonymous object to find therein an imaginative stimulus, is close to that of the Rayogram; sometimes the elements used are the same: scrap of woven fabric, thread, etc.

quality of their grey-toned plates which make the first *frottages* identifiable most clearly as products of the unconscious. So it can be said that the birth-date of surrealist painting, properly so-called, is that of the *frottages*. Nevertheless the author of *Beyond Painting* has quite legitimately made use of identical terms in recounting both discoveries, that of *collages* and that of *frottages*.[1]

In Max Ernst's work, disorientation is not premeditated. It appears at the moment when the

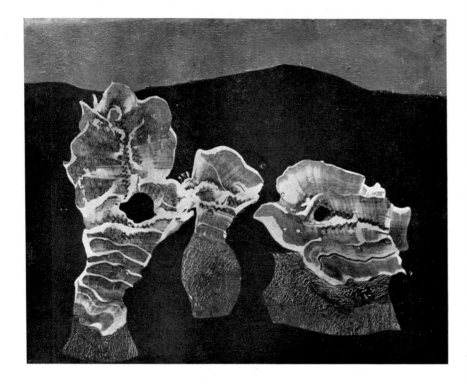

Max Ernst: *Shell-Flowers.* 1927.

poet adapts, delimits and situates the phantasms. Thanks to this retouching, without which Leonardo's wall would of course be nothing but a wall, the poem-picture acquires the *vibration* which is its very life; it attains a true lyricism in which the lights of an hallucinated consciousness shimmer.[2]

The creatures released by Max Ernst's imagination are new gods. If they have any relation with the past it is on the plane of poetic analogy; they are not more or less transposed imitations of a pre-existent document. Men in ancient times believed that insects and serpents sprang spontaneously from the damp earth; Ernst gives a positive force to this old illusion: in his hands, pictorial material comes alive and gives birth to new reptiles, mantises and hitherto unknown birds of prey.

The first *frottages* were published in 1926, under the title *Histoire Naturelle*.[3] The preface which Jean Arp wrote for his friend's album recreated the state of mind which had heralded the appearance of Ernst's first 'projections': '...like a lion who scents a succulent pair of newlyweds the seismic plant desires to make a meal of the dead man. in his millennial den made up as a foetus it whirls with lust like the white juice of the end with the black juice of the start and the ferocity of its gaze chases the navels around the earth. the lime-tree grows tractably on boarded plains. the chestnut and the oak start out under the banner of d.a.d.a.. that is to say, domine anno domine anno. the cypress is not a dancer's calf in the ecclesiastical ballet....'[4]

'In a country the colour of a *pigeon's breast*,' Ernst writes, 'I acclaimed the flight of *100,000 doves*. I saw them invade the *forests*, black with desires, and the *walls* and *seas* without end.—I saw an *ivy leaf float upon the ocean* and I felt a *very gentle earthquake*. I saw a *pale, white dove, flower of the desert. She refused to understand. Along the length of a cloud* a superb man and woman *danced the Carmagnole of love. The Dove folded herself in her wings* and swallowed the key forever.—*A string lying on my table* made me see a number of *young men trampling upon their mother*, while several *young girls* amused themselves with *beautiful poses.*—*Some exceedingly beautiful women crossed a river, shrieking. A man, walking on the water, took a young girl by the hand and shoved past another.* Some persons of a rather reassuring aspect—in fact, *they had lain too long in the forest*—made their *savage gestures only to be charming.* Someone said: *The immobile father.*'[5]

Comparing the titles of the *frottages* which make up this fairy story with those already mentioned in connection with *collages*, we can perceive on the one hand the discontinuation of the mechanist theme and, on the other, a darkening of the humour,

1. As can be seen by comparing the quotations on pp. 77 and 127.

2. *Vibration* in painting, or *pulsation* in literary expression, is always the conscious-unconscious interaction which brings the picture or poem to life—and, psychically, the human being.

3. Jeanne Bucher, Paris.

4. See Jean Arp: *On My Way, poetry and essays 1912-1947,* (*op. cit.*).

5. *Beyond Painting.*

Max Ernst: *The Orange-Blossom*. 1930.

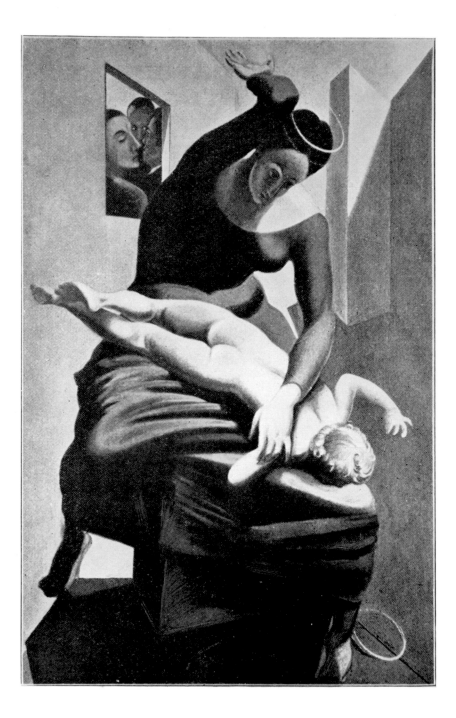

Max Ernst: *The Virgin Spanking the Infant Jesus before Three Witnesses: A.B., P.E., and the Artist.* 1928.

which becomes introverted, 'black'. In 1928, a Max Ernst exhibition opened at the Galerie Georges Bernheim in Paris, with an impressive 'entry of the flowers'. Conjured up by *grattage*, there grew here in strange gardens hard 'bone-flowers, scale-flowers, tubular flowers, flowers struggling under the water, flowers pierced through the neck by stones'. The artist also exhibited 'his birds, his flying forests, his maledictions, his Satanas....'

Period of Flowers, period of Birds, period of Hordes—period of planets hovering above dark Forests. 'Men feel a natural instinct of terror about passions and sensations that seem stronger than themselves,' wrote Oscar Wilde (in *The Portrait of Dorian Gray*). While René Crevel, writing the preface to the 1928 exhibition, saw in *Histoire Naturelle* 'the terrible marvels of a universe whose secrets we cannot even attempt to crush underfoot, a universe greater than us'. But the artist had a 'clear conscience' with regard to these terrifying scenes that he was revealing: he made no attempt to veil these mysteries of the inner universe—on the contrary, he invented a thousand ways of forcing them to show themselves in broad daylight.

As we have already seen, many of the pictures painted by Max Ernst between 1921 and 1925, before the *frottages*, proceeded from a similar conception to that of the *collages* without in fact containing any glued elements *(éléments collés)*. They often expressed a non-pictorial subversive intention, such as the painting entitled (obviously by antiphrasis) *Vive la France*; or the one called *Revolution by Night*. *Two Children Menaced by a Nightingale* includes objects attached to the canvas which complete the scene in a realistic-humorous manner: the painting is more the model of an hallucination than its image.... *But Men Shall Never Know It* is a myth-picture showing the spheres of the sun and moon hovering over a black sky in which a scabrous intertwining of men's and women's naked legs shimmers: from this apparition a little whistle is hanging which, says the inscription written on the back of the canvas, 'because people are paying attention to him, imagines he is soaring to the sun'.

The one picture with a really premeditated theme painted by Max Ernst during this period is *The Virgin Spanking the Infant Jesus before Three Witnesses: André Breton, Paul Eluard and the Artist*. Breton had suggested the idea for this painting, in which Mary is vigorously smacking a little Jesus whose halo has fallen to the ground. Exhibited at the Salon des Indépendants in 1926, the picture

soon acquired a visiting-card in one corner of its frame bearing the words: 'Protest by the Catholic Artists'. When, some time later, Max Ernst wanted to include this picture among other pain-

Max Ernst: *Monument to the Birds*. 1927.

tings of his in a show in his own country, the reactions of the faithful were more violent. The Cologne diocese succeeded in having the exhibition closed, and the author of the sacrilegious painting was practically excommunicated by an assembly of Catholic notables (including Herr Ernst senior!). After an exordium by the archbishop in person, the assembly, reviving the medieval '*clameur de haro*' (ritual denunciation), pronounced in chorus a '*Fuj!*' of final contempt directed towards the impious painter.[1]

'From Rimbaud's famous love for the decorative panels over doors, for silly refrains, and the revolutions of morals,' wrote Breton in *Le Surréalisme et la Peinture*,[2] 'from the systematic taste that Lautréamont is supposed to have had for a sort of

1. Much later, in Hollywood, where the artist held an exhibition in 1948, a priest—Protestant, it is true—who seemed extremely well-informed in every aspect of surrealist painting, undertook to demonstrate to Max Ernst that the painting of the Virgin remained somewhat timorous in terms of blasphemy. This pious individual observed that the picture would have been far more scandalous if Jesus had been spanked with the aid of his own halo.

2. No. 9-10 of *La Révolution Surréaliste* (1927).

Max Ernst: *Two Children are Menaced by a Nightingale*. 1924.

spiritual trench extending from Young to certain medical reports, from Jarry's taunting knowledge of heraldry, and even from the inspiration which Apollinaire sought in catalogues, Max Ernst seems to have inherited the sense of a culture that is extraordinary, captivating, paradoxical and priceless.' The iconography of *La Révolution Surréaliste* was to devote considerable space to such a culture, beyond Culture and Taste, and the choice of the many strange and usually anonymous documents that the review published was made very much in the spirit of Max Ernst: illustrations of fair-ground attractions, one-man bands, under-water crocodile tamers, scenes from old films, wax heads, absurd folding-screens.... The theme of disorientation assumes a thousand shapes: a *View of Malaga* represents a lamp-post in front of a huge wall; *Versailles* is a female figure in an entrance-way; a *Maison-attentat* is the blank façade of a building carrying a single sign: FORTUNE; a Mack Sennett bathing belle is paired with an old engraving representing the figure of a black-smith constructed entirely from cog-wheels and connecting-rods; the papal nuncio emerges from the Elysées Palace between a captain of gendarmerie and an ambassador both loaded with gold braid and decorations (this is not a photographic *collage* like the view of the Paris Opera House with a herd of cows passing by, also reproduced in the review); another photograph, brought back from Japan ('contributed by Mme André Malraux' says the title), consists of pieces of watermelon cut in the shape of little pyramids; and, to complete this very partial list, the moving reproductions of *Attitudes in Hysteria in 1878*, taken from the archives of the Salpêtrière mental hospital in Paris.

If Giorgio de Chirico has influenced so many painters who have revealed the different faces of the new plastic poetry, Max Ernst as much as Tanguy, Magritte or Dali—and, through these, others who appeared later—it is largely, one must repeat, because of the extraordinarily *condensed* character which hallucinatory disorientation assumes in his work. The images of Chirico's first period showed man-made objects, but no human beings, no natural landscapes. The world was reduced to a single class of elements, and a large part of concrete reality seemed to present no interest whatsoever to the author of these silent paintings. The inner condensation compensated this

apparent impoverishment; the objects represented assumed a far greater significance than their models in real life, and Chirico's images were the potential sources of an infinity of other pictures.

The world outside of ourselves is only interesting to us because we can discover in it the partners necessary to our existence. The *narcissistic* mentality, of which Chirico is a remarkable example, discovers his own universe in himself, in the form of apparitions: at the origin of narcissistic hallucination lies the reflection of the individual image. In Chirico's work, interior and exterior mirrors had multiplied and transformed the reflection. But suddenly this painting began to show the premonitory signs of a profound evolution. An *Evangelical Still-life* of 1918 shows the scaffoldings made of rulers and set squares and the placards covered with mysterious signs open up before an unexpected urban landscape: skyscrapers pierced by a hundred black windows, with a tiny figure standing at their foot, looking vaguely like a soldier wearing a helmet—perhaps the soldier from Ferrara about to depart for fresh adventures?

By the end of 1918 the war was over. Chirico, a civilian once more, went to Rome where he show-ed for the first time the mannequins of *Hector and Andromache, The Troubadours* and *The Disquieting Muses* as well as the *Metaphysical Interiors*. The show was a complete failure; one single painting found a purchaser, and that was the only one which was not 'metaphysical': a portrait of a young man. It was then, during the summer of 1919, that Chirico experienced his 'revelation of great painting' while standing before a picture by Titian in the Villa Borghese museum in Rome.[1] He began to work in the museums, copying old masters. At the same time he wrote studies on Raphaël, Böcklin and Klinger for the review *Il Convegno*. Was he attempting to find a point of contact, a 'meeting-place', between German Romanticism, the literary painters and the 'masters'? In any event, it is clear that thenceforward his paintings embodied a new disquiet, very different from that which typified his anterior work.

A strange situation indeed: Chirico, while claiming to be returning to conventional teachings, seemed to be forcing himself into spontaneity. A would-be virtuoso manner—the 'wiped' style, in art-students' parlance—began to drown the luminous dreams of his early years in a vague mist. The exaltation to which the conscious elements seemed previously to succumb had vanished: thus forced perspectives disappeared and spatial lines were henceforward drawn strictly according to the rules. It was as if the conscious and the unconscious no longer illuminated each other, were no longer transfigured by reciprocal influence, but, on the contrary, contradicted and fought each other; as if that dynamic conjunction, the hallucinated conscious mind, in its drive towards creation, had undergone a new *schizis*. Had 'alienation' taken the place of hallucination?

It is no longer the invisible presences of a late afternoon which people the new images; now human figures appear, real ghosts this time, divorced from our time, outcasts of the past. They are memories of classical allegories, ancient figures whose shadows fade out on a leaden ground; beings carrying an evil omen, for they have *lost their shadows*. These are still-lives, landscapes, the well-known world of Art, in which the portrayer of hallucinations seems more astray than in his old labyrinths. The naïve gifts, simplicity, precision, even the lyrical quality of 'awkwardness', have disappeared. The manner becomes that of an unskilled adult. Never again is one to see the pure, clear images,

1. G. de Chirico: *Memorie della mia Vita (op. cit.)*

Max Ernst: *The Night of Love.* 1927.

Versailles.

Maison-attentat.

the villas and apartments motionless and vibrating with enigmas.

During this period Chirico painted several pictures on the theme of the 'return of the prodigal', of which one (1919) constitutes a disheartening imitation of classical painting, while another (1922) depicts a 'metaphysical' mannequin in front of an arcaded palace, clutching a woolly-looking ghost in a frock-coat (this painting in fact copies the theme of one of his 1917 drawings). After experiencing so many adventures, was Chirico's imagination preparing to 'settle down'? *The Departure of the Argonauts* (1922) is a family portrait: in a square drawn in sober perspective are two warriors, one of whom is brandishing the staff of that well-known little oriflamme, a woman in the background, and an old man stretched out on the ground contemplating with an expression of infinite sadness a quadrangular milestone bearing the name of the artist: G. de Chirico. May we not see the two brothers, Giorgio and Savinio, in this painting, with the mother enigmatic and severe, and the father merely a reclining figure on a tombstone?[1]

Chirico still produced occasional successful compositions, such as the *Roman Villa* of 1922, blending sunny architecture with fantastically swirling mists. But the portraits of his mother that he painted from 1919 onwards—he sometimes showed himself in the background—are handled with a terribly painstaking precision, with paint that is no longer smooth but has become slick; as for the Latin mottoes underlining certain self-portraits, they pay to the Enigma a tribute which is a little too explicit to be anything but retrospective.

The *Metaphysical Interiors*, all dating from after the declaration of war in 1914, signified the idea of *refuge*. Chirico took refuge in their tightly sealed rooms and accumulated there his 'windfalls of memory', Parisian reminiscences, impressions gleaned in the industrial cities of Emilia. When he returned to the French capital in 1925 he found a very different atmosphere from that of peacetime

Paris, and one by no means favourable to the narcissism of former years. Apollinaire was dead, the one leader of the modern movement who had the capacity to combine graciousness and authority amid the intrigues and disputes of the various cliques. In the newly constituted surrealist group, the humour and gaiety of Dada had turned into fierce irony. *La Révolution Surréaliste* proclaimed itself 'the most scandalous review in the world'. 'Like a sunrise, the yellow car suddenly appeared in the Rue Ordener; we drove it in such a state of spiritual intoxication that no other considerations seemed important': with these words, in a story which attempted to unveil the secret faces of Anarchy—and its traitors—Louis Aragon recalled in 1924 the exploit, ten years earlier, of the famous Bonnot gang.[2] In 1924, too, the appearance of *La Révolution Surréaliste* in the bookshops, inside its red cover, may well have inspired a feeling of panic or dizziness in the passerby who decided to glance through its pages. While *Relâche* lit for the last time the joyous flame of the dada spirit, the new review was capable, if necessary, of using their own principal weapon against serious people —seriousness. A few established critics had thought fit to show an occasionally benevolent interest at the time of the publication of the *Surrealist Manifesto*, but the surrealists had preferred to keep their distance. From the atmosphere of Dada, in which some of them had hurled insults at their public, a point had been reached where they had —so to speak—climbed down into the auditorium and were heckling the actors of the old repertoire. They declared their hostility towards the concepts of family, country, religion. They called art, literature, the social system and money to account. *La Révolution Surréaliste* proclaimed itself loudly to be the free power of dream and hallucination, of poetry and of love. And manifestoes such as the 'Address to the Dalai Lama' and the 'Letter to the Schools of Buddha' showed that the spirit of the East had not lost its grip on the young intellectual avant-garde.

But the glory of the *Urban Landscapes* and the *Interiors* still continued to exercise an undiminished influence over this new generation of painters and poets. Since the end of the war Chirico had entered into correspondance with Breton and Eluard, who both wanted to obtain paintings of his early period; Eluard and his wife Gala had travelled to

1. These lines were already written when I became acquainted with Mr James Thrall Soby's work *Giorgio de Chirico*. I was immediately struck by the resemblance (involuntary on the part of the painter?) between the reclining old man of the *Departure of the Argonauts* and Chirico's father as he appears in the photograph reproduced on p. 17 of Mr Soby's book.

2. Louis Aragon: 'When the game is up' (*Le Libertinage*, N.R.F., Paris, 1924), supposed confession of an accomplice of Bonnot's who had sold out to the police.

Italy in 1923 to see an exhibition of Chirico's work at the second Biennale of Rome, and while there had even bought several of his most recent pictures. It must be said that these acquisitions were roundly condemned by André Breton, who had already had difficulties with Chirico as a result of a request for illustrations to a book of poems; he had been disappointed and annoyed by what the artist had sent and had not wanted to use them.

The meeting of the surrealists and Chirico rapidly turned to disaster. The latter's evolution in no way corresponded to the expectations of those who considered him to be one of the two 'fixed points' of Surrealism (the other being Lautréamont in literature).[1] There was also no doubt a clash of temperaments between Chirico and Breton, who appreciated the artist's humour but certainly not his narcissism, especially when it took the form of a pride hardly compatible with his own. 'Is not boasting something necessary, even indispensable?' Chirico was to write later, and not without malice, in *Hebdomeros*. 'And is it not better to boast, even at the risk of annoying one's contemporaries, than to become like that famous courtier whose memory was finally affected by the too prolonged exercise of his profession?'

Old incidents were raked up as a means of damning Chirico retrospectively. He had written from Italy to Breton's wife, who wanted to buy *The Sacred Fish* and *The Disquieting Muses*, that these paintings were in the hands of collectors who wanted rather high prices for them, 3,500 and 5,000 lire respectively, but that he could make copies of them for 1,000 lire each. 'These copies,' he added, 'will have no other fault than that of being executed with more beautiful materials and a more skilful technique.'[2] This proposition was not considered exorbitant, a little later on, by Paul Eluard, for whom Chirico painted in Paris a copy of *The Disquieting Muses*. But Breton took a different view and had this to say in *Le Surréalisme et la Peinture*: 'I have actually been present at this painful scene: Chirico attempting to reproduce one of his own early paintings with his present heavy hand, not indeed because he sought some illusion or disillusion in this act which might have been touching, but because by cheating on its ex-

ternal appearance he could hope to sell the same picture twice. It was so far from being the same, alas!'[3] Breton adds that Chirico had also made various antedated versions of his earliest paintings and in this way put on the market 'a great number of falsely marked and therefore *fake* pictures'.

However, Chirico had lost none of his sarcastic intelligence, and one can discover more or less clear, and clearly spiteful, echoes in *Hebdomeros* of his feelings concerning certain habits and hobbies of the surrealists. No doubt he found a number of his early paintings hanging on their walls, and heard them praised to the skies. But according to *Hebdomeros*: 'He had no wish to arouse complicated feelings in his friends, in fact he even dreaded their admiration; all that "*It's magnificent! It's fantastic! It's astonishing!*" only caused him a very moderate pleasure and in the long run ended by irritating him. His one happiness was in being left absolutely alone by everyone; to be dressed like everybody else, pass unnoticed, never to feel the arrow of a glance, even a well-meaning one, in his back or side. Or again, yes, he would have liked to be taken notice of, but in a *completely different way*. To have the advantages and satisfactions of glory without experiencing its boredoms. Sybaritism, in fact!' What Hebdomeros-Chirico loved most of all was 'rooms, cozy rooms in which one can shut oneself, curtains drawn and doors closed; and, above all, the corners of rooms and low ceilings'.

As a sequel to the first World War, political upheavals took place throughout the world, resulting in savage attacks being made on contemporary thought in an attempt to uproot the new mental attitudes in poetry and science so as to instal official compulsory art. Are these not some of the menaces contained mysteriously in Chirico's first paintings: menaces of the invisible man, of the invisible sea, of barbarian hordes lurking behind the horizon, towns whose inhabitants have fled, abandoning in the streets, the squares, even in their own rooms, the hoarded mementoes from the deep-lying realm of childhood?

The surrealists tried to persuade Chirico to return to this early inspiration, and one painting of his reproduced in the second issue of *La Révolu-*

---

1. *Le Surréalisme et la Peinture.*

2. Mr Soby, in his *Giorgio de Chirico*, quotes this letter as having been addressed to Gala Eluard. But I have seen the letter in question with its envelope addressed to Mme André Breton (the first wife of the poet, now Madame Simone Collinet, director of the Fürstenberg Gallery in Paris).

3. A reproduction of the copy in question, identifiable by a dark band across the base of the canvas—Chirico had used a slightly longer stretcher than for the original and this band fills up the extra space—can be found in *Fantastic Art, Dada, Surrealism* (Museum of Modern Art, New York, 3rd edition, 1947).

tion *Surréaliste* (January, 1925) certainly represents one of the artist's rare attempts to evoke his earlier state of mind: this *Metaphysical Interior* gives the impression, with its muzzy technique, of dating from a later period. But the artist was drawing farther and farther away from these themes, perhaps because he felt obscurely that their prophecies had in a certain sense been realized. To continue to submit to them became forced labour for him: on a picture entitled *The Fruits of the Poet* (1925) representing three apples in front of a 'metaphysical' assemblage of rules and set-squares, he inscribed the legend: 'I like the fruits, I detest the decor.' It had, in fact, become merely a decor.

Chirico had elaborated a whole theory to explain his evolution. The fact that neither logical argument nor violent opposition had the slightest effect on his unconvincing rationalizations is sufficient to show their genuinely paranoiac nature. He claimed to have realized the defects of oil painting and to have discovered the beauties of 'emulsion'; he was seeking 'matter' and 'quality'. He had written to André Breton from Italy saying that he was tormented by the problem of *craftmanship*, was copying in the museums and reading all the old treatises on painting. 'I have discovered that the chronic and mortal sickness of painting today is *oil*.' He had started 'with the patience of an alchemist' to filter his varnishes, grind his colours, and so on. He found that in this way the mystery of colour and the magic of painting was profoundly increased.[1]

It was in vain that Max Morise answered him, fairly and indeed amicably, in *La Révolution Surréaliste* (No. 4, July, 1925):[2] 'If a painter knows, consciously or not, what he wants to express, then, I assure you, he will employ whatever methods are best suited to his purposes without it being necessary for him to question himself deeply on this particular problem.... When the technique of a picture is analyzed, the mystery of its creation remains intact.... One realizes that a picture is "well painted" *because* it is beautiful; the converse is false.' (A reasoning which might be summed up in Picasso's aphorism: 'Craftmanship can't be learnt.') Chirico could not and would not listen. Less than a year after his meeting the surrealists the break occurred, with an almost panic violence which showed the

extent of the disillusionment felt on both sides. Held to be irresponsible, in *Le Surréalisme et la Peinture* (published in *La Révolution Surréaliste*, no. 7, June, 1926), as far as all his previous work was concerned, but absolutely responsible for the 'meretricious painting' of his recent period, called a coward, cheat, viper, and accused of amorality and greed, Chirico was denounced, on top of all that, for having one of his exhibitions prefaced by 'the ignoble cretin Albert C. Barnes' (the celebrated American collector). 'This preface would suffice, I think, to dishonour him,' wrote Breton.[3]

These attacks were taken up again or repeated over a period of years, and Soby was able to write in *The Early Chirico* that the quarrel between Chirico and the surrealists constituted 'one of the most unpleasant episodes in the history of modern art'.

Chirico's reply to these insults was to speak, perhaps with conviction, as disparagingly as possible about his former production. Later on he declared some of his earliest paintings to be forgeries, although they were absolutely authentic, and also condemned others which were in fact forgeries! Since a large number of false Chiricos were turned out during the second World War, it is true that some disorder has prevailed in cataloguing the artist's early work. (In this respect, Soby's *Giorgio de Chirico* may be profitably consulted: the book reproduces almost all the authentic early Chiricos, and none of the many forgeries at present in circulation).

In 1928, in the guise of a counter-demonstration to offset a Chirico exhibition at Léonce Rosenberg's gallery, the surrealists brought together in their own gallery all the pictures they possessed from the artist's early period, and installed among them a model entitled: *Here lies Giorgio de Chirico*, consisting of a plaster reproduction of the tower of Pisa surrounded by little horses in india-rubber, and doll's furniture.[4] Louis Aragon heaped insults upon the enemy in his preface to the catalogue of this exhibition;[5] he pointed out in passing the role which the unflagging maternal presence must have played in the artist's evolution (but indirect in any

---

1. Letter published in *Littérature* (new series, No. 1, March 1, 1922).

2. Max Morise: 'Concerning the Chirico exhibition.' This was the artist's first exhibition since his return to Paris.

3. The passage concerning Dr Barnes is suppressed in the American edition of *Le Surréalisme et la Peinture*.

4. Allusions to Chirico's *Horse* and *Furniture* themes, which are mentioned later in this chapter.

5. Louis Aragon: 'The Pamphlet changes authors.' See *Documents Surréalistes*, in which this text is erroneously included among those of 1927.

case—it is unlikely that Mme de Chirico ever gave any advice about painting to her son), and accuses Chirico of being a 'false Oedipus'. Hardly. It would be only too easy to demonstrate, in terms of complexes and symbols, that Chirico blinded himself for having killed his father and loved his mother. Viewed in this perspective, his adventure would appear, rather, to be one of the most fascinating illustrations of an authentic Oedipus complex.

Raymond Queneau went one better in *La Révolution Surréaliste* (No. 11): 'His work can be divided into two parts: the first and the bad.... Giorgio de Chirico's early work does not excuse the sinister clown of today the muddy colours of his recent pictures, and together with these pictures we shall throw into the garbage-bins of oblivion this painter who was the first to discover a mysterious and new aspect of mystery.'

'About 1926,' wrote Marcel Duchamp in the *Catalogue of the Collection of the Société Anonyme*, 'Chirico abandoned his "metaphysical" conception and turned to a less disciplined brush-stroke. His admirers could not follow him and decided that Chirico of the second manner had lost the flame of the first. But posterity may have a word to say.'

The relaxed brush-stroke can be encountered from 1919 onwards, but it is around 1926 in fact that the old themes were finally abandoned by the one-time painter of Arcades. New mannequins took up prostrated, inconsolable poses, immense statues in classical drapery on the edge of a vague shore, the head oval and smooth, the torso formed of an accumulation of ruins, porticos and crumbling frontages. But *Seated Mannequins, The Archaeologists* (in the Amsterdam Municipal Museum) and other paintings of this series do not deserve all the severe treatment they got at the hands of the surrealists. In another departure, Chirico was the first to make use of themes borrowed from Gallic coins, whence his pictures of *Horses*—one white, one black, rearing up on a beach among the stumps of fallen columns. Yet again, groups of wrestlers (in their case the faulty drawing produces a strange feeling of embarrassment) grapple between the panelled walls of a room. These same rooms with low ceilings, solemn and bare, witness the passage of cohorts of lictors and warriors (*The Triumpher*, 1928), paintings unpleasantly contemporaneous

with the success of Mussolini's fascio.... In another picture (*Interior*, 1926) a cypress grove is growing in a room with a closed door, with sea-waves lapping up against the tree-trunks and soaking through the grooves between the floorboards. And the idea of

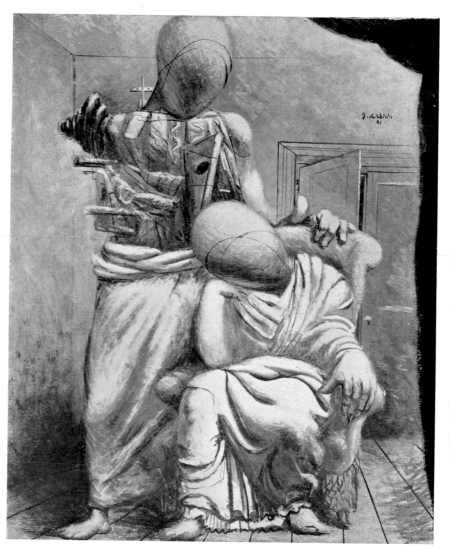

the revenge of natural forces now subjugated and domesticated is expressed in the pictures of *Furniture* (1926-29), glass-cupboards, armchairs, iron bedsteads, piled in a heap on a small square of floor in the middle of a deserted landscape, as if after a shipwreck, an earthquake or the destructions of war.

The strangeness remains, the feeling of an inner drama bound up with exterior menaces, while the

Giorgio de Chirico: *The Poet and His Muse.* 1921.

metaphysical trophies, once so new and well-defined, the scientific and dream objects, even the silent towns seems to be ageing and falling into dust, leaving out of all their accumulated riches only a suite of heterogeneous furniture. The pictures of *Furniture* contained a new prophecy: one could see them reproduced, very realistically, on an infinite number of occasions, during the second World War—and even after that—among the chaos of bombed cities.

Finally, from 1930 onwards there are still-lives, landscapes, streets, sharing a realistic style in which something ironic and mad, some kind of humour still lurks. As for the self-portraits in which Chirico depicts himself today garbed as a condottiere, a sixteenth century lord of the manor, and so on, these effigies bear quite openly the marks of narcissistic obsession, and can be considered as psychological documents.

Many years later, when passions were calmed, the writer-painter Robert Motherwell suggested a coherent explanation of what had happened. In the first number (June, 1942) of the magazine *VVV*, published by the surrealists in New York during the second World War, Motherwell wrote that 'something happened to alter Chirico's conception of painting', not his discovery of painting in the grand style, which seems to have been only a secondary phenomenon, but quite simply, after the months of barracks and isolation in Ferrara, that of 'Parisian painting at a moment when it was turning from many years of experiment ... to a painting relying on the weight of traditional images understood by everyone, as in the "classic" period of Picasso, Derain, and so on. It is not difficult to suppose that Chirico was ravished by the "objective" authority of such painting, and determined to participate in its creation. His pictures after 1918, being failures, are generally ignored by critics, but they afford the clue...'. Motherwell goes on to say that he was, of course, inevitably defeated in his effort to create a painting that was authoritarian, normative (intelligible to any 'normal' person) and plastic, because his gift was the precise opposite, unique, personal and poetic.

The tragedy of the situation was, as I have said, that the poetic gift did not allow itself to be smothered so easily. So strange an imagination, concealing so many secrets, did not succumb without a struggle to the artist's 'deliberate attempts to cater to the luxury trade'.[1] And by far the most surprising aspect of the whole adventure is the survival, in Chirico's written work, of the very special atmosphere of his first paintings. His critical writings of 1920-21 are masterpieces of sensitivity and intelligence, but the admirable novel *Hebdomeros* recreated in 1929 the atmosphere of the first pictures while encompassing also the more recent themes. Roman landscapes, Returns of the Prodigal, Myrmidons shut into rooms with moulded cornices (one may well believe Hebdomeros when he says that 'the enigma of this ineffable group of warriors and pugilists, difficult to make out and forming in one corner of the room a polychromatic and immobile block in stances of attack and defence, was only truly understood by himself'), horses galloping between broken pillars ('the great dysenteric mares,' says Hebdomeros elsewhere, 'among the drums of the collapsed columns'); these new spells are lighted by the calm solar light which bathed the old hallucinations, the squares with porticoes, the old men carved in stone, and the metaphysical objects, 'scaffoldings that are curious, severe and amusing at the same time'. *Hebdomeros* embraces the whole of Chirico's painting, the old and the new, related in the naïve, humorous, melancholy and precise manner which fits very well the description of one of the paintings of Arcades.

The war, in *Hebdomeros*, is no longer a ruinous chaos but an endless and peaceful siege which allows time to think of many things, recall memories and make long speeches to friends. This is a nostalgic, lazy war, like the one described by Apollinaire in *Calligrammes*:

> *Ah God how pleasant is war*
> *With its songs and long idle days*

Hebdomeros is basically a *roman à clef*, containing some most curious characters, such as the flute-playing sculptor; Casca, the happy painter from the south; the lover of twilight; the good man ('he had been seen crying') who only lends money to the rich; the generous friend who swindles his debtors. These figures and still others are as transposed and as recognizable (if one holds the clue) as an Italian square in the Arcade dreams. Thus, the hermit-gastronome who adores scientific tinkering *(Hebdomeros,* pp. 72-74*)* and sometimes climbs up into his tower, and is 'not at home to anyone' while his servant pretends that he is out

1. Robert Motherwell: 'Notes on Mondrian and Chirico' in *VVV*, No. 1, New York, 1942.

Man Ray: A scene from the film *L'Etoile de Mer*. 1927.

Francis Picabia: *Hera*. 1928.

on an errand, telling obstinate visitors who wish to await his return: 'When Monsieur goes out on an errand he remains away for several days', can be identified by referring to *Memorie della mia Vita* (p. 161): the person in question is André Derain.

'*Hebdomeros*, or the painter's genius in writing' was the description of the book by the review *Bifur* which had sponsored its publication. Experts have combined to praise the pictorial splendours of the Towns, the Mannequins, the Interiors, the delicacy of the impasto, the quality of their pigment. 'Literary painter' is a clumsy description: a poet-painter, rather, who possessed all the painterly qualities while he was purely a poet, Chirico proves himself a poet-writer in *Hebdomeros*, despite the fact that he was writing in a language which was not his native idiom. But, in his writing, the French phrase follows closely the meanderings of his dream-like thoughts, remains sometimes in suspense, then passes with incomparable simplicity from humour to melancholy, from drama to philosophy, from the real to the imaginary. As in the towns of childhood memories, the inner image and the real are no longer distinguishable.

Since the end of 1925, the relationship between Surrealism and painting had been sufficiently clear to justify the title of a collective exhibition of *Surrealist Painting* at the Galerie Pierre, which brought together work by Arp, Chirico, Max Ernst, Paul Klee, Masson, Miró, Picasso, Man Ray, Pierre Roy, prefaced by André Breton and Robert Desnos. This relationship had permitted the creation in 1926 of a Surrealist Gallery (directed first by Roland Tual, then by Marcel Noll), in the rue Jacques Callot, on premises previously occupied by the Communist-influenced review *Clarté*, and here collective and one-man shows took place. The gallery opened on March 26, 1926, with an exhibition of paintings by Man Ray and of 'Island Objects'. By the side of objects of primitive Oceanian art from the collections of Breton, Eluard, Aragon, Tual and various Parisian experts, Man Ray showed twenty-four pictures, including his very first paintings, a 1908 *Study*, the 1912 *Dream*, *MCMXIV*, as well as the *Revolving Doors* and such objects as *The Impossibility* of 1917 and *Something to Write With* (1924)—a bird's feather, embedded in corrugated cardboard; also, the *Portrait* of *Rrose Sélavy* (1923), some rayograms

and a few later paintings. The preface to the catalogue consisted of phrases about birds: 'I saw then that at the sound of a bell—A nun was put into a wine-barrel—For having given the pox to the Dispenser's bird' (Giorgio Baffo). 'Calm bird whose flight is reversed bird nidifying in mid-air' (Guillaume Apollinaire). 'Scissors of the law, break yourselves like glass against the bird's eyelash' (Robert Desnos). 'So the white bird is now in the temple of the great flame-coloured monkey' (Diderot). 'We valued highly this bird which was, for us, a sort of guardian spirit of the house' (Lautréamont). etc.

Man Ray's work was reproduced more often than that of any other artist in the pages of *La Révolution Surréaliste*. With him, the theory of the 'machine-poet' was illustrated by admirable examples: airb-rush paintings, objects, rayograms, and photographs, which can be said to have given modern photography its essential impulse.

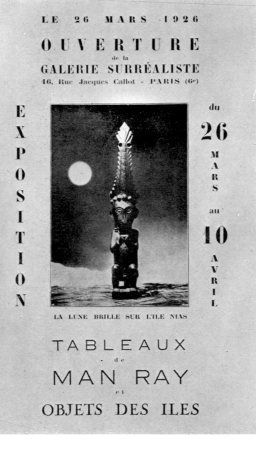

Cover of the catalogue for the opening exhibition of the Galerie Surréaliste. 1926.

The Galerie Surréaliste, rue Jacques-Callot. 1926.

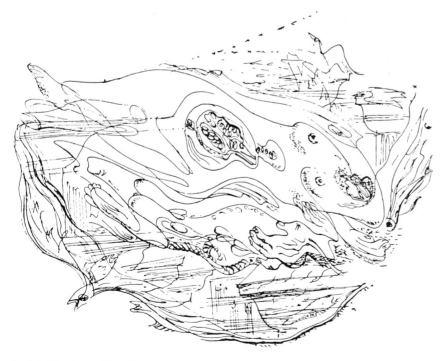

André Masson : Drawing. 1925.

Sensitive plate, developer, fixing bath, projection screen were not symbols for Man Ray but the very tools of creation. Photographs by him reproduced in the review include: *Motor Race*, grey and crossed by flashes of light like a futurist 'spiritual state'; *The Boulevard Edgar Quinet at Night*, very abstract with its superimposed white circles; some artificial landscapes (such as *Marine*) that the lens makes more evocative than real nature; various banal or ridiculous architectural structures suddenly rendered poetic (such as *Compte-rendu de l'Exposition des Arts Décoratifs*); and the mannequin meditating between a sphere and a cone. Several of these images were included in a film shot by Man Ray in 1927 with a scenario by Robert Desnos: *L'Etoile de Mer* ('The Star-Fish'), in which everything is in a state of metamorphosis and seems touched continuously by a wizard's magic wand.[1]

Almost all the adherents of the surrealist movement made use throughout the years of the label 'Editions Surréalistes' for subscribed editions or editions printed at author's expense. In 1926, the Editions Surréalistes announced the inauguration of a series of *Snowballs*, souvenir-objects in the shape of glass globes containing a tiny reproduction of a Picasso still-life or a porcelain eye, placed there by Man Ray, which could be viewed through their miniature snow-storm instead of the usual Eiffel Tower or Sacré-Cœur. The 'series' only comprised these two items.

The final article of *Le Surréalisme et la Peinture* appearing in *La Révolution Surréaliste* (No. 9-10, October, 1927) is devoted mainly to the praise of Max Ernst, Man Ray and André Masson. Born in 1896, Masson decided early in life to become a painter, attended the courses at the École des Beaux-Arts, and then became attracted to the modern movement. In 1924 Breton bought one of his paintings, *The Four Elements*, from Kahnweiler; a little later Masson became one of the first participants in the young surrealist movement.

La Révolution Surréaliste published a great number of his drawings, ostentatiously automatic in character. These complex arabesques blend fragments of architecture with fleeting symbols such as hands, birds, fishes, and look strangely like cerebral convolutions from which the images are escaping. Their author was visibly trying

1. From the same period, *Les Mystères du Château de Dé* (film shot by Man Ray in the villa of the Vicomte de Noailles in the south of France) containing photographic trick effects that remain unsurpassed.

142

to adapt to the world of graphic art the method of writing recommended by the *Manifesto*. 'Pigeon flies! Fish flies! Pigeon flies against fish flies! Fish flies (certain fish). Fish also does not fly! Apple rises and falls! Jet of water supports egg which falls and does not rise. Woman cherishes man who loves woman who fears man. Vaudevilles!'

Could this commentary, and the whole article in *Le Surréalisme et la Peinture* dealing with the 'chemistry of the intellect' in relation to Masson reveal the presence in the artist's work of the two Disquieting Muses: surprise and disorientation —and humour as well? In any case, the influences of Chirico and Dada are remarkable by their absence in Masson's work. On the other hand, his liking for symbolism is less reminiscent of Redon than of the 'symbolist' Matisse of 1911. During 1924-26, his pictures were allegories *(The Constellations, Death of a Bird, The Armour, Nudes and Architectures*, etc*)* carried out in the manner of the cubist 'Scaffoldings', but in mastic or bluish tones. Later, he took different guides (as, for example, Miró's plastic technique).

Taken to task in 1929 in *The Second Surrealist Manifesto* and in the special number of the review *Variétés*, Masson took no further part in the activities of the group, and renewed his participation only at the time of the 1938 International Surrealist Exhibition in Paris. Breton again devoted enthusiastic pages to him during their common stay in America during the second World War, and condemned him once again in 1947, consigning him to the category of 'surrealists despite themselves'.[1]

As a matter of fact, Masson seems, in general, to be essentially an *erudite* man, and I feel that his paintings often express the conflict between plastic influences and literary reminiscences. He hardly ever makes use of the agents of synthesis which are the 'ways of forcing inspiration' so much employed by the surrealists. One might add that during the course of recent *Interviews*,[2] the artist defined himself as a follower of Cézanne and Matisse and a 'dissident surrealist'.

André Masson: *The Bird Hunt*. 1926.

Picabia continued to paint, as always, 'for pleasure', and by 1924-25 the author of *Very Rare Picture upon Earth* had abandoned mechanist painting. In

1. See below, p. 342.
2. Published by Julliard, Paris, 1958.

Francis Picabia, 1928.

festivals and sunshine, and he returned to the theme of the beautiful Spanish women that he used to draw in Barcelona; in addition, he sketched light ironical-poetic allegories (*Ambition* is a young man, naked, with a bird on his head). He exhibited a series of humorous *Bull Fights* at Théophile Briant's gallery in Paris: pictures of bull-fighters seized with panic and quaking ignominiously before the wild beast. In 1928, he showed his first *Transparencies*, at the Galerie Fabre in Cannes and again at Briant's.

Carib and Butterfly,[1] from the beginning of this period, is formed of three superimposed images: a head, a butterfly with spread wings, and a human figure seen in profile. Thereafter the themes become transparent, composed of line drawings washed with diaphanous colours. *Côte d'Azur* shows regattas passing across the bodies of girls bathing. The figure in *The Shadow* is a light-coloured phantom against a grey background, overcome with terror before a butterfly and duplicating himself in a new silhouette, cut out in blue cellophane and fixed to the first one—but slightly to one side—thus producing through its transparency a play of white, blue and blue-grey zones similar to a mirror's trembling reflection.[2] The panoramas of the *Transparencies* unfolded themselves always in these tones of thick glass, blue or greenish-blue, paintings superimposing a whole series of scenes, accumulating picture upon picture, so that—in the words of Marcel Duchamp—one has 'the impression of a third dimension without the aid of perspective'. This dimension is not only spatial; it is also psychic: it is the dimension of the dream, of those deep, monochromatic kingdoms of sleep. The nightmares of the period of Monsters have given way to calmer reflections, and one calls to mind here Paul Eluard's tender poetry, to which the adjective 'transparent' has been so often applied, and also the crystalline, singular images of André Breton.

Eluard's windows, Breton's crystals, Picabia's transparencies: these washes create depths in which the inhabitants of an oneiric aquarium plunge and dart, a 'drawing-room at the bottom of a lake'. It would have been more appropriate if Picabia, rather than illustrating a de luxe edition in 1931 of a somewhat languid science-fiction novel

1. The only painting by Picabia reproduced in *La Révolution Surréaliste* (No. 12, December, 1929).

2. This image eventually became a real phantom: the cellophane cracked and Picabia destroyed what remained of the picture.

any case, twelve years after Orphism, machines had ceased to be objects of horror for artists, and the mechanist theme had become public property: the assembling instructions for radiophonic apparatus, now in its infancy, seemed to be mere copies of Picabia's earlier works. The artist changed his style yet again, producing perhaps the strangest paintings of his whole career. This was the Period of Monsters: human figures with six eyes, horribly expressive faces, smears, dots, shadows, daubs of a brush out of control, riots of arabesques and serpentine forms cut into fragments. *After the Rain*, *Woman with Parasol*, *Figures in Rain*: the titles, too, were there for pleasure—the pleasure of painting and being a poet, a pleasure that had become cruel.

In 1927, Picabia left Paris, keeping only a *pied-à-terre* in the Avenue du Bois, and went to live in the south of France at his villa in Mougins, the Château de Mai. He possessed substantial private means at that time which allowed him to live on his yacht, sailing from one port to another along the Riviera. His painting of this period shows the influence of

Francis Picabia: *Woman with Monocle.* 1924.

Francis Picabia: *The Shadow*. 1928.

1. Éditions Antoine Roche, Paris.

The mountain the sea and the beautiful girl bathing
  In the house of the poor
  Behind the faded sky which is all the shade they have
  Thousands and thousands of dark lamps are hiding
  A field of reflections unites the tears[2]

and especially:

  In Madame des Ricochet's salon
  The mirrors are beads of crushed dew
  The console is made of an arm plunged into ivy
  And the carpet dies like waves[3]

Like Picabia, Paul Klee took no part at all in Surrealism as an organized movement, which is no doubt why his name, although it had been mentioned in the *Surrealist Manifesto*,[4] is not to be found in *Le Surréalisme et la Peinture*. All the same, the third number of *La Révolution Surréaliste*, in 1925, reproduced *Seventeen Strays*, *The Miser's Parsimonious Words*, *The Believers' Castle* and others of his compositions. Klee also participated in the first exhibition of surrealist painting at the Galerie Pierre, and, as I have said, his original supporters in France were the surrealists. The first work on Klee to be printed in France, by W. Grohmann, was published by the Éditions des Cahiers d'Art in 1929, with articles by Aragon, Crevel, Eluard, Lurçat, Soupault, Tzara and Vitrac. In that country the first monograph on Klee was produced by Gallimard in 1930 ('The New Painters' series) with a preface by René Crevel.

Klee's art is essentially graphic, whatever the medium used: drawing, water-colour, gouache or oil. Nearly all his pictures, which are mostly small, show the primary importance of the brush-stroke or pen-stroke; the themes are indicated by lines, defining areas of colour or shadow where necessary. His art is one of *graffito*, in which, wrote René Crevel, 'there is not one line which does not quiver with power.—The nail-marks which scratched out rocks and pebbles at the whim of a cyclopean fancy, all the graffiti of other worlds, the marionettes in a trance and the ectoplasmic flowers have been drawn and photographed, without any lighting tricks, without fraudulent romanticism or a mendaciously bombastic form of expression.—

by André Maurois, *Le Peseur d'Ames*,[1] could have lent to Breton's and Eluard's verses the images of a translucent world in which beautiful faces, languishing bodies and hybrid objects are dreaming:

2. Paul Eluard: 'L'Univers-Solitude' in *A toute Épreuve* (Editions Surréalistes, Paris, 1930).

3. A. Breton: 'World' in *Poèmes* (Gallimard, Paris, 1948).

4. See above, p. 121.

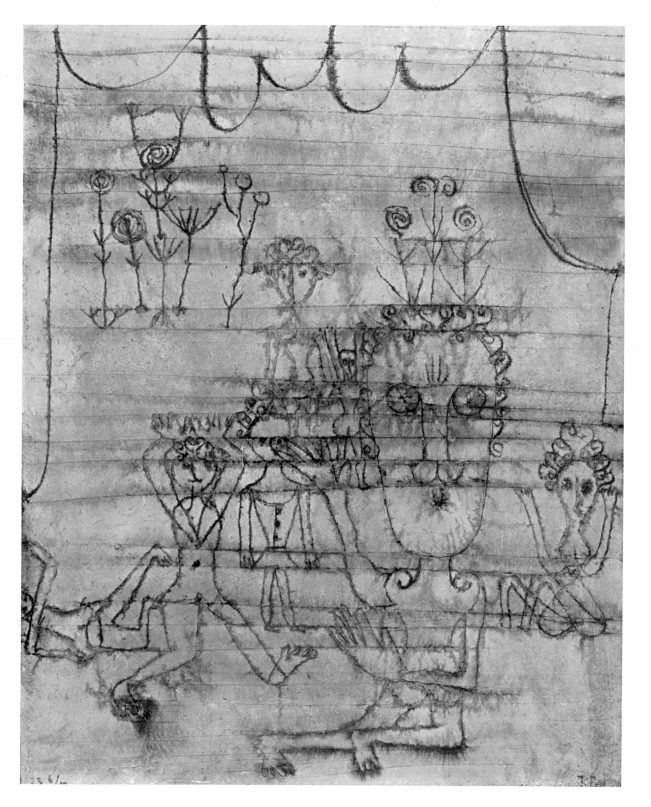

Paul Klee: *Ballet Group*, or *The Family*. 1923.

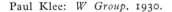

Paul Klee: *W Group*. 1930.

Paul Klee: *Dance of Horror*.

And here indeed,' concludes Crevel, 'is the most intimate and precise surreality.'

'A secret museum of dreams', in Crevel's words... These images were often executed on prepared crackled, irregular or blotted surfaces against which the drawing seemed almost engraved, white or black on a dark or light base: they remind one, too, of ideograms, or of the inscriptions in Arabic lettering that Klee would have seen during his visit to Tunisia in 1914—a voyage which in fact marked an important stage in his evolution. But infantile symptoms were still ever-present: the small scale of his works, line-drawing, colouring and plastic values indicated by hatching or stippling—this is what has been called—not disparagingly—Klee's *scrawls*. 'I wanted to be like a new-born child,' he wrote at the dawn of his career, in 1902, 'knowing nothing, absolutely nothing of Europe, ignorant of poets or fashions; like a savage, almost.'

Nevertheless, this essentially instinctive painter made every effort to theorize his impulses, becoming a professor of painting—his particular painting—at the Bauhaus in Weimar[1] during the early twenties, though this institution could hardly be considered a Temple of the Unconscious. His theses, based on the expressive values of constructive elements, recall those of Post-Impressionism: for instance, his 'colour circle' does not differ much from Charles Henry's famous 'chromatic circle'.[2] At other times his theories seem to have an affinity with Taine's concept of sensation as being 'at the central point of knowledge, a kind of link placed between the infinite ramifications of the branch and those of the root'.[3] For Klee, it is the artist himself who represents the tree-trunk, the trunk at the centre of the tree of art, plunging his roots into the heart of experiences and sensations and developing them in a different shape, as different as the leaves are from the roots, but just as ramified.

All this constitutes an entirely logical explanation of the extraordinary variety in the appearance of his pictures, but there is one additional link between all these paintings, drawings and engravings, each so

1. The Bauhaus later moved to Dessau.
2. Cf. *On Modern Art*, by Paul Klee, a text dating from 1924, but published during his lifetime only in an English translation (with an introduction by Herbert Read, Faber & Faber, London, 1937). After Klee's death at Locarno in 1942, the original German text was published eventually in 1945 (*Uber die moderne Kunst*, Benteli, Berne), and even later, in 1948, an 'adaptation' was published in Brussels (*De l'Art Moderne*, Editions de la Connaissance). Klee may perhaps have known of Charles Henry's theories through the latter's essays on 'Colour, light and form' which appeared in 1921 in the review *L'Esprit Nouveau* (Nos. 6, 8 and 9).
3. Taine: *On Intelligence*, in Part One, Book III, Chapter I (*op. cit.*).

different from the others: humour. In the mono-graph by Crevel already mentioned, a short biography tells us that for Klee, in 1900, 'Italy became a history lesson full of life, and his epigonic nature was a woeful revelation to him. He tried to combat his pessimism by invoking irony against himself'. The element of pessimism in his work was already notice-able before 1914, when he had begun to introduce a satirical, even sardonic note into German Expressionism (*At Table*, and numerous caricature-engravings: *Spirit and Matter*, etc.) and this ironic pessimism does not spare his own work—the specific sign of humour. This tendency finds consistent expression in the choice of a title, after the picture is finished, designed to indicate its new subject matter. Even when, rarely, the work does not contain a comical element not far removed from caricature, childishness or expressions of delirium, the title still presents almost invariably a defiance to all logic if not indeed to the picture it commentates. *Drawing for the Dance of a Grieving Child*, *Silver Moon-Mushroom Blossom*, *The Steamboat Passes the Botanical Gardens*, *Animals on Trek*, *Whose Fault is It?* are the titles of some of the compositions illustrating Klee's 1924 lectures on art in the 1948 Belgian edition; they are similar in character to those published by *La Révolution Surréaliste* in 1925. There are very many others in the same vein.

Klee discloses the poetic nature of his compositions as soon as they have completed the cycle of plastic metamorphoses. His tree, branching out over the fields of dream and childhood, draws its sap from humour and the juice of its fruits is also humour.

Pierre Roy, who took part in the surrealist exhibition of 1925, was one of Chirico's most constant imitators and a precursor of the surrealist convention in painting. This artist who in 1914 had already engraved on wood the well-known drawing of *The Human Target*,[1] seemed to have retained nothing from his studies of Chirico but the idea of *trompel'œil* as a justification for the simultaneous presence of disparate elements in a picture. His successes in this sphere (*Cetacean Fisheries*, *The End of the Off Days*[2]) only manage, however, to remove any feeling of life from his compositions. Nevertheless, as a quite accomplished vulgarizer of the Metaphysical Interiors, Roy was deemed worthy of a

Pierre Roy: *Metric System*. 1930.

1. See p. 47.
2. *La Révolution Surréaliste*, No. 7.

Emile Savitry: *The Meeting*. 1928.

Georges Malkine: *Ecstasy*. 1926.

preface by Louis Aragon, written in Dada style, to his 1926 exhibition at the Galerie Pierre. The title: *He who sticks to it.* '... We are living in the era of rock-candy sticks. They emerge from the earth at every seismic shock, they are the mental menhirs of conversation. Oh porphyries. Oh clotted blood. I raise a monument to the word AS. I raise a monument *to those who died of love.*

LONG LIVE FÉLIX FAURE!

Félix Faure was a kangaroo, a real kangaroo, Ladies. He died AS one should die.[1] I write a preface to the catalogue of the painter Félix Faure.'

Pierre Roy continued to paint *trompe-l'œil* compositions throughout his career. He died in 1946.

One may also mention the Belgian painters Delbrouck and M. Defize—husband and wife—who exhibited at the Galerie Van Leer in 1929, with a catalogue preface by André Breton, then returned to Belgium and oblivion. The uneven but always curious works of Georges Malkine were reproduced in surrealist reviews until 1930.

The special number of the Belgian review *Variétés* devoted to Surrealism reproduced two paintings by Émile Savitry, and *The Meeting*, in particular, produces a disquietingly bewitching

effect: in a landscape of desert dunes, an enormous knotted ribbon, apparently made of wood, rears up facing another tiny knotted ribbon which gives the impression of being terrorized by the sudden apparition of its immense brother.... A Savitry exhibition in 1929 was honoured by another dadaist preface by Aragon:

'Yes I saw... but the noise of the saw, the delicious noise of saw on ashlar no longer makes the world grind its teeth it has turned the saw into a violin more violate than... yes then sawteeth, and nowadays go grind your teeth then, it seems that the cretinizing machine is polishing its nails, every little nobody knows the who why of my dust, briefly: that painting imitates or doesn't imitate the na or picture interests the new recruit, the nurse-maid or the cucumbers.' etc.[2]

Savitry had a huge success: all the paintings on show were quickly bought by various collectors. The ease of this achievement unnerved the artist, who immediately lost all interest in an activity so devoid of risks and left for Oceania with the money from the sales. Some years later, he reappeared to become one of France's best professional photographers. The strangest part of the story is that though Savitry never touches a paintbrush nowadays, his wife paints very beautiful pictures: the fresh, charming images which Elsa Henriquez composes with a genuine naïvety are well-known.

The final issue of *La Révolution Surréaliste* (December, 1929), detailing the group's activity over a period of four years, mentions no fewer than twelve exhibitions held during this time (Miró, Surrealist painting, Max Ernst (three exhibitions), Man Ray, Tanguy, Arp, Chirico, Savitry, Delbrouck and Defize, Dali), but omits those of André Masson, Pierre Roy and some others and ignores shows by Picabia and Klee.

In 1928 an exhibition was organized at the Paris gallery 'Le Sacré du Printemps', bringing together works by Arp, Chirico, Ernst, Malkine, Masson, Miró, Picabia, Roy, Tanguy, under the title: *Does Surrealism Exist?* (Already, each year, critics and columnists were burying the movement.) Max Ernst had designed for the catalogue cover a daisy losing its petals in the manner of the old game: a little, a lot, passionately, not at all. The last flying petal gave the answer: Surrealism, and its painting, existed—passionately.

1. Félix Faure died in the arms of a courtesan, in 1899, while President of the French Republic.

2. For the complete text see *Documents Surréalistes*, pp. 143-144.

Joan Miró: *Woman Standing*. 1937.

Joan Miró: *Head of a Woman.* 1938.

CHAPTER VI

HISTORY OF TWO MAGI
AND OTHER MEMORABLE ADVENTURES

By amplifying reality to an astonishing degree, painters have the capacity to teach us or remind us of many aspects of the truly essential elements of this reality conventionalized by habit. Through a strange retroactive effect, this enlarged reality becomes again essentially primordial and primitive. Life in its successive phases, human evolution, the tentative or fugitive aspects of existence, of which scholars can give us only a theoretical understanding, must appear in an entirely different light at that moment when painting is capable of revivifying the creative activities of the most ancient civilizations.

Joan Miró was born on April 20, 1893 at Montroig, in Spanish Catalonia. In 1907 he became a student at the School of Fine Arts in Barcelona; for some time he worked as a store-clerk, then in 1912 he entered the Gali Academy. His first exhibition was held in 1918 at the Dalmau Gallery in Barcelona, consisting of landscapes and still-lives in the 'fauvist' manner. He was influenced by Cubism at the time of his first visit to Paris in 1919 —his first exhibition in Paris was at the Galerie La Licorne in 1921. But soon, Miró was mixing with the dadaists, who were in the process of becoming surrealists; he had a studio in the rue Blomet, not far from that of André Masson; and his paintings, first seen by Masson who showed them to Max Ernst, Breton and the other members of the group, already gave clear indications of his later style and preoccupations: the origins of life and the great desires of the human spirit.

It has been said of Miró's work that his images are those of a child, are indeed 'childish'; this is at least a recognition of his spontaneously child-like delight in colours and shapes. Such comparisons deserve to be given closer study, since in the case of Miró his extremely individual naïvety does not spring solely from surface appearances; in reality, his work incarnates, through an instinctive identification on his part, certain basic characteristics of the existence of organic beings.

The first period of human existence is called the 'oral' stage by psychologists, because, being devoted almost entirely to nutritive functions, it is centred on the mouth: the child's sole contact with the outer world is its mother, and more specifically its mother's breast. The passing of this stage does not necessarily mean its annulment, and sometimes character is determined throughout life by particular dispositions in infancy. Thus, optimism or pessimism—the dispositions which, throughout the adult's entire life, influence his general attitude to existence—derive to some extent from the first emotional reactions of the child at the breast: 'it's good', or 'it's bad'. May one not classify among the survivals of infantile optimism those abstract paintings (for example, those of one of the pioneers of abstract art, Max Bill) which are mainly composed of circles: schematic images of the maternal breast, the source of the infant's good nourishment multiplied many times, like manna in the desert? An abstract painter once showed me a small study that he had painted at the beginning of his career: it was a nude, in which the woman's body was entirely covered by a network of juxtaposed circles, all of them the same dimension as the breasts themselves.

One of Miró's favourite motifs was also to be the circle, but he went far beyond that tranquillizing aspect. The 'oral' existence of infancy takes a particular form in human beings, one that is present to a curious extent in this artist's work. I refer to *parasitism*, for the infant at the breast

Joan Miró, c. 1930.

Joan Miró: *The Far-mer's Wife*. 1922-1923.

can be considered the 'parasite' of its mother who is, indeed, biologically and psychologically constructed to encourage its enterprises. Many of Miró's paintings have the sometimes comical but more often menacing appearance of parasitic insects much larger than life. Nothing is lacking: the mouth bristling with sharp teeth, the articulated body's delicate limbs, the feelers like hooks or claws or shaped like suckers. The frightening *Head of a Woman* of 1938, with its wiry tangled hairs, huge paws, ovoid thorax, serrated mouth and ferocious little eye, is surely the portrait of the 'flea with a shrivelled pupil' of the *Chants de Maldoror*: a flea seen through a microscope, as it were. Other paintings remind one of parasitic colonies enormously enlarged.

Are we not entering, then, into an inhuman or anti-human world whose laws are fundamentally different from our own? We all know that no aspect of human nature is foreign to the classical humanist. But modern painters place themselves in a more perilous situation: no aspect of living matter is foreign to them. They do not restrict man to his own species; they see him as a microcosm, a *minor mundus* in the words of Pico della Mirandola (whose own name resembles a picture of Miró's), containing not only the brute sensation of the animal but also the vegetative soul of plants. In this way, tendencies which in earlier ages were revealed only to inner contemplation become manifest to some extent; esoteric concepts begin to impregnate the work of creators who never considered themselves 'initiates' but who are nevertheless *artists* in the alchemical sense of the term.

Portraits projecting elements of infantile sensation now assume a fresh significance and appear to us as magical signs, as means of achieving desires: in one word, as a *style*. To assume a possibility, a 'mask' —the mask *(persona)* is the principal means of representing a personal style plastically—had always been the prerogative of chiefs in primitive societies; in this way they could distinguish themselves from the generality of men in the clan, who lived more or less anonymously and did not express personal desires. (In any case, at this stage of evolution the desires are mainly directed towards the fundamental need for food; there exists, therefore, the same relationship between man and the world as between the baby at the breast and its mother.) For the tribal chief, the realization of desire depended above all on a faultless style. A single clumsy, inadequate or abortive word or gesture, and the whole enterprise was doomed to failure, the chief lost his authority and the possibility of expressing his personal desires. Magical rites evolved originally from the transformation of a representative of a clan into a stylized being retaining an inner relationship with the emotional life and psychic structure of the tribesman.

The personality-individual assumed the collective personality of the whole clan by means of style which, in its turn, engendered prohibitions and taboos: it was necessary to prevent the other members of the group from being affected by that dangerous idea which consists in having personal desires. In later civilizations, of course, this arrangement became vulgarized and was reduced to simple imitation: everyone wants a table with tapering or square legs, according to the fashion dictates of the 'chief' in power at the time; the sign becomes an external symbol and style becomes decoration. The tables' intended purpose has not been changed: their ornamental appearance has simply been modified.

Miró's pictures do not represent a lady or a Catalan landscape or some other subject. Yet they are as far removed as possible from abstraction, incarnating as they do unalloyed style: that is to say, the 'mark' of the creator, his magic and personal sign. And this magic world of Miró's, this world of coloured signs, is also a world of objects—but not objects of art like period furniture. The fundamental concept of realistic representation is that the real is formed of objects. But the object has disappeared from modern physics, which sees a whole range of energies and an interplay of continuous happenings as the motivating force of a complex and many-faceted reality. To create a discontinuous order within this continuous whole, to determine and specify a given personality at the very centre of reality's indecision and absolute indetermination, is the real role allotted to personal style. The creator systematizes the outer world in a human sense: he humanizes it truly by imposing his own inner structure and desires upon it.

Miró's disquieting and compelling images spring from the source of that emotional current which we have seen Max Ernst feed with his marvellous malefices. Miró's style of painting, that of the *magus*—if one can schematize it in this way—possesses a fixed, perfected streak of violence; while painting of Ernst's type, that of the *seer*, is in perpetual evolution. The relationship between these two great surrealist painters is almost like the contrast between marvel and prophecy, between miraculous simplicity and divinatory intelligence.

Joan Miró: *Catalan Landscape (The Hunter)*. 1923-1924.

The following story, however, will show the two painters associated, and jointly reproved by their

Joan Miró: *Collage*.
1933.

surrealist friends, as a result of their collaboration in 1926 in the productions of Serge de Diaghilev's Ballets Russes.

The previous year *Le Surréalisme et la Peinture* had, as we have already seen, paid homage to Picasso for his scenic designs for the ballet *Mercure*, and it was Picasso himself who had advised Diaghilev to commission Miró and Ernst to create the decor for another ballet, *Romeo and Juliet*. The project cannot have met initially with any opposition on the part of the surrealists, otherwise the two painters would hardly have accepted the invitation; but no doubt, on reflection, the 'taste for agitation' gained the upper hand. In any case, on the evening of the première (May 18, 1926) at the Théâtre Sarah-Bernhardt, the curtain had scarcely risen when the surrealists, sitting in a group among the audience, began to raise a storm of cries and protests, while leaflets rained down on the astonished theatregoers, asserting that 'the participation of the painters Max Ernst and Joan Miró in the productions of the Ballets Russes by no means implicates Surrealism in such a betrayal of its basic ideas. These ideas are essentially subversive and can never come to terms with such enterprises, whose aim has always been to tame the dreams and rebellions of physical and intellectual hunger in the interests of the international aristocracy'.[1] The demonstration, in fact, had 'revolutionary' intentions, and the participants included certain Communist or fellow-travelling intellectuals who were fairly close to Surrealism at that time.

The confusion soon reached its peak. Yves Tanguy was in the second balcony, in a state of some trepidation—it was his first 'surrealist demonstration' and his plain suit had barred him from the orchestra stalls where the main group and its allies was installed in strength—having been given the task of unfurling a banner bearing the words: LONG LIVE LAUTRÉAMONT! As the banner could not be stretched out at full length some members of the audience got the impression that it read: 'Long live the emperor!' The invectives which Aragon was yelling from a stage-box were lost in the fantastic uproar. Breton, Crevel, Prévert, Pierre de Massot and a number of others blew whistles with all their might. The police, called by the theatre management, were far from gentle in handling the culprits; Jean Bernier, of the review *Clarté*, was beaten up, while Robert Desnos, half-unconscious and with his dinner-jacket shirt front covered in blood, literally flew towards the exit hurled by members of the audience. An individual

1. For the complete text of this tract, signed by Aragon and Breton, see *Documents Surréalistes* (reproduced from *La Révolution Surréaliste*, No. 7).

(who had not wanted to take part in the demonstration) in the December, 1926 issue of *La Révolution Surréaliste* refused haughtily to throw any light on the motives of this new change of front: '*La Révolution Surréaliste* publishes reproductions in this number of two pictures by Max Ernst. Once again it is necessary for us to understand each other, and once again our enemies have to give up the idea of judging us. We can see them sneering, but we can also notice with contempt the ever-growing fear which is disfiguring them. We live in an atmosphere which they cannot breathe. The purest spirits remain with us.'

in evening dress who was encouraging the representatives of law and order was vigorously slapped by Marcel Duhamel, who realized a trifle late that his adversary was a police superintendent with no lack of supporters in the auditorium; the future director of the 'Série Noire'[1] soon found himself in a daze on the pavement of the Place du Châtelet, where he received a final blow from one of the dancers in the ballet company who had craftily positioned himself at the exit to 'greet' the expelled trouble-makers on their way out.

The newspaper *Comoedia* of May 19, 1926 gave the following account of the events: 'An incident at the Ballets Russes.—It was expected that the performance at the Théâtre Sarah-Bernhardt of Mr Constant Lambert's ballet, *Romeo and Juliet* would give rise to demonstrations. These duly occurred. The plot was not directed against the composer, but against the set-designers, MM Max Ernst and Jean Neyro.[2] The surrealists, who have now taken the place of the dadaists, greeted the rise of the curtain with broadsides of whistle-blowing, thus showing that they were only attacking the designers. Sitting together in a compact group, they provoked an uproar which was soon followed by acts of violence. The public reacted vigorously against them. The demonstrators were finally expelled. Calm having been re-established, the work was favourably received.'

The imbroglio was still not resolved. The two 'culprits'—out of town at the time of the incidents—soon returned to favour. A note by Paul Eluard

1. In France, a well-known series of novels of detection and crime, published by Gallimard, whose title *Série Noire* ('Black Series') can also mean 'a chapter of accidents'.

2. *Sic*.

By making far-reaching use of the techniques of *papier collé* and *collage*, Miró produced a most audacious series of pictures and objects in mixed media. Tar-paper or cardboard torn haphazardly, ropes, nails, wire and so on were all utilized in the construction of these extraordinary, definitive—and ephemeral—fetishes. Nothing remains, as far as I know, of the *Portrait of a Dancer* of 1929—a cork pierced by a hat-pin and adorned with a feather, stuck in the middle of a blank canvas—except the canvas itself bearing the artist's signature. And what has become of that *Spanish Dancer*: a profile in cardboard surrounded by a string whose sinuo-

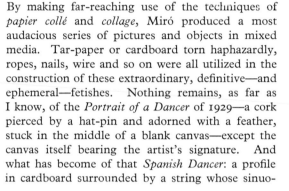

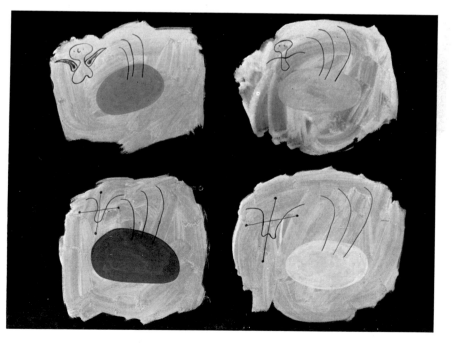

Joan Miró: *Rope and Persons*. 1935

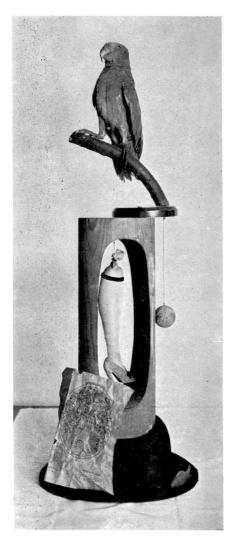

Joan Miró: *Object-Sculpture*. 1936.

Joan Miró: *Spanish Dancer*. 1928.

sity vaguely suggests a *tutu*, resting on a set-square which, one might say, 'stands on tip-toe'? Even less easy to describe is another *Spanish Dancer* consisting essentially of a plumbline. Or his 1931 *Personage*: a plywood board with the edges cut out in the shape of symmetrical scrolls, the sex represented by a wooden log and the nose by a coat-peg, an open umbrella fastened to the 'shoulders', and the whole construction crowned with a bouquet of artificial flowers.

Comical and cruel, gaily and innocently scandalous, Miró's magical style astonishes and convinces like a child's blurted comment.

The village of Locronan, in Finistère, home of the family of Yves Tanguy, is only three leagues distant from the site of the town of Ys, engulfed in the fifth century, so it is said, when the daughter of King

Joan Miró: *Nocturne.*
1938.

159

Gradlon, in a love-pact with the devil, opened with a golden key the flood-gates protecting the city from the sea. Tanguy was born on January 5, 1900 in the buildings of the Ministère de la Marine, place de la Concorde in Paris, where his father, a retired sea-captain, worked in one of its offices. But fairy-tale legends surrounded his birthplace too. There exists an engraving by Méryon, that strange nineteenth-century artist who was certainly something of an alchemist, which might almost be a prophetic view of Tanguy's birthplace: facing the colonnades of the Palais Gabriel in this old print, and higher than the Obelisk's slender gnomon, flying mares, canoes, and sharks ridden by shadowy human forms are poised in mid-air, sweeping in with the clouds from the west. . . .

Yves Tanguy's father had seen his career compromised as a result of his pro-Dreyfus opinions, which he had never attempted to conceal from his immediate superiors at the time of the celebrated Affair; he had consequently been relegated to minor functions and his salary reduced accordingly. So his son had few illusions about the charms of an administrative career, even a maritime one, when, in keeping with family tradition he went to sea in 1918 and sailed to Africa and South America in cargo-ships, as an apprentice officer in the merchant marine. In 1920 harsher fortune befell him when he was conscripted for military service and sent to the 37th Infantry Regiment at Lunéville. Completely disheartened by barracks-life, Tanguy—like Sengle, the hero of Alfred Jarry's Les Jours et les Nuits—very soon turned into a passive deserter of the hypochondriacal variety. Jarry, who was known to drink red ink with his dinner to astonish his eating companions, would not have disapproved of the bad jokes which Tanguy played upon himself, as when he started eating his socks during a morning coffee-break, or when he ate with apparent relish a sandwich with a filling of spiders: less, indeed, to amuse the other recruits than to keep them at a distance. Who can tell to what extremes this role of voluntary plague-victim might have led him, had not Jacques Prévert,[1] inducted into the same regiment, occupied the adjacent bunk in sleeping-quarters? Prévert understood Tanguy's state of mind, and in fact shared it, but his natural gaiety and sense of humour had enabled him to weather the demoralizing horrors of garrison life; these qualities provided a vital tonic for his companion's depression. Maybe the fact that both their families were from

Brittany also helped to cement their friendship. In any case, they soon decided to 'volunteer' for a posting—anywhere, so long as they could get out of Lunéville; this decision had the unexpected result of parting them for a time. Tanguy jumped at the first chance and was soon off to Tunisia. Prévert had his name put down, soon afterwards, for a contingent due to leave for Syria, without pausing to consider that the French mandate had resulted in public disturbances in that country and that, in fact, fighting was going on all over the place. Luckily, the future author of La Bataille de Fontenoy succeeded, just in time, in having himself transferred to Constantinople, which was occupied peacefully at that moment by Allied troops.

The part of Paris which had particularly attracted Tanguy ever since his youth was Montparnasse, named a 'quartier de louftingues' (eccentrics' district) by Apollinaire in his La Femme Assise; he had spent most of his free time there during the war and began to frequent it once again, in Prévert's company, after they were released from military service in 1922. The two young men had become inseparable companions. Neither of them dreamed of writing or painting at that stage, although they made expeditions to bookshops specializing in modern literature—rather than to art galleries, which were still cluttered up with the Post-Fauvism and Sub-Cubism of the École de Paris. One day they came across Les Chants de Maldoror[2] at Adrienne Monnier's bookshop. At the same place, they discovered, a little later, La Révolution Surréaliste, and were enchanted by this new review's violence and richness of expression. They also showed themselves capable of gulping down prodigious quantities of alcohols of all colours at the cafés terrasses.

Since their financial resources were practically nil, they also made an attempt to earn a living —with no success whatever; easy jobs did not come easily to them. Their most extended experience in this field lasted a whole six months, at the 'Courrier de la Presse' agency, from which they were finally dismissed after Prévert had allowed his imagination rather too much freedom in the selection of press-cuttings that he sent to the subscribers. Meanwhile, Tanguy was employed as a broker's runner (he lasted a week), and a tramcar driver, but this career was ended violently after two weeks by

1. Later famous as a poet. His book of poems, Paroles, became a best-seller in France after the last war.

2. By Isidore Ducasse, 'Comte de Lautréamont' (1846-1870). First published in Paris in 1869. An English version by John Rodker appeared in 1924 (Casanova Society, London), and an American version by Guy Wernham in 1943.

Jacques Prévert and Yves Tanguy, Lunéville. 1921.

Marcel Duhamel. 1926.　　　Jacques Prévert in front of the house in the rue du Château. 1925.　　　Yves Tanguy. 1925.

a hay-wagon which the apprentice driver had been unable to avoid. Most of the time, they were faced with complete penury. They were far from attracted by the idea of living with their families, and in any case neither of them could expect much financial assistance from that quarter. Tanguy, whose father had died, and whose mother had returned to Locronan, had no relations in Paris except for a sister with whom he did not get along and a brother whom he detested. Prévert himself has told me how, one winter night, Tanguy was obliged to sleep in a cellar with a raging toothache and nothing to eat but one frozen sausage! He himself was often not much better off.

Meanwhile, Tanguy took to making occasional pencil sketches on the paper table-cloths of Montparnasse cafés, sketches of imaginary people and places whose quality of poetic fantasy did not go unnoticed. The painter Vlaminck, among others, was attracted by these curious drawings and showed them to the art critic Florent Fels who was deeply impressed by them. Tanguy underwent a decisive experience in 1923, on the day when, from the platform of a bus, he caught sight of a picture in the window of Paul Guillaume's gallery in the rue la Boétie which intrigued him so much that he immediately jumped off the moving vehicle and hurried to the display-window: he was looking for the first time at one of Giorgio de Chirico's early paintings. This story has been repeated often,

Yves Tanguy: *La rue de la Santé*. 1925.

with the conclusion that from that day Tanguy resolved to devote himself to painting, without having previously ever touched a paint-

brush in his life. In fact, such a 'resolve' had been taking shape for some time. But no doubt, this first sight of Chirico's work showed him the possibilities inherent in this kind of suddenly revealed poetry, making a lasting impression that was bound to influence gradually his whole artistic development.

The two friends were eventually helped out of their difficulties by Marcel Duhamel, whom Prévert had met in the army, in Constantinople, and who had recently returned to Paris and was currently presiding over the destinies of a Parisian hotel, the Grosvenor, belonging to an uncle of his. Duhamel decided that the best solution to the problems of the moment was to find an apartment where he could invite his friends to share more or less permanent accommodation with him. He thought, too, that Yves might start painting seriously, and Jacques begin to write. So, early in 1924, he rented an ancient but fairly roomy cottage at 54 rue du Château, behind the Gare Montparnasse, and here the three companions installed themselves with their respective girl-friends; this small group was soon augmented by acquaintances in search of provisional lodgings.

Provided with a magnificent supply of artists' materials by Duhamel, Tanguy set himself to painting with great energy and enthusiasm. He painted his first picture on return from a night-time tour of Paris by car with Fels and Duhamel. *La Rue de la Santé* was vigorously constructed in a rather expressionist manner; one can perhaps detect Chirico's influence in, for instance, the ascending perspective of the street dotted with minute figures. A second painting represented a tower rising high up above a vast plain. Then Tanguy painted everything which came into his head: bouquets of flowers, country scenes, and, especially, compositions filled with an inexhaustible fantasy. A *Globe of the World* depicted a circle in which a whole number of scenes, plants, animals and fish were finely worked into the impasto. *La Rue Gibbs* was crossed diagonally by real telegraph wires. *The Portrait of the Artist* included a staircase represented by match-sticks placed one on top of another, being climbed by a figure composed entirely of red and blue arteries and veins; in a corner of the composition was fastened a medallion containing a portrait of the infant Yves. *Lighthouse* shows the same match-stick-staircase and the same anatomical figure, with a cardboard lighthouse and a child's boat of folded paper glued to the canvas. It can be seen that Tanguy preferred to use the

n the 'Prieuré', home of Yves Tanguy's mother in Locronan. In striped jerseys, from left to right: Marcel Duhamel, Pierre Prévert, Yves Tanguy. 1927.

Marriage of Yves Tanguy, at the *mairie* of the 14th arrondissement, Paris. From left to right: Yves Tanguy, Jeannette Tanguy, Marcel Duhamel, Jacques Prévert. 1927.

Yves Tanguy, 1927.

Inside the house in the rue du Château, 1925.

processes of *collage*[1] in their most 'literary' sense, using realistic-humorous substitutes for elements which could equally well have been painted, as did Picabia during the Dada epoch, and Max Ernst in *Two Children Menaced by a Nightingale* (1924), for instance.

The critic Fels considered these productions with sorrow. 'You're finished,' he said to Tanguy, 'you're going to end up a surrealist!' Indeed, the artist and his two companions were becoming increasingly attracted by the surrealist movement. They had met Robert Desnos in Montparnasse, and he kept them informed of the inside activity and public manifestations of the group, he being at that time one of the group's most active participants. And Tanguy had copied out in elegant handwriting on one of the walls of the large sitting-room of their house in the rue du Château Louis Aragon's poem: 'The Tidal Wave.'

The Tidal wave came into the room where the whole
  little family was gathered together
It said Hello everyone and promptly shut their ma up
  in the cupboard
. . . .

The father said to it See here now
But the wave refused to let itself be buggered about
It put a little salt water in the mouth of the unhappy
  progenitor
And the worthy man expired god rest his soul
Then came the turn of the daughters
The first on her knees
The second on her two cheeks
The third like an animal believe me
The fourth the same way
The fifth I shudder with horror and my pen refuses to
  describe such abominations
Lord lord would you be less merciful than these
Ah I was forgetting
The chicken was devoured in its turn
By the wave the ignoble tidal wave.

It was after the notorious affair of the Closerie des Lilas, in 1925, when a literary banquet arranged in honour of Saint-Pol-Roux was well and truly sabotaged by the surrealists, that the three friends decided to get in touch with Breton. An appointment having been made, Yves Tanguy and Marcel Duhamel (Prévert was unable to come for some reason) climbed the stairs to the studio in the rue Fontaine one fine evening, after having called upon

certain 'means of forcing inspiration' which owed nothing to automatic writing. Rather astonished by his guests' volubility, Breton kept them till a late hour; they only separated at about two in the morning, already firm friends. His meeting with Prévert soon afterwards completed a mutual conquest. From then on, the surrealists' friendship caused the inhabitants of the rue du Château to desert the Montparnasse haunts—and, as a result of their adhesion, Surrealism itself experienced a kind of heyday.

The house no longer exists, having been demolished as a result of extensions to the Gare Montparnasse, but 54 rue du Château was one of the main shrines of Surrealism during its heroic epoch. It was not only the focal point for some of the most brilliant painters and poets of the younger generation—nearly all unknown at that time—but it was also a place where a certain way of behaving and living which was far removed from art and literature could be freely indulged in. The whole atmosphere was most agreeable and friendly, with lots of cats playing everywhere and a well-stocked bar carefully supervised and replenished by Duhamel. A strange fetish, discovered by Tanguy in a second-hand shop, glittered with its thirteen enigmatic pearls at one end of an immense table which he had built on the spot and which was so huge that it had to be sawn in half when they wanted to move it from the room later on. On the walls were cinema posters, sign-boards and placards—trophies brought back from nocturnal expeditions—whose inscriptions, out of their element, took on a new significance, amusing or sinister. According to André Breton: 'Surrealism never showed such an organic unity or experienced a greater effervescence than at this period. . . . Absolute non-conformism, total irreverence and also the greatest high spirits reigned at those reunions of ours which were held in the old house in the rue du Château.'

It was at 54 rue du Château that the 'surrealist games' were originally played, the first being that of the *cadavre exquis* ('Exquisite Corpse'), defined later in the *Dictionnaire Abrégé du Surréalisme* as a 'game of paper-folding, which involves the composition of phrases or drawings by several people, without any of the participants having any idea of the preceding contribution or contributions. The classic example, which has given its name to the game, is that of the first sentence obtained in this

1. Jacques Prévert was not writing a line at that period but made a number of *collages*, of which only a very few have survived.

Yves Tanguy: *Water-table*. 1929.

Yves Tanguy: *Genesis*. 1926.

way: "the exquisite—corpse—shall drink—the young —wine".

Beginning by being a mere amusement, this game (which is not very different from party-games such as 'Consequences') became, by reason of the many variations of which it was capable, a sort of revelatory indicator of the group's 'mental-emotional state'. The written or drawn contributions achieved a remarkable and unforeseen homogeneity; the vitality, the viability, even, of the hybrid beings thus formed was as great as that of individual creations. It even seemed that the imagination of a single individual could not have achieved so powerful a degree of disorientation, nor so organic a unity and logic in the welding together of disparate and illogical elements.

The first 'Exquisite Corpse' drawings were published in No. 9-10 of *La Révolution Surréaliste* (October, 1927), their authors remaining anonymous, as also were the authors of a series of sentences composed according to a similar system: 'The winged mist seduces the locked bird,' 'The oyster from Senegal will eat the tricoloured bread' and so on. The special issue of the review *Variétés*, 'Surrealism in 1929', reproduced new collective drawings with the authors' names indicated: Joan Miró, Max Morise, Man Ray, Yves Tanguy; and it reproduced also the results of a game of 'hypotheses and consequences' (the participants are identified in the review by their initials). 'S.M. : When the capital letters start nagging the small letters,—E.P. : the exclamation marks will no longer have much meaning. A.M. : If Poincaré died, –J.T. : I would bathe in the sea and become a swallow.—B.P. : If orchids grew in the palm of my hand,—A.B.: the masseurs would really have something to deal with.—S.M. : If your shadow's shadow visited a hall of mirrors,—A.B. : the sequel would be indefinitely postponed to the following issue.—P.U. : The day one raises a statue to the association of ideas,—L.A. : the angel of the bizarre will invent the art of billiards.—Y.T. : The day that children start slapping their fathers,—A.B. : young people will all have white hair...'[1]

The 'surrealist games' were considerably extended

later on: various versions of 'questions and answers', the game of truth (which served as an excuse for innumerable discussions and quarrels), a 'word of mouth' game, a game of 'murderers' and still others were played, at the same time as the 'Exquisite Corpse' game in its various forms, until the outbreak of the Second World War.

Tanguy's evolution after meeting the surrealists can be followed in the pages of *La Révolution Surréaliste*, which published reproductions of his work in No. 7 (June 15, 1926) and subsequent issues. The first of his pictures reproduced is still based on the processes of *collage* and graphic fantasy of his earliest paintings, and the human—or rather, anthropomorphic—figure and animals remain the most important subjects (see also *Lost Animals* in *La Révolution Surréaliste*, No. 8). But Tanguy was soon to abandon anecdote and interiorize his vision. He adapted the lessons of automatism with a growing mastery, in the sense that he allowed his painting to grow like a plant and to bloom slowly until the point of perfection was reached. He adopted various means of painting 'blind': for instance, he painted some of his pictures with the canvas upside down so that he might experience the surprise of his own creation when he placed the picture the right way up again.

Henceforward, the beautiful milky, sparkling light of Tanguy's pictures begins to spread out like an aurora, a light in which grey predominates, and the shades are all blue-grey with infinitely subtle transitions. The earth and the sky blend together in waves surging one on top of the other. Sometimes his use of *grattage* is reminiscent of Max Ernst or Klee, but its development in his work has always a subtle personal quality. A smear, a stain, a slashed line justify their involuntary existence by the magic of a shadow or reflection which adds the essential finishing touch. The brushstrokes in this flowing colour conjure up storms and create rainbows. Already, the reproductions of his painting *Second Message* and of a drawing in *La Révolution Surréaliste* No. 9 (October, 1927) gave some indication of the haunting images central to his work, objects with an appearance and shape that are at the same time familiar and unknown. But the horizons of Yves Tanguy's world really opened up with the painting reproduced in the eleventh issue of the review (March, 1928) in which organic shapes project a hard, thick shadow,

1. S.M.: Suzanne Muzard. E.P.: Elise Péret. A.B.: André Breton. J.T. : Jeannette Tanguy. B.P. : Benjamin Péret. L.A.: Louis Aragon. P.U.: Pierre Unik. Y.T.: Yves Tanguy. For other examples see *Histoire du Surréalisme* by Maurice Nadeau (Éditions du Seuil, Paris, 1945). The commentaries on the 'Exquisite Corpse' and 'Questions and answers' games in *Histoire du Surréalisme* (pp. 277 and 279) are by André Breton and first appeared anonymously in *La Révolution Surréaliste*, No. 9-10 (1927) and No. 11 (1928), as well as in *Variétés* (1929).

Yves Tanguy at the
Ile de Sein, 1930.

But it is just such art, so instinctive and yet so
assured, so naïve in the most authentic sense of
the word, that lends itself most directly to reflection.

The concept of cycles of civilization is one of man's
most ancient approaches to time. The Egyptians
and Hindus both shared a theory according to
which the world develops from a fixed beginning
to an absolute end, determined throughout by
cyclical laws. At the close of a particular period
Nothingness resumes its universal reign. But the
creative cycle recommences after this phase of
non-existence and, thus, creation and annihilation
follow each other through eternity. Buddhism, in
its northern school, reaffirms this doctrine by assign-
ing a Buddha to each period of creation.

Such a concept differs essentially from the
European idea of time. In western thought, time
is comparable to an infinite straight line which any
actual moment of time, moving along this straight
line at a uniform speed, invariably cuts into two
equal parts: past and future. The Hindu time-
concept could better be compared to a spiral line;
each happening is destined to take place at a precise
moment and repeat itself thereafter according to an
invariable order.

The idea of a cyclical universe includes that of
the return of the seasons, and explains man's
attachment to the earth, to that *Magna Mater* who
nourishes her children, the world of living beings,
according to well-established rhythms. 'Mothers!
We share Faust's terror, we too experience an
electric shock at the very sound of these syllables
that conceal powerful goddesses not subject to
time or place',[3] primordial beings who engender
each new being. With Tanguy, the Mother symbol
becomes something very real, just as the idea of
the Mother is represented in the new-born child by
an entirely material image of nourishment.

People believe—Tanguy never made much effort
to share this belief—that in order to survive one
must 'earn one's living', exchange some merchandise against money so that the money may in turn
be transformed into whatever one needs to exist.
Commerce is founded on the belief that one can
truly *live* by this abstract activity: Tanguy always
understood that man really exists in terms of colours.
Some people think that colours themselves are

strongly reminiscent of Chirico, on to misty veils
that are living things as well as symbols, earth as
much as smoke. Some of the first paintings in this
definitive style of his are: *Mama, Papa is Wounded!*
(1927), *The Agreement* (1928), *Your Tapers
Taper ('Tes bougies bougent')* (1929) and *Inspiration*
(1929).

If the creation of a new vision as a more all-
embracing synthesis of reality necessarily involves
also a return to a primitive vision springing from the
profound recesses of man's soul, this corollary must
be especially applicable to Yves Tanguy's painting.
Discussing Tanguy's picture *Ancient Horizon*,
André Breton wrote in *Le Surréalisme et la Peinture*[1]: 'The potential expansion of an artist's
imagination is closely related to the variety of
cosmic phenomena.' And Tanguy himself has
said: 'I expect nothing from reflection, but I have
full confidence in my reflexes.'[2]

1. In 'Genesis and Perspectives of Surrealism'.
2. Quoted from the catalogue to an exhibition of surrealist
drawings in December, 1935 at the Galerie des Quatre
Chemins, Paris.

3. André Breton: *Le Surréalisme et la Peinture* ('What
Tanguy Veils and Reveals').

Yves Tanguy: *The Ribbon of Extremes*. 1932.

Yves Tanguy: *Ennui and Tranquillity*. 1938.

merely a merchandise that can be bought, or represent some other abstract, intellectualized element. But if Tanguy's namesake, *le Père* Tanguy, who used to earn his living selling artists' colours, is still remembered today it is because Van Gogh painted his portrait: colours are magical things and can change into life and into living works of art. Some people think that pictures are composed according to abstract rules and thanks to the artist's abstract reflections: Tanguy was convinced that, to a great extent, pictures are the product of colours. In Tanguy's work, the basic quality of his colour is a sort of milky consistency. His universe is that of primitive man or the child, a universe as edible as the gingerbread palace that can be found in infinite variations in children's songs throughout the world.

Grown-ups are rather frightened to identify the idea of the Earth with that of the Mother, since this mother can be extremely cruel towards her sons. But, despite bitter experience, people still cherish the secret hope of reconciling their inner desires with the glacial hardness of reality. And if the Egyptians worshipped the scarab as a god, it was perhaps because this insect represented for them the symbol of a possible reconciliation. Between the sacred scarab's legs, the ball in which it will deposit its eggs gradually assumes the appearance of a sphere. As it rolls along, each part of the sphere, having reached the lowest level, ascends once again in an endless repetition. If one considers that the matter of which the scarab's ball is composed, and upon which the larvae will feed so as to reach the status of perfect insects, is already the lowest level of another cycle, one can understand the importance that the Egyptians attached to the symbol of the Scarab. The circle of life rises and descends, life sets out unceasingly on its new journey in a different circle: the Egyptian sages saw in the Scarab's ball a counterpart of the earth as well as the microcosm of the sky's transparent, superposed canopies.

The phrase *Milky Way* is an exact designation of our Cosmos, but it equally expresses the same ancestral desire as the symbols of the Great Mother or the Scarab. This is perhaps a secret truth which few people have been privileged to discern: Yves Tanguy had an instinctive perception of the fact. When asked to contribute to a new illustrated edition of *Les Chants de Maldoror*,[1] he immediately chose as his theme the 'scarab stanza', and this choice, or rather the impulse which made this particular passage the inevitable choice, may be seen as a conjunction of the ancient symbols of the Scarab and the Milky Way: that is to say, the Earth and the galaxy of which it is one of the molecules.

Yves Tanguy: *The Glance of Amber.* 1929.

Tanguy's paintings place us inside a globe swelling with milk, at the centre of a huge maternal breast. The horizon, which was carefully distinguished in his early paintings (although the milky texture and colour of sky and earth were identical), gradually disappears; soon the earth no longer possesses clearly defined frontiers but blends continuously into the sky. Transition is constant, opposition and

1. Editions G.L.M., Paris, 1937.

contest disappear, and we enter into the realm of Perfection.

Tanguy painted his pictures with industrious patience and an extraordinary and almost miserly care as far as the material means were concerned. He was known to regret the fact that he could not put the unused colours back into their tubes; his palette was always kept meticulously clean, and his studio, painted in an immaculate white, was strictly empty apart from the easel and the canvas meet and where opposites become identical, 'where a feather weighs as much as a lead bullet, where everything can fly as easily as it can bury itself in the ground, where the most irreconcilable objects can confront each other without disaster'.[1] And here is the point where the Mother is one with the Earth, and the Earth becomes a nebulous spiral, where the organic is ultimately inorganic and dawn resembles high noon or the midnight sun. Tanguy's pictures are lit by the aurora borealis, his beings are

Yves Tanguy: *Your Tapers Taper*. 1929.

in process of execution. In this atmosphere he created his rounded, delicate shapes, so full of warmth and life; then he placed them inside another huge sphere. The sky of Tanguy's world is the Milky Way.

Here, then, is a man who really placed himself at the exact point where the most dissimilar elements living and crystalline, and his landscapes are astral, or submarine. His work achieves an infinite recreation of forms and their arrangements (is one leaf ever like another leaf, or a tree like another tree?) and, at the same time, possesses a basic uniformity

1. A. Breton: *Le Surréalisme et la Peinture*, in his essay on Yves Tanguy.

172

Yves Tanguy :
Gouache. 1936.

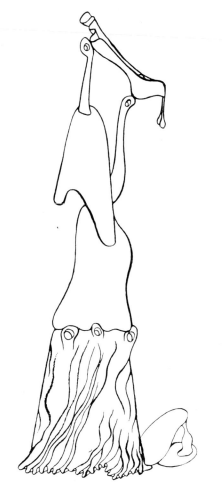

as an unavoidable consequence of Perfection which is the ultimate unity resulting from a complete synthesis, attained by a reciprocal assimilation of all existing things.

Reality becomes at the same time extremely simple and extremely complex. And at this magical point where all contradictions are resolved and all desires fulfilled, man finds himself once again at the beginning of his life and his cycle of existence. Even the vital act of eating is at the same time extremely complex and extremely simple. The various senses—of distance, as hearing, vision and smell, of nearness, as touch and taste—melt into an undifferentiated unity. Nourishment is an external object, but loses this exteriority as a result of the human being's assimilative activity. The frontiers between the external and the internal are in fact obliterated.

Tanguy's infallible reflexes have accompanied the development of reality to the very summit where everything is well-wrought and perfect, finally resembling beach shingles or the candy decorating the witch's succulent palace. In some of his early work, Chirico used to reproduce scrupulously the appearance of those sweetmeats which he doted on as a child. But Tanguy's painting is *all* nourishment: one can call it truly *materialist*, because appearance and existence are identified therein in a total functional unity. It is Perfection because it contains all and at the same time possesses the solution of everything that it contains. It is the Ideal identical to the Assimilable.

Yves Tanguy: Drawing for *Cri de la Méduse*, by Henri Pastoureau. 1937.

'Exquisite Corpses'.

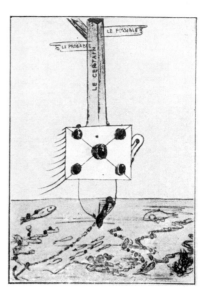

1927.

1927.

c. 1930. By André Breton, Tristan Tzara, Valentine Hugo, Greta Knutson.

174

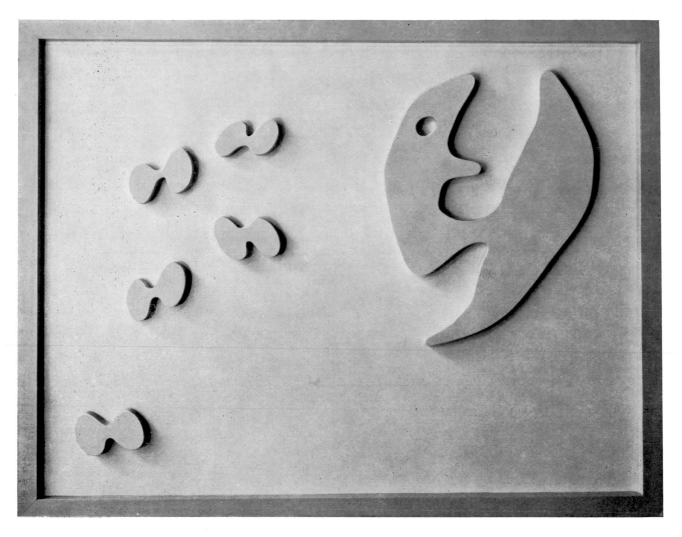

Jean Arp: *Head and Bow-ties.* 1929.

Jean Arp, too, has created a body of work that seems to contain a great proportion of happiness in the shape of realized desire. Like Tanguy and Miró, and even before they started painting, Arp discovered the perfection of that suppleness, vivacity and hardness inherent in those forms subject to the gentle erosion which time imposes upon objects in nature. He was the first to create these truly celestial worlds which we have seen Miró and Tanguy bring to life according to their own personal visions. Arp's reliefs are—according to the titles of some of them—*Navels*: the organ of nutrition in the warm darkness of prenatal life, as is indicated by the French word for navels, *nombrils*, which suggests the word *ombres* (darkness) and also the word *nombres* (numbers). Indeed, we may consider these reliefs to be subject to the law of numbers, and so constellations belonging naturally to the Milky Way. The similarity between the forms in so many works by Arp, Miró, and Tanguy is very striking; but basically they are simply similar universes discovered individually, separately and instinctively by each artist.

Jean Arp returned from Zurich in 1926. Weary of his bellicose native countries, he had tried unsuccessfully to become a Swiss citizen: no doubt his naturalization dossier carried the stigma of all the bohemian eccentricities of the Cabaret Voltaire, and Arp had to remain an Alsatian. But the surrealist movement quite naturally adopted him at once. *La Révolution Surréaliste* published reproductions of his new Reliefs: 'Still lives' such as *Table, Mountain, Anchor and Navel*; *Paolo and Francesca*; *Comma*; and *Endless Moustache*.

René Magritte: *Perpetual Motion.* 1934.

In René Magritte's work may be found, as with so many other exponents of pictorial Surrealism, the dual influence of Dada and Chirico. It is true that Dada had remained almost entirely unnoticed in Magritte's native Belgium. Only Clément Pansaers had incarnated the dadaist spirit in brilliant poem-pamphlets illustrated by himself: *Bar Nicanor*, *Le Pan-pan au Cul du Nu Nègre*, etc, and he had died young, in 1922, leaving no followers in his own country. René Magritte and his friend E.L.T. Mesens first encountered Dadaism through its adherents in Paris. During visits to Paris in 1921, Mesens had made friends with Tristan Tzara and had got to know Philippe Soupault and Georges Ribemont-Dessaignes. He occasionally met Marcel Duchamp who by then was already concerning himself far more with chess tournaments than with artistic and literary battles; he also met Picabia, and Erik Satie in whose company he visited Man Ray's first exhibition at the Librairie Six. Mesens was a poet[1] who was at that time devoting himself to musical composition, writing melodies for modern poems: among others, Soupault's *Garage* was published in 1921 in Brussels with music by Mesens. Subsequently, when he came to read the Chirico manuscript belonging to Paul Eluard,[2] its call for 'no music' influenced him powerfully enough to make him give up musical composition altogether.

René-François-Ghislain Magritte was born on November 28, 1898 at Lessines, in the province of Hainault. His first childhood memory was the sight of men in helmets: soldiers who had arrived to take away the gas-bag of an observation balloon that had come to grief on the roof of his parents' house, dragging the enormous partly-deflated skin

1. E.L.T. Mesens: *Poèmes* (1923-1958), Editions du Terrain Vague, Paris, 1959.

2. See above, p. 54.

down the stairs and through the courtyard. In 1912 the family suffered a tragic drama: Mme Magritte became nervously depressed and committed suicide by throwing herself into the River Sambre at Châtelet. The following year, René Magritte met at a fair-ground in Charleroi, a young girl, Georgette, who was to become his wife.

Until 1918 he studied at the Brussels Academy of Fine Arts. Then in 1922 he got married and, to gain his living, had to take a job as a designer in a wall-paper factory where he spent the whole day turning out bouquets of cabbage-roses destined for the adornment of Belgian living-room walls. He then attempted various other equally boring jobs which involved drawing advertising publicity sketches. He spent his free hours painting. For a time he practised abstractionism together with Victor

Servranckx whom he had met during the wallpaper period. Meanwhile, Mesens was bringing back pamphlets and reviews from his visits to Paris which he showed to a circle of young people grouped around Magritte and himself: Philippe Soupault's

René Magritte: *The Migrant Angel*. 1926.

Westwego was one of the first ambassadors in Brussels of the new poetry. The *collages* of Max Ernst made a strong impression on Magritte as soon as he first saw the illustrations to Paul Eluard's *Malheurs des Immortels*. In 1922, Magritte painted a picture which he entitled *Portrait of Pascal*: a naked figure with immense pale blue eyes, seen from the waist up, the torso a dark ochre colour —a phantom curiously reminiscent of the one with closed eyes in *The Child's Brain*, a picture which Magritte had not yet seen. It was only some months later that he was first able to see one of Chirico's compositions. He came across a reproduction of *Love Song* in an issue of the review *Les Cahiers Libres*: the head of a statue with blind eyes staring skywards, lying beside a red rubber glove in front of the arcades of an Italian square.

But the review *Oesophage* with its motto: 'Hop là! Hop là!', which Mesens and Magritte brought out in 1925, was chiefly impregnated by the spirit of Picabia. Its single number was followed by three issues of *Marie*, 'a fortnightly newspaper for glamorous youth' to which some of the Paris dadaists contributed. The tone of these reviews, especially that of *Oesophage* which reproduced some anti-Breton cartoons by Picabia taken from *391*, was extremely non-committal towards those who were just beginning to form the surrealist movement in France. Independently, Marcel Lecomte, Camille Goemans (later the director of the first gallery devoted to surrealist painting) and Paul Nougé had made contact with the Paris group; they were publishing monthly tracts in Brussels under the general title *Correspondance*, of which about twenty appeared, all polemical-philosophical in character and written for the most part in a terribly obscure style. However, the two groups soon joined forces. 'The real problem for us,' Mesens has written,[1] 'was to intervene in as many spheres as possible of human activity, of *life*. As did the French surrealists, we met together not only to put the others to the test but to test ourselves as well.' In October, 1926, in fact, official contact was made in Paris between Mesens and the French surrealist group, with Louis Aragon acting as intermediary.

Very few of Magritte's early paintings remain today. The *Portrait of Pascal* has been destroyed, but 'one can recall,' writes a biographer, 'the silhouette of a woman with a rose in place of her

René Magritte, Georgette Magritte, and E.L.T. Mesens, 1922.

heart, and another woman imprisoned by immovable screens.'[1] Magritte has said[2] that he 'found his first real painting in 1924: it represented a window seen from inside a room. On the other side of the window, a hand seems to be trying to grasp a flying bird.' Then he painted white, naked figures with empty eyes, or strangely shaped torsos, or solitary hands, evoking Chirico's favourite themes, and the 'tragic aspect of statuary' to which that artist alludes in his essay on Böcklin. Even Magritte's treatment of architectural elements tends to suggest 'the metaphysical meanings of perspective' which Chirico described in his study on Courbet. We can see a distant but precise echo of *Love Song* as recently as 1948 in the painting entitled *Memory*, in which the forehead of a marble bust standing on a window-ledge is welling blood.

From 1926 onwards, Magritte was able to devote himself entirely to painting, thanks to the support of the Brussels gallery 'Le Centaure'. In August 1927 the artist went to Paris (returning to Brussels in 1930) and began to take part in the life of the Parisian group. He lived in the suburbs, at Perreux-sur-Marne, working hard and producing during the course of a single year about sixty pictures, including some very large ones: a remarkable accomplishment, if we consider that each of his paintings represents *an idea*.

Other painters have sought to achieve surrealist disorientation by means of 'derangement', by modifying usual pictorial procedures and traditions in order to provoke and then transcribe the appearance of hallucinatory scenes. These painters have created new worlds and new beings in an unknown atmosphere. The voice of reason could, as a result, very easily deny any validity to these universes, while science, in its turn, rejected them in terms of its own statutory, precise world. But Magritte's pictures, painted with an absolute modesty of means, painstakingly executed, conscientiously coloured scenes that are not even naïve, resembling school-book diagrams or technical illustrations, are at the same time curiously disturbing riddles. And any attempt to decipher their cryptic meanings soon involves one's conscious and reasoning mind in a self-induced disorientation.

1. E.L.T. Mesens: 'The Apprentice Magicians in the Land of Plethora', in *Le Fantastique dans l'Art Belge*, special number of the French review *Les Arts Plastiques* (June, 1954).

1. Louis Scutenaire, in a study of Magritte published in Anvers, Belgium, 1948.

2. In the autobiography which appeared in *René Magritte* (Editions de la Connaissance, Brussels, 1954).

René Magritte: *The Human Condition.* 1934.

René Magritte: *The Rape.* 1934.

Variétés, no. 8, 1929.

Dictionnaire Abrégé du Surréalisme. 1938.

Variétés, no. 8, 1929.

Une forme quelconque peut remplacer l'image d'un objet :

Un objet ne fait jamais le même office que son nom ou que son image :

Or, les contours visibles des objets, dans la réalité, se touchent comme s'ils formaient une mosaïque :

Les figures vagues ont une signification aussi nécessaire aussi parfaite que les précises :

Parfois, les noms écrits dans un tableau désignent des choses précises, et les images des choses vagues :

Ou bien le contraire :

René MAGRITTE,

La Révolution Surréaliste, no. 12, 1929.

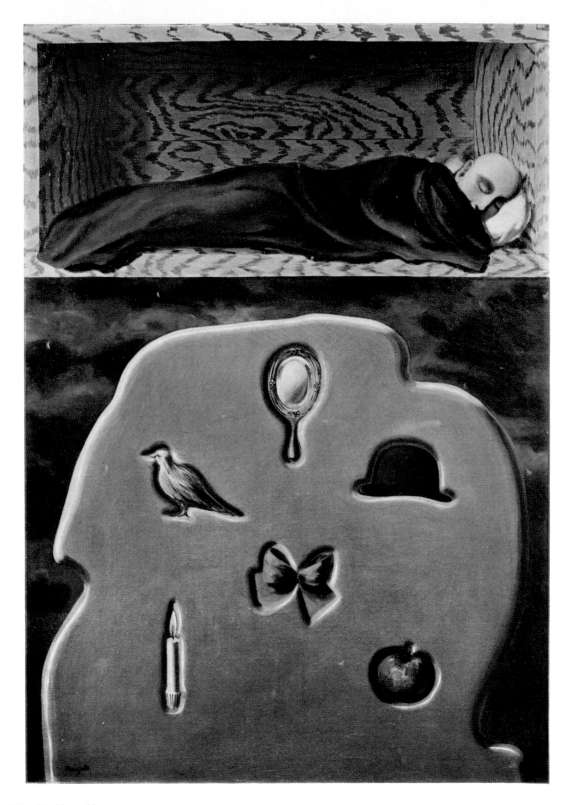

René Magritte: *The Reckless Sleeper*. c. 1930.

Clement of Alexandria, following the Gospel according to Matthew and the Greek philosophers, has said that the beginning of knowledge is *admiration*. At least the word *thaumazein* has been translated in this sense, although it can also mean *terror*. Admiration and terror would seem to be fairly far apart as concepts; nevertheless, in terms of the psychological mechanisms which they each release, they are not so dissimilar. Admiration is an attitude which tends eventually to go beyond the admirative process, and thus in a certain sense encompasses its own annihilation; terror can be defined in identical terms. In general it is difficult to bear the feelings of admiration or terror over a long period of time. Like needs or desires, they have somehow to be suppressed or fulfilled.

Knowledge would seem to be the means of satisfying these strange, compulsive desires. In this light, the development of the sciences appears as the specific reaction to a certain class of stimulants: a rather more complex reaction, certainly, than the reflex movements of the amoeba. In order to neutralize the admirable and terrifying desires that we feel in the heart of our miraculous universe, the sciences have developed a whole mass of explanatory systems, kinds of intellectual vaccines; among these venerable arcana, precision has shown itself in recent times to be one of the most effective. The sciences have thus become remarkable means of disillusionment, and with the aid of their openly flourished weapons some people have even claimed to have put paid to a great number of appearances evoking admiration or terror: the gods, for example, or the neuroses. We have become pretty well accustomed by now to this *virtus antidormitiva*, as a modern Molière might say.[1]

Such a state of affairs is, however, challenged by artistic activity, which possesses among other functions that of ceaselessly creating well-springs of knowledge, both admirable and terrifying (although works of art are in principle inexhaustible springs, it still seems that—contrary to all the laws of physics—the vitality of the ancient springs depends in this instance on that of the newly discovered springs). Reason dogs the steps of art with its measuring instruments, attempting to canalize methodically the disquieting torrents with which art nourishes man's spirit despite all obstacles. This eternal steeplechase, this relatively pacific

competition, has no application to René Magritte. One gets the impression that he has determined to fight reason with its own weapons.

Reason is the daemon of the Immutable Laws, the guardian angel of the Absolute. Everything it touches becomes determinate, coming within the scope of an unambiguous order that is utterly different from that indeterminate world in which man plunges into experiments with only his senses and his fantasies to keep him afloat. But Magritte tries to reduce the opposition between the rational on one side and the irrational (in both its fantastic and concrete aspects) on the other. His pictures resemble images of dreams—the dreams of reason—for dreams can sometimes possess a frightening precision. Is it really healthy to seek the alleviation of such sensations? Are these not on the contrary excellent means of putting life to the proof, our own lives even? Magritte has proved that precision, far from being an arcanum of alleviation, is on the contrary a powerful means of renewing the well-springs of admiration and terror.

These paintings imply a rationally conceived ulterior motive, through which, by inverse function, they destroy the possibility of being destroyed by reasoning: it is something like the disillusionment of disillusionment. The artist does not seek a miracle by miraculous means, by automatism or by mechanical techniques: he simply confines himself to the structure of the human soul as philosophy or text-books of psychology describe it. Our head, with our brain, is one object among others; yet this is perhaps the one that creates all the other objects in the world: it has been argued that these other objects have no real existence except in so far as our brain itself exists. Does our brain perceive objects, or does it conceive them? A curious problem, which discussion has by no means resolved as yet. To achieve a surrealist picture, that is to say one with a tremendous power of disorientation, Magritte had only to translate this situation into images.

The picture which is called, naturally enough, *Perpetual Motion* shows a figure holding up a dumb-bell at head level; one of the dumb-bell's two balls constitutes the figure's own head. Thus the world is only an extension of what is taking place inside one's head. But the interpretation might be reversed: our brain would then be only an extension of an exterior and truly real world (in which case one might well consider that a champion weight-lifter is bound to be a bit of a dumb-bell!).

But let us be quite clear about it: if it is true that

---

1. Cf. Molière: *Le Malade Imaginaire...* '*Cur opium facit dormire?*' '*Quia est in eo virtus dormitiva quae facit dormire,*' a question and answer which have come to symbolize all scientific explanations which explain nothing....

René Magritte: *The Annunciation*. 1929.

the images we record are of a real exterior world, then this reality immediately divides into two; there is the real world and the world of images. But there is a third reality, which is the relation between the real and its image, and a fourth, the relation of this relation.... This division into two can go on endlessly in this way, like two mirrors placed face to face. We have already encountered the first stage of this horrific labyrinth, created by the indefinite repetition of one single structure, in the work of Giorgio de Chirico, with his 'picture within a picture' effects. Another picture by Magritte illustrates this new situation. *The Human Condition*, of 1934 (again, the title is exactly adapted to the subject), represents a picture in a landscape of which it reproduces one of the details. The picture is placed in the landscape in such a manner that it covers and replaces the real detail with absolute exactitude. The picture and the picture within the picture, reality and its image, are blended in a simple and multiple unity. *The Human Condition* is surely as admirable as *Perpetual Motion* and just as terrifying. 'Hebdomeros opened his window wide on to the spectacle of life, on to the world's scene. But he had to wait, because it was still only a dream, and even a dream within a dream.'

perched on her shoulder. *Revolution* (1928) shows a canvas on an easel, depicting simply white clouds in a blue sky.

André Breton wrote in 1941, in 'Genesis and Perspective of Surrealism': 'Magritte's procedure, not automatic, but entirely deliberate, supports Surrealism from 1929 onwards.' No. 12 of *La Révolution Surréaliste* had reproduced Magritte's picture puzzle, *I do not See the — Hidden in the*

René Magritte: *The Storm.* 1933.

Eulogy of Dialectics (1937) represents the façade of a house, with one window open, through which can be seen, inside the room, the same façade with all the windows closed. In *Threatening Weather* (1928), three gigantic objects are floating, as well-defined and misty as storm clouds, above a marine horizon—a woman's torso, a musical instrument and a chair. *Black Magic* (1934) is a woman painted in white, with the blank eyes of a statue, a dove

Forest, surrounded by photographs of the members of the group, all with their eyes closed. (This may also be taken as a tribute to the early Chirico.)[1]

During this period, Magritte revived the idea of pictures with inscriptions: the object and its name inscribed on the canvas present a violent contrast of meaning. Two shapeless blobs are

1. See p. 54: 'There is only what I see with my eyes open and even better closed.'

called respectively 'the wind' and 'Normandy': the whole picture is called *Word Usage*. In *The Key to Dreams*, an egg is 'the acacia', a shoe 'the moon', image, an object meets its name. It can happen that the image and the name of this object meet' (the drawing shows a forest on one side, and on the

René Magritte: *Threatening Weather.* 1928.

a hat 'the snow', a candle 'the ceiling', a glass 'the storm', a hammer 'the desert'. 'Certain objects need no name,' wrote Magritte in *La Révolution Surréaliste*, No. 12, giving illustrations in support of his claim. 'Sometimes a name serves only to describe itself' (the drawing represents the word: sky). '...One sees images and words differently in a picture' (a flower upon which is written the word: mountain). '... An object meets its

other the word: forest). 'It seems probable that there is little connection between an object and what represents it' (two identical houses, one entitled: the real object, the other: the represented object; this is the concept above analyzed in reference to *The Human Condition*). 'An object never performs the same functions as its name or its image' (a horse—a picture representing a horse—a person pronouncing the word: horse).

186

'... Sometimes, the names written in a picture designate precise things, and the images vague things' (the word: cannon, beside an indistinct scribble) 'or else the contrary' (the word: fog, designates an ink-well).

What remains of words and their concepts, and of concepts and their words, after the diabolical Magritte has passed by? Among all the philosophers, it must be admitted that the only one to grasp the essential truth was the pataphysician Jarry: the universe is truly that which is the exception to oneself.

In May, 1928 a review appeared in Belgium which, for two years, gave proof of the international expansion of the surrealist movement: *Variétés*, founded by P.G. Van Hecke with Mesens as one of the editors, called itself an 'illustrated monthly review of contemporary thought'. This magazine aimed at being eclectic to some extent, dealing with sport, fashion, events of the day, music, novels and theatre, as well as avant-garde painting and poetry: but the 'contemporary thought' which it revealed was, above all, Surrealism. Distributed throughout Europe, the review played an important role in the diffusion of surrealist ideas and images. Its pages featured drawings by Magritte or his imitators (Marc Eemans, Auguste Mambour), and it published Mesens' first *collages*. In 1929, *Variétés* published a special issue, under the direction of the Paris group, devoted entirely to Surrealism. One of the main attractions of this review lay in its very numerous photographic reproductions showing the work of the new school of painting, but it also followed the example of *La Révolution Surréaliste* by illustrating the theme of disorientation from many different angles: antiquated photographs, comic photographs, mysterious photographs; Man Ray's first emulators revealed 'unappreciated landscapes' (suburbs, yards, rooftops, etc).

Picasso's work first started revealing specifically surrealist influences in about 1927. From this period derive the sketches for 'Crucifixions' (which recall only very distantly the celebrated theme: the cross which was the instrument of the divine agony seems to have interested the artist more than the Saviour himself, whose face is reduced to the

size of a pin-head) in which the interlacing graphic line has affinities with Arp's Reliefs and Miró's arabesques. For comparison with the Crucifixions, see, for example, *Hand Catching a Bird, Nude*, etc, painted by Miró in 1926, and other earlier pictures by the same artist. Was it a matter of influence or of chance when Picasso followed Miró in constructing objects with the aid of nails, planks and huge cords? And those 'Heads' and 'Figures' made from very simple, 'childish' visual symbols: an almond marked with a single point for the eye, a dotted line or a straight line crossed with downward strokes for the mouth, a few parallel lines for the hair, and so on, the whole figure encircled by an undulating outline passing over coloured flat-tints? The markings are distributed extremely casually, but the faces seem alive even when the mouth is placed at the top of the head or when a single figure has three eyes.[1]

The surrealist aspect of Picasso's work continued to grow in importance from that time onwards. In July, 1928, the 'Dinard period' began with drawings representing projects for monumental sculptures. These drawings had been preceded, during a time when the artist was staying in Cannes, by charcoal sketches for sculpted groups which Picasso saw in his imagination as being put up all along the promenade de la Croisette. At Dinard he took up these themes once more, in pen sketches that proposed multiple variations (published for the first time in the review *Cahiers d'Art* at the end of 1929) of groups of imposing forms, as slender and firm as living flesh, new 'Scaffoldings' surmounted by small spheres pierced by sockets that look, listen and speak, worked out with a *trompe-l'œil* technique and bathed in an atmosphere which deepens Chirico's and Böcklin's sense of mystery.

With these amazing imaginary statues, Picasso's genius seems to have transformed the dejection of the mannequins of Chirico's later period (1925-26), those sad, monumental figures set up on the shores of misty oceans, into a genuinely apocalyptic tragic quality. The finely and impetuously interlaced pen-strokes create deep, menacing shadows in which hard lights gleam. Sometimes the ghost of an arcade forms a dark hollow in the background; sometimes, in a 'literary' effect deriving authentically from Chirico, a cast shadow signals the presence of a being *outside* the picture: the shadow is that of a 'real' personage, but the monstrous

1. André Breton says in 'Genesis and Perspective of Surrealism': 'It can be said that Miró's influence on Picasso... was to a large extent a determining one.'

edifice contemplating it is more alive and more real than the shadow of the real.

Then the pen drawings gave place to pictures which their titles termed Bathers, though they

Pablo Picasso: Drawing. 1928.

are more like tripods or peculiarly constructed footbridges, sometimes holding a perfectly normal key at the end of an appendage, about to open the door of a beach-cabin. During this same period the artist produced a series of brightly coloured small paintings, also called Bathers, but consisting this time of forms with the undulating, creased contours of sheets flapping in the wind; while all the sculpture-paintings which have sometimes been called 'Metamorphoses' are painted in the greyish tints appropriate to dreams and apparitions. Against the background of a sketched in, half-suggested reality, a vaguely cloudy sky and the appearance of a beach, his tragic, dreaming Eves, hardly existing as yet, prepare to disintegrate and fashion themselves anew according to other combinations of spindles, spheres and frameworks which Picasso seems to have copied from nature—a purely inner nature.... For instance, *On the Beach* (1928), *Woman*, *Woman with a Veil*, *Bather with Arms Raised* 1929, etc.

When the artist reverted once more to his Ingres-inspired manner, it was to abandon classical pastoral scenes in favour of a new liberty of expression exemplified in his engravings for Ovid's *Metamorphoses*. (This work illustrated by Picasso was one of the first enterprises of the Swiss editor Albert Skira.) His entire artistic production changed, gaining a fresh energy. He had forged metal struts and stays to support the absurd limbs of his imagined statues; now the frameworks themselves began to grow into statues, intertwined with the creepers of gigantic philodendrons. They seem to grow with the plant and from the plant; or is it perhaps the vegetable element which is springing from the sculpture?

The metal sculptures, the plant-objects, the engravings for Ovid's *Metamorphoses* and a large number of new paintings were shown in a big Picasso Exhibition which, in many respects, could be considered as ranking among Surrealism's most important manifestations and for which the Galerie Georges Petit threw open its vast and ancient doors in Paris in 1932.

Thus a tremendous shift in the scope of human awareness was taking place, as a result of which the infinite potentiality of reality and the possibility of overcoming the limits usually assigned to man's aspirations became clear. The surrealists constituted the outer flank in this vast wheeling movement, but, thanks to an increasingly complete identification with inner reality, their work began to assume a more precise and in some ways more sculptural character (an evolution that is particularly noticeable with Tanguy), resulting from the harmony between the inner object and its representation. It could be said that the surrealists' productions had originally been *presentative*, since they had helped to create the reality they described—a still indeterminate reality shaped almost entirely from the future. Later they acquired more *representative* qualities, and hence specific and permanent traits, and characteristic, autonomous signs.

Professional criticism found it difficult to follow this 'revolution-evolution'. On the few occasions when it occupied itself with Surrealism it was to bury it, with an equally remarkable constancy and inefficacy. The critics were prepared to recognize some talent in the movement's writers, but the painters were treated with contemptuous disdain. The review *Cahiers d'Art*, in many ways an estimable publication, which had some justification in claiming after two years of existence that it 'occupied the first place among art periodicals' (in many respects it took the place of the defunct *Esprit Nouveau*), prefaced an article by Jean de Bosschère on Max Ernst (No. 2, 1928) by a note declaring that though the editors thought it 'their duty' to acquaint their readers with 'so-called surrealist painting', they were convinced that surrealist painting did not exist—but for reasons different from those advanced previously by Pierre Naville. According to the *Cahiers d'Art*, it was quite simply because 'the painters of this school are entirely lacking in pictorial qualities'.

In 1930, in the same review, the critic E. Tériade's 'Documentary Account of Contemporary Painting' (fourth article: 'The Literary Reaction') dealt, invariably in the past tense, with the 'brief career of pictorial Surrealism' which appeared even briefer in so far as the author made no mention of Tanguy, Magritte or Dali. Masson and Miró were considered to be the only painters who had been able to 'detach themselves from their surrealist environment'. The illustrations were in keeping with the tone of the article; for instance, only two early paintings of Chirico's were reproduced, in postage-stamp size: *Prophecy of the Savant*, without any title, and *The Song of Love* under the title of *Head*.

Miró is also treated very roughly in the same number. The account of an exhibition he had just held at the Galerie Pierre states flatly that 'the mere gymnastics of his paint-brush do not in the very least allow Miró to enter even the most humble regions of painting'. Miró has 'reached the bottom of the dead-end, all contact lost with painting'. To sum up, 'no artist, even if he may be slightly gifted, has the right to use what talents he has in a deliberate effort to amuse imbeciles'. But there is no point in pursuing this class of quotation; one could extract some far more insulting ones from the other reviews and the newspapers of the time. (However, a few months later, *Cahiers d'Art* changed its attitude with regard to Surrealism: in subsequent chapters I shall have occasion to refer frequently to this review.)

From the 'socialist' painting of Courbet, through Seurat's 'mathematics', Gustave Moreau's (later on, Chirico's and the surrealists') 'literature' to Picasso's 'panoplies' and the 'mechanism' of the futurists and Dada, these new forms, and others too, have never lacked the pejorative epithets of the critics of the era. While it was invariably claimed at their first appearance that 'this is not painting', such discoveries revealed themselves finally as being *painting itself* in its very essence, and were responsible for the poetic as well as for the plastic renewal of painting. But if we consider the 'eternal values of art' in an attempt to recognize what painting 'is', may we not heed Leonardo da Vinci's advice when he states that the three principles of painting are: the object, the object's shadow, and the object's perspective? And is this not an exact definition of the art of Chirico? Naturally, since the surrealists are concerned with a new reality, their representations are entirely different from those of classic realism.

By 1930, most of the important personalities of the surrealist movement had already made an appearance. The reality of the surreal, which had been deepened by its development into something palpable, was to attract the support of a sculptor, Alberto Giacometti; and Salvador Dali was about to start describing it in the most precise fashion.

By circumnavigating the personal quarrels and moral considerations which take up so large a part of André Breton's *Second Surrealist Manifesto* (published originally in the twelfth and last issue of *La Révolution Surréaliste* in December, 1929), and which make this work such a splendid example of literary polemic, it is possible to detect the twofold anxiety to fight against the vulgarization of its first discoveries and to renew the themes of Surrealism. The negative reaction of the critics did not prevent the author from advising an attitude of mistrust towards any public support; in capital letters, he called for 'THE TRULY PROFOUND OCCULTATION OF SURREALISM'. Invoking the teachings of the secret sciences, and astrological and alchemical themes, he stated that Surrealism sought nothing less than a 'spiritual point' where all contradictions disappear—a point that could represent the summit of the Hegelian dialectical pyramid. But a little later on Breton referred to a 'supreme point', an expression deriving rather from alchemical theory. In short, the slogan no longer seemed to be automatism but esoterism.

The group accentuated its tendency to become a 'private chapel' while still deploring, contradictorily, the forced occultation to which many of its productions were being subjected. Aragon writes: 'Neither Crevel nor myself are allowed to be printed any longer. And naturally it is the contents of our writings which have made the publishers hostile towards us.'[1] From 1930 onwards most of the works published by the surrealists appeared as being issued by 'Editions Surréalistes', which meant simply that they had had to publish the books at their own expense. The title did not indicate a legally existing firm, but it was used until the outbreak of the second World War without, in fact, ever being usurped by outsiders.

On other planes, though, there was no noticeable introversion of activity. The political manœuvres of the surrealists began to assume a new degree of violence. The surrealist revolution did its best to put itself 'at the service of the Revolution'—but fresh disillusionments awaited the faithful in their dealings with the extreme left-wing political organizations, as had been the fate of the dadaists before them.

Le Surréalisme au Service de la Révolution was the name given to the new review which the group launched in July, 1930. From the second issue on, the title was printed in phosphorescent letters which shone in the dark, as did also an heraldic escutcheon printed on the cover, bearing the superimposed astrological symbols of the planets Uranus and Saturn.

The new publication inaugurated an ingenious method of page-setting in which the texts were printed in one, two or three columns as desired, allowing theoretical, poetic, polemical and documentary articles, and various news items, to be printed side by side if necessary, but without any resulting confusion. The notes of the day gave news, when the occasion arose, of the development of the movement in Europe: thus the reader was informed in 1930 of the constitution of a Yugoslav

group publishing a review: *Surrealism Here and Now*, and in 1933 of the existence of a Czechoslovak group.

Poetically and philosophically, the hero-image of the surrealists at that time was D. A. F. de Sade: Sade the rebel and revolutionary, the atheist, the apostle of love, the great nobleman who became president of the Section des Piques during the Revolution, only to be imprisoned by Robespierre as he had been under the monarchy and was later to be by Napoleon. Now, thanks to the researches of Maurice Heine, the friend and collaborator of the surrealists, Sade's life and work were at last divested of their veils of legend and fantasy and placed in a true perspective.

The illustrations in *Le Surréalisme A.S.D.L.R.* followed an entirely different pattern from those one had been accustomed to see in *La Révolution Surréaliste* and which had been popularized by *Variétés*. No more anachronistic or bizarre images and very few drawings were reproduced; instead, there were several pages of plates, consisting of documentary photographs carrying a political or polemical message, and reproductions of surrealist works: paintings, *collages*, objects. In the first issue, there were reproductions of scenes from the film *L'Age d'Or*, and some photographs by Man Ray which had lost none of their quality of excitement: notably, a *Homage to D. A. F. de Sade*. In the third issue (December, 1931) appeared one of Man Ray's first 'solarizations', called *Primacy of Mind over Matter*.

Like the other automatic (mechanical) processes used by surrealist artists, *solarization*[2] is the systematic use for poetic ends of a process that had already been observed in photography, but that had been regarded hitherto as a joke or an accident. In fact it was accidentally—as had been the case with the rayograms—that Man Ray re-exposed a negative which he was in the course of developing, so that the white areas turned grey while remaining surrounded by a lighter ring (an effect which is, of course, reversed in the positive print). Instead of throwing away a print that anyone else would have considered useless, Man Ray took full advantage of the unsuspected possibilities resulting from this accident, and produced a whole series of photo-

Escutcheon displayed on the covers of *Le Surréalisme au Service de la Révolution.*

Man Ray. Photographic self-portrait. 1934.

1. Aragon: 'Surrealism and Revolutionary Prospects', in *Le Surréalisme au Service de la Révolution*, No. 3, December, 1931 (Cf. *Histoire du Surréalisme*, p. 201).

2. Described in photographic manuals by the term 'Sabattier effect', from the name of the photographer who first wrote a description of it.

Pablo Picasso: *Abstraction, with Cloudy Blue Sky.* 1930.

Man Ray: *Primacy of Matter over Mind.* 1931.

graphs which transfigured the play of shadows and light on a face, an object, a landscape. Through over- or under-developing his solarizations, or through partial solarization, he was able to repeat in a new form his constant rediscovery of that exalted beauty which lies beyond the beauty of physical appearance. *Primacy of Matter over Mind* reshapes the contours of a naked woman, revealing unknown wonders of the female body.

In the sixth issue of the review (May, 1933), there are some drawings by Arp accompanied by a poem:

The stones are filled with guts. bravo. the stones are filled with air.
the stones are branches of water.
there's a bone-leaf sprouting from the stone that's a mouth. bravo.

. . . .

the stones are clouds for their second nature is dancing on their third nose. bravo.
when the stones scratch themselves their roots grow nails. bravo. bravo.
the stones have ears to eat the exact time.

Jean Arp was applauding himself, and he had reason. With his *Concretions* he had just brought 'his specific contribution to Surrealism'.[1] He had achieved the hard and solid concretization of the imaginary in the three dimensions of space. A longitudinal section of one of these objects or object-beings would reveal the outline of one of his Reliefs, as if those curious puzzles that constitute the Reliefs had always been since their conception the flat projection of three-dimensional creatures which their creator intended to re-present one day. Shaped with endless patience, by that same process of moulding and rubbing, the Concretions seem to bring to life the delectable beings that exist in Tanguy's pictures, beings which in their turn inevitably evoke the Reliefs: not by reason of any exterior 'influence' but because of that *inner* harmony between poet-images discussed earlier.

The *papiers déchirés* which Arp was to develop a little later combined 'presentation' and 'representation'. One day, after tearing up a sketch that failed to satisfy him, Arp noticed that the fragments of his drawing, lying on the floor, seemed to reconstitute themselves in a way that was as insistent as it was unexpected: he had only to draw certain strokes connecting the scattered lines of the destroyed

1. Marcel Duchamp: *Catalogue of the Collection of the Société Anonyme*, (op. cit.).

Jean Arp: *Papier déchiré*. 1937.

work to obtain a new drawing which also contained the old one. So he started tearing up a whole lot of drawings enthusiastically, and saw them change shape and give birth to new designs that were both surprising and familiar.

Sophie Taeuber and Jean Arp had gone to live in 1926 among the hills of Meudon, where they had a studio-house built for them which soon became peopled in the strangest fashion. On the lawns and terraces, between the rose-bushes and lavender-clumps, the Concretions displayed their immaculately white bodies like naked witches. Some perched on

Jean Arp's studio, 1959.

Jean Arp: *Head of an Imp.* 1930.

pedestals, others acquired their bronzed complexions in the sun. Some grew old and their bodies became furrowed with wrinkles. They invaded the rooms, too, while Jean's Reliefs and Sophie's paintings covered the walls with clouds and planets. There was an almost alarming atmosphere of swarming creatures in the studio; on the floor, tiny sculptures pressed closely against each other, heaped up like grain; others, already adolescent, were standing in rows on the shelves.

The double number 5-6 of *Le Surréalisme A.S.D.L.R.* (May 15, 1933) contained two poems by Maurice Henry and his drawing representing a woman asleep in a four-poster bed by the seashore, one arm hanging down with the hand wearing an enormous glove. Maurice Henry had already met the surrealists in 1929; at that time he was publishing poems in the review *Le Grand Jeu*. The *Grand Jeu* group had had a stormy passage with the surrealists during the course of a meeting organized by both groups in the rue du Château.[1] This had not prevented Maurice Henry from continuing to interest himself in the surrealists' activities; he crossed their path again in 1933 at the Association of Revolutionary Writers and Artists, quit this organization at the same time as they did and thenceforward participated in the group's activities.

Some sketches with a satirical-political flavour which he had made for reviews published by the above Association led him to take an interest in the field of humorous drawing. I particularly remember the picture called *The Private View* which he sent to the 1933 Surrealist Exhibition at the Galerie Pierre Colle: a solitary figure stands in the middle of a vast plain, surrounded by an army of plinths each of which is supporting an enormous block of rough stone. Soon after that, Maurice Henry started publishing his work in various newspapers: drawings containing an extremely subtle graphic naïvety, with disconcerting captions. The least of his quietly mordant sketches contains some intellectual satire and provokes a curious degree of disquiet, or, as Jacques Prévert has said, 'injects its own kind of panic into Ceremony'.[2]

The albums of *collages* which Max Ernst published in 1929 and 1930, *La Femme 100 Têtes*[3] and

1. Cf. *Histoire du Surréalisme*, and *Documents Surréalistes*.
2. Jacques Prévert: 'One fine day...', preface to an exhibition of drawings by Maurice Henry at the Galerie des Deux Iles, Paris, December, 1946.
3. *The 100-headed Woman*; but the French is pronounced 'La Femme sans tête', i.e. 'The Headless Woman'.

Rêve d'une Petite Fille qui Voulut Entrer au Carmel, accomplish perfectly the synthesis between hallucination and an entirely conscious desire for general subversion. One can find in them the anticlericalism which the detractors of Surrealism have always deplored as being 'elementary', as well as repeated

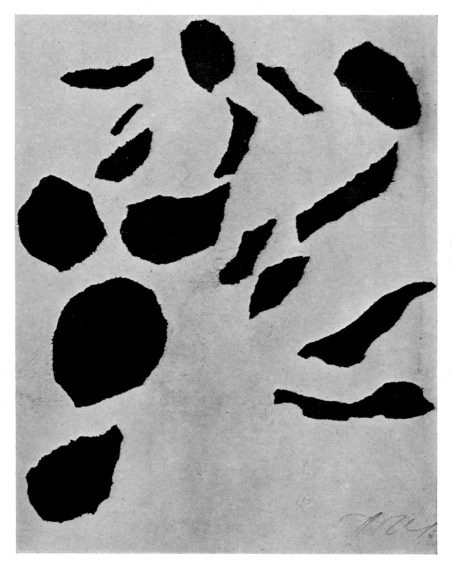

attacks against the ideas of Country and Family: 'Never, within living memory, did the *Femme 100 Têtes* have any relationship with the creature who speculates upon the vanity of the dead: the spectre of repopulation.' A mechanist-humorous note is occasionally apparent in these reconstruc-

Jean Arp: *First papier déchiré*. 1932.

Maurice Henry, 1957.

tions of engravings from children's books, old works of popular science and catalogues. The juxtaposed elements combine to form images that are utterly coherent, both technically and poetically, renewing and recreating the spirit of the 'readymade'. Sometimes the original engravings are hardly 'assisted' at all, as for instance in the series that makes use

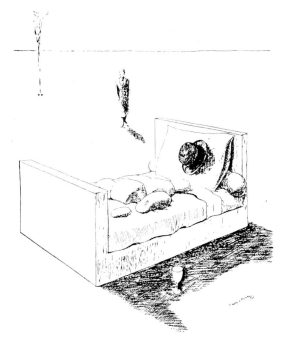

Maurice Henry: *When One is Sleepy*. 1933.

of strange illustrations showing a sort of bone market. Humorous or tragic, each discovery possesses the quality of exaltation.

These are the great picture-books of revolutionary-poetic thought. In the accompanying texts one can detect the breath of revolt of Rimbaud's *Les Mains de Jeanne-Marie* and the sarcastic tone of his *Un cœur sous une Soutane*, as well as a marvellous humour: 'And Loplop, the superior of the birds, is made flesh without flesh and shall live among us—His smile will have a restrained elegance —His weapon will be drunkenness, his bite fire—His gaze will plunge straight into the debris of desiccated towns—Living alone on her phantom-globe, beautiful and robed in her dreams, Perturbation, my sister, the Hundred-headed woman—Each bloody riot will give her life full of grace and truth—Her smile, which is fire, will fall in the shape of black jelly and white rust onto the sides of the mountain —And her phantom-globe will find us again—At all the ports of call.'[1]

In the sixth issue of *Le Surréalisme A.S.D.L.R.*, the author of the present *History of Surrealist Painting* made his first contribution to the publications of the group with which he had come into contact a few months earlier. The review reproduced one of the illustrations from *Mourir pour la Patrie*, a collection of twenty-four drawings which I had made in 1930.[2] The book included a preface, also published in the review, which paid tribute to Jules Verne—and to Max Ernst, whose *collages* in *La Femme 100 Têtes* had provided the original inspiration for my enterprise. While the captions in *La Femme 100 Têtes* provided a commentary on the pictures, my drawings performed the opposite function of constituting the echo of phrases, words and sentences picked at random from books and catalogues.

Among these unpremeditated images, one in particular demonstrated—long afterwards—that complex of automatism and fate, 'objective hazard', which had already governed the choice of captions. The first drawing in the collection represented a game of *round dice*—an entirely original idea, as I thought at the time: three billiard-balls on which were marked the black numerical spots of playing dice. But, without my knowledge, these unusual dice had already been thrown, though I did not

1. *La Femme 100 Têtes*, end of Chapter IV.

2. *Mourir pour la Patrie* ('To die for one's country'), by André and Marcel Jean. Drawings by Marcel Jean based on texts chosen by André Jean. (Éditions des Cahiers d'Art, Paris, 1935).

'There remains then he who speculates upon the vanity of
the dead, the spectre of repopulation.'
Max Ernst: *La Femme 100 Têtes*. 1929.

learn the fact until much later when, strolling with Max Ernst some time in 1954 through the 'scrap-iron market' in Paris, I discovered on a stall heaped with junk a small box containing some ivory balls yellowed by time and marked like playing dice. Instruc-

Marcel Jean: Engraving for the album *Mourir pour la Patrie*. 1935.

tions on the box explained that this was a game to be played like billiards, except that the spots uppermost on the balls were counted in addition to the breaks; six small flattened surfaces on the balls allowed them to roll to a stop and show a number on top without any possibility of argument.

It seems, sometimes, that a particular painting or drawing—or a particular literary work or even a pattern of behaviour—represents a materialization of future encounters and events: I have already mentioned Chirico's prophetic portrait of Apollinaire, indicated that artist's interest in omens, and discussed that particular quality in his work which blends memory of the past with intuition of the future. Chirico's reflections on the classical epochs are of this nature: once upon a time the world was 'full of gods' and, also, full of omens, and innumerable allusions to dreams by writers in ancient times related, in fact, to *premonitions* which concerned equally the individual and the human community.

In our day, an opposite tendency is evident: the dream is studied as a *retrospective* phenomenon, illuminating an individual psyche (Freud) or revealing 'archetypes' (Jung). The surrealist writers themselves, when analyzing dreams, coincidences and even premonitions, did so from a subjective-psychological point of view, following the methods of Freud.

The only man in our time to have studied premonition, especially in dreams, as an objective fact, has been the English engineer and writer John W. Dunne. With a strictness which by no means excluded a sense of humour, Dunne made use of his medical and mathematical knowledge to study his own dreams (which in his case were often most sensational and disquieting, and Dunne apologized to his readers for this dramatic aspect which might conceivably obscure the scientific character of his study) and the dreams of his contemporaries. He was able to establish that the prophetic dream is as widespread a faculty as the retrospective dream, despite the fact that the prophetic element is rarely suspected. His observations up to 1927, and the conclusions which he drew from them about the nature of time, were published in his work *An Experiment with Time*.[1] Most of the dreams described by the author 'came true' in a few days or a few weeks; nevertheless, one of them, 'the most perfect example of the kind I have ever experienced' says Dunne of that particular 'long-range association', took about twenty years to achieve its prophetic message in actuality (it was originally a retrospective dream induced by the illustrations of imaginary flying-machines in Jules Verne's *Clipper of the Clouds*).[2]

There seems no doubt that one could observe many more facts of this nature by following the

1. Faber & Faber, London, third edition, 1958. Macmillan, New York, fourth edition, 1938.
2. Cf. *An Experiment with Time*, Chapter XII.

Salvador Dali: *The Lugubrious Game.* 1929.

Salvador Dali: *Accomodation of Desire*. 1929.

purple.'[1] At that particular moment, a review of which Dali was then a devoted reader, *L'Esprit Nouveau*, was making fun of the Parisian art-students who were putting on great airs because they were painting purple shadows....

There is no doubt that in a Paris or Madrid official art school in the twenties, it was impossible for a student to show an interest in anything more recent than Impressionism without arousing the dark suspicions of his professors and fellow-students. But Dali's penchant for Cubism was not his only originality. He possessed a very lively sense of paradox and a natural propensity for making jokes at the expense of those around him: these talents he exercised fully at Art School. For example, having to copy a Gothic statue of the Virgin during a drawing class, Dali drew a pair of scales with meticulous care and explained to the outraged teacher: 'Maybe you see the Holy Virgin there, as everyone else does. But all I can see is a pair of scales.'

However, the information that this over-brilliant pupil was able to glean from foreign magazines remained rather inadequate as far as the latest avant-garde movements were concerned, since, though *L'Esprit Nouveau* might well be considered progressive in relation to academicism, it was still at least two revolutions behind the times. As Francis Picabia wrote ironically (in *Littérature*): '*Littérature* is for simple souls; *L'Esprit Nouveau* is for complex souls.' The review directed by Ozenfant and Le Corbusier usually passed over in silence all the various activities which eventually led to the formation of the surrealist movement. Yet, by a strange coincidence, *L'Esprit Nouveau* died just after it had announced, in January, 1925, the appearance, not, it is true, of the *Surrealist Manifesto* or *La Révolution Surréaliste*, but simply of *Surréalisme*, an ephemeral bulletin published three months previously by the poet Ivan Goll.[2]

In any case there are absolutely no signs of any preoccupation with dadaist or surrealist themes in Dali's early artistic experiments, which showed themselves to be influenced by very disparate tendencies: at one moment, Vermeer's inspiration can be seen in *Girl Sewing* and *The Basket of Bread*, then Synthetic Cubism becomes his model, or

Ingres in the manner of Picasso, or the *Scuola metafisica* (*Neo-Cubist Academy*, *Figures on the Sand*). These works achieved a considerable measure of success in Catalonia. Dali had by now been expelled from the School of Fine Arts (apparently for taking part in a conspiracy against one of the professors) and, in his native province, his personality had already helped to cause him to be considered a 'case'.

Apparently Dali discovered Surrealism only during the course of 1927, no doubt through reviews or catalogues; *Variétés* must have brought him a wealth of information in 1928. Two paintings dated 1927 show a remarkable change of front in their author's attitude: *Apparatus and Hand* and *Blood is Sweeter than Honey* (notice the literary

Salvador Dali: *Landscape*. 1931.

air of the second title and its sadistic note) are both images with a strongly surrealist tendency and, according to James Thrall Soby, 'must be read as a forecast of what we now know as the Dalinian style'.[3] And the artist's own account, in his *Secret Life*, of his working methods during that period show the degree to which he had been impressed by the theses in the *Surrealist Manifesto*; he attempted, in his turn, to adapt the processes of automatic writing to painting: 'I spent the whole

1. S. Dali: *The Secret Life of Salvador Dali* (Vision Press, London, 1948; Dial Press, New York, 1942).

2. The first and only number of *Surréalisme* appeared just before Breton's *Manifesto* (thus provoking a violent quarrel between Breton and Goll), in October, 1924, with the collaboration of Marcel Arland, Paul Albert Birot, René Crevel, Joseph Delteil, Robert Delaunay, Paul Dermée, Jean Painlevé, Pierre Reverdy and—posthumously—Apollinaire.

3. Cf. James Thrall Soby: *Salvador Dali* (Museum of Modern Art, New York, 1946). The early paintings mentioned above are reproduced in this work.

day seated before my easel, my eyes staring fixedly, trying to "see", like a medium, the images that would spring up in my imagination. Often I saw these images exactly situated in the painting. Then, at the point commended by them, I would paint, paint with a hot taste in my mouth.... At times I would wait whole hours without any such images occurring. Then, not painting, I would remain in suspense, the brush hanging motionless from one hand.... Sometimes nothing resulted...'.

On a first visit to Paris, Dali went to see Picasso. Then, during a second stay he met his compatriot Joan Miró, who told the surrealists about his strange compositions. In 1929, the dealer Camille Goemans visited Cadaques, a little Catalan village near the French frontier, where Dali was living. René and Georgette Magritte joined him there, followed by Paul Eluard and his wife Gala. Dali fell in love with Gala, who soon left Eluard and became the young painter's wife and astute business-manager. In 1929, Dali finished *The Lugubrious Game*, a completely surrealist little painting: it is a mixture of objects, female figures, birds' heads, hands, hats, pebbles, tentacles, all flowing out of an architecture viewed in perspective and rearing up like a monstrous plume in front of a statue garnished with an enormous hand, on the plinth of which is engraved: 'Gramme, centigramme, milligramme'—the motto of Salvador Dali's minutely detailed painting.

Dali collaborated with Luis Buñuel, whom he had known in Madrid in a student circle, in the making of their film *Un Chien Andalou*. When the film was completed, he joined Buñuel in Paris for its first showing, and duly put in an appearance at the Café Cyrano, in the Place Blanche, where the surrealist group was meeting at the time. At first he was careful to observe the modest attitude appropriate to a neophyte. His reserve contrasted strongly with his new friends' usual boisterousness, although he was able occasionally to make a definite impression on a gathering most of whose members were either poor or pretended to be so. For instance, he invariably paid for his drinks with a hundred franc note, appearing to consider coins simply as paper-weights, designed to keep the bank-notes from blowing off the café table; and he enquired about the possibilities of living in Paris on only ten thousand francs a month (about £50 or $200 in 1929!). In addition, he had a contract from the Galerie Goemans in his pocket for his first Paris exhibition, and Breton and Eluard had already bought several paintings from him. Aragon even had the idea of making use of his own society friends to promote a 'Dali lottery': twenty people or so would each hand over a hundred francs a month to the artist, and a monthly draw would make someone the owner of a Dali painting!

'What is worth saving from the interminable reels of film which have been unwound for our benefit up to the present time and have as surely disintegrated: those occasional fragments which were, after all, only a harmless way of passing an evening; some others that induced utter depression and a sense of fantastic cretinization; others again that were responsible for a brief, inexplicable exaltation? What is worth remembering of all this, except the voice of the arbitrary evoked in a few of Mack Sennett's comedies; the voice of defiance in *Entr'acte*; the voice of a savage love in *White Shadows*; the equally illimitable voices of hope and despair in the films of Chaplin? Apart from these, nothing, except *The Battleship Potemkin's* indomitable call to revolution. Nothing except *Un Chien Andalou* and *L'Age d'Or*, which are in a category all their own.'

How many titles could we add, after thirty years, to that exceedingly brief honours list, extracted from the 1930 introductory programme to *L'Age d'Or*? The word *film* expresses perfectly the nature of an art which has rightly been called 'epidermic', a synthesis and substitute, for better or usually for worse, of the adventure-serial of previous eras and the documentary or suggestive postcard. Buñuel had had the idea (according to Dali in his *Secret Life*) of taking a daily newspaper for the theme of his first film, in which all the images would be animated, from the local news right through to the comic strips: in the end, the newspaper would be swept up and thrown into the garbage-bin. But *Un Chien Andalou* turned out to be a very different conception; dream-like adventures bound together by a secret necessity, demanding the spectator's participation outside the limits of direct understanding; a thread of irrational consequences which never breaks; the imaginary following inexorably a desperate, irrefutable logic.

Luis Buñuel was born in 1900, spent his youth under the enforced discipline typical of the feudal regime which still reigns in Spanish Jesuit schools, and came to Paris in 1920 to study music. He immediately became attracted by the cinema, and got a job as assistant director for Jean Epstein on the film *La Chute de la Maison Usher*; but he soon

Salvador Dali: *Birth of Liquid Desires.* 1932.

realized that he would have to become his own producer. *Un Chien Andalou* was filmed in Paris in 1928 (that is to say, before either of the two authors had met the surrealists) and shown at the Studio 28 cinema, rue Tholozé, from October 1 to December 23.

Dali played a major part in the writing of the scenario, but it was Buñuel who succeeded in endowing his friend's ideas, and his own, with an extraordinary sense of actuality. Scorning the technical pretensions and failures which characterize so-called avant-garde films, his production was simple and precise, with an infallible sense of *tempo* (no doubt Buñuel's musical

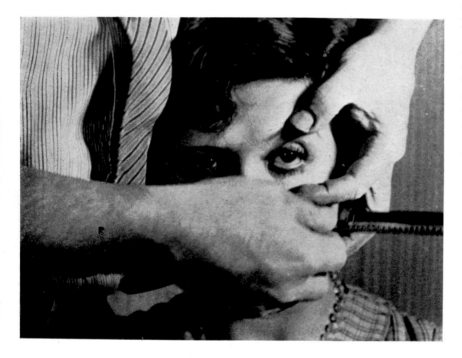

A scene from the film by Luis Buñuel and Salvador Dali, *Un Chien Andalou*, 1929.

training was of use to him in this respect); the result was more than an arresting spectacle—it was a stupefying experience. In the opening scene, a razor-blade seen in close-up slices through a young woman's eye with the same precision as the thin wispy cloud passes across the face of the moon in the preceding image. Neither the admirers of beautiful photography nor the lovers of realism had the time to worry about 'how it was done'; already other scenes were introducing the spectator into an increasingly tragic atmosphere. Buñuel was so emotionally involved in the film's realization that he was ill for several days after slicing through

the cow's eye which provided the illusion of a human eye on the screen.

Un Chien Andalou was something so obviously out of the usual cinematic rut that, by sheer force of contrast, it achieved an immediate success—of which the surrealists promptly made full use. Some difficulties had already arisen as a result of the publication of the scenario, which Buñuel had quite innocently offered to the publisher Gallimard for his *Revue du Cinéma*. The surrealists indignantly protested to their new friend that this constituted a 'distraint' upon a work which they claimed for themselves, and there was even talk of a punitive expedition to the printing-works to break up the type for the article. Finally, Eluard and Buñuel contented themselves with going to Gallimard to ask for the return of the text, a request which was refused. Thereupon, the scenario was reprinted in *La Révolution Surréaliste* (No. 12) with this introductory note by Buñuel:

'The publication of this scenario in *La Révolution Surréaliste* is the *only one authorized by myself*. It expresses, without any reservation whatsoever, my complete adherence to the ideas and activities of Surrealism. *Un Chien Andalou* would not have existed if Surrealism had not existed.

'*A successful film*' seems to be the opinion of most of the people who have seen it. But what can I do about those who go mad about anything new, even if the novelty in question outrages their deepest convictions? What can I do about a bribed or at least hypocritical press, and this cretinous mob which labelled as *beautiful* or *poetic* what is basically nothing but a desperate, passionate incitement to murder.'

206

Shortly before *Un Chien Andalou* was first shown, the first exhibition in Paris of Dali's paintings took place at the Galerie Goemans (September, 1929). André Breton wrote the preface: '. . . These new creatures, whose evil intentions are apparent, have just started moving. We experience a dark pleasure at the realization that nothing on their path exists any more except themselves, and we recognize that their habit of multiplying themselves and *melting away*[1] identifies them as beasts of prey.' *The Lugubrious Game* was shown, together with *Apparatus and Hand, Accommodations of Desire, Illumined Pleasures* and some other paintings.

The artist made use of his own manual dexterity as a 'means of forcing inspiration' in a few of his earlier pictures which are certainly the most genuinely surrealist paintings of his whole career: *The Font* (1930), *The Profanation of the Host* (1930), *The Dream* (1931). Against a background of coloured waves, swirling currents intermingle and focus themselves finally into figures and objects. They are not so much dream-images as illustrations of a kind for a still unwritten manual of psychoanalysis: even the titles sometimes provide a commentary with Freudian undertones. A predilection for suggestive or even remarkably unsymbolized sexual themes is noticeable in his work (Dali is the author of some extraordinary erotic drawings).

In 1930, the Editions Surréalistes published Salvador Dali's *La Femme Visible* (followed in 1931 by *L'Amour et la Mémoire*, under the same imprint). The frontispiece consisted of an engraving by the author, a jumble of strange shapes, blazing chalices and coprophagous androgynes, with the following lines, just above the artist's signature, taken from the chapter entitled 'The Great Masturbator':

> *. . . in the cruel ornaments of false gold*
> *which cover his soft delicate forehead*
> *imitating*
> *the shape of an imperial crown*
> *whose fine leaves of bronzed acanthus*
> *reach as far*
> *as his smooth rosy cheeks*
> *and extend their hard fibres downwards*
> *until they dissolve*
> *into the snow-white nape of his neck*

This is one of the appearances of the 'Great Masturbator', a favourite theme at that time in Dali's pictures. In his same role of poet, he describes

with equal satisfaction 'the Avenue of Spirito-artistic Sciences' in which can be found

> *the usual sculpted couple*
> *with tender nostalgic faces*
> *and it is the man who devours*
> *the immeasurable shit*
> *which the woman*
> *craps*
> *lovingly*
> *into his mouth*

coprophagy, like putrescence, being an important factor for the artist at that period (in his artistic and literary activities, of course).

La Femme Visible includes a 'theoretical' section under the headings 'The Putrescent Donkey', 'The Sanitary Goat' and 'Love', concerned mainly with the *paranoiac-critical method* which Max Ernst described, later on, as a 'rather pretty term, which will probably have some success because of its paradoxical content'.[2] Dali's definition is equally paradoxical, and all his terms are more or less contradictory: 'Paranoiac-critical activity: spontaneous method of original knowledge based upon the interpretative-critical association of delirious phenomena'.[3]

Critical paranoia might be compared to an image-interpretation test, a test repeated interminably, and invariably producing different results: a given reality suggests two, three or more different ones (depending on the individual's imaginative capacity), each one as acceptable as the original since each variation can be perceived and accepted as real by others. For instance, one can see, or persuade others to see, all sorts of shapes in a cloud: a horse, a human body, a dragon, a face, a palace, and so on. Any sight or object of the physical world can be treated in this manner. From which the proposed conclusion is that it is impossible to concede any value whatsoever to immediate reality, since it may represent or mean anything at all.

Envisaged in this way, critical paranoia is not only a creative method in which we can easily recognize the 'means of forcing inspiration' and the gazing at old walls advocated by Leonardo, but, in addition, an attempt to disorganize the outside world, a sort of paroxysmal impetus towards disorientation. And Dali, who claims to hate simplicity,

---

1. In the French: *fondre*, 'to melt away', also 'to swoop upon'.

2. *Beyond Painting (op. cit.).*

3. An alternative definition by Dali is: 'A spontaneous method of *irrational knowledge* based upon the critical and systematic objectification of delirious associations and interpretations'.

takes pains in *La Femme Visible* to disorient his readers first of all, by presenting his theses in a humorous-philosophic style copied from the 'digressive passages' in *Les Chants de Maldoror*.[1] For example, he tells a story of a fake pianist who knows that he does not know how to play, but manages to play on a fake piano with every semblance of conviction—a story certainly designed, in the words of Lautréamont, to 'reduce the reader to a state of utter idiocy'.

Critical paranoia has still other associations: for instance, with the 'fringe' etymological system which I have discussed in relation to André Breton. He and Paul Eluard even managed to inject an Hegelian-Freudian synthesis into Dali's 'theories': in the foreword to *La Femme Visible* they invoked 'the dialectical concept allied to the psychoanalytical concept, both crowned by what Dali calls, so strikingly, the paranoiac-critical concept',[2] the most vital concept, they added, of a revolutionary point of view. 'Dali's very great capacities—capacities which are defined on the artistic plane—will prove to be the most important factor today in the liquidation of a long outmoded formula, the only one left to the bourgeois world which, we must realize, is reduced to this single weapon, increasingly sharpened and so increasingly breakable: censorship.' The least one can say about these declarations is that they fail to recognize the artists's sense of humour; in particular, the part which humour played in the practical application of the theories expounded in *La Femme Visible*.

Dali had much in common with those circus performers who, with an imperturbable seriousness, perform sketches based on themes as banal as climbing a ladder or playing a trumpet solo. He was a dazzlingly intellectual acrobat with a matchless instinct for 'sensitizing' the most worthless themes. The most vulgar clichés were grist to his inventive mill. And soon he began to discover the element of surprise in the familiar, in the terribly familiar: all this with a deliberately cretinizing intention which did not spare his own friends.

In 1933, Dali transformed Millet's *Angelus* into a positive geyser of associative images: he had discovered that the figure on the left was hiding his turgescent sex under his hat, that the woman was pregnant, that the wheelbarrow suggested an erotic attitude, that the pitch-fork was stuck into the 'meat' of the earth, which represented nourishment, etc.[3] According to Dali, it was these hidden meanings which were responsible for the picture's fame, rather than its more apparent aspect as a commonplace religious image. The artist painted a series of pictures in which he achieved a more or less complete metamorphosis of *The Angelus*, including *Meditation upon the Harp* and *Gala and the Angelus of Millet Immediately Preceding the Arrival of the Conic Anamorphoses*, reproduced in *Le Surréalisme A.S.D.L.R.*, No. 6 (May 15, 1933). Another series of pictures had exploited the theme of William Tell, with the Swiss patriot appearing as the hero of an 'enigma' or of some complex (presumably of frustration). One of the images in this cycle is remarkable for the sheer fantasy of its flying pyramids of obsessional objects, old women with beards, pianos with tails, putrescent donkeys, and so on.

After that, the author of *The Lugubrious Game* made a great commotion about 'anamorphic' images, resembling the vapid reflections of the distorting mirrors of fairground sideshows, which do in fact provide rather Dalinian views of reality: anyone contemplating himself in such mirrors may see all the marks of invincible genius or congenital cretinism, passing through the whole spectrum of the most unlikely morphological accidents. Then came another sideshow, 'anaglyphs'; Dali discovered a curious book on this subject[5] which he recommended to all his friends. He announced that he intended to paint anaglyphic pictures: these would appear to be three-dimensional when looked at through special glasses. But the project was not executed.

Most notorious of all, perhaps, were his dithyrambic eulogies of Meissonier, that finicky calendar illustrator who was one of the best paid painters of his time and is considered today to be one of the most worthless of any age. Dali undertook to rehabilitate this nullity, and lavished the full resources of his fertile imagination on the scheme. When I mentioned the 'chronogram' photographs[3] in the first issue of *Minotaure*, he

1. Concerning Lautréamont's 'digressive passages', I refer the reader to the analysis by Arpad Mezei and myself in our *Maldoror*, Ch. XVI.

2. A remark which gave the extreme left-wing intellectual groups a splendid opportunity, fully exploited, to accuse the entire surrealist movement of 'Freudo-Marxism'.

3. A study by Dali on 'The Myth of Millet's *Angelus*' has remained unpublished, except for the Introduction, which was printed in the first issue of the review *Minotaure*.

4. Reproduced in *Le Surréalisme A.S.D.L.R.* No. 4 (December, 1931).

5. *Les Anaglyphes Géométriques*, by H. Vuibert (Librairie Vuibert, Paris, 1924).

6. See above, p. 19, note 3.

immediately assured me that Meissonier's picture, *1812*, depicting Napoleon and his general staff on horseback in a landscape of churned-up ruts and mud, was a chronogram of the movements of a horse, 'because the horses in this picture all had their legs in different positions'.

The artist was in the habit of communicating his discoveries to the surrealists by means of missives written in a carefully delirious handwriting, addressed to the leader of the group; these started invariably with the words: 'Dear friend Breton', and ended by assuring the recipient of his 'surrealist unconditionality'. Breton in his turn read out these texts to his assembled friends, in his incomparable style and with a gravity which was soon tempered by the laughter of his audience. I shall return on a later page to Dali's special message about the philosophical and passionate significance of pork chops, pigs' trotters and lobsters. At that time, famine was very much the order of the day (pictorially speaking) in Dali's plan of campaign: he painted half-eaten telephones on plates, and similar pictures which impelled those art critics who had finally been won over to Surrealism to exclaim fervently: 'What voracity!'

But it is impossible to catalogue here all the facets of an activity which the ex-student from the Madrid School of Fine Arts was busy deploying at that time on a larger and more public platform, helped greatly by his own exceptionally lively and sharp intelligence. Indeed, several of his proposals deserved better than the burlesque-flavoured sauce with which he dished them up. It is worth pausing briefly to consider his rediscovery of *art nouveau* (or 'modern style' as it is called in France) which certainly merits attention. In 1933, Dali wrote: 'I believe that I was the first—in 1929, at the commencement of *La Femme Visible*—to consider, without a shadow of humour, the delirious architecture of *art nouveau* to be the most original and extraordinary phenomenon in the history of art.'[1] (However, Dali protested against 'the facile literary use made of the 1900 epoch... which is liable to provoke a particularly repugnant sort of smile.')

'Perhaps no other simulacrum,' wrote Dali in *La Femme Visible*, 'has ever created a general effect to which the adjective *ideal* is more exactly appropriate than that great simulacrum which constitutes the astonishing ornamental architecture called *art nouveau*.' In evoking this art, for which Barcelona is the holy town and which must, in fact, have provided a genuine childhood memory for him, Dali abandoned for once his usual labyrinthine style: 'No collective effort has succeeded in creating so pure and disturbing a dream-world as these *art nouveau* buildings which, on the fringe of architecture, constitute in themselves alone absolutely valid realizations of desires made concrete, in which the cruellest and most violent automatism painfully betrays a hatred of reality and a need for refuge in an ideal world, as in the typical structure of childhood neurosis.—Here is something we can still love, the imposing sum of these cold, delirious buildings spread throughout Europe, scorned and ignored by anthologies and surveys. Here is something worth supporting in opposition to the fat pigs of contemporary esthetics, those defenders of execrable "modern art", here, indeed, is something worth opposing to the whole history of art.'

So-called functional buildings, apartment houses and other machines-for-living, deteriorate and grow old like all machines in less than a generation, but with the added inconvenience that, being constructed from reinforced concrete, these particular machines soon become far more of a nuisance than out-of-date cars or railway-engines. This architecture of self-punishment, in Dali's phrase, manifests in the most blatant fashion the profound inferiority complex of those who have conceived it: the '*cité-radieuse*' type of buildings resemble nothing so much as sanatoria perched on top of block-houses. But *art nouveau*, the last great architectural and decorative style, adapted all kinds of material to its whims—stone, wood, metal, ceramic—with a liberty attained earlier only by Far Eastern art. Houses, furniture and even the least important objects were covered by flowers with languishing stems and by marvellously beautiful women with flowing robes and hair, swooning away in waves or in smoke, into the warm embrace of the night. 'The ornamental objects of *art nouveau* reveal to us in the most material way the persistence of dreams in the face of reality.'[2]

Antonio Gaudi was one of those who transformed these dreams into architectural structures. Right up to his death in 1926, he peopled the Catalan capital with fantastic works. Whether it was a question of dwelling-houses, or of collective units

Salvador Dali: *Millet's Angelus*. 1934.

1. 'Concerning the terrifying and edible beauty of *art nouveau* architecture' in *Minotaure*, No. 3-4 (December, 1933).

2. Preface by Dali for his exhibition at the Galerie Pierre Colle, June, 1933.

with a social purpose like the Park Güell (named after the patron who supported Gaudi throughout his career), or of the never-completed and unusable basilica of the Church of the Holy Family (*La Sagrada Familia*), he placed his technical ingenuity at the service of an inexhaustible imagination.

Along the terraces of the Park Güell long benches of cement undulate according to the curves of the hill, winding like immense multicoloured serpents, their surfaces incrusted with ceramic fragments from a pottery, an adornment which is not only economical but, on this scale, genuinely beautiful, with innumerable shades of colour blending into a rich and subtle iridescence. Beneath the terraces, and supporting them, rises a forest of columns pointing in various directions, blending every possible architectural order, from the Doric to the 'dishevelled'. Abundant ornamentation covers outside walls, doors—'tender doors of calves' liver'[1]—and railings turned into huge metallic thistles. In the city itself, in the Paseo de Gracia, the modern houses created by Gaudi have a strangely antediluvian flavour: as though gigantic tides had left behind them all along the balconies 'fossilized waves and foam in forged iron.... An inhabitable building made of the twilight reflections of clouds on to the surface of a lake...'.[2] The ceilings of the rooms are patterned with the outlines of waves upside down. On the roofs, the 'abstract' shapes of the chimneys suggest monsters with gaping jaws.

Gaudi, fervent Catholic though he was, was less inspired by the sacred images of Christianity: the saints in the niches of the portal of his Church of the Holy Family are the most vulgar types of mass-produced 'holy objects'. And the architecture of this monument is, fundamentally, that of a pagoda: soaring spires like the pyramids of a Hindu temple, labyrinthine and colossal, stones which turn into rockeries, lace-work, tree-bark, smoke, carapaces; there are trees of green mosaic, pillars as scaly as the limbs of a prehistoric animal supporting the structure, monstrous insects and shell-fish crawling along the flying-buttresses.

A curious kinship exists between Gaudi's conceptions and those of another builder, whose compulsive constructions were first revealed to us by J.B. Brunius in the review *Variétés* (June 15, 1929): this was Ferdinand Cheval, known as the *facteur* Cheval,[3] creator of a dream palace, his *Palais idéal*, in Hauterives in the Drôme region of France.

1. S. Dali in *Minotaure*, No. 3-4.

2. *Ibid.*

3. J. B. Brunius has since written further articles on the *facteur* Cheval: in *Cahiers d'Art*, special number devoted to 'the surrealist object' (Paris, 1936), and *The Architectural Review* (Vol. 80, London, 1936). The film written and directed by Brunius in 1939, *Violon d'Ingres*, takes the *Palais idéal* and its creator as one of its main themes.

Antonio Gaudi: The Church of the Holy Family, Barcelona.

Salvador Dali: *The Persistence of Memory.* 1931.

A country postman who died in 1924, Cheval was about thirty when he suddenly had a vision of an imaginary palace: this he proceeded to turn gradually into reality, and between 1879 and 1912 he undertook the task of building this palace on the ground adjoining his cottage, entirely unassisted and using as materials stones that he picked up along the country lanes during his rounds, combined with cement. In this way he constructed, pebble by pebble, a temple of realized desire which made no concession whatsoever to usefulness apart from a recess built into one of the walls, where he could lay out his mason's tools. The Palace's walls are decorated by inscriptions, such as 'The fairies of the East have come to fraternize with the West'. The dream of this 'naïve' architect, the *facteur* Cheval, with its profusion of ornamentation and the serenity of the columns and stratified entablatures, brings to mind the imposing and exuberant constructions of the Hindus and the Indonesians. It would perhaps be appropriate to describe the Dream Palace as an exotic Forest by Henri Rousseau transformed into architecture.

Dali's ceaseless interventions contributed in no small measure to the movement's continued effervescence, and he soon achieved a position of prime importance in Surrealism. René Crevel devoted an enthusiastic study to him in *Dali ou l'Anti-obscurantisme* (Editions Surréalistes, Paris, 1931). Max Ernst had drawn an ex-libris for Paul Eluard in the manner of his Bird period, with the motto *Après moi le sommeil* ('Then let sleep come'). This inspired Dali to design a vignette for André Breton's collection of rare books showing him as an ant-eater—'André Breton the tamanoir'. No doubt the author of *Nadja*, a charmer who also liked to fancy himself as the 'great *persona non grata*', was delighted to see himself symbolized by this hairy creature with its prehensile claws, that catches ants for its meals with its tongue.

But Breton had been well aware, from the beginning, of the dangers lying in wait for this new recruit. In his introduction to the 1929 exhibition at the Galerie Goemans, he had written: 'Dali is like a man hesitating (his future will show that he did not hesitate) between talent and genius, or, as one would have said in a previous age, between vice and virtue.' Couched in these terms, the prophecy could hardly fail to turn out true in one way or another, but Breton's preface became more

explicit in a later paragraph: 'On one side there are the mites which attempt to cling to his clothes and never to leave him even when he goes out into the street; these particular mites say that Spain and even Catalonia is fine, that it is thrilling that a man can paint such small things so well (and that it is even better when he *enlarges*), that one person with his shirt stained with shit, like the one in *The Lugubrious Game*, is worth thirty well-dressed men and even more than a hundred naked men and

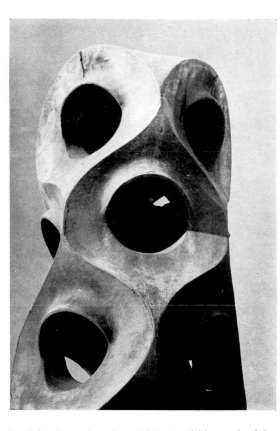

that it is about time the rabble should be cock of the walk in our beloved country and its fallow capital. . . . On the other side there is hope; the hope that everything will not crash into ruins after all and that, to start with, the sound of Dali's admirable voice may continue to ring true in his own ears, despite the interest that certain "materialists" have in persuading him to confuse it with the creaking of his patent-leather shoes.'

The provocative scatology of some of Dali's themes, his declarations on the virtues of putrefaction in which he praised what he claimed to be its 'terrorizing' effect, might lead one to think that he was too apt to confuse terror and disgust, the latter sentiment being in general unpropitious for opening the path to knowledge. On the other hand, his ultra-finicky technique was very popular with a number of collectors of modern art whose nostalgia for academicism was thus gratified. But despite all this, Surrealism pinned its hopes on this artist who was so anxious to place 'the ideal images of Surrealism' (his own paintings) at the service of 'the imminent crisis of consciousness', at the service of the Revolution; who denounced any activity of a *foreseen* nature in categorical terms: music ('song takes on the thousand atheistic forms of the praises of God'), the cult of classical beauty, of harmony ('this is harmony, this is filth, this is the realm of sheer shame'); who, in due course, came out against family, country, religion, and for love: 'I am thinking of the abominable, ignoble native country where I spent my youth.... With families, the parents' room with the windows closed in the morning, giving off a fearful stench of uric acid, cheap tobacco, lofty sentiments and shit.... Far away from love, far away from you, O violent, sterilized woman';[1] who finally drew a picture of the Saviour with a flaming heart and this inscription underneath: 'Sometimes I spit on the portrait of my mother from sheer pleasure!'[2]

With their second film, *L'Age d'Or*, which was shown at the end of 1930 at Studio 28, Luis Buñuel and Salvador Dali achieved far more than a simple demonstration of their continued attachment to Surrealism: they provided new fuel for 'the soul of the group' with their sensationally direct approach and images of violence and revolt pitched to the highest possible degree of intensity. To some extent the new film was a collective enterprise: Max Ernst played the part of the leader of the outlaws in it, while the programme preface constituted nothing less than a 'Manifesto of Surrealism in the service of the Revolution'. Above the signatures of Alexandre, Aragon, Breton, Char, Crevel, Dali, Eluard, Péret, Sadoul, Thirion, Tzara, Unik and Valentin, it undertook to measure 'the wingspan of this bird of prey so utterly unexpected today in the lowering sky, the lowering western sky:

L'Age d'Or.' This rapacious bird proceeded to spread its black wings, in the preface, over every domain—psychology, the instincts, different mythologies, love, disorientation, and finally over social problems: 'In an era of prosperity, *L'Age d'Or* must be made use of socially, and its value must thus be established by the satisfaction for oppressed classes of their need to destroy, and perhaps too by flattering the masochistic tendencies of the oppressors.' The preface then took up Dali's profession of faith mentioned above: 'The sculptural reproductions of various edifying allegories will take their place in a perfectly normal manner in the moral mythologies of the future, and among them the most exemplary will prove to be that of two blind people devouring each other and that of a youth with a nostalgic gaze spitting on the portrait of his mother from sheer pleasure.... Provocation is as good a precaution as any other,' the text continued, 'although the means of expression capable of discouraging swindling can hardly be contained any longer within the framework of a book, a picture or a film.' But in this respect *L'Age d'Or* was eminently capable of 'disappointing anyone who hoped to extract a convenient pabulum from it'.[3]

While this film deliberately refused in advance the kind of success achieved by *Le Chien Andalou*, it was nevertheless stamped with the same simplicity of expression and technical virtuosity as its predecessor. Its scandalous potentiality was so much the greater, and the years have not weakened its power: it is still impossible to show *L'Age d'Or* today except in the small auditoriums of a few cinema clubs. The scenes include 'a blind man being ill-treated, a dog squashed, a son killed almost wantonly by his father, an old lady slapped, an unconsummated love-scene dominated by the violence of frustrated actions,' and symbolic images like that in which the heroine sucks with rapture the big toe of a marble statue of Apollo. As a final shock to the sensibilities, the Comte de Blangis, Sade's protagonist in *Les 120 Journées de Sodome*, appears in the guise of Jesus Christ ('this latter episode is accompanied by a *pasodoble*'); the last image in the film is of a crucifix on which several women's scalps are nailed.

Nevertheless, in presenting this film to the general public, the surrealists had overestimated 'the masochism of the oppressors'. Their ideas had been tolerated as long as they were restricted

---

1. This quotation and the preceding ones are taken from *La Femme Visible*.

2. 'Amalgamated' with later pro-Catholic declarations by Dali, this picture was reproduced in the *Almanach Surréaliste du Demi-siècle* (special number of the review *La Nef*, Paris, 1950).

3. The complete text of this preface can be found in *Documents Surréalistes* (pp. 169-178).

to pamphlets and reviews with a limited distribution, but as soon as they were brought to the screen and benefited from the cinema's special emotional qualities, they were immediately viewed as a real danger which had to be suppressed at all costs. After a few showings during which there were only timid and isolated gestures of protest, the counterstroke was organized. In this connection the town councillor Le Provost de Launay, wrote to Chiappe, the prefect of police, that 'more and more of us have decided to react against a poisoning of society and French youth which is becoming systematic'. One evening, an extreme right-wing pre-Hitlerian group, the 'Camelots du Roy', attached to the royalist newspaper *Action Française*, and a league of 'anti-Jewish Youth', sent its commando troops to Studio 28.

Part of the film was projected without incident, but the riot broke out at a point in the 'story' where a liveried chauffeur emerged from a luxurious car carrying a monstrance and put it down on the pavement, while a pair of woman's legs emerged from inside the car. The demonstrators took that as their signal to hurl bottles of ink at the screen, throw stink-bombs, attack the non-demonstrating section of the audience, break up the seats and smash windows. An exhibition of books and pictures set up in the cinema foyer was torn apart and paintings by Miró, Ernst, Dali and Tanguy trampled underfoot.

As a result of this raid, the surrealist group published an illustrated pamphlet which showed the state of the premises 'after the departure of young Frenchmen of good family, respectful of art and property'; a photograph of the screen stained with ink carried the caption: *Christian illiteracy*, and there were various other edifying documents. But the scandal caused serious difficulties for several of those who had been concerned with *L'Age d'Or*. The first to be affected was Studio 28 itself: it had been the first cinema in Paris to show avant-garde films regularly, and had resuscitated and shown old films of Méliès, etc, but it never really recovered from this disaster and led an uncertain existence from then on. The Vicomte de Noailles, who was the patron of a number of surrealist enterprises and had financed Buñuel, was threatened with excommunication and other more effective measures of retaliation if he permitted the continued showing of *L'Age d'Or*— which was, in any case, soon banned by the police. The surrealists and the collectors who had lent paintings or books for the devastated exhibition

A scene from the film by Luis Buñuel and Salvador Dali, *L'Age d'Or*, 1930.

necessarily suffered serious losses. And the ill-fame of his film pursued the producer for many years: in 1943, after the publication of Dali's *Secret Life*, certain American journalists, who had noticed that the man responsible for this unmentionable film was Luis Buñuel, created so much unfavourable publicity that he was forced to resign from the post he held at the time in the film library of the Museum of Modern Art of New York.

Salvador Dali: *Paranoiac Face* (interpreted photograph). 1931.

From the pictorial point of view, Dali's paranoiac-critical method achieves concrete form in the process of the *double image*. This, basically, is the often engaging game of puzzle pictures: 'I've lost my sheep, where can they be?' asks the shepherdess, and the sheep are revealed in the outlines of the branches of a tree, in the grass or in rocks. From the double image one passes to the multiple image, in which the same picture can represent several different images at the same time. To illustrate this theory, Dali accomplished several genuinely curious *tours de force*: *The Phantom Cart* (1933), *Nostalgic Echo* (1935), *Spain* (1938), *Old Age, Adolescence, Infancy* (1940), etc.

It is questionable whether an absolute freedom of interpretation and creation is really the concern of concrete things. What would total liberty represent, ultimately, except nothingness? Even if it were possible for a person to do exactly what he wanted, his activity would inevitably be devoid of any sense or form. The very concept of the *object*, as we have seen, presupposes the idea of an obstacle. True creation, creative freedom, is a struggle to liberate oneself from a fixed and determined past, but at the same time it is based upon another determination—that of its own future.

What is involved essentially is the reality of symbols. The picture which represents one anecdote can convey another or several others, but with the whole contained within a more general theme. Dali's multiple image is a superimposition of anecdotes, but it is simple in the sense that it expresses a single symbol under various pretexts. The cluster of meanings contained within a single picture is far from being arbitrary. In the Rorschach test, for instance, one subject may interpret an image symbolically which another subject will envisage entirely differently, but the two different visions derive from more general systems which embody yet other types of interpretation.

Dali seems to have foreseen this objection

Salvador Dali: *Hysterical and Aerodynamic Feminine Nude*. 1934.

because, in his book *La Femme Visible*, the symbolic construction appears also as a pyramid of associations culminating in a 'gratuitous point... absolutely proof against any psycho-sensory influence'. In *The Conquest of the Irrational*, the paranoiac-critical method is even reversed and the author declares that 'pictures as different as *La Gioconda*, Millet's *Angelus* and Watteau's *The Embarkation for Cythera* signify exactly the same thing'.[1]

It seems, in fact, that the structure of Symbols is much closer to being a genuine *language*, relatively free and creative, certainly, and capable for this very reason of expressing its individual and subjective aspects. The paradox in Dali's case lies in his attempt to uproot symbols in order to ascribe an arbitrary sense to them. But we are never as 'gratuitous' as we would like to be. Take, for instance, one of the artist's most curious inventions, that of the *soft watches (montres molles)* which are to be seen for the first time in *The Persistence of Memory*, painted in 1931, as objects in a landscape that resemble watches but have the consistency of limp rags. 'You may be quite sure,' wrote Dali in *Conquest of the Irrational*, 'that the famous soft watches are nothing else than the tender, extravagant, solitary paranoiac-critical camembert of time and space.' Although Dali's commentators have apparently all accepted this version, we may have on the tip of our tongue (appropriately enough!) an entirely different explanation from that of the relativist cheese. If the paranoiac-critical method is anything more than an imposture, it can bring us in this instance an infinitely more coherent interpretation.

The word *montre* (watch) is a word-image with a double meaning: in French, it is the imperative of the verb *montrer* (to show) and the name of the apparatus *montrant* (showing) the time. But there is a very common childhood experience: the doctor asks the sick child to '*montrer sa langue*' ('show his tongue'), which obviously is soft. The child, we may say, *la montre molle* (shows it soft: with the double sense that in French this phrase can also mean 'the soft watch'). The irrational and even anguishing nature of this act for the child, in view of the circumstances, could certainly constitute an experience capable of leaving profound impressions in the psyche. Here, then, is a most concrete origin for the image of the soft watches, an

origin founded in an authentic childhood memory; this seems to be confirmed by the title of the picture, which may not have been premeditated by the artist but remains far from 'gratuitous', as can be seen. The watches in *The Persistence of Memory* resemble tongues more than anything else.

The word-play is untranslatable into Spanish, but the picture was painted in Paris when French had already become Dali's second language. A later picture of his, painted in America, with the rather farcical title *Uranium and Atomica Melancholica Idyll*, depicts among other things a watch ending in a tongue. In English, the phrase: 'Watch your tongue', while not an equivalent of '*montre ta langue*', conveys the same sense of adult supervision of the child's activity.

It would have been most interesting if the artist had indicated clearly the true explanation, but one can easily understand why, consciously or not, he has preferred to conceal it behind the deceptive symbol of Einsteinian camembert. The image of the soft watch is not only double but multiple: the tongue itself is a symbol, that of a soft penis. Dali has always been haunted by ideas of deficiency. The

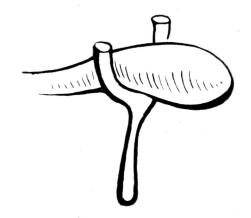

great number of crutches and of figures deformed by soft extensions or substitutions, which he has always enjoyed painting, is revealing. The case of Dali provides a good illustration of Adler's theory that anxiety about insufficiency is balanced by compensatory ideas of power : his paintings often include human figures whose heads are fantastically swollen.

Salvador Dali: Drawing. 1938.

1. S. Dali: *La Conquête de l'Irrationnel* (Editions Surréalistes, Paris, 1935); published in English translation as *Conquest of the Irrational* (Julien Levy, New York, 1935), and later, as an appendix to *The Secret Life of Salvador Dali* (op. cit.).

Dali's so-called gratuitous point, the summit of all reality, turned out, in fact, to be Dali himself.

His theories probably inspired Breton and Eluard in 1930 to collaborate in writing the 'simulations of delirium' collected in *L'Immaculée Conception*; equally, his gratuitous point seems to be a mere echo of the 'spiritual point' (later to be termed 'supreme point') presented by the *Second Surrealist Manifesto* as the ultimate aim of surrealist research. As far as individual psychology is concerned, the concept of a supreme point is simply a manifestation of egocentricity, and in Dali's case it took only a few years for his 'imperialism' to bear fruit, and for the 'mites', which Breton had detected at the very beginning, to start their long journey across the artist's fashionable garments. Was his destiny governed ultimately by a taste for paradox and eccentricity combined with the desire to ingratiate himself with a particular clientèle? Just before the surrealist exhibition which took place at the Galerie Pierre Colle between June 7 and 18, 1933,[1] Dali suggested, in the form of one of his communications to his 'dear friend Breton', a project for a catalogue preface beginning with the words 'Do you remember a very filthy painter who called himself Cézanne...' and continuing with an eulogy of Meissonier. The reception this proposal received among the group can be guessed from the tone of Dali's subsequent text, which formed the preface to his own one-man show at the same gallery, from June 19 to 29, 1933: '... But, my dear Breton, you know too, and as well as myself, that my solitude becomes immense and incurable the very moment that I think suddenly, my heart beating faster, of Napoleon at the head of his army in the Russian campaign, and of the horses with all their regulation straps and buckles among this fine snow with its little thirst, covering the landscape *just as* Meissonier painted it in his well-known and immortal picture and with that delicacy of academic technique which is unique to him and which appears to me at the moment to be the most complicated, the most intelligent and the most extra-pictorial method to use for the forthcoming deliria of irrational exactness in which I

believe Surrealism must inevitably be involved in the immediate future.'

Dali was, indeed, alone in his views as far as Meissonier was concerned. Max Ernst, Giacometti and others were categorically opposed to the idea that any public manifestation by the group should present this academician as the ancestor and model of surrealist painting. Dali's proposed text for the surrealist exhibition having been ruled out, the preface contented itself with being enumerative: 'Disagreeable objects, chairs, drawings, sexes, paintings, manuscripts, objects to sniff, surreptitious automatic objects, wood, plaster, phobias, intra-uterine memories, elements of prophetic dreams, dematerializations of desires, eye-glasses, finger-nails, symbolically functioning friendships, picture-frames, rotting chimneys, books, ordinary objects, taciturn conflicts, maps, hands, retrospective female busts, sausages, exquisite corpses, palaces, coats, libertines, butterflies in pairs, aural perversions, blackbirds, fried eggs, atmospheric spoons, pharmacies, unsuccessful portraits, loaves of bread, photographs', and even 'tongues'.... Such were the ingredients of the exhibition in the rue Cambacérès.

The happenings in the outside world during this period—Hitler's rise to power in Germany, and the political reactions of the left-wing parties to this new menace—gave rise to repeated discussions within the group. But Dali appeared less and less often at these conventicles, and in 1933 refrained from following his friends into the Association of Revolutionary Writers and Artists (the *A.E.A.R.*) which had just been founded. Their previous dealings with the politicians of the extreme left-wing allowed the surrealists no illusions as to the possibility of their achieving effective action in this alliance which came under Communist control from the start; but they did not think fit to refuse *a priori* their participation in the enterprise, having already proposed the same idea themselves: they had, indeed, not long before, attempted to set up an organization of this type which would have grouped writers and artists of revolutionary convictions. The surrealists were, in any case, very quickly excluded from the *A.E.A.R.*, or they resigned, as a result of a whole series of incidents which almost immediately led them into conflict with its Communist leaders. But even if Dali's refusal to embark on this sad adventure can thus be justified in retrospect, a much more disquieting aspect of his political tendencies was the interest he began to show in Nazism and in the personality

1. With the participation of Arp, Breton, Dali, Duchamp (his 1914 readymade *Pharmacy* was exhibited), Eluard, Max and Marie-Berthe Ernst, Giacometti, Maurice Henry, Marcel Jean, Magritte, Miró, Picasso, Man Ray, Tanguy, etc.
It may be mentioned that, at Paul Eluard's suggestion, the painters of the surrealist group exhibited that same year at the *Salon des Surindépendants* which had been founded a few years earlier by M. René Mendès-France. By the side of Arp, Dali, Max Ernst, Giacometti, Valentine Hugo, Magritte, Miró, Méret Oppenheim, Man Ray, Tanguy, were to be found a few 'sympathizers' such as Viollier, and Malespine who had himself participated in the surrealists' activities during 1929-30.

of Hitler. It was charitably considered to be humour—which it was, no doubt, but of a dubious kind—when themes such as the 'Hitlerian nurse' began appearing in his pictures. Dali's contribution to a pamphlet devoted to Violette Nozières[1] was considered by some of the surrealists to be a joke in extremely bad taste, consisting as it did in a 'paranoiac portrait of Violette Nazières (Nozières)', a repulsive-looking figure with sagging breasts, and an immense nose supported by a crutch, with the explanation: 'Nazi, Dinazos, Nazière.—Nez.'[2]

Another approximation of the same kind was contained in a huge picture which Dali painted shortly afterwards, entitled *The Enigma of William Tell*, in which Lenin appears without his trousers, one of his buttocks fantastically elongated and resting, of course, on a crutch—a very different painting from the kind of mystical vision which the leader of the Russian revolution had previously inspired in him: *Six Apparitions of Lenin on a Piano*.[3]

In January, 1934 it was decided to call Dali to account, and he was summoned to the rue Fontaine where the group was assembled in André Breton's studio. The tone of the discussions, which was calm to start with, very soon became heated, and it must be admitted that the show (there were several performances) was well worth seeing. The number of gags which the painter of *The Lugubrious Game* invented on these occasions would have made the fortune of a variety theatre. Pretending to have flu, he declaimed with a thermometer in his mouth, occasionally interrupting himself to read his temperature. He kept pulling up his socks, and, like the character in Molière's *Précieuses Ridicules*, started peeling off layers of extra undergarments, he knelt down at Breton's feet as though he were confronting the Blessed Sacrament, he began reading out a preposterous communication intended to demonstrate

The studios in the rue Fontaine, seen from the Boulevard de Clichy.

the surrealist and Maldoror-like character of his admiration for Hitler. But he had gone too far. At the point in his speech where he reached the phrase: 'But, in my view, Hitler has four balls and six foreskins...' Breton interrupted him brutally with: 'Do you intend to bore us much longer with this damn nonsense about Hitler?' Dali was so taken aback that he stopped his peroration, and nobody ever knew what other characteristics he might have ascribed to the Führer's morphology.

Beneath its eccentric mask, his argument was limpidly dogmatic. Basing himself on the original definition of Surrealism as the dictation of thought outside all esthetic or moral considerations, etc, Dali was in effect saying: I transcribe my dreams, therefore I have no right to exercise any conscious control over their contents; is it my fault if I dream of Hitler, or Millet's *Angelus*? Turning to Breton, he shouted, above the laughter of the company: 'Every night I dream that I'm buggering you' (he used a more forcible term) 'so I have the right to paint my dream, and I shall paint it!' Needless to say, he did not.

At this stage of the debate it might have been pointed out to him that Surrealism was not obliged to sponsor any or all of his private obsessions. It might also have been added that the initial theories of Surrealism seemed rather out of date by now; that, in addition, the purely oneiric origin of his pictures was by no means convincingly established; and that, finally, concerning the Hitler-Maldoror 'analogy', the regime of terror instituted by Germany's new masters represented essentially the wrong exit from a patriotic-economic dead-end, which really had absolutely nothing to do with Lautréamont. It must be said in Dali's defence that his opponents in the room were far from having reached a unanimous, or, for some of them, simply a clear opinion on these questions. Also, to his eternal credit, he had succeeded in creating an atmosphere remarkably unconducive to any rational and logical argument. Nevertheless, some of those present, more annoyed than amused by the stratagems of the one-time author of *L'Age d'Or*, made no attempt to hide from him their opinion that his Hitlerian fantasies seemed to indicate to them, in view of the menacing future, a carefully calculated submission in which Surrealism wanted no part and to which it would lend no support. 'But,' replied Dali, this was just 'primary surrealism.' 'And who are these primary surrealists?' thundered Breton: 'name them!' 'It is André Breton at the moment,' retorted Dali.

1. The surrealists decided to pay homage to this young girl accused of having poisoned her parents (the case caused a considerable stir in France at the time, as it was complicated by presumptions of incest and several other peculiar circumstances) after a visit by Breton to Picasso, in which the latter declared his intention of painting a picture dedicated to Violette Nozières. The brochure, published by Éditions Nicolas Flamel in Belgium in December, 1933, with a cover designed by Man Ray, contained poems by Breton, Char, Eluard, Maurice Henry, Mesens, César Moro, Péret and Rosey; and drawings by Dali, Tanguy, Max Ernst, Brauner, Magritte, Marcel Jean, Arp and Giacometti.

2. 'Dinazos' was the term used to designate the members of a Belgian Hitlerite group.

3. This picture is now in the Paris Museum of Modern Art under the title of *Composition*.

Salvador Dali: *Meditation on the Harp.* 1933.

Salvador Dali: *Six Apparitions of Lenin on a Piano*. 1933.

In fact, Breton was by no means anxious to separate himself so hastily from such an excellent publicity-agent for Surrealism: he was more concerned with checking Dali's ebullience. And, for their part, Dali and his wife Gala would have been extremely inconvenienced by a condemnation, which might have had serious effects on the sale of his pictures. During these goings-on, Tzara, Eluard and Crevel were all on the Riviera and had written to oppose any idea of excluding Dali during their absence. However, during the course of one last heated discussion, Dali was indeed excluded, and soon afterwards a few members of the surrealist group, including Breton, agreed in writing to 'fight him by every possible means'.

Finally, the affair petered out. The fascist riots in Paris of February 6, 1934, and the ensuing counter-attack by left-wing groups, engaged the whole of the surrealists' attention and time. Given the alert on February 7 by a group of young intellectuals, the surrealists collaborated in the formulation of a *Call to Action* which brought together a great number of signatures and provided the first step towards the formation of the Committee of Vigilance of Anti-fascist Intellectuals.

The Dali case became of secondary importance, while the artist, from then on, ceased attending the regular meetings of the group. But he was still invited to contribute to most of the surrealist exhibitions, and was even able to hang *The Enigma of William Tell*, prominently and without any untoward incident, in the guise of a 'phenomenon of affective cannibalism' among the other paintings in his exhibition at the Galerie Jacques Bonjean, from June 20 to July 15, 1934.

This exhibition was a great success. Paris society and Paris art-critics were united in their enthusiasm for the objects made from chocolate, a sculpture covered with dead flies (the artist would have wanted them to be made of precious stones) and pictures entitled: *Apparition of my Cousin Carolinette on the Beach at Rosas (Fluidic Presentiment)*; *Atmospheric Skull Sodomizing a Grand Piano*;[1] *Night Table Used as a Diurnal Fly (Theory of Flies in the 'Weaning of Furniture')*, etc. There was also an *Hysterical and Aerodynamic Feminine Nude* based on a commonplace plaster statuette which the artist had augmented with streamlined appendages resembling those of an airplane or a racing car.

---

1. In French 'un piano à queue', literally, 'a piano with a tail'.

In 1930, Louis Aragon and Salvador Dali went to see an *Exhibition by Revolutionary Artists* which was being held at the Parc des Expositions near the Porte de Versailles in Paris: they were both struck by a strange painting, signed Clovis Trouille and entitled *Remembrance*, which depicted a priest hitching up his soutane to show a woman's frilly knickers and silk stockings, next to an academician hugging tightly a monstrous and rather undescribable figure (its buttocks, uppermost, are also its face), and two skeletons wearing German and French uniforms holding enormous white rabbits in their arms, while, above their heads, a kind of female snail rains down a shower of medals and decorations.

The picture was reproduced in No. 3 (December, 1931) of *Le Surréalisme A.S.D.L.R.* The author of this strange allegory was indeed drawing on personal memories: a priest-ridden childhood, seven years of military service, of which five coincided with the first World War, and a period as a student in a provincial art school. Clovis Trouille was born on October 24, 1889 at La Fère (Aisne). He studied drawing and design at Amiens and became an advertising artist. From 1924 until very recently he has been working as a technician for a concern manufacturing wax mannequins for shop-windows. A tranquil man with a violent imagination, Trouille elaborated his very personal artistic conceptions in silence and isolation until his meeting with the surrealists, and in the course of time he has achieved a considerable body of work.

He has never participated regularly in the activities of the group, though he has acknowledged his debt towards Dali, who provided him with the taste for 1900 style, and whose example he followed in developing a pictorial technique which he has always wanted to be ultra-precise. He paints the scenes that he conjures up with a photographic exactness. Like Dali, he does not hesitate to carry out certain parts of his designs from documents, copying photographs or colour-prints, and making expert use of the process of painted *collage*. This is not to 'please his customers'—Trouille has no customers—but because he believes that a picture should be absolutely explicit, and express the author's thoughts in the most exact and direct manner.

In these violently anti-social, anti-religious, anti-moral images, the technique is always subordinated to a deliberately scandalous intention. Though Trouille has played a normal part in everyday life

223

and accepted the usual need to exercise a trade or profession, still the banal horrors of existence seem to exert conflicting influences on him in his art: revulsion, amusement and excitement. He delineates a world that is badly made as far as daily existence is concerned but which is admirably propitious for love-making.

Trouille has told me that he is conscious of the attractions exercised by the decoration and pomp of the costumes of Roman Catholicism, and that he finds an equivocal beauty in these solemn robes and ritualistic disguises which seems to him to combine most naturally and effectively with the profane charm of feminine underclothing. His nuns are street-walkers, and his monks debauchees, in the best traditions of 'primary anticlericalism'. His humour protects him effectively from professors of psychoanalysis and all inveterate apologists who might otherwise try to lecture him about repression or ambivalence. He likes women, but not priests, warriors, or officials, and his paintings state this fact clearly. His pictures have nearly always been judged too extreme to be shown in public, and yet none of them, not even his 1930 painting *Partouze*, belong to the category of under-the-counter pornography. They are far more reminiscent of those splendidly humorous and sensual postcards of the beginning of the century, in which the suggestion remains on the border of realization.

In 1926, Clovis Trouille painted *Naguerre, ou le 106 n'est pas consigné à la troupe*[1] in which beribboned conscripts and half-naked girls are drinking together merrily in front of the famous and terrifying poster advertising *Chéri-Bibi*: 'Oh no! not the hands! not the hands!'[2] His 1930 composition, *The Ferocious Accusation*, is a complicated dramatic allegory with guillotine, skulls, owls, monsters playing guitars, transfixed communion hosts and flashes of lightning. Subsequently, he painted a great number of scandalous and aggressive scenes, such as the picture in which Christ is seen standing in a cathedral chancel,

having descended from his cross complete with his crown of thorns and wounds, and roaring with laughter; or *My Obsequies*, a scene filled with cruel and ludicrous details: the superb catafalque making its way through a solemn or indecently dressed throng of priests, various leading figures of society, women and ordinary people.

Clovis Trouille's is indeed *popular* art—nothing in common with museum folklore—a true 'people's' art according to the very French tradition of priest-hating and the liking for wine and pretty girls. But his reverend sisters with their skirts tucked up above their thighs, his priests enraptured by alluring seductresses, his gorgeous or pathetic women offering themselves freely, also possess a fantastic and sometimes poignant charm. In a letter written by Gustave Flaubert to the woman he called his 'Muse' can be detected the resonance of a poetry which—if one added humour—is also that of Clovis Trouille, a poetry created from eroticism, violence and despair: 'And even though it is only an immodest costume, chimeric temptation, the unknown, *the aura of evil*, the old poetry of corruption and venality.... I have never been able to watch these women in low-bodiced blouses passing in the rain, under the gas-lights of the lamp-posts, without my heart beating faster; just as the robes of monks with their girdles of knotted cords excite me in I know not what ascetic, deep recesses of my soul. The point of intersection is so complex in this idea of prostitution! Lust, bitterness, nullity of human relationship, muscular frenzy and the clink of gold: so that, gazing into its depths, one is seized with giddiness, and yet one learns so much! And one is so sad! And one dreams of love so well! O devisers of elegies, it is not on ruins that you should lay your head, but on the breasts of these gay ladies.'

Trouille has so far refused to show his paintings in a one-man exhibition. He has occasionally sent pictures to some of the Salons, and invariably experienced difficulties with the organizers. After repeated requests from a gallery which wanted to show his work—nearly all of which is hitherto unreproduced and unexhibited—he made it known to them, after considerable delay, that on the whole he preferred not to have an exhibition, because, he said, for one thing he was not in need of money, and for another thing he valued his paintings at such a high price that no collector could afford to buy them.

---

1. 'No. 106 is not off-limits': *naguerre* is an invented word combining the meanings of *naguère* (not long ago) and *guerre* (war).

2. Chéri-Bibi: hero of the pre-1914 serial novel of the same name by Gaston Leroux. Chéri-Bibi was a terrible but essentially good-hearted criminal pursued inexorably by Fate.... The poster in question illustrates a scene from his adventures in which he has a whole new skin grafted on to his body so as to alter his appearance. The grafting operation was particularly agonizing when it came to the hands, and the picture shows Chéri-Bibi undergoing this final operation, streaming with blood and screaming: 'Oh no! not the hands!....'

Clovis Trouille: *My Burial Vault*. 1947.

Alberto Giacometti: *The Hour of Traces*. 1930.

What is called an 'external object' constitutes a closed unity resistant to our imagination and our desire to alter it at whim. This unity and consistency are the essence of the object. The word itself expresses an idea analogous to 'objection', just as the German word for 'object', *Gegenstand*, means literally 'counter-stand, resistance'.

The object's manner of resistance and its means of forming a closed unity vary endlessly. An object may take on a thousand different forms but it invariably expresses the concept of the closed, the resistant, the unified. Therefore, as soon as a reality shows a regular pattern and begins to possess a constant rhythm, it has the capacity to become an object. In the early thirties, when the surrealist world was beginning to develop into a reality of this nature, the surrealists started to focus their attention upon the creation of *objects*, remarkable points of reference of a universe which is separate from everyday life but still connected to it by the taut, solid threads of desire. The writers in the group also took part in these researches, or, like André Breton, composed *object-poems*: intriguing little pictures combining objects and poetic phrases.

In December, 1936, *La Révolution Surréaliste* No. 8 announced a forthcoming exhibition of objects, whose catalogue would have provided 'a formal definition of the surrealist object'. This exhibition never took place, doubtless because of a lack of sufficient material. Later, new creations began to appear on the scene, which were to increase rapidly in number, as will be seen during the course of this chapter. In 1930 Salvador Dali recommended 'the construction of objects with an erotic significance, in other words, of objects designed to produce a particular sexual emotion by indirect means'. Shortly beforehand, Alberto Giacometti had created a curious structure which attained the simplicity and 'efficiency' of a piece of physical apparatus, a 'mute and mobile object' that can be considered as the first specifically surrealist object. It consisted of a ball bearing a narrow groove along its lower surface, suspended by a cord tied to a rod lying across the top of a framework, and able to swing to and fro above a sharply-angled construction situated beneath it in such a way that the tension of the cord never allows the ball to dovetail completely into the wedge's sharp surface.

The third number of the review *Le Surréalisme A.S.D.L.R.* reproduced this object, as well as the first efforts that it had inspired—Valentine Hugo: a gloved hand and a red hand interlaced; Gala Eluard: two sponges brushing against a bowl of flour; Dali: a woman's shoe holding a glass full of milk in which a lump of sugar is about to dip itself; Breton: a bicycle saddle surrounded by foliage. These are very simplified descriptions of the constructions in question which were all, in fact, extremely complex: in this respect they lacked the essential quality of Giacometti's invention, the sense of unity of a true object.

Alberto Giacometti is Swiss, born in 1910 in Stampa, a small village in the canton of Grisons. His father was a post-impressionist painter well-known in his own country. Alberto, the eldest son, started painting, drawing and sculpting from a very early age. He studied at the École des Arts et Métiers in Geneva, spent nearly two years in Italy, then went to Paris in 1923, working in the studio of Bourdelle and in the academies. In 1930 he met the surrealists.

The third number of *Le Surréalisme A.S.D.L.R.* published a double page of sketches by Giacometti representing several 'mute and mobile objects', including the suspended ball, described above, which was later to be entitled *The Hour of Traces* (another of his objects, also including a suspended ball, originally carried this title; it was reproduced in *Le Surréalisme A.S.D.L.R.* No. 6).

'For some years now,' wrote Giacometti in 1934 in the review *Minotaure*, No. 3, 'I have made only

Alberto Giacometti:
The Palace at 4 a.m.
1933.

sculptures which offered themselves already completed to my imagination; I have limited myself to reproducing them in space without changing anything... (if I even undertake to modify a single aspect or have to calculate one dimension, I am completely lost at once and the whole effect is destroyed). Nothing has ever appeared to me in the form of a picture, and seldom even in the form of a drawing. The attempts I have occasionally made to produce a picture or even a sculpture consciously have always failed.' *The Palace at 4 a.m.*, for example, a fragile little mansion constructed from thin wooden rods, 'took shape slowly towards the end of summer 1932.... By autumn,

its outer reality was so complete that its execution in space took only one day.' Such productions are like the photographs of an invisible reality. Giacometti, in the text quoted above, explains at length the meaning of each section of the Palace, which must remain an arbitrary structure, therefore, only for those who do not understand its inner reality. In fact, the work is entirely *representational*, or, to be more precise, there is an *identity* between the work and inner reality: the contents of the unconscious mind can impregnate certain sectors of the conscious mind so strongly as to be forced to materialize themselves in the shape of objects.

The object-sculptures created by Giacometti between 1930 and 1934 include: *Disagreeable Object* (1931), a sort of elephant's tusk furnished with spikes at its pointed end; *Three Mobile Figures on One Plane* (1932), as ironical as an alarm-clock; *Head-Landscape* (1932); *The Game's Over* (1933); and a *Table* (1933), from which a hand and a half-veiled woman's head are protruding; finally, in 1934, the statue whose origin and meaning André Breton recounted in 'Equation of the Discovered Object'[1] *(objet trouvé)*: a female figure whose hands seem to be clutching an invisible object, explained by Breton as 'an emanation of the desire to love and be loved, in quest of its true human object and in all the agony of this quest'.

The Invisible Object was Giacometti's last surrealist work. At the end of 1934, the sculptor dissociated himself from his former productions and soon renounced them in explicit terms: I myself heard him declare at that point that everything he had done until then was 'masturbation' and that for the time being he had no other objective than to try and 'put into place' a human head. He thereupon began to spend his days modelling busts of his brother Diego.

This sudden conscious preoccupation with materials and techniques, combined with a disdain for his former activity, is inevitably and immediately reminiscent of Chirico's career; all the more so because Giacometti, like Chirico, abandoned his pure, direct style in favour of a less clearly defined approach, more sketchy and impressionistic. Finally, the sculptor's new orientation resulted in the construction of filiform personages, statuettes whose most curious feature is their tremulous sur-

1. Essay published in 1934 in *Intervention Surréaliste*, a special number of the Belgian review *Documents 34* (edited by Jean Stéphane and E.L.T. Mesens).

face and minute size: all of them, moreover, being practically identical.

The conflict with the surrealists that resulted from this change of front was limited to a few mildly acidulous discussions and the signing by some members of the group of a 'motion of defiance' which was never made public. Giacometti's final contribution to Surrealism consisted of two sketches in the margin of a prospectus for conferences scheduled for June, 1935, although the project was never realized.[1]

The anti-surrealist reaction of the author of *The Invisible Object* became as strong and as tenacious as that of Chirico. Giacometti said later—and with no trace of humour—that his surrealist period proved catastrophic for him and was an intolerable impasse; that his objects of this period were 'worthless, fit for the junk-heap'.[2]

But do not his present impressionist statuettes resemble those vague human outlines that architectural draughtsmen include in their project-

Alberto Giacometti: Drawing. 1951.

sketches in order to give the scale of the envisaged constructions? Perhaps the ghost Giacometti elaborates interminably is meaningful only in terms of the emptiness surrounding it: it provides the dimensions of an invisible palace which will never be built.

Yves Tanguy also suggested a series of objects in *Le Surréalisme A.S.D.L.R.* No. 3, in the form of drawings entitled *Weights and Colours*, with explanatory captions describing small comical creatures, in pink plush, in purple plaster, in pale green moulded cotton-wool, in flesh-coloured soft wax. One of these objects was to be 'filled with mercury and covered with bright red plaited straw so as to appear almost weightless'; another 'in sky-blue chalk with hairs on its top' was to function with a symbolic simplicity: 'This object is to be used to write on a blackboard. It will be used from its bottom end, so that finally nothing will be left of it but the tuft of hair on top.'

The name of the true originator of surrealist objects, Marcel Duchamp, figures in the table of contents of the second and fifth issues of the review. The first pages of No. 5 (May, 1933) are devoted to a few of the notes (those concerning the 'Waterfall' and the 'Lighting Gas') written during the construction of the Large Glass of *The Bride Stripped Bare by her Bachelors, Even*; at that moment Duchamp was in the process of collecting the material for his Green Box, which was to include these texts. In No. 2 (October, 1930) are reproduced two pages of a chess study elaborated by Duchamp in collaboration with the master Halberstadt: *Opposition and Sister Squares are Reconciled*,[3] the first work offered to the public by the creator of *The Bride...* for some years. This study would seem at first to be of rather specialized interest, since it concerns a problem of end-game play in chess (as did the concise and original formula for the well-known bishop and knight mate proposed by Raymond Roussel at about the same time).[4] The pawn end-game analyzed by Duchamp and Halberstadt had been the subject of controversy in chess circles for twenty years, and the method used by the two authors was designed, according to the opening phrases of the essay, 'to remove its pseudo-esoteric appearance from the problem'. The title of the booklet, which seems mysterious, is in fact no more so than the terms of a mathematical problem: the difficulty is to find a solution. But it is by no means necessary to be a top-ranking chess-player to follow the argument and understand

Alberto Giacometti: *The Invisible Object*. 1934.

1. This bulletin contained a programme of proposed lectures and demonstrations (for the complete text, see *Documents Surréalistes*; cf also *Histoire du Surréalisme*, p. 231) in a facsimile reproduction in Breton's handwriting, illustrated by Arp, Dali, Dominguez, Max Ernst, Giacometti, Valentine Hugo, Marcel Jean, Man Ray, Tanguy. Duchamp had contributed to the ornamentation by autographing his own thumbprint.
At the end of 1935, Dali gave a lecture in the Théâtre du Vieux Colombier, accompanying it with photographic projections and various other attractions, such as the presentation of an old woman on whose head he balanced an omelette cooked in front of the audience.

2. In the review *L'Œil*, January 15, 1955.

3. Published in a trilingual edition (French, English, German) by Éditions de l'Échiquier (Brussels and Paris, 1932).

4. Cf Raymond Roussel: *Comment j'ai écrit certains de mes Livres* (Lemerre, Paris, 1935).

the developing interplay of relations and forces governing the disposition of the chess pieces and their movements. The ingenious typographical design of the pages adds greatly to the clarity of the demonstrations, and humour is finally evident in the authors' concluding admission, that their system leads inevitably to drawn games.

In the sixth issue of the review (May, 1933) appeared reproductions of a *Surrealist Object* by

L'objet de gauche est en cire molle imitation chair. L'appendice du haut est flottant et d'une couleur plus brune. Les trois formes arrondies du centre sont en matière dure, d'un blanc mat.
L'objet de droite est en craie bleu ciel. Dans le haut, des poils. Cet objet doit servir à écrire sur un tableau noir. Il sera usé par la base, pour qu'il ne finisse par subsister que la touffe de poils du haut.   **Yves TANGUY.**

Max Ernst and *Life of an Object* by Yves Tanguy. The latter is a drawing into which is incorporated a text taken from a botanical treatise: 'The object is capable of defending itself against drought by pushing its roots deep into the soil so as to absorb moisture present at a considerable distance from the surface...'; the banal phrase becomes suggestive when associated with the invented form. An article by Max Ernst, 'Inspiration to Order'[1] (a first brief version of *Beyond Painting*), shows the *collage* to be one of the original forms of the

surrealist object. The description of an object of this kind, notes Max Ernst, can be found in Lautréamont's famous image: 'Beautiful as the chance meeting upon a dissecting table of a sewing-machine with an umbrella', an image that could easily be materialized by the process of *collage* and results, he continues, from 'the pairing of two realities which apparently cannot be paired on a plane unsuited to them'.[2] Other descendants of the *collage* were the *cadavre exquis* ('exquisite corpse') and Salvador Dali's multiple image. It is by this means, Ernst concludes, 'that Surrealism has enabled painting to travel with seven-league boots a long way from Renoir's three apples, Manet's four sticks of asparagus, Derain's little chocolate women, and the Cubists' tobacco-packet.... Needless to say, this has been a great blow to art critics, who are terrified to see the importance of the "author" being reduced to a minimum and the conception of "talent" abolished. Against them, however, we maintain that surrealist painting is within the reach of everybody who is attracted by real revelations and is therefore ready to assist inspiration or make it work to order.'

With the final two numbers of *Le Surréalisme A.S.D.L.R.*, both published in May, 1933, the last purely surrealist review disappeared. This effacement may well have been due to material causes the economic crisis, the soaring costs of publishing, perhaps a lack of patronage (the publication of *Le Surréalisme A.S.D.L.R.* had been dependent upon subsidies from the Vicomte de Noailles). And yet, there were more collaborators than ever: about sixty names figure in the list of contributors to the last number, including some belonging to groups set up outside France. So that at the very moment when Surrealism was arousing a growing interest in Europe and throughout the world, it lost its own autonomous means of expression—but not its hopes of re-establishing a similar vehicle. In 1934, a new review was planned, *Le Surréalisme International*, for which Man Ray had composed a cover: three flags flying, one red, one black, the third red and bearing the hammer and sickle, representing Socialism, Anarchism and Communism respectively (this was the era of

---

1. 'Inspiration to Order' is published in R. Motherwell's compilation *Max Ernst: Beyond Painting* (*op. cit.*)

2. Which recalls Pierre Reverdy's definition of the poetic image, quoted in the *Surrealist Manifesto*.

'united fronts' leading up to the Popular Front). But the project came to nothing.

The very fact of the development and expansion of surrealist ideas can also provide an explanation for this disappearance of their own private forum: certain aspects of Surrealism inevitably underwent the same vulgarization as any other great and fertile concept, and that particular period had already commenced. The situation was very far from providing the 'occultation' demanded in the *Second Manifesto* when Breton and Eluard, at the invitation of the Geneva editor Albert Skira, agreed to collaborate with their friends and on a permanent basis to an art magazine not designed as a surrealist review but allowing Surrealism full access. On May 25, 1933, ten days after the appearance of No. 5-6 of *Le Surréalisme A.S.D.L.R.*, the first issue of the luxurious *Minotaure* was published.

By its title alone (suggested originally by Georges Bataille and André Masson) the new review placed itself under the sign of Surrealism. Minotaur is the ancient symbol and classic example of the hybrid, a being considered in the western world as a 'monster'. The word *hubris* in Greek conveys the meaning of 'a proud insolence towards the gods'. The Greeks saw divinities throughout the universe who bestowed upon people and things their characteristics and their limits. To break these limits, to extend or go beyond the frontiers of being, was to deny external laws and offend the gods.

Minotaur incarnates *hubris* as a consequence of and punishment for an offence against the gods. King Minos had not kept his promise to sacrifice his miraculous bull to the gods: the gods took revenge by making his wife, the Queen, fall in love with the beast and finally give birth to a child with the head of a bull. But though Minotaur is 'against nature' he is alive, terribly alive and dangerous. Mythology then pits Theseus against him, the 'pure man' who is able to find his way through the twists and turns of the Labyrinth's passages thanks to the thread given him by Ariadne: to achieve continuity so to speak, in Minotaur's home, a domain of mutations and sudden turnings, and finally even to slay Minotaur.

So the concept of stable, regular continuity triumphs over the monster, and racial purity over the hybrid. But the story is far from ended and this limpid picture becomes finally very cloudy. Theseus, this reasonable man, returns home and commits an incredible blunder which results in the death of his father; it is true that he has meanwhile abandoned Ariadne on the Island of Naxos, where the god Dionysus lands and weds her. Since Minos' bull had also emerged originally from the sea, it would seem that there exists a hidden identity between Dionysus and Minotaur.

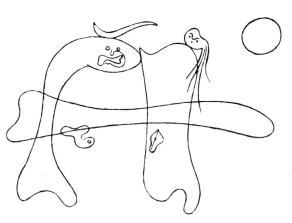

Joan Miró: Drawing. 1933.

The development of the myth seems to indicate that in the end it is Minotaur who triumphs and who wins Ariadne.

Surrealism had appropriated the obscure import of this story, but the relationship becomes clearer if one identifies Theseus with the conscious mind and Minotaur with the unconscious, as the myth suggests. No doubt Surrealism has attempted to bridge these two worlds, but always with a marked predilection for *hubris* and with a constant return to unconscious sources, as is indicated by Max Ernst's text from which a few passages have already been quoted. For if it is true that some interbreedings may prove unfavourable, and that certain combinations may be lethal in terms of heredity —and also in what one might call the heredity of ideas—it is equally true that evolution remains the privilege of hybrids, while pure races stagnate.

Minotaure was hybrid, like its spiritual ancestor, and, to begin with, eclectic. It reproduced pictures by Miró, Dali, Picasso, Braque, Matisse, as well as some post-fauvist 'colts' from the stable of M. Tériade, the nominal editor of the review. André Masson was represented from the very first issue, having just designed the scenery and costumes for a Diaghilev ballet, *Les Présages* (music by Tchaïkowsky), an entertainment which for M. Tériade 'constituted an important date'. In this and subsequent issues, Maurice Raynal, faithful friend of the cubists since their heroic epoch, discussed Despiau and Maillol, Laurens and Lipchitz, Brancusi and Giacometti. There were comprehensive studies of Cézanne, Degas,

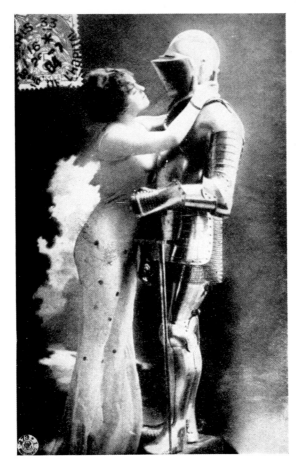

Postcard from the collection of Paul Eluard.

and Fauvism, and a contribution by Le Corbusier devoted to the drawings of a madman, the Swiss Louis Sutter. Classical art was represented by Tintoretto, Poussin, Rubens, Corneille de Lyon, Pol de Limbourg, Georges de la Tour, Holbein. Contemporary writers included Reverdy, Valéry, Saint-Exupéry, Ramuz, etc. Occasional articles on music were also published, and an essay by Giorgio de Chirico, 'On Silence'.

In fact *Minotaure* would have been no different from any other art review if the collaboration of the surrealists had not imposed upon it a particularly intense pattern. Chief editor in all but name, André Breton published some of his most

brilliant essays in the magazine: on automatism, chance, dreams, predestination—'The Automatic Message' accompanied by a number of drawings by mediums; 'Beauty shall be Convulsive' illustrated by Man Ray's photographs; 'The Sunflower Night' *('La Nuit du Tournesol')* with images by the photographer Brassaï; 'The Starry Castle' *('Le Château Étoilé')* embellished with new *frottages* by Max Ernst; etc.

Maurice Heine contributed comments on the Gothic novels and the naïvely frightening illustrations in their early editions; on the *'femme féique'*, the type of fairy-like ideal woman which Restif de la Bretonne insisted should be depicted in the engravings Binet made as illustrations for his works; on martyrologies unearthed from old books; on the apocalyptic *Prodigies* of Duvet, the engraver from Langres, who anticipated Dürer in this field; on the terrifying, impassioned expressions of the Tibetan Minotaur-gods. He also contributed more specialized studies examining various problems of psychopathology.

In one issue of *Minotaure*, Paul Eluard spread through fifteen pages, with many colour reproductions, the riches of those 'treasures of nothingness', illustrated postcards: floral designs, messages of good wishes, travel cards, cards reproducing news items of the times, humorous cards, cards with insets and flaps ('the postcard has often made use of *collage*, and nearly always with most happy results'), licentious cards, cards dedicated to love and women.[1] His poem *Juste Milieu* was published surrounded by the drawings of madmen, while his 'Physique of Poetry' reviewed the work of poets who were also illustrators—Jarry, William Blake, and Lewis Carroll; or the illustrators of poets—Delacroix of *Faust*; Aubrey Beardsley of Wilde; Rops, Renoir, and Matisse of Mallarmé; Klee and Arp of Tzara; Picasso of Apollinaire and Benjamin Péret; Tanguy and Max Ernst of Eluard; Derain of Reverdy and Breton; etc.

Benjamin Péret wrote on automatons, armour, ruins, and Max Ernst described 'The Mysteries of the Forest', René Crevel studied strange aspects of the world of fashion ('The Great Model Seeks and Finds her Skin'), while Tristan Tzara examin-

1. In 1937, a series of twenty-one *Surrealist Postcards* was printed and put on sale through the initiative of Georges Hugnet, reproducing paintings, drawings, *collages* or objects by Arp, Bellmer, Breton, Jacqueline Breton, Dali, Dominguez, Duchamp, Eluard, Nusch Eluard, Ernst, Hugnet, Marcel Jean, Dora Maar, Magritte, Miró, Méret Oppenheim, Paalen, Penrose, Man Ray, and Tanguy.

ed the psychic determinants of women's fashions in an article on hats: 'Why a Woman's Taste is Always Right'. Pierre Mabille was another writer whose interest in Surrealism led him to contribute to *Minotaure*: his essays in the review dealt with anthropology, symbols, 'luminous consciousness', and he introduced unpublished drawings by Seurat.

Dali, above all, found an ideal spring-board in *Minotaure*. His reply in No. 3-4 to a questionnaire sent by Tériade to various artists concerning the problems of the model in painting, of spontaneity and chance, is worth quoting. While the other painters who had been consulted restricted themselves to solid generalities such as: 'Circumstances are always favourable for someone who is in his right place' (Braque), 'One must give a picture its chance' (Borès), 'I aim first at a physical sensation so as to reach the soul subsequently' (Miró), and so on, Dali replied to the questionnaire point by point and let it be known that, for him, the *model* was a 'succulent and gelatinous pig's trotter *au gratin* in which, as everyone knows, the soft superfine meat serves only to enfold within its delirious nutritive softness the true and authentic gnawed bone of objectivity.' 'If,' continued Dali, 'the model has disappeared today, it is most probably because the painter has eaten it.... How could that particular pig's trotter continue to exist today when we know that the surrealists, going beyond the cannibalism of meat, have reached the stage of bone cannibalism, to a point where they devour objects and object-beings?' Furthermore, *spontaneity* 'is also a pig's trotter, but a pig's trotter turned inside out, in other words a lobster which, contrary to the pig's trotter, presents an external skeleton while the superfine delicate meat, that is to say delirium, fills the interior.' As for *chance*, 'it might very well be nothing but a serious and important grilled cutlet, brim-full of flavour and biological afterthoughts, because chance represents and constitutes exactly the mean point of softness between the "model" and "spontaneity", that is to say between the pig's trotter *au gratin* and the lobster *à l'américaine*. One may observe, in fact, that in the case of the grilled cutlet the bones are half inside, half outside, in other words co-existent....'

Before publication, Breton had read this page to his friends. Everyone was delighted, except Roger Caillois who objected that the reasoning appeared to him to be somewhat sophistic, to say the least, a proposition entirely accepted by the others but considered unimportant in view of the bewildering effect such a text was bound to produce in *Minotaure*. The most disconcerted person of all was no doubt the questioner himself, who capped Dali's reply with this final *mea culpa*: 'Painters are more qualified than anyone to cast light on certain things which art-criticism has constantly ignored but which, as a result of this

Salvador Dali: Cover for *Minotaure*, no. 8, June, 1936.

first perspective, seem nevertheless essential.'[1]

Dali's later contributions were in the same vein. They were entitled: 'A Paranoiac-Critical Interpretation of the Obsessive Image of Millet's *Angelus*', 'Concerning the Terrifying and Edible Beauty of *Art Nouveau*', 'The New Colours of Spectral Sex-Appeal', 'The Aerodynamic Apparition of Object-Beings', 'Non-Euclidean Psychology of a Photograph', 'The Spectral Surrealism of Eternal Pre-Raphaelite Femineity'. Finally he formulated the 'First Morphological Law Relating to Soft Structures' (dealing with bearded women) in the ninth issue, October 1936—it was his last contribution.

Man Ray published in *Minotaure* some 'Portraits of Women' taken from an album published in 1933,[2] as well as *Dance-Horizons*, images of different dances and dancers, and a number of other documents. In *The Bouquet* he used the magic of solarization to change a firework display into a spray of flowers in broad daylight. *Explosante-Fixe* is a photo of a dancer in action, used as a frontispiece to Breton's article 'Beauty Shall be Convulsive'. And the review also reproduced his *Revolving Doors*, the album of abstract drawings which he had composed in New York in 1916-17.[3]

In the role of a temporary art critic, Jacques Prévert spoke sentimentally of the tiny ancient statues of Beotia: 'Those who constructed you with their hands constructed you in their own image.... I would like to see those men, take them by the arm and speak joyfully to them... drink a glass with them....—Then, slightly tipsy, we would go together to look at the statues of today... and we would become helpless with laughter in front of the monuments to the dead, in front of the monuments to the sick... in front of the monuments to old men... to eunuchs... to assassins... to the Marshal of France... to Maurras... to senile idiots... to the mad... to fire... to help... to the Archbishop of Paris... to Monsieur Seguin's goat... to Gallifet... to cretins... to the etc, etc, etc.'

Under the sign of Sade and Freud, several critics and scholars contributed essays revealing the extent and significance of the strange, terrible or marvellous aspects of instinctual expression in works of the past. Pierre Courthion discussed 'The Sadism of Urs Graf', and the element of cruelty in Géricault's paintings. G. Pudelko wrote about Uccello and 'Piero di Cosimo, an Eccentric Painter', Paul Recht about 'Botticelli and the Plague'. Max Raphaël published his sociological and psychological reflections on Baroque art. Edward James faithfully repeated Dali's preoccupations by extolling 'The Marvel of Minuteness' in the work of some old masters. Thanks to the reproductions in *Minotaure*, a renewed interest (which has continued to grow) was shown in the work of the master of composite heads, Arcimboldo, and in the school he inspired, with the pyramids of fruit, flowers, vegetables, foliage, fish, and animals, and even the landscapes, that all turn into human faces.

The cover of the first number of *Minotaure* reproduced an object-picture by Picasso:[4] against a background of corrugated cardboard a drawing of the minotaur is superimposed on an arrangement of ribbons, lace doilies, silver paper, and artificial leaves. In the inaugural number, an article by André Breton presented hybrids and objects, the hybrid-objects constructed by Picasso. In 1930, in *La Peinture au Défi*,[5] Louis Aragon had described Picasso bringing to life 'old pieces of netting and cardboard, strings and corrugated iron, rags from the refuse-heap'. In his article, Breton speaks now of plant-sculptures blending plant-life and forged iron; he describes a personage made from thin strips of iron, festooned with children's toys, whose foot is a cobbler's last; a fig-tree root topped by a red feather; and a small picture representing a leaf (a real leaf) and a butterfly (a real butterfly): 'It is only in 1933 that a real butterfly has been able to enter the field of a picture, and has been able to do this, moreover, without its entire surroundings crumbling immediately into dust,' remarks Breton.... 'A mind so constantly

1. Dali's culinary metaphysics had a dadaist precursor. Raoul Haussmann, the Dadasopher, edited a manifesto in Berlin in 1920, 'A Return to Objectivity in Art', in which he claimed that Italian Futurism was the expression of a people 'accustomed to dry food', that 'Cubism had taken shape in France as a result of this nation's fondness for soup', and that 'the incomprehensible German soul' had given birth to the hybrid Expressionism because it was comparable to 'soup with meat-balls'. (Cf. R. Haussmann: *Courrier Dada, op.cit.*)

2. By James Thrall Soby, Hartford, Connecticut, for *Cahiers d'Art*, Paris, and Random House, New York.

3. See above, p. 60.

4. The covers of *Minotaure* were illustrated successively by Picasso, G.-L. Roux, Derain, Borès, Duchamp, Miró, Dali, Matisse, Magritte, Max Ernst and Masson.

5. A preface to the catalogue of an Exhibition of *Collages* (more accurately *papiers collés* and *collages*) at the Galerie Goemans, which brought together works by Arp, Braque, Dali, Duchamp, Ernst, Gris, Miró, Magritte, Man Ray, Picabia, Picasso, Tanguy. Included among the reproductions in the catalogue were photo-montages by Lissitski and Rodtchenko designed for political propaganda.

J. de Momper : *Landscape-Head*. Eighteenth century.

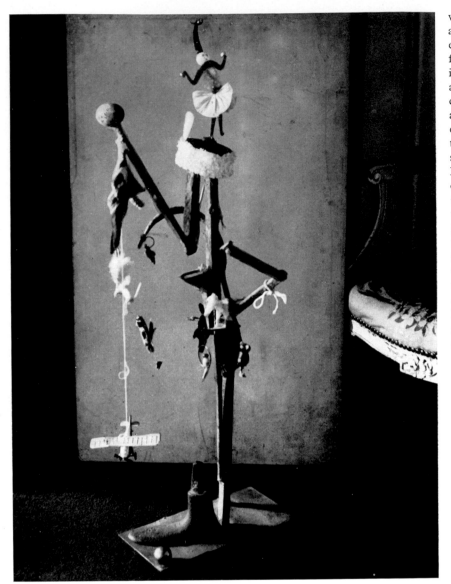

which was apparently supposed, to represent—an excrement, 'as, indeed, would become quite evident once Picasso had placed the relevant flies in position'. Yet the subject of this picture inspired a bucolic optimism in Breton rather than a Dalinian 'terror'. Apparently the artist 'deplored the necessity of using colour for want of a suitably durable genuine dried excrement, and regretted especially the impossibility of reproducing these particularly *inimitable* excrements that he sometimes noticed in the country where children had been eating cherries without bothering to spit out the stones.' 'The deliberate taste for cherry-stones in this situation,' continued Breton, 'seems to me, I must say, to provide the most objective proof possible of the very particular interest which the relationship between the unassimilated and the assimilated should arouse: a relationship whose variations, in terms of the benefit of mankind, may well be considered the essential motivating force of artistic creation.' It would appear that the humour of this passage is one of 'reception' rather than 'transmission', in other words, apparent to the reader but not to the author.

The article was copiously illustrated: photographs by Brassaï of sculptures in cast iron, bronze, plaster, steel rods and sprung wire; reproductions of sketches and preliminary studies after Grünewald's *Crucifixion*, and twenty-eight drawings in the style of the 'Metamorphoses': variations on the human body transformed into balls, planks, basins, rain-gutters, horns and trumpets, wheels, tables, chairs, etc.

Pablo Picasso: *Object*. 1933.

and exclusively inspired is capable of turning everything into poetry, of ennobling everything.'[1]

The article, entitled 'Picasso in his Element', ended by extolling a small unfinished painting

Thus, the fame and influence of the movement was continuing to grow, yet many of the painters (and poets) remained far from affluent. During the years of economic crisis, none of the surrealists was even remotely enchanted by the sort of Bohemian existence to which most of them found themselves reduced. After the collapse of the Galerie Goemans, Dali himself had considered the idea of trying to earn some money as a commercial artist. On the advice of Clovis Trouille, he had submitted a project to the management of Trouille's mannequin-manufacturing company for a series of display figures, mannequins made from leaves or wire, mannequin-aquariums in which goldfish would have been seen swimming, and so on. These ideas, some of which have become

1. Which brings to mind Arp's poem, 'What the Violins are Singing in their Bed of Lard' (1939) from his collection *Le Siège de l'Air* (op. cit.):
    ...Le papillon empaillé devient un papapillon empapaillé. Le papapillon empapaillé devient un grandpapapillon grandempapaillé....

236

commonplace today, were rejected by the firm in question as scandalous and impracticable. Max Ernst and Miró were both just as financially embarrassed at times. And Tanguy, after a period of relative prosperity during which he had developed his talents to their full power, found buyers for his paintings becoming so rare that he was once more on the verge of destitution.

All this did not prevent new painters from joining the surrealists; Victor Brauner, for instance, who was born in Bucharest in 1903: his parents' house was in a street appropriately named Calea Victoriei. In 1933 Brauner was living in the rue du Moulin-Vert, in the Montrouge district of Paris. His studio was in the same building as those of Yves Tanguy and Giacometti—they were three very different establishments: Giacometti's studio black and dusty, cluttered with tools, sculptures and scattered objects; Tanguy's studio clear, clean, and bare except for his paintings on the walls, a bed, a table, a few chairs, and the easel, palette and brushes which he kept in a state of rigorous clean-

Rue du Moulin-Vert, Paris, where Yves Tanguy, Alberto Giacometti, and Victor Brauner lived in 1933.

liness and order; Brauner's studio, with canvases piled high against the walls, and sculptures too (I can remember a sort of Gorgon's head egurgitating a green celluloid frog). From one corner of the latter room a dilapidated lemur in a cage punctuated the conversation with unnerving groans and squeaks, while Margit—the artist's first wife—cooked highly indigestible but extremely tasty Judeo-Rumanian dishes for the visitors.

During the course of the years Brauner's work had been influenced in turn by movements as diverse as Cubism, Dadaism and Expressionism. He had composed a series of large cryptic pictures that were both comical and scandalous. *The Strange Case of Mr K.* was an enormous painting divided into regular squares, each separate square illustrating one of the metamorphoses of the Mr K. of the title: an obese, mustachioed figure, the caricature of some banker or policeman from the pages of Kafka and Jarry, first depicted stark naked, then, later, glittering with decorations, wearing crucifixes, in a tail-coat, in a cassock, finally becoming a map, an Arcimboldian mosaic of objects, architectures, machines, etc. *Mr K.'s Power of Concentration*, an immense diptych, showed the same character against an alternately black and white background, covered with tiny celluloid babies looking just like pink maggots.

Brauner was most anxious to be introduced to the surrealists, and so his neighbour Yves Tanguy yielded to his entreaties and, one day during 1933, took him along to the Café de la Place Blanche, which had become the group's meeting-place. Victor Brauner's first contribution to a surrealist publication was a drawing made for the booklet *Violette Nozières*.

After his meeting with the surrealists, Brauner began to employ perspectives and cast shadows

The Café de la Place Blanche.

Victor Brauner, 1935.

Victor Brauner: *Composition.* 1937.

Victor Brauner: *Kabiline in Movement.* 1937.

reminiscent of Chirico, to emphasize the imaginary or remembered objects of his new paintings. Chirico had derived inspiration from the displays of scientific instruments in the shop-windows of Ferrara; perhaps the window of some orthopedic establishment in Bucharest's Strada Doamnei, or the chemists' shop-fronts, provided Brauner with his point of departure for pictures such as *We are Betrayed*, painted in Paris in 1934: in the glare of a hard light coming from some invisible window a most strange paralytic, constructed from boot-trees, coat-racks and hat-blocks, is sitting stiffly

upright in an armchair, like one of Chirico's mannequins in different garb; but in the background an amusing and disquieting animal, with extraordinary long ears and tail, is certainly the product of a more private mythology. The vampire-monk of *Kabiline in Movement* (1934) must have been haunting some pharmacist, on whose premises the tiled floor stretches back in perspective towards a back-shop filled with strange objects.

Brauner had his first Paris exhibition in December, 1934, at the Galerie Pierre.[1] The material results were disappointing and he returned to Bucharest soon afterwards. We shall re-encounter him in Paris in 1938.

Oscar Dominguez was twenty-eight when he made his first appearance at the Café de la Place Blanche towards the end of 1934, wrapped in an enormous overcoat that made him look like a bear. The Parisian winter had always had a depressing effect on this native of Tenerife, where the temperature never drops below 70°F. at any time of year. Dominguez had already paid several visits to Paris. After the death of his father, a land-owner who had bequeathed his children nothing but debts, he spent some time as a commercial artist, experiencing success and boredom in equal measure. Painting was his passion, and he had not waited to be accepted into the Paris group before considering himself a surrealist. In May, 1933 he had had a 'surrealist exhibition' at the Circulo de Bellas

1. For the text of the preface, by André Breton, see *Documents Surréalistes.*

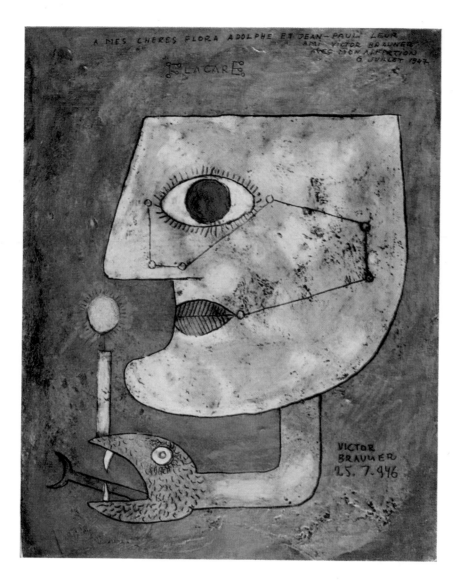

Victor Brauner: *Composition in Wax*. 1946.

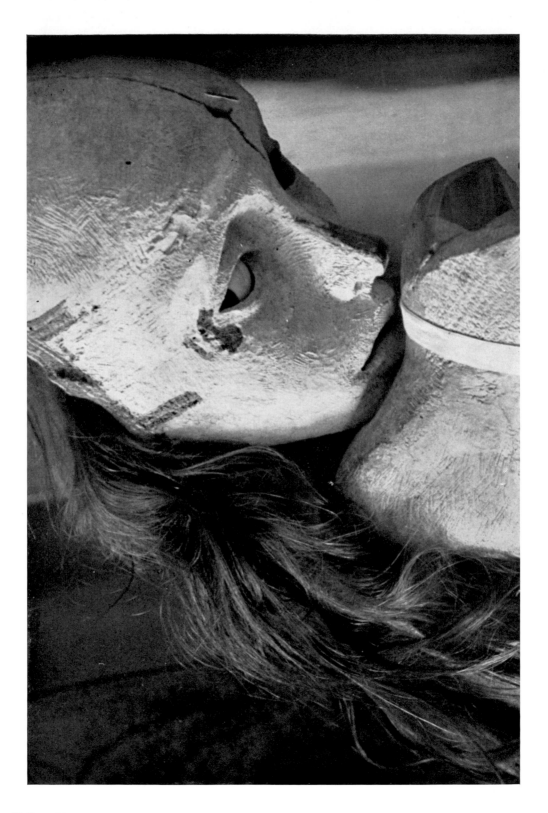

Hans Bellmer: *The Doll*. 1934.

Artes in Tenerife, under the auspices of the review *Gaceta de Arte*; the catalogue reproduced two of his paintings, *Sueño* (1929) and *Souvenir de Paris* (1930), which are comparable and by no means inferior to Dali's first surrealistic works of 1927. Max Ernst's influence is discernible, and other models can be guessed from certain titles: *Mujer Invisible, El Enigma de la Inspiración, Efecto Surrealista*, etc.

When he met the Parisian surrealists he was living in the Rue des Abbesses in Montmartre, in a very high-ceilinged studio, together with his companion Roma, a Polish girl who fed him almost entirely on minced beef. He was painting fairly large pictures which gave expression to a strange humour: a bull, half skeleton, cradling a naked woman in the rib-cage of his chest as though she were in a hammock; a female torso emerging from a blue fog, balancing a gigantic safety-pin on her head. Then followed a series of paintings of much smaller size, in which his mastery of technique and his precision almost equalled Dali's and possessed the same care for detail and facility of execution. From this period one may mention *The Hunter*, which represents a hand-shaped cage imprisoning a bird. Later, Dominguez conjured up such images as an anthropomorphic heating apparatus, a steam-roller breaking into pieces as it tries vainly to flatten a rose, a gnarled tree growing through the body of a brand new car: blendings and conflicts between nature and machines. The eternal Spanish theme was to reappear in his picture of a ghostly bull-fight, in which the beast's horns send out flashes of lightning to a coffin containing the toreador's body.

The sixth issue of *Minotaure* (December, 1934) featured two pages of photographs of *dolls*, 'variations on the assembling of an articulated minor'. But these figurines, with an air of lewd abandon that one might associate with a victim of Jack the Ripper, seem more ready to be disassembled: their limbs are sometimes connected by ball-joints to a torso with budding breasts, but usually the body is dismembered and its parts lost in a tangle of ribbons and lace. Sometimes the doll is nothing more than a skeleton of rods and framework, its clothes disordered, giving a suggestive wink over one dislocated shoulder.

The author of these scandalous reveries was a German, Hans Bellmer, living in Berlin where he had been an advertising artist. Hitler's rise to power forced him to abandon this occupation, since he had refused to join any of the Nazi organizations. In the resulting isolation he had begun to construct the fetishes of the most 'degenerate' of arts, according to Hitlerian terminology. '...What sweated through the staircase or the cracks in the doors when these girls were playing at being doctors, what dripped from those clysters filled with raspberry-juice, intermingled to provide something

René Magritte: Cover for *Minotaure*, no. 10, December, 1937.

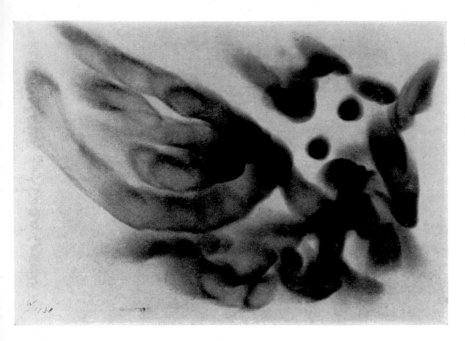

Wolfgang Paalen: *Fumage*. 1938.

Kurt Seligmann: *End of the Automobile.* 1938.

(*Totemic Landscape of My Childhood*, for example, in *Minotaure* No. 12-13, May, 1939). Esteban Francés and Remedios Lissarraga, friends of Dominguez from Barcelona, came to Paris in 1937; Francés turned the process of *grattage* to his own uses.[2] Kurt Seligmann was the first surrealist painter to derive inspiration from the art of heraldry.[3]

One should also mention Balthus, whose exhibition at the Galerie Pierre in 1934 attracted the attention of the surrealists, although he has never belonged to the surrealist group or participated in any of their activities. His composition *The Street*[4] is almost shockingly unusual because of

2. *The River*, reproduced in *Minotaure* No. 12-13. *Desire*, by Remedios, appeared in No. 10.

3. *Les Vagabondages Héraldiques*, fifteen engravings by K. Seligmann, with poems by Pierre Courthion (Chroniques du Jour, Paris, 1934). See also his painting *Jubivillad* in *Minotaure* No. 12-13.

4. Reproduced in the special number of *Documents 34*, June, 1934.

very like the essence of seduction, well able to excite desire.'[1]

After learning of the existence of *Minotaure*, Bellmer had sent a selection of reproductions of his creations to the review. In 1936 he went to Paris to meet the surrealists, accompanied by his wife, whose delicate features were curiously evocative of the emaciated faces of her husband's dolls; Margarethe died soon after their return to Germany. Because of this, and because of the increasingly unbearable atmosphere in his own country, Bellmer decided to leave for good and take refuge in Paris. The only tangible evidence of his Berlin activity that he brought away with him was in the shape of a few copies of a tiny little book bound in pale blue watered silk, *Die Puppe*, a collection of photographs taken by him of his dolls in characteristic poses. He joined the surrealist group, invented fresh permutations and situations for his figurines, and at the same time developed a graphic style whose acuteness, precision and elegance are dedicated to an erotism that is often cruel.

In 1935, Wolfgang Paalen, after trudging for years through the wastelands of abstract art, suddenly saw the light—of Surrealism. He introduced the process of *fumage*, interpreting the smoke-trails deposited on a surface by a candle-flame

1. From an article by Bellmer on his dolls published in *Cahiers d'Art*, June, 1936.

the strange contrasts in appearance and manner between the various stylized figures, the erotic nature of certain details, and the perfectly commonplace street-scene that provides the frame for these disquieting elements. One is reminded of the unreal, dream-like effect of certain images by the romantic painter Fuseli, in which the objects in the same picture are all depicted on different scales: animals are enormous or tiny, women dwarf-like or normal in size, flowers have immense calyces, and so on—especially in Fuseli's series of pictures inspired by Shakespeare's *Midsummer Night's Dream*. This same displacement is to be found in *The Street*[3], but in terms of intellect: each individual in Balthus' painting seems to live a separate existence, to belong to a world apart, a special dimension, resulting in an atmosphere of *absence* which is the secret of the sense of disorientation inherent in all of this artist's work. Balthus has created a number of illustrations for Emily Brontë's *Wuthering Heights*,[1] and has drawn upon this theme for several subsequent paintings. More recently he has painted very large pictures in which a violent immodesty is evident (as, for instance, *The Window*, 1956).

The word 'object' is, as I have already remarked, primarily a synonym for 'resistance'; no aspect of existence devoid of resistances could contain objects. Impressionist painting, in which things tend to blend into each other, provides some conception of a world without resistances and without objects, an entirely subjective, individual world—'idealist' in the language of philosophy.

And yet the point of departure for Surrealism is the subjective world; Impressionism lies at the origin of surrealist painting, and Chirico, who has discussed Impressionism learnedly in various critical essays, is not more 'objective' than Monet—on the contrary. Despite this fact, the surrealists, and Chirico himself in particular, rediscovered the object: a new object containing a large admixture of subjectivity, in the shape of Desire. But desire also implies resistance, is a limited, defined tendency, and by its very nature presupposes a certain degree of restraint. So that an object, in the surrealist sense of the word, is a complex of fantasy and restraint, of desire and resistance, which possesses a material substance.

1. See *Minotaure*, nos. 5 and 7.

It is possible to obtain such a materialization through the resources of painting. Surrealist painting illustrates the reciprocity and antagonism of objective reality and subjective reality: for example, surrealist painters often locate their new beings, their desire-objects in a more or less realistic landscape. In his *Treatise on Painting*, Leonardo da Vinci says that 'a most important part of painting is the background of painted objects... in which the outlines of natural bodies have a convex curvature.' In the work of the surrealists, these backgrounds—deserts, oceans, mountains, clouds—may also be interiorized, symbolized in some way, sometimes merely suggested, with the desire-objects standing out against these organic-inorganic scenes.

Balthus: *Two Young Girls*. 1949.

In the work of Max Ernst, the relationship between object and landscape is constant. Beginning in 1934, Ernst painted a series of pictures of fields, terraced and partitioned by low walls, where long white wings have crashed, from whose snapped joints visceral growths are blossoming: the *Garden*

Max Ernst: *Garden Airplane Trap.* 1936.

Airplane Traps deal with air disasters, a theme rarely exploited hitherto in painting. Tanguy has given the object-landscape relationship its purest surrealist expression; in his paintings the invented object, both desire and memory, is delineated in landscapes of inner reality. Picasso's surrealist phase (the 'Metamorphoses') is characterized by the presence of such objects in a realistic landscape. During 1935, Miró composed paintings entitled *Person in the Presence of Nature*, *Animated Landscape*, etc, and from earlier years one can mention, among many others, *Catalan Landscape* (1923-1924, a picture including written phrases), and *Person Throwing a Stone at a Bird* (1926). As for Dali, he has never used any other process; his pictures invariably represent more or less metamorphosed objects in a meticulously realistic landscape.

Beyond its purely sensory harmonic and plastic stage, painting is capable of transforming desire into concrete forms which then possess a reality extending beyond subjective reality. Here one can discern a concept close to that of Jung's *archetypes*. This heretical psychoanalyst has shown that certain 'complexes' are almost identical in a large number of individuals and only alter very slowly during a sequence of generations. According to this theory, the female image which exists in each human being, the *anima* in Jung's terminology, is invariably an archetype, but since most men are not very individualized, their anima remains so vague that it is difficult to describe it exactly and its 'solidification' into a well-defined object retains a contradictory character. Surrealist objects, in so far as they are 'complex-objects', may well incarnate an archetype. Although most of them are mysterious, unstable, animated and contradictory, they occasionally become 'archetypal portraits', and it is indeed the most convincing of these archetypal portraits which achieve the completeness and stability enabling them to become 'collective portraits' that are *good likenesses*, that is to say images in which each of us can *recognize his own desire*.

In the creation of surrealist objects, Dominguez demonstrated an infallible inventive power and dexterity. He elaborated an endless succession of constructions in which the most disparate elements met on an entirely unsuitable plane—which suddenly turned out to suit them very well indeed. No description can do justice to the sheer perfection of detail of these creations—though by now most of them have disappeared—in which the concept

of the readymade is splendidly renewed: *Le Tireur* is a plaster reproduction of the celebrated Roman statuette *Tireur d'Epine* minus its head and legs, the torso divided by a vertical pane of glass. *The Typist*'s two charming little ivory hands with long handles (they are back-scratchers) are poised above rows of glass fragments. *Exact Sensibility* is a white globe out of which a hand protrudes, gripping a hypodermic syringe that it is in the act of plunging into the globe; the object in question extends into other structures that finally blend

Oscar Dominguez: *Exact Sensibility*. 1935.

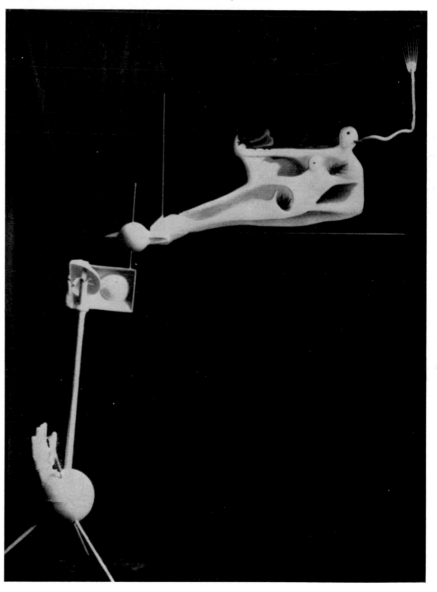

245

Oscar Dominguez: *Arrivée de la Belle Epoque.* 1936.

into a picture and still continue to develop into new objects outside the picture's frame: this combination (of which only the picture itself has survived) achieves a curious synthesis between object and picture. *Arrivée de la Belle Epoque* is a small statue of a woman separated at the waist by a rectangular frame between the upper and lower sections: inside the frame a slender cone in red galalith and a perforated point-protector stand side by side. Other objects represent a rubber horse passing through a toy bicycle; a figure with a head made from a ping-pong ball, completely tied up with string, apart from one dangling doll's leg inside the glass-fronted framework of a clock; another little horse, seen through a magnifying glass, which splits slowly in two, operated by the mechanism of a photographic shutter-release; a celluloid swan floating in a pool of moulded plaster inside something resembling a chalice.

One day Dominguez discovered an enormous and obsolete musical instrument in the *foire aux puces*, which the dealer told him was an ophicleide: with a female head fixed on top and a coat of white paint, this ruin was transformed into the most luxurious, fashionable evening gown. For *Opening*, the word 'Paris' cut through a zinc plate seems to be bristling with comical hair-curlers—the strips of metal from the cut-out letters are wound around sardine-can openers; behind their 'openings' can be glimpsed a violin's scrolled neck transformed into Cinderella's fragile slipper. Dominguez built an immense black table shaped like a grand piano for the studio in the Boulevard Montparnasse where he was living in 1936, as well as a comfortable armchair obtained by padding the inner surface of a wheelbarrow with red satin (this last object was particularly admired by some connoisseurs, for whom Dominguez executed several replicas of his upholstered wheelbarrow).[1] This surrealist furnishing scheme was completed by an ancient gramophone painted white, and quite soundless, since the turn-table revolved eternally beneath a poised hand which had taken the place of the pickup arm, while two female legs emerged from the contraption's horn. Its title was *Never*.

In the author's studio, 1936: Marcel Jean with Oscar Dominguez, who had just completed his object *Opening*.

An *Exhibition of Surrealist objects* was thus not only a possibility in 1936 but had become imperative. It took place during that year, between May 22 and 29, at the Paris residence in the Rue de Marignan of Charles Ratton, an expert in primitive arts. This exhibition provided the review *Cahiers d'Art* with the opportunity of publishing a special number[2] in which an article by André Breton, 'Crisis of the Object', discussed the surrealist concept of the object in Hegelian terms; Claude Cahun, in 'Beware of Tame Objects', attempted to assess the social significance of surrealist objects; I emphasized their symbolic-sexual importance in an essay whose title was borrowed from Domin-

---

1. *Minotaure* no. 10 reproduced a photograph by Man Ray (from a series entitled *Dawn of Objects*) depicting an elegant lady in evening dress reclining in an upholstered wheelbarrow. The gown was by the couturier Lucien Lelong—and the wheelbarrow by Dominguez.

2. *Cahiers d'Art* had already devoted an issue to Surrealism in 1935, with contributions by members of the French and foreign groups. Another issue published Max Ernst's *Beyond Painting* in 1936. A later issue devoted to Picasso's poems, with contributions mainly by the surrealists, will be discussed in a later chapter.

Photograph by Man Ray, gown by Lucien Lelong, wheelbarrow by Oscar Dominguez. 1937.

guez' object *Arrivée de la Belle Epoque*. The article that Dali had contributed to this number alluded to the swastika, although with prudent reservations, but he concerned himself chiefly with Plato: and here he was on surer ground, since this Greek philosopher has always been a target for the gibes of the surrealists. In Dali's words:

'When Plato writes, "Non-geometers, keep out!" we are all quite aware that this philosopher is indulging in his usual half mocking half good-humoured facetiousness and garrulousness, since, in fact, no one cared less about geometry than he did.... If the truth be told, he was really the *Dame aux Camélias* of Mediterranean thought... who,

Serge Brignoni: Interpreted *Objets Trouvés*. 1936.

Bismuth crystals.

Natural object.

Bird-man from Easter Island.

Marcel Jean: *The Spectre of the Gardenia* (reproduced on stamps). 1936.

Mathematical object.

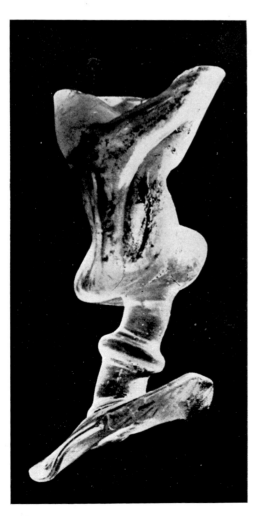

Perturbed object: A wine-glass found after the eruption of Mont Pelé in Martinique.

without realizing it, inaugurated brilliantly the first great official brothel of esthetics.'

In the Charles Ratton exhibition were to be seen:

Natural objects: mineral kingdom—agates, and crystals containing pockets of fossil water;[1] vegetable kingdom—sensitive and carnivorous plants; animal kingdom—a stuffed ant-bear and a gigantic oepyornis' egg.

Interpreted natural objects: a 'monkey-shaped fern', as found in florists' shops. *Incorporated natural objects*: shells and pebbles integrated into sculptures and objects by Max Ernst. *Perturbed objects*, such as the completely distorted household articles found in the ruins of St Pierre de la Martinique after the eruption of Mont Pelé in 1902. *Objets trouvés* ('discovered objects'): 'Any discarded object within reach of our hands should be considered a precipitate of our desire,' claimed André Breton in the preface to the Exhibition catalogue.[2] These 'discovered objects' were incongruous, unexpected, strange or simply of unknown origin: books, fetishes, pipes, biscuits, and so on—but the book had spent some time in the sea and was encrusted with shell-fish, the fetish had no doubt presided over some black mass, the bowl of the cherry-wood pipe was fashioned into a grimacing head, and the star-shaped biscuit was signed 'Raymond Roussel'.

Interpreted objets trouvés: roots, round pebbles and various rock structures were displayed and arranged in such a way that they took on an added meaning or seemed to reveal some hidden message. *American objects*: Eskimo, Hopi Indian, Mexican, Peruvian, etc, and *Oceanian objects* from Torres Strait, New Guinea, New Ireland, New Britain, the New Hebrides, the Loyalty Islands, etc. *Readymades* by Duchamp: the *Bottle Rack* and *Why not Sneeze?* The *Mathematical objects* provided one of the revelations of the exhibition; they were constructions designed for teaching purposes, putting into concrete form certain formulas of space geometry, such as 'Enneper's surface of negative constant curve, the differential coefficient of the pseudo-sphere', the 'Aspect of the elliptic function $P''(U)$ for $G_2 = O$ and $G_3 = 4'$, 'Kummer's surface of sixteen double points, of which eight are real', etc. There was something astonishing and moving in these shapes whose lines and curves expressed an exact mathematical problem and yet, at the same time, suggested a whole number of analogies and of associations between ideas and images. Max Ernst had originally come across these constructions in the Institut Henri Poincaré and had mentioned them to the director of *Cahiers d'Art*, Christian Zervos, who in his turn had asked Man Ray to photograph them. Man Ray selected a few from the dozens of such objects crowded together in dusty glass cases and created beautifully exact and evocative photographic reproductions of them.

Last came the *surrealist objects*, which included Jean Arp's *Survivor's Kit*, bits of wood without any purpose carefully secured to a panel as though they were vitally important tools; and a sculpture made out of newspaper called *Mutilé et Apatride*. Bellmer's ball-and-socket-joint creations were on show, as were some object-poems by Breton, an object by Jacqueline Breton called *The Fair-haired Woman*, Dali's *Aphrodisiac Jacket* decorated with forty glasses filled with peppermint, and various objects by Dominguez. Max Ernst contributed a *Mobile Object*, and there were two objects from Giacometti's surrealist period, *The Hour of Traces* and *Three Mobile Figures on One Plane*. A painting by Magritte entitled *This is a Piece of Cheese* did in fact depict a piece of cheese, while Maurice Henry's *Homage to Paganini* consisted of a little sick violin swathed in elastic bandages. My own contribution was *The Spectre of the Gardenia*, a woman's head with a surface of black fabric, and zip-fasteners in place of the eyelids. A large number of objects by S. W. Hayter, the Anglo-Parisian engraver and painter, were also to be seen in the exhibition, including a *Winged Victory*, the cast of a hand clutching a lump of setting plaster. Georges Hugnet showed a series of *Book-objects* designed by himself and brilliantly executed by the bookbinder (now deceased) Louis Christy.[3] Man Ray had sent *The Orator*, an immense mouth cut right through a panel of blackwood, and *What We All Need*, a clay pipe with an iridescent glass bubble rising out of the bowl.[4] An object by Miró typified the extraordi-

Man Ray: *Object for Destruction.* 1932.

1. See also the special number of *Cahiers d'Art* for reproductions of certain minerals from the collection at the Natural History Museum in Paris: stibnites from Transylvania resembling hedgehogs, a lump of bismuth whose surface seems to have been set up in printing-type, limonites that appear to be exotic tubers, a formation of calcite looking just like a snowman.

2. For the complete text see *Documents Surréalistes*.

3. See reproductions in *Minotaure*, No. 10.

4. It was naturally impossible to exhibit Man Ray's *Destroyed Object*; *Cahiers d'Art* published four photographs showing the successive phases of its disappearance.

nary constructions he was putting together at the time: a stuffed parrot perched on a hollowed-out block of wood containing a doll's leg and flanked by a pendulum and a map. From Picasso came a small painted sculpture dating from 1914, *The Absinthe Glass*, and from Marcel Duchamp *The Brawl at Austerlitz* (1921). Tanguy's *From the*

M a n   R a y :   *Cadeau*
(1936 model).

Other Side of the Bridge comprised a pink, padded vampire's hand, with long tapered fingers disappearing into the holes of a solitaire board. Méret Oppenheim's *Fur-covered Cup, Saucer and Spoon* proved to be the great success of the exhibition; the visitors immediately imagined themselves drinking their chocolate out of this unusual cup.[1]

There were other objects, by Serge Brignoni, Claude Cahun, Gala Dali, Angel Ferrant, Marinello, E. L. T. Mesens, Paul Nougé, W. Paalen, Roland Penrose, Jean Scutenaire, and Max Servais.

Léo Malet had discovered the highly suggestive possibilities which resulted from holding a mirror upright and resting it on certain photographs

(of faces, hands, etc) so that the portion of the image facing the mirror-surface and its reflection in the mirror combined to produce 'Reflection-objects': the examples he exhibited of this process were so erotic that they were hung high up on the gallery walls so as not to offend public morals.

Alexander Calder showed a *Mobile*. Calder is American, and a son and grandson of sculptors; he was the author of an ingenious *Miniature Circus* in which the mechanical models ran through most of the classical repertoire of the circus-ring.[2] In 1929 he had shown some abstract sculptures, which Jean Arp had named *Stabiles*, at the Galerie Percier. Later he embarked upon the paradoxical venture of introducing movement into sculpture, resulting in his *Mobiles* (so named by Marcel Duchamp). At first the Mobiles were worked by motors, and when they were shown at the Julien Levy Gallery in New York in May-June, 1932 they promptly blew all the fuses. Soon after this period Calder began to develop his aerial constructions consisting of shaped metal plates cunningly balanced at the ends of long rods, which he first exhibited in 1933 at the Galerie Pierre Colle in Paris. The least breath of air or the slightest touch set in motion the delicately complex structure of these enchanting machines, suspended in the air like downward hanging plants, quivering and revolving with fascinating grace—in Duchamp's words: 'the sublimation of a tree in the wind'. Duchamp quotes Plato's *Philebus* in connection with Calder's 'mobiles': such objects 'carry within them their own pleasures, which are quite different from the pleasures of scratching oneself'.[3]

Objects, again.... During the early thirties Marcel Duchamp had offered a very few of his creations to the attention of a deliberately restricted and chosen public. His chess study, published in 1932, has already been mentioned. In October, 1934 he produced a subscribed edition of one hundred copies of that astonishing object, the Green Box, containing the notes for *The Bride Stripped Bare by her Bachelors, Even*, to which André Breton devoted his essay 'Lighthouse of the Bride' in

1. Most of the above objects, and some others, are reproduced in the special number of *Cahiers d'Art*.

2. Calder's *Circus* can be seen working in Hans Richter's film: *Dreams that Money can Buy* (see below, p. 330). The *Circus* was exhibited in 1927 at the Salon des Humoristes during Calder's first stay in Paris.

3. Marcel Duchamp: *Catalogue of the Collection of the Société Anonyme*.

Minotaure No. 6. The cover of this number was composed by Duchamp and reproduces one of the *Rotoreliefs* which were published during the following year by his friend H. P. Roché, who, in 1954, wrote a light-hearted summing-up of that particular enterprise.[1]

In the special issue of *Cahiers d'Art* devoted to objects, Mme Gabrielle Buffet-Picabia analyzed the relationship between the spectral and the objectively real in the *Rotoreliefs*: 'They result from a sort of deliberate confusion of the values

and arbitrary limits with which conventional thought distinguishes between the concrete and the abstract, Art and Everyday life. Basically, these are just ordinary gramophone records on which Duchamp has designed flat geometrical coloured drawings of spirals and circles. Their rotation on a gramophone turntable creates an optical illusion in which unexpected forms of objects develop, appearing in relief: the boiled egg, the goldfish bowl, the champagne cup and the others are really picture-puzzles resolving themselves in the same way as word-puzzles. ...But, while seeking to provide nothing more than an intellectual pastime based on illusion, he

Marcel Duchamp: *Rotoreliefs.* 1935.

1. H. P. Roché: 'Diskoptiksdemarcelduchamp', in the review *Phases*, No. 1 (Paris).

had in fact happened upon a new technique for inducing visual hallucination, a new means of supplementing the impressions to be derived from work executed in relief.'[1]

'The first task of painting,' writes Leonardo da Vinci in his *Treatise on Painting*, 'is that the objects

Méret Oppenheim: *Fur-Covered Cup, Saucer and Spoon.* 1936.

it presents should appear in relief.... It is the purpose of the painter to make his bodies stand out against their background.... He who surpasses others in this ability deserves to be considered most skilful in his profession.' It seems certain that Duchamp created his discs without the least concern for such historical data; but the fact remains that, with derisive ease, he has produced animated paintings whose geometric designs outlined on a plane surface appear to be real objects in relief. And this perhaps brings them closer to what Leonardo calls 'the soul of painting' than so many works of art appreciated 'by those whose common taste and ignorance esteem only the brightness and boldness of the colours, not considering the relief of the object, which is the beauty and the marvel of art.'

The concentric or eccentric revolving spirals sometimes used for advertising purposes or in fairground attractions, and the hairdressers' signs whose obliquely striped rotating cylinders unreel endless white and red ribbons, remain two-dimensional effects; whereas Duchamp's optical discs create a relief out of two-dimensional designs through rotation. Movement, that is to say, time, provides their *third* dimension, and it is this dimension which transforms a flat composition into a spatial reality in movement.

The *Rotoreliefs* were presented by their author at the Concours Lépine, an annual inventors' show in Paris where the ingenious and sometimes crazy contrivances of a host of dedicated amateurs can be inspected. The *Rotorelief* 'stand' was between those of a portable apparatus for compressing garbage and a painless potato peeler. The people who stopped to look at the optical discs, which Duchamp himself was amiably spinning, reiterated one question: 'What's it for?' The whole set was priced at thirty francs (about 7s. or $1 at the time) and did not find a single purchaser during the course of these demonstrations.[2]

'A subject can be dressed in harsh colours and still astound those who contemplate it, because of the illusion of relief,' states Leonardo. In the case of *Cœurs Volants* (reproduced on the cover of the issue of *Cahiers d'Art* mentioned above), the effect of relief is created by the harsh—in fact blinding—colours. Inside a vermilion shape representing a heart, Duchamp outlines another blue heart. The two shades of colour are very intense and of equal depth. Since the eye tends to perceive the colour red as 'advancing' and blue as 'withdrawing', the hearts literally move apart from each other and become almost unendurably vibrating objects. What is remarkable is that neither the *Rotoreliefs* nor the *Cœurs Volants* depend upon binocular vision for their three-dimensional effect: on the contrary, the effect is enhanced when they are looked at with only one eye. 'It is impossible for a painting, even though executed with the greatest perfection of outline, shadow, light, and colour, to seem in the same relief as the natural model, unless the painting is looked at with one eye.' (*Treatise on Painting*.)

During 1935, Picasso launched himself enthusiastically into the process of automatic writing,

1. Gabrielle Buffet: '*Cœurs Volants*' ('Fluttering Hearts') in *Cahiers d'Art*, June, 1936, accompanied by a colour-reproduction of the Rotorelief *Verre de Bohême (Bohemian Glass)*.

2. Which led H. P. Roché to the following conclusion in his article in *Phases*: 'Cesdisks-làsontmaintnantcherchésparleskolectioneurpasparlepeuplemaitoutdemêmelepeuplyles verra l'dimanchesiyvaaumusée.'

and spent several months devoting himself entirely to this pastime. As the contributors to the first numbers of *La Révolution Surréaliste* had done ten years previously, he covered page after page with phrases uncontrolled by conscious thought: 'A worse scandalmonger had never been known except if the wheedling friend licks the little woollen bitch twisted by the palette of the ash-grey painter dressed in shades of hard-boiled egg and armed with the foam which performs a thousand monkeytricks in his bed when the tomato no longer warms him what does he care if the dew that does not know the winning lottery number which the carnation gives a knock at the mare...' and so on. The artist treated his writings in the same way as his pictures, developing multiple variations from them, and noting down the place, the date and sometimes even the hour of each composition. Experimenting with the 'processes of the process', he turned litanies into monologues, making systematic use of the future tense, for instance: '... I will cradle the lamb in my arms and will give him my breast to devour I will bathe him with my tears of joy and sorrow and I will lull him to sleep with the song of my solitude' etc, or mixed words and numerals: 'Young girl correctly dressed in a beige coat with violet facings 150,000—300—22—95 centimes calico combinations corrected and inspected by allusion of ermine fur 143—60—32 an open brassière on the wound's fringes held gaping apart by hand-pulleys making the sign of the cross perfumed with *reblochon* cheese 1300—75—03—49—317,000—25 centimes' etc, or chanted the dirge of the child-dedicated-to-wear-blue-and-white: 'Listen to the hour in your childhood which white in the blue memory white border in his very blue eyes and a scrap of indigo of the silver sky the white glances cross cobalt the white paper which the blue ink tears out bluish' etc.

The review *Cahiers d'Art* reproduced these texts in a special publication devoted to Picasso's work between 1930 and 1935, with a long essay by André Breton, 'Picasso as Poet' and tributes (some in the Catalan language, including those by Miró and Dali) from most of the surrealist writers and painters. The publication also included a great number of reproductions of his pictures and drawings, variations on themes such as the circus, the Norman or Mediterranean countryside, birds, women painting or reading or sleeping, and finally bull-fights. The most important of these latter studies was a large engraving (subsequently often reproduced) called *Toreromachy* or *Minotauro-machy* (1935), whose symbolism is somewhat complex. In it, a female torero is conquered by Minotaur, which might be an expression of the triumph of sensuality and the instincts; to the left of the composition a figure closely resembling Jesus Christ is hurriedly climbing out of the arena with the help of a ladder, while two Spanish beauties look on with indifference. But between the escaping Jesus and triumphant Minotaur a little girl can be seen who may well provide the essential key to the whole adventure: she seems indeed to incarnate the surrealist Lucifer, the 'child-woman' carrying a light which dazzles and halts Minotaur.

New albums appeared. Max Ernst's five-volume work, *Une Semaine de Bonté, ou Les Sept Éléments Capitaux* ('A week of Gifts, or The Seven Capital Elements') was published in 1934 by Jeanne Bucher,

Max Ernst: Collage from *Une Semaine de Bonté* (Part Two: Monday—element, Water; example, water). 1934.

Paris. This is a series of 188 *collages* subdivided into seven parts. *Sunday*—element: mud; example: the Lion of Belfort. *Monday*—element: water; example: water. *Tuesday*—element: fire; example: the cour du Dragon.[1] *Wednesday*—element:

black; examples: 1) the laughter of the Cock, 2) Easter Island. *Friday*—element: vision; example: inner vision (four visible poems). *Saturday*—the unknown element; example: the key of songs.

The *collages* are reproduced slightly enlarged, which gives them an added sharpness and intensity. There are no captions, but the author himself presented his new album as a 'novel'. The pictures speak for themselves and reveal the same subversive and poetic spirit already manifest in *La Femme 100 Têtes* and *Rêve d'une Petite Fille....* The 'visible poems' of the sixth day are now famous, with their perspectives of hands and eyes, their pyramids of ankle-boots, their statues, their birds, their skeletons making strange gesticulations in twilit landscapes.

The same publisher issued an album by Georges Hugnet in 1936, a sort of serap-book entitled *La Septième Face du Dé* ('The Seventh Face of the Dice') for which Marcel Duchamp composed a '*couverture-cigarettes*' ('cover made of cigarettes'), consisting of a very large-scale reproduction of unrolled and therefore unsmokable cigarettes.

In 1937, a volume of drawings by Man Ray, *Les Mains Libres* ('The Free Hands'), was published —also by Jeanne Bucher—with poems by Paul Eluard. In his preface, Eluard writes: 'Man Ray's drawing, always desire, not need. Not one piece of fluff, not one cloud, but wings, teeth, claws. —A mouth around which the world turns.—Man Ray draws to be loved.' The collection features faces, eyes, hands, women as silhouettes, women as landscapes, women as pillars, women as castles, feminine shapes superimposed on objects that are displaced or modified in strange ways. There are also two imaginary portraits, which seem impressively authentic, of the Marquis de Sade, that fantastic and revolutionary writer of whom no portrait has survived. Together with Max Ernst and Marcel Duchamp, Man Ray was one of the first to exploit the surprising results that could be obtained by enlarging photographs, drawings or engravings *without retouching*.[1] His book includes several reproductions of greatly enlarged details from certain drawings—thus disorienting his own work.

One of Paul Eluard's poems in *Les Mains Libres*, entitled 'Objects', contains these lines:

In this room where I live
I gather all the landscapes.

Max Ernst: Collage from *Une Semaine de Bonté* (Part One: Sunday — element, Mud; example, the Lion of Belfort). 1934.

blood; example: Oedipus. *Thursday*—element:

1. This ancient courtyard no longer exists. It opened on to the rue de Rennes, near St Germain des Prés, and its entrance was crowned by a sculpture representing a dragon. But the huge bronze Lion of Belfort (commemorating the siege of Belfort by the German armies during the 1870-1871 war) still towers above the place Denfert-Rochereau in Paris.

1. Some of the photographs in the album by Man Ray mentioned on p. 234 are examples of the effects obtained by simply enlarging the negative.

256

Joan Miró : *Person in the Presence of Nature.* 1935.

International Surrealist Exhibition, Galerie Beaux-Arts, Paris. 1938.

CHAPTER IX

AROUND THE WORLD WITH SURREALIST PAINTING

Outside France, apart from Belgium where, as we have seen, artists and writers participated in the movement's activities from the beginning, the first countries to organize official surrealist groups were those in Central Europe and the Balkans—the countries where French influence was strongest between the two World Wars, and which had the closest ties with Paris. In Prague, the *Devetsil* group of poets, led by Vitezlav Nezval, had been in touch with the Parisian surrealists since 1928. In Bucharest, the painters Gherasim Luca, Perahim and Paul Paûn, and the writers Baranga and Pals, edited a surrealistically-inclined review *Alge* ('Seaweed') from 1930 to 1933. Finally, in Yugoslavia a properly-constituted surrealist group existed, and in 1930 published a collection of texts and illustrations under the title of *Nemogoutché* ('The Impossible') at the 'Surrealist Press' in Belgrade. This publication, which included articles by French surrealists with whom they were in correspondence, such as Breton, Aragon, Eluard, Thirion and Péret, was the 'first collective manifestation of Surrealism in Yugoslavia'. Its appearance was not dissimilar to that of *La Révolution Surréaliste* and it featured a number of unusual photographs, some rayograms, *collages*, an 'exquisite corpse' executed in Paris, and reproductions of pictures in tragic tones by Vane Bor, others by Zivanovitch-Noe very much influenced by André Masson, and drawings by Stoyanovitch, Jovanovitch, and Davitcho.

Three issues of a review *Nadrelizam Danas i Ovde* ('Surrealism Here and Now') were published by the same group of poets and painters between 1931 and 1932, giving a perspective of the activities of the Yugoslav group during that period. This new review seemed to be modelled more on *Le Surréalisme A.S.D.L.R.*, with whole pages at the end of each number devoted to political and controversial illustrations, and reproductions of works by French and Yugoslav painters. In No. 3, an 'essay in the simulation of paranoiac delirium' showed the photograph of an old wall interpreted variously by six painters and poets.

The sixth issue of *Le Surréalisme A.S.D.L.R.* (1933) contained a letter from Vane Bor to Salvador Dali, on the subject of the fascination which (in the Yugoslav artist's personal experience) oil paints could exercise, as a result of their intrinsic qualities of consistency and smell, the size and shape of the tubes from which they are dispensed, the names of the different colours, etc. It is, indeed, entirely conceivable that some painters' artistic vocations were determined by this singular, though very real 'magic of colours'.

The Yugoslav surrealists, who were mostly orthodox Communists, seem to have vacillated somewhat in their relationship with the Paris group when the differences between the French surrealists and the Communist Party resulted in an unavoidable final break. From 1935 onwards, their activities became more sporadic; in any case, their opinions made them marked men to an acutely suspicious police system, and, as a result, some of them had to serve prison terms.

The first important exhibition of surrealist painting outside France took place in the United States, in 1931, when the Wadsworth Atheneum of Hartford, Connecticut, whose director, the late A. Everett Austin, had transformed it during the course of the years into a lively centre for the modern arts, showed works by Dali, Chirico, Ernst, Masson, Miró, Picasso, Pierre Roy, Survage and others. In 1932, the New York gallery which

Salvador Dali: *Turbulent Cover*. 1935.

Julien Levy had opened the previous year presented an exhibition of paintings by Dali, Ernst, Picasso, Man Ray, Pierre Roy, Charles Howard, Viollier, *collages* by Max Ernst and Joseph Cornell, photographs by Atget, Boiffard, Man Ray, George Platt Lynes, Moholy-Nagy, Tabard—and Man Ray's 'Snowball'. During the following years, New York was able to see shows devoted to Miró, Man Ray, Dali, Masson, Arp and so on, all organized by Julien Levy, whose gallery had become an important point of diffusion for Surrealism in the United States. Levy exhibited not only all the surrealist painters, but also a number of others more or less influenced by Surrealism, the 'neo-Romantics'; and he gave private screenings in the gallery of films by Buñuel, Man Ray and others. His study, *Surrealism*,[1] was the first book in America to deal with the movement.

In December, 1933, a one-man show by Dali in Barcelona was instrumental in launching a surrealist group in Catalonia, while the year 1934 saw an exhibition in Zurich of works by Arp, Ernst, Giacometti and Miró, and the Spanish sculptor Gonzales. But it was Belgium which was to see the first big collective exhibition under the sign of Surrealism.

As a result of E.L.T. Mesens' initiative in persuading the directors of the Palais des Beaux-Arts in Brussels of the interest which an exhibition of surrealist paintings would arouse, a '*Minotaure* Exhibition' took place in this gallery, from May 12 to June 3, 1934, bringing together all the artists whose work had been reproduced in the pages of the review *Minotaure*. Entrusted with the hanging arrangements, Mesens grouped in the first room paintings by Beaudin, Borès, Suzanne Roger, Roux, Rattner, etc, sculptures by Despiau, Maillol, Laurens, Lipchitz, and Gargallo, as well as works by Braque, Derain and Matisse. In the second room, which was the largest, and in a third room, were displayed the surrealists: Arp, Brauner, Chirico, Dali, Ernst, Giacometti, Valentine Hugo, Magritte, Man Ray, Tanguy, with the addition of Balthus, Duchamp, Brancusi, Kandinsky, Klee and Picasso. It had been necessary to set aside a fourth room, a special 'reserved section' for works judged by those in authority to be too provocative for the people of Brussels: Salvador Dali's *Enigma of William Tell*, for example. These pictures were hidden behind a curtain which was only supposed to be drawn aside at special request! As may well be imagined, this 'reserved section' was the most popular of all, and the curtain was seldom left undrawn during the run of the exhibition.

1. Black Sun Press, New York, 1936.

260

Salvador Dali first visited the United States at the end of 1934, in time for the presentation at the Julien Levy Gallery[1] of his 'subconscious images, surrealist, extravagant, paranoiac, hypnagogical, extrapictorial, phenomenal, super-abundant, super-sensitive'—according to the catalogue—such as: *Imperial Monument to the Child-woman, Gala; Skull and its Lyrical Appendix Leaning Against a Night Table Which Should Have the Temperature of a Cardinal's Nest; Night Table Used as a Diurnal Fly (Theory of Flies in the 'Weaning of Furniture')*; etc.

Strange rumours began to filter back to Europe. It seemed that Dali had launched one of those crazes which regularly grip everyone in America, from top to bottom of the social scale, like an epidemic: the Dalinian version of Surrealism was apparently the latest brilliant successor to the Coué method, mah-jongg, the Charleston, the song *Valencia*, and so many other dazzling and ephemeral fashions. The artist and his paranoiac-critical jargon had conquered the reporters; it was said that the newspapers were full of stories about his exploits. His eccentric proposals were the delight of New York's snobbish coteries, while at the same time he was drawing for the 'tabloids' whole pages of concrete irrationalities, plant-armchairs and lobster-telephones, whose success rivalled that of the comic-strips.

It was known, too, that he had annexed the Marx Brothers, and Harpo in particular, and a press photo showed him with an exalted expression, sketching the man in the curly wig. (It must be

said that from the moment the first Marx Brothers film was shown in Europe, the surrealists had shown unbounded enthusiasm for these inspired clowns.) Dali also launched forth into commentaries on the sex appeal of various film stars: William Powell's was 'spectral', he explained, and Greta Garbo's 'phantasmal'. It was even claimed that, thanks to him, Surrealism was so successful that antique dealers were able to get rid of unsellable stocks of false Chippendale simply by rechristening them 'surrealist furniture'!

From 1935 onwards, surrealist exhibitions, usually accompanied by conferences and publications, became frequent outside France. Thenceforward, these were to constitute the principal means of spreading Surrealism in various countries.

The Copenhagen review *Konkretion* (four numbers) gave considerable space to Surrealism during 1935 and 1936. Its final number, 'Surrealism in Paris' (March, 1936), was entirely devoted to the writers and painters of the Paris group. A 'Surrealist-Cubist Exhibition', which was mainly surrealist, was held in Copenhagen in January, 1935; in addition to a large number of pictures by artists working in France, there were contributions from Swedish painters of the *Halmstadgruppen*. The Halmstad group (named after the seaport of that name, not far from Gothenburg) had been formed after the first World War on the initiative of G. A. Nilson, and was instrumental in acquainting Scandinavia with Cubism and, later, with pictorial Surrealism. Stellan Mörner, Erik Olsen, E. Thoren, as well as Sven Jonson, W. Lorentzen, and O. Olson, were engaged in experiments in painting based on the work of the Paris surrealists. Denmark itself was represented at the Copenhagen exhibition by Vilhelm Bjerke-Petersen, who was the organizer of many surrealist public activities and the author of several studies devoted to the movement, by Rita Kern-Larsen, Harry Carlsson and others, and finally, by Wilhelm Freddie.

Freddie was twenty-one when he exhibited a painting called *Liberty, Equality, Fraternity* at the Copenhagen Salon d'Automne in 1930. After an abstract period, Freddie's technique and inspiration became influenced by the work of Dali. The appearance of the above-mentioned painting at the Salon d'Automne provided the Danish public with its first sight of a picture in surrealist style. The symbolism of Freddie's images, which scar-

Salvador Dali: *Shirley Temple.* 1939.

1. Dali's first American exhibition took place at the same gallery in November-December, 1933.

cely veiled—if, indeed, it did not enhance—their erotic element, created scandals that involved the artist in a whole series of brushes with the authorities of the various countries where his work was shown.

In 1937, his *Sex-Surreal* exhibition in

Wilhelm Freddie: *War Memorial.* 1936.

Copenhagen presented 'sado-masochistic' or 'sensual interiors', 'psycho-photographic phenomena', and objects such as the *Sex-paralysappeal*, the *Internal Portrait of Grace Moore*, and *Zola's Writ-*

ing Desk (a dressmaker's dummy on which were placed a revolver and an ink-well) which, together, provoked a general outcry. At the private view, a stranger even tried to strangle the artist! The police ordered the exhibition closed, and confiscated all the works on show, including seven paintings and a sculpture which were placed in the criminological collection at the Danish police headquarters—where they still remain, surrounded by the revolvers and daggers of famous murderers. As for the artist, he was condemned to ten days hard labour for pornography.

Freddie was to have further troubles in various towns in Denmark, in Oslo, and, as we shall see later, in London. The Nazi authorities forbade him entry into Germany for 'insults to the Chief of State', in other words, Hitler: he had exhibited a large composition entitled *Meditation upon Anti-Nazi Love*. It was only in Stockholm that Freddie was able to show his work during this period without bringing down the wrath of the authorities on his head.

However, in 1940, not long before his country was occupied by the Germans, an exhibition of his in Copenhagen was a huge success, and although there was an entry fee, about twenty thousand people visited it. Even in October, 1940, Freddie was able to organize a surrealist exhibition featuring Vilhelm Bjerke-Petersen, Harry Carlsson, Erik Olson and Elsa Thoresen; but soon the Danish Nazi newspapers began to pay him such delicate tributes in print as: 'The ancient Greeks would have hurled him off a cliff-top into the sea, and that is just what *we* shall do, once our new Europe has become a reality'.[1] Later, Freddie had to spend many months in hiding and finally—helped, this time, by the Danish police—took refuge in Sweden at the beginning of 1944, and remained there until the final defeat of the Nazis.

He is the author of a ballet, *The Triumph of Love*, performed at Elsinor in 1940, and of two short films, *Definitive Refusal of a Demand for a Kiss* (1949), and *The Eaten Horizons* (1950).[2]

At the beginning of 1935, André Breton and Paul Eluard went to Prague at the invitation of the

1. Quoted by the critic Steen Colding in on article on Freddie, published in the English review *The Studio* (March, 1948).

2. Shown at the 1951 Paris Festival of Short Films (Cf S. Colding: '*Rayons dans l'Œil de la Lune*', in the review *L'Age du Cinéma*, No. 6, 1951).

Czechoslovak group, which was extremely active at the time. The Czech surrealists were mostly Communists, and Breton and Eluard had the unusual experience of being in a country where the Communist Party press spoke of their work and activity with praise, and where the Party contained members who were not only sympathizers but fervent supporters of the surrealists. 'The two greatest poets of present-day France', according to *Rudé Pravo* (the Czech Communist daily), gave a whole series of lectures combined with poetry-readings in Prague.

An *International Surrealist Bulletin* in Czech, with French translations, was published (on April 9, 1935) as a sequel to this visit. Quotations from Breton and Eluard, together with declarations by the poet Nezval, and by Zavis Kalandra, a member of the Communist press directorate, stated the relations between art and revolution as the surrealists understood them: solidarity of artists with the revolutionary forces, but the right to preserve 'the independence of their experimental methods'.

There was no collective exhibition in Czechoslovakia during the visit of the two leaders of the movement, but the *Bulletin* reproduced works by Styrsky, Toyen and Makovsky, who represented painting and sculpture among the Czech surrealists. These artists were particularly interested in the *object*, more especially in relation to *collage*, which both the writers and the painters of the group were practising then. In April, 1935, the Prague review *Svetozor* published a number devoted to *collages*, photomontages, and strange or ancient photos, the latter in the style of the Belgian review *Variétés*. In France, the tenth issue of *Minotaure* (1937) reproduced a *collage* by Styrsky of a lady gazing despondently at a gentleman fastening his suspenders. Later on, Toyen's albums[1] accomplished the paradox of 'drawn *collage*': the images have the appearance of montages entirely redrawn by hand. For his part, the sculptor Makovsky combined extremely diverse materials, such as stone, canvas, string and cardboard.

Both the paintings of Styrsky and those of Toyen often depicted, during this period, creatures like stony, ruined ghosts: Styrsky's *Ice Eater* (1933), Toyen's *The Yellow Spectre* (1933).[2]

1. *Les Spectres du Désert* (Prague, 1939); *Le Tir* and *Cachetoi, Guerre* (Prague, 1946).
2. Both reproduced in the *Dictionnaire Abrégé du Surréalisme* (Galerie Beaux Arts, Paris, 1938).

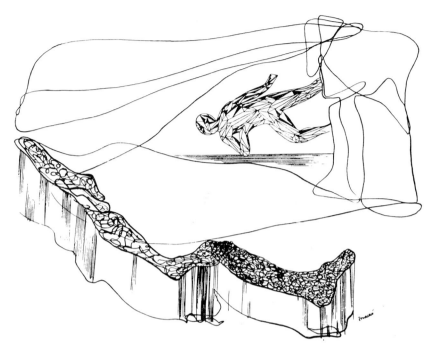

Jindrich Styrsky: Drawing. 1934.

In May, 1935, another invitation was extended to the Paris surrealists, this time from friends of Oscar Dominguez in Tenerife who for four years had been publishing a review of modern art, *Gaceta de Arte*. Breton and Péret went to the Canaries, and met Eduardo Westerdahl, the director of the review, and the poets Domingo Pérez Minik, Domingo Lopez Torres, Pedro Garcia Cabrera and Agustin Espinoza. *Gaceta de Arte* organized an exhibition at the Ateneo Gallery of paintings, water-colours, drawings, *collages*, engravings, and photographs, including work by Arp, Bellmer, Brauner, Chirico, Dali, Dominguez, Duchamp, Max Ernst, Giacometti, Maurice Henry, Valentine Hugo, Marcel Jean, Dora Maar, Magritte, Miró, Méret Oppenheim, Picasso, Man Ray, Styrsky, Tanguy. Conferences were held, and Buñuel and Dali's film *L'Age d'Or* was shown.

A second bilingual edition of the *International Surrealist Bulletin*, this time in Spanish and French, appeared in October 1935 at Santa Cruz de Tenerife, dealing with the same issues—the relationship between art and revolution—as the Czech number. It contained reproductions of *The Hunter* by Dominguez, and *The Death of Marat*, an engraving by Picasso for a collection of poems by Benjamin Péret.

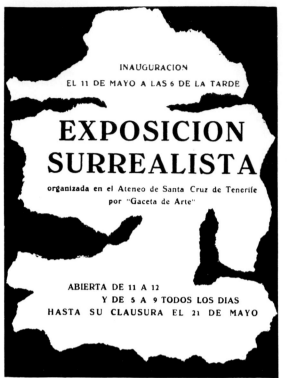

Cover of the catalogue for the Surrealist Exhibition in Tenerife, 1935.

In Tenerife, nature itself seemed surrealist to the visitors from Paris, as they admired the extraordinary flora on the slopes of the Teyde Volcano, whose snow-covered peak dominates this island ringed by shores of black sand. Back in France, Breton described these memories in 'Le Château Etoilé',[1] mentioning the flamboyants with their flame-coloured leaves, the dragon-tree's geometric radiation, the small *pitanga* tomato's 'exquisite taste of poison', the Datura, the giant Euphorbia, the *sempervivum* which no mutilation can kill, and dies only when boiled, the imperial fig-tree with its balloon-like fruit, the meadows of sensitive plants which droop gradually at the slightest physical disturbance, then revive, the *retama* or white mountain Genista whose flowers evoked for Breton the strange plant-growths of Max Ernst's *Garden Airplane Traps*.

1. In *Minotaure*, No. 8 (June, 1936), with illustrations by Max Ernst. This essay was reprinted as Chapter 5 of Breton's *L'Amour Fou* (op. cit.)

Great systems of thought have always had the ambition to become universal. Geographic extension is already a form of universality. While, in this sense, the Dada movement had been universal from birth, in the case of Surrealism the existence of local groups during the thirties fashioned in the likeness of the one in Paris, facilitated the spread of Surrealism throughout the world. And the surrealist exhibitions outside France nearly always relied heavily on contributions from the painters in Paris.

This extension of Surrealism had been preceded by a sort of condensation, since the Paris surrealists themselves came from all points of the horizon; the French always remained a minority, especially among the painters. However, the tendency towards universality is not in itself sufficient to distinguish surrealist thought from that of all the other modern movements, not to mention the various philosophies, scientific doctrines and religions which present the same 'ecumenic' character. The specific difference lies in the factor of the *marvellous*, but Surrealism has sought a marvellous inherent in the real and the concrete, an *experimental* marvellous: 'disorientation' being only one means—though one of the most effective means—of carrying out the experiment successfully. The surrealist painters have approached the theme of the marvellous in a personal, original manner, so that in the alternating process of condensation and extension of the movement, and even in its geographic diffusion, the adepts of Surrealism have had it within their power to rediscover the arcanum of miracles.

In this respect the island of Tenerife has every appearance of being a predestined place. Its flora, its geology and its origin seem equally miraculous. The tales and the dubious records concerning Atlantis have never ceased to engage man's interest from ancient times right up to the present day, in the face of all sceptical refutations; some geologists, as is well known, have been struck with the congruency of the contours of the facing American and African coast-lines and consequently have postulated a theory that the two continents originally formed one single land-mass, whose separation must have resulted from one of the greatest natural catastrophes in the life of this planet. In this case, the Canary Islands, those of Cape Verde, and the Azores would represent the vestiges of a convulsion that must have occurred very long ago in terms of the history of mankind. Legends such as that of Atlantis—or, indeed of the town of Ys—

cannot be accurate accounts of historical facts, but they may very well be accurate as expressions of very remote geological events. The mysterious relationship between Yves Tanguy's painting and the legend about the disappearance of an ancient city of Brittany beneath the waves does not constitute a particularly unusual phenomenon in Surrealism. In the regions of these vanished lands, near the gulfs or on the islands which perhaps mark their site, the minds of those endowed at birth with a special sensitivity may be moved, in the deepest recesses and the most hidden mechanisms of the unconscious, as though by vibrations originating in the beginnings of time.

In 1935, Oscar Dominguez showed his friends some images obtained by a method he had just discovered unintentionally: they were the first *decalcomanias-without-object*. He spread gouache with a paint-brush on a sheet of smooth paper, placed a second sheet of paper on top of the wet colour, then separated the two sheets. The crushed colour produced landscapes of rocks, water, corals, and so on. The process became extremely popular among the surrealists, and soon everyone was busily creating decalcomanias. In 1936, several of the results obtained[1] were presented in the eighth issue of *Minotaure*, prefaced by Breton and accompanied by a fantastic story which they had inspired Benjamin Péret to write.

If the surrealists had been acquainted with

1. By André Breton, Jacqueline Breton, Dominguez, Marcel Jean, Georges Hugnet and Yves Tanguy.

Oscar Dominguez: Decalcomania. 1936.

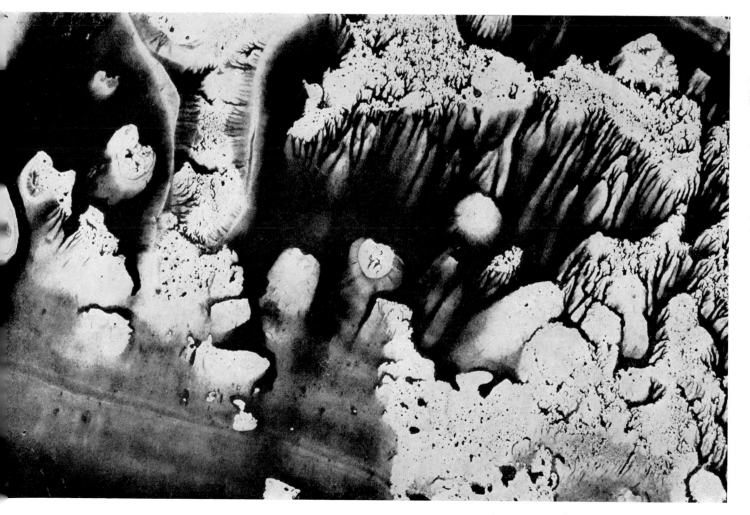

the Rorschach test at that time,[1] they would have noticed the resemblance between their decalcomanias and Rorschach's *Zufallsbilder* (which he obtained by using the same process, except that the paper was folded in two after the water-colour had been applied, resulting in symmetrical images). Other antecedents, too, may be found, such as the 'dendrites' which George Sand and her circle of friends amused themselves by constructing during the evening gatherings at Nohant. The same method seems to have been used for a part of the composition in William Blake's *Portrait of Newton* (at the Tate Gallery, London). It is the same case, then, with the decalcomanias-without-object as with so many other processes: the surrealists turned to poetic uses mediums which had hitherto remained almost invariably games or curiosities. In any case Dominguez was not aware of any precedent when he discovered these new images.

'I should have been drowned...' are the opening words in *Minotaure* of Péret's story based on decalcomania-images, and he ends with the words '...I had just entered Eldorado'. The plates executed according to Dominguez' method almost invariably show endless sheets of water, an immense oceanic depth, a sheer wall of water breaking into cataracts and, beneath this falling mass, sparkling rocks in which one could almost recognize the ore of Atlantis' fabulous metal, orichalc. These scenes have the appearance of engulfed reefs or submerged continents; the one time that Yves Tanguy used the technique of decalcomania, he re-created exactly the appearance of one of his own paintings.[2]

But making monotonously splendid decalcomanias was to produce just one more 'ancient wall', once the initial astonishment had passed off. How might one *interpret* this almost over-beautiful wall? It was with this aim in mind that I experimented with the use of screens and stencils, and in collaboration with Dominguez was able to give the appearance and texture of rocks, lakes, or underwater ruins to silhouettes of lions, windows, gramophones, hands and faces.[3] After this, my friend discovered the secret of obtaining decalcomanias on canvas, and developed poetic combinations of objects in these landscapes. But it was reserved to Max Ernst, in 1940, to transfigure these new images of desire according to their essential nature.[4]

Through pure laziness, because he found it less tiring to let himself 'drift' with the tide of paint, Dominguez obtained new unconscious images one day, almost without thinking. By pursuing to its ultimate conclusions the process of 'gliding' paint, and of form created mechanically through the play of the brush in the pigment, he succeeded in revealing an aspect of the psyche outside the control of the conscious mind. Without even claiming to be in a state of inspiration, he was able to detach his conscious activity, to some extent, from his creative faculty: it seemed exactly as though the two states existed side by side in him without interference. In his studio in the Boulevard Montparnasse, during 1937, friends and visitors came and went, and Dominguez could pay attention to their conversations and took part in them himself, without his paint-brush ever ceasing to glide and sweep along the canvas. He would have preferred it, in fact, if the different shades of colour had been able to flow spontaneously from the brush, since even mixing them on his palette still occupied his 'inattention' too much. What is remarkable is that he did not simply paint indiscriminate shapes, or more or less felicitous blobs of colour. In subtle blue-grey tones recalling Tanguy's galactic light, he created an undulating, stratified matter which soon transformed itself into well-defined, dense spheres.

Without doubt, these globes resembling worlds in process of formation were images of infancy, an evocation of the maternal breast, a very distant memory—or regret.[5] But disquieting fissures appeared in these magnificent spheres, like splits in the original matter. A prolonged and fascinated contemplation of the paintings of the 'cosmic' period by this man of the Canary Islands, Oscar Dominguez, may well lead us to evoke once again the hermetically veiled echo of a geological catastrophe.

---

1. Dr Rorschach died in 1916, while still a young man, but his theoretical writings were not published in France until 1948. Before the second World War, the 'Rorschach test' was very little known in France, even in specialist circles, and the surrealists were unaware of its existence.

2. See *Minotaure*, No. 8.

3. These plates made up an album, *Grisou* ('Fire-damp'), 'automatic decalcomanias interpreted deliberately', as yet unpublished. The project for the cover, composed in ' magnetic typography', was reproduced in the supplement to the *Dictionnaire Abrégé du Surréalisme*, 1938.

4. These productions of Max Ernst will be discussed later, in connection with his 'American' period, since most of this artist's decalcomania-paintings were executed while he was in the United States during the second World War.

5. Dominguez' mother died when he was one year old (see below, pp. 355-356).

Oscar Dominguez: *Lancelot 28° 33'*. 1939.

Oscar Dominguez : *Memory of the Future.* 1939.

One of the pictures whose analysis discloses a particular symbolic richness—it is, in fact, the first, chronologically, of the cosmic series, and the spheres have not yet appeared—represents a cliff whose rock-face surges upwards in stratified waves, sliced by deep black abysses. The appearance of these surfaces also brings to mind those huge sheets of paper which race through the rollers of a rotary printing-press. The rocks are like the pages of a newspaper, and the inorganic matter is a book for those who know how to read it; but, inversely, man's machine construction is able to transform a living idea into an inorganic complex. The symbol which is revealed in this rather equivocal manner is expressed more manifestly by a typewriter, a small and solitary object, placed by the artist at the top of the immense cliff. But this machine is 'sprouting': the metal stems of the keyboard, terminating in the buds of the keys, are extended like twigs in spring. Against a landscape which is that of the dawn of time, the one living thing, the sole hope, one might say, is a machine. And, again, with its tail of long waving stems, and a sort of beak formed by the sheet of white paper curling over as it emerges from the roller, the strange mechanism resembles a bird perched on the cliff-edge—a swallow, perhaps, 'announcing spring', or the dove after the flood, or perhaps ... a canary.

There is no doubt that the earth possesses more continents for Surrealism than for other forms of synthetic thought. Certain works of Dominguez state explicitly the legend which has been sketched out, above, in general outline. For instance, he chose as the theme for his illustration in the G. L. M. edition of *Les Chants de Maldoror*[1] a phrase from the strophe of the 'two mysterious brothers' riding along the seashore, a strophe in which Lautréamont speaks of extinct volcanoes and of other signs of a great geological convulsion. In his drawing, a woman can be seen in the centre of vast waters, before a gigantic wall of liquid; she wears a head-dress of bananas (the fruit of the Canaries), a symbolic figure standing erect like the commemorative monument of some seismic disturbance that must have taken place where the Islands now lie.

During the months preceding the outbreak of the second World War, the cosmic painting of Dominguez evolved towards a kind of crystallization. The signs of aridity increased. Influenced,

Oscar Dominguez: *Nostalgia of Space.* 1939.

perhaps, by the appearance of the 'Polyhedra', one of the mathematical objects photographed by Man Ray,[2] the artist allowed a steppe vegetation to start growing on his planets, sharp-bladed plants which finally fill the whole space of the picture with their tangled prismatic masses, networks of long, cutting needles like the shapes of death in crystalline form.

In October 1935, another surrealist exhibition was held in Belgium, this time in La Louvière, an industrial town of Borinage; it opened with a lecture by Mesens, followed by a poetry-reading. This public display had been organized by a group of young trade-unionists and workers, and took place in the local municipal hall. It brought together 'objects, paintings, water-colours, drawings, *collages*, and photographs', by Chirico and Klee, and by Arp, Brauner, Dali, Max Ernst, Marcel Jean, Miró, Man Ray and Tanguy, as well as the Belgians Magritte, Mesens, Paul Colinet, Max Servais, Camille Bryen, and Raoul Michelet.

'Raoul Michelet' was Raoul Ubac, who published

1. Illustrated with drawings by Brauner, Dominguez, Ernst, Espinoza, Magritte, Masson, Matta, Miró, Paalen, Man Ray, Seligmann, Tanguy (Paris, 1938).

2. See p. 251.

during this period a book to which Magritte contributed illustrations, *L'Invention Collective*. And *Minotaure* revealed his talents as a photographer,[1] in particular his use of the technique consisting of placing the negative and positive of the same subject one on top of the other, very slightly out of alignment, when making a print; the images thus obtained gave a curious impression of bas-relief. This procedure is described in early manuals of photography, but here again the poetic possibilities had remained unexplored. All the nuances of a photograph treated in this way assume a special density and quality: sky becomes sand, water turns into marble, a woman's tresses are waves of polished steel, and steel itself is soft limestone.[2] In the field of engraving, Ubac adapted this technique to the printing of etchings. The sculptures in slate which he executed at a later date shared with his photoreliefs the same visual qualities of texture and 'grained' surface.

The series of large-scale international exhibitions devoted to surrealist painting was inaugurated in June, 1936 by the International Surrealist Exhibition of London, held in the vast halls of the New Burlington Galleries. The initiative had been taken by Roland Penrose, an English friend of Max Ernst, who owned a remarkable collection of modern painting, was himself a painter, and was married at that time to a Frenchwoman, the poet Valentine Penrose.[3] Roland Penrose, with the help of various prominent English sympathizers and the collaboration of the French and Belgian groups, busied himself with organizing this international exhibition, which finally included work by more than sixty artists from fourteen different countries.

Together with pictures, objects, drawings, *collages*, and sculptures by twenty or so Paris surrealists, and works by Brancusi, Chirico, Duchamp, Klee, Picabia, and Picasso, were paintings by members of the Belgian, Scandinavian and Czech groups; there were also contributions by the Catalan Angel Planells, a disciple of Dali, the Madrid painter Maruja Mallo, the German Richard Oelze, who worked in Paris and produced ghost-like and precise scenes strangely full of a sense of indecision, and a number of English artists of whom Paul Nash was the 'surrealist in chief' (he achieved considerable success in England later on by adopting in turn every conceivable pictorial formula). The sculptor Henry Moore, who was already well-known for work influenced successively by Jacob Epstein's enormous stone carvings such as *Adam*, then by Zadkine and Brancusi, demonstrated his abilities as a poet-plastician in sculptures having an affinity to Arp's work: round, monumental, perforated forms. There were also Eileen Agar with her talented fantasies, Charles Howard, who was engaged in a sort of fantastic constructivism, Mervyn Evans, more 'vorticist' than surrealist, Humphrey Jennings, Julian Trevelyan, and Edward Burra, who was known chiefly for his satirical sketches extolling the Negro race, and was influenced in painting by Ernst, Chirico and Klee. Drawings by Reuben Mednikoff and Grace Pailthorpe (the latter a doctor and psychiatrist) derived from pure automatism. Cecil Collins carried on the Romantic tradition of Blake and Fuseli.

Children's drawings, and Oceanian, African and

International Surrealist Exhibition, London, 1936. The flower-headed woman in Trafalgar Square.

1. In No. 10, Raoul Ubac's *Triumph of Sterility*: two photographic *collages* rephotographed and one of them solarized.

2. Cf *Minotaure*, Nos. 11 and 12-13; in the latter number are 'fossils', as seen by Ubac, of the Eiffel Tower, the Paris Stock Exchange, and the Opéra.

3. *Herbe à la Lune*, by Valentine Penrose, had appeared in 1935 (Editions G. L. M., Paris), and *Le Nouveau Candide* in 1936 (G. L. M.)

American primitive objects were also on show, as well as a great number of *objets trouvés*, interpreted natural objects and surrealist objects. Roland Penrose's object, *Captain Cook's Last Voyage*, was a wire globe with a woman's bust inside. And, to carry out an idea of Dali's, a charming young woman, Sheila Legge, agreed to conceal her face under a great bouquet of roses on opening day, and circulate among the guests as a flower-headed woman.[1]

The surrealist display created a sensation in the British capital, and, in the words of the weekly *Bystander* 'set more tongues wagging in passionate disagreement than any exhibition since the Post-Impressionists first bewildered London.'[2] Crowds flocked in at the rate of fifteen hundred a day during the two weeks the exhibition lasted; scenes shot inside the gallery were shown in newsreels, while innumerable articles in the press alternated between sarcasm and indignation. 'A Shocking Show,' shrieked the *Daily Mail*'s headline. The show might have been even more shocking if Wilhelm Freddie's paintings could have been exhibited, but, on their arrival in England, they had very nearly been incinerated by the customs authorities, since British law makes any article deemed 'improper' liable to be burnt. Only a few drawings by the Danish artist managed to find their way to the New Burlington Galleries by unofficial routes.

The fourth and last issue of the *International Surrealist Bulletin*[3] (in English and French) appeared in September, 1936 and announced the formation of an English surrealist group. On the front page, a photograph placed the flower-headed woman among the pigeons of Trafalgar Square. On the back page, scenes taken from a newsreel showed the English surrealists and their friends from Paris together in the exhibition halls. The *Bulletin* reproduced paintings, sculptures and objects by Penrose, Moore, Jennings, Nash, Rupert Lee, Dr Pailthorpe, Evans, and Eileen Agar.

Raoul Ubac: *Fossil of the Paris Stock Exchange.* 1937.

Humphrey Jennings: *A Woman.* 1934.

1. Dali illustrated this theme in several paintings of 1936: *The Man with the Head of Blue Hortensias, Three Young Surrealist Women Holding the Debris of an Orchestra in their Arms,* etc.

2. June 17, 1936.

3. The third issue of the *Bulletin* appeared in Brussels, with a cover by Magritte, on August 20, 1935, with a manifesto-declaration by the Belgian group and the text of the speech which André Breton had been prevented from delivering at the *Congress for the Defence of Culture* organized in Paris by the Communists.

271

Roland Penrose: *Captain Cook's Last Voyage*. 1936.

The 'Fantastic Art' section formed an important part of the exhibition, showing the links that existed between Surrealism and certain precursors of its concept of the marvellous, as well as its kinship with ornamenters and anecdotists of the past, and even with humorists, and curious or extravagant illustrators. One could see originals or reproductions of works by Baldung, Dürer, Bosch, and Giovanni di Paolo; the 'composite images' of Arcimboldo; a number of strange drawings and engravings, such as Oronce Finé's woodcuts illustrating his book, *Raison d'Architecture Antique*; ornaments by Cornelis Floris and Giovanni d'Udine; mysterious engravings attributed to Jean Goujon; *Temptations of Saint Anthony* by Peter Huys and the German engraver Schongauer; extracts from the Flemish Christopher Jamnitzer's *Neuw Grottessken Buch*, from the *Perspectiva Corporum Regularium* of his Austrian namesake Wenzel Jamnitzer, and from da Vinci's *Divina Proportione*; allegorical engravings by Musi, Penni, and followers of Dürer such as Schön and Vogtherr; a work by Ligier Richier; emblematic symbols from Lombardy, an Italian *Fall of Phäethon*, and several of those curious pictures using 'fantastic perspective', where the subject appears in its real proportions only when viewed from the edge of the canvas (the best-known example is the elongated skull depicted at the base of Holbein's painting, *The Ambassadors*).[2] Then there were designs for jewellers by de la Barre, and for goldsmiths by van Vianen; a *Rebus* by della Bella; an *Ornament* by van den Eeckhout; extraordinary scenes etched by Filippo Morghen; *Figures* attributed to Magnasco; fantastic metamorphoses and animated objects by Bracelli; imaginary costumes by Nicolas Larmessin; architectural compositions by Piranesi, Hogarth, and Callot. In this same section were engravings by William Blake, romantic subjects by Bresdin (called '*Chien-Caillou*'), an invented landscape, *The Titan's Goblet*, by the American Thomas Cole, witchcraft scenes by William Heath, le Poitevin, and Ramelet, an 'interpreted blot' by Victor Hugo, works by Ensor, Fuseli, Redon, Kubin, Mlle Lenormand's *Dream* predicting the burning down of the Tuileries, and the *Dream* painted by the Douanier Rousseau, etchings by Meryon, selections from Goya's *Los Caprichos*, drawings by Lewis Carroll, lithographs and engravings by

In December, 1936, America in its turn organized an International Surrealist Exhibition. Alfred H. Barr, Jr, director of the New York Museum of Modern Art—an institution created in 1929 by a group of art-patrons and collectors—decided to give the American public a comprehensive view of the movement's accomplishments in the plastic field. The exhibition which opened at the Museum's premises at 11 West Fifty-third Street (since replaced by a new building on the same site) extended its scope to include Dada, as well as the 'precursors' of previous ages, and 'related' contemporaries. Conceived in these terms, the exhibition assembled an enormous mass of material: seven hundred original works or reproductions were on show, and nearly a hundred artists represented. It was indeed 'the biggest surrealist show on earth'. Its title, *Fantastic Art, Dada, Surrealism*,[1] introduced the term 'fantastic art' to denote works presenting a literary or metaphysical side, or an ultra- or extra-pictorial character.

1. Also the title of the volume prepared by the Museum to 'record and explain' the exhibition: edited by Alfred H. Barr, Jr, first edition, 1936; second enlarged edition, 1937.

2. National Gallery, London. This painting provided the inspiration for many of Dali's pictures with 'atmospheric' skulls.

Grandville, and wood-engravings by Edward Lear. There were a large number of satirical drawings (there was even one by Delacroix) and caricatures: Daumier and André Gill from France, Joseph Beale from America, Cruikshank, Gillray and E. V. Lucas from England, Naegele and Busch from Germany. Three variations (French, German and Italian) on the theme of *The World Upside Down* were on show; finally, there was an anonymous portrait-caricature of King Louis-Philippe, *The Marvellous Potato*, 'French school, early nineteenth century', in the words of the exhibition catalogue.

After this procession of 'ancestors', the section called 'Twentieth Century Pioneers' offered Chagall, with paintings of 1911 and 1913; a great number of early Chiricos (twenty-five compositions, including eight drawings); Marcel Duchamp, represented by the *Coffee Mill*, *The Bride*, *The King and Queen Traversed by Swift Nudes* (watercolour), *Pharmacy* (corrected readymade), *The Bachelors* (pencil and watercolour), a photograph of the *Bottle Rack* readymade, the 'rotary glass plate' called *Precision Optics*, the yardsticks of the *Three Standard Stoppages*, the object *Why not Sneeze?* and the *collage Monte Carlo Bonds*; three works by Kandinsky, nineteen by Paul Klee (1904 to 1935), and twenty or more pictures, *papiers collés* and drawings by Picasso, his etching *Minotauromachy*, and his illustrations for Balzac's *Le Chef d'Œuvre Inconnu*.

The section presented under the heading 'Dada and Surrealism' constituted the heart of the exhibition. Dada was represented by Baader, Baargeld, Grosz, Haussmann, Hannah Höch, Ribemont-Dessaignes, and Christian Schad who, in 1918, using the process rediscovered soon afterwards by Man Ray, had reproduced outlines of objects directly onto sensitized paper so as to form abstract-geometric compositions that were later called *Schadographs*.

Arp's contributions consisted of nearly thirty different items: reliefs, concretions, *collages*, drawings and engravings. Thirteen paintings and drawings by Dali ranged in date of execution from 1929, *Illumined Pleasures*, to 1936, *City of Drawers*, and included his 1933 object, *Retrospective Bust*. There were no less than forty-six works by Max Ernst, giving a complete panorama of the artist's activity from 1918 to 1936. Giacometti was represented by three sculptures, Magritte by seven paintings, Masson by thirteen compositions in various mediums, Miró by fifteen paintings, relief constructions and objects. Picabia (who might equally well

have been placed among the pioneers) showed *Catch as Catch Can, Amorous Procession, Infant Carburettor, Totalizer, Dada Movement,* and *The Kiss* of 1925. Man Ray's manifold activities were exemplified by *collages*, paintings, rayograms, drawings, works from his American Dada period, his 1932 *Object of Destruction*, his 1935 *Orator*, etc. Six paintings by Tanguy were exhibited, in addition to one object, *From the Other Side of the Bridge*, and some drawings. Also to be seen were an early *collage* by Aragon, and others by Breton, Eluard, and Mesens; a drawing by Tzara; pictures, objects, drawings, photographs, and decalcomanias by other participants in the surrealist movement in France: Bellmer, Brauner, Dominguez, Méret Oppenheim, Marcel Jean, Hayter, Dora Maar, Sophie Taeuber-Arp, Paalen, Leonor Fini, Valentine Hugo. England was represented by Henry Moore, Paul Nash, Roland Penrose, Eileen Agar, John Banting, Reuben Mednikoff, and Grace Pailthorpe; America by Joseph Cornell; Germany by Richard Oelze.

Other sections enlarged this gathering even further. Under the heading 'Artists Independent of the Dada and Surrealist Movements', were placed Pierre Roy, Alexander Calder, and Kurt Seligmann (who might have figured among the surrealists), the Russian and Hungarian abstractionists, Malevitch and Moholy-Nagy, the Mexican Siquieros, the Spaniards Fernandez and Gonzalez, the Dutchmen Domela and Tonny, the English vorticist Wyndham Lewis (who had become more cubist than anything else), and even works by 'Kukrynitsky', a composite name used by three illustrators from Moscow's *Pravda*. Katherine Dreier, the co-founder with Duchamp and Man Ray, in 1920, of the *Museum of Modern Art, Société Anonyme, Inc.*, appeared in this section with two paintings. The section also grouped a large number of other artists: Russell Aitken, Julian Alberts, Herbert Bayer (professor at the Bauhaus in Dessau), Fred Becker, Meyer Bernstein, Allan Gilbert, Louis Guglielmi, Waldo Kaufer, Benjamin Kopman, Helen Lundeberg, the photographer George Platt Lynes, Loren McIver, George Marinko, Isamu Noguchi (a sculptor born in Los Angeles of Japanese parents, who became friendly later on with the surrealists living in America during the second World War, and composed large-scale symbolic works), André Smith, Harry Sternberg, and George Wotherspoon. The catalogue reproduced works by Peter Blume, a curious allegorist, Federico Castellan, Georgia O'Keefe (the wife of Stie-

273

glitz), Arthur Dove, Lorser Feitelson (described as the 'leader of the California post-surrealists'), Knud Merrild, belonging to this West Coast group, Wallace Putnam, Walker Evans, and C. C. Beall (author of a *Composite Head of President Roosevelt*). Humorous drawings were represented by James Thurber and Rube Goldberg, and by two frames showing the 'Wolf Pacifier' from a 1936 animated cartoon by Walt Disney.

The 'Comparative Material' assembled the art of children and the insane, folk art, Man Ray's photographs of mathematical objects in the Poincaré Institute of Paris, and examples of 'commercial and journalistic art' which hardly give an inkling of the subsequent invasion of the advertising field by the surrealist influence. The plates of the Rorschach test, a china 'cat clothed in roses', and an *Oval Wheel* made by a French wheelwright named Benquet in 1878 ('ordinarily such wheels are round', explained the catalogue), were classed as 'Miscellaneous Objects of Surrealist Character'. Finally, a section of 'Fantastic Architecture' showed photographs of constructions by Gaudi, the Facteur Cheval's *Dream Palace*, Schwitters' *Merzbau*, and architectural projects by Emilio Terry who, in opposition to the concept of the house as a 'machine for living in', felt that a building should be 'a dream come true'.

The catalogue formed a 250 page volume with 150 reproductions, notes on each artist exhibited, a 'brief chronology of the Dada and Surrealist movements from 1910 to 1936', and an introduction by Alfred H. Barr, Jr. The cover design was taken from a drawing by Arp, and the jacket reproduced a rayogram by Man Ray.

Many of the visitors were so fascinated by Méret Oppenheim's object, the *Fur-covered Cup, Saucer and Spoon*, that they seemed to take it as a symbol of the Exhibition and of the Museum itself, just as the *Nude Descending a Staircase* had once incarnated the Armory Show.[1] The critics were non-committal or sarcastic for the most part, and those who showed enthusiasm or even simple objectivity were in a minority. Without doubt the New York exhibition, with its genealogy of 'influences', and its classifications by schools and styles, occasionally suggested rather far-fetched origins or descendants of surrealist and fantastic themes. Nevertheless, as a direct result of the importance accorded to the supplementary sections which are described in the preceding pages, the Museum of Modern Art's enterprise showed Surrealism, without any ambiguity, to be a means of expression standing largely apart from the harmonic-visual arts. And, at the same time, the exhibition attempted to *situate* Surrealism in the main stream of contemporary life.

In his capacity as director of the Museum of Modern Art, Alfred H. Barr, Jr had never ceased to emphasize the allied concepts of art as an integral component of life, a museum as a living organism, and exhibitions as 'work hypotheses'. His efforts in this direction have helped enormously in the task of making modern art in general both known and understood in the United States.

Certain members of the Museum's Board of Trustees, who had been somewhat puzzled by the *Fur-covered Cup*, the *Why not Sneeze?* and the *Oval Wheel*, attempted to impose a selection when the exhibition was sent on tour to other American cities. But, thanks to Barr's intervention, this proposed censorship did not take place.

In 1936, Belgium produced a new recruit for Surrealism: the painter Paul Delvaux. Delvaux was born in Antheit-les-Huys, in Liège province, on September 23, 1897; his father was a Brussels lawyer. As an artist, his initial inclinations were expressionist-naturalist, very far indeed from the modern movement. In fact, he did not conceal his profound lack of interest in the most acclaimed artists of the day. According to E. L. T. Mesens, 'he declared that he saw absolutely nothing in Picasso's finest cubist paintings, and suspected some of the most authentic innovators at that time of being hoaxers.'[2] He never involved himself in the activities of the surrealist movement, but he can still legitimately be classed as a surrealist painter.

During 1936 he made frequent visits to the Brussels Palais des Beaux-Arts, of which his friend Robert Giron was director, and where another friend of his, the writer Claude Spaak, was also an official. There he became acquainted with Mesens who also held a position at the Palais des Beaux-Arts. These visits gave Delvaux the opportunity to digest thoroughly the collections of classic and modern art on display, and, finally, to encounter surrealist painting. He was deeply impressed by the mysterious quality of the objects

1. Cf Dwight Macdonald's 'Action on West Fifty-third Street', a 'profile' of Alfred H. Barr, Jr (*The New Yorker*, December 12 and 19, 1953).

2. *Op. cit.*, cf p. 178, note 1.

and perspectives in Chirico's work, and fascinated by Dali's minutiae; but he was hostile at first to Magritte's paintings, though he was gradually won over, through stages of disquiet and then interest, to an eventual admiration that was still subject to returns of doubt and perplexity.[1] Meanwhile, these contacts led rapidly to a complete change in his pictorial concepts. Thanks to Surrealism, Delvaux discovered the possibility of revealing the unity of the world of complex feelings which preoccupied him.

The classically robed woman leaning forward towards a rose-bud sprouting through the floorboards of an endless corridor, contemplated by another woman—her twin sister or perhaps her reflection (*Woman with a Rose*, 1936), and the bevy of women in lace gowns moving towards a triumphal vista of ancient buildings (*The Procession in Lace*, 1936), are all the same woman, duplicated, multiplied by invisible mirrors. Now these women are poised in front of magnificent mansions, quite naked, beautiful as always, their eyes calm and steady, with heavy breasts and slim bodies (*The Pink Bows*, 1936; *Nocturne*, 1939; *The Echo*, 1932): always the same woman, whose aimless movements disclose nothing but the fact that each image of her is intensely alive.

Two voyages which Delvaux made to Italy before the last World War confirmed his taste for classic architecture, and his admiration for the perfectly proportioned female body. Delvaux has 'sat Beauty on his knees', but he has never insulted it because, for him, beauty is Love: a sensuality that is free and calm just because it is sovereign, a pagan passion ignorant of the idea of sin, a desire so violent and whose triumph is so assured that it seems to impregnate and immobilize the landscapes.

The particular atmosphere of Delvaux's paintings derives from the perspectives which give a 'metaphysical' density to the scenes; perspectives which are absolutely strict, and very rarely forced as they are with Chirico (one exception is *The Black Town*, 1946). The atmosphere emanates from his imagined cities, night-enshrouded and moonlit, from the luminous bodies of his women, from the porticoes and structures painted with extraordinary precision, from the mountains 'looking from afar like giant boulders lying helpless in the dark'.[2] It still exists in his daytime scenes.

It becomes interiorized with his antiquated, immaculate Walloon living-rooms, with their wainscoting and ceilings decorated with mouldings, and their gas lighting (*The Night Train*, 1947).

Delvaux suggests the existence of short-circuits in the flux of duration: his personages meet themselves at each turning of a temporal labyrinth. There are never any clocks in his pictures: what timepiece could possibly count the hours in this Palace of Mirrors whose reflections are slightly displaced in time, where the same woman stands out simultaneously in the various attitudes she is able to assume in the space of a few seconds? While with Balthus—to whom Delvaux has sometimes been compared—space separates itself into juxtaposed compartments,[1] with Delvaux several fractions of time exist at the same moment in the same space.

Delvaux's work is distinguished less by 'periods' than by a whole series of 'echoes'. Only a biographer on terms of intimacy with the artist could trace the sentimental sonorities in his work, and evoke, perhaps, an adolescent love, rediscovered as an adult, lost again, then reconquered once and for all in his original object—an adventure which began the very moment that Delvaux found his means of expression. Delvaux paints the echoes of a single love, and it is the mark of a great painter to have been able to veil and yet reveal his personality in all the fullness of his allegories.

Children and old men are usually absent from the scenes he paints, as also are domestic animals: there is just the same woman, always young and beautiful, sometimes a man who is also young (*The Temple*, 1944)—or skeletons. The poet cares nothing for ages of man which are not those of sensual love, and even death is for him an indefinitely repeated echo in the spaces of time. The only realities are the time of love and the duration of death. 'I shall never leave you again,' Delvaux has said to Love. And that is what Death says to all men sooner or later. In the *Lunar Town* or the apartment of the *Courtesans*, the commensal of these grave, beautiful women is a skeleton imitating their simple gestures.

The *Entombment* of 1951 shows Death reigning supreme, but here the artist's intentions are clear: all the characters in this celebrated episode are skeletons. On another occasion, against a less precise, seemingly aged background there is no one in the room except the symbols of death (*The*

1. Cf Claude Spaak, *Delvaux*, monograph published in Antwerp, Belgium, 1948.

2. Lautréamont.

1. See above, p. 243.

Skeletons, 1944), and, in one corner, a dress-maker's dummy. But through a glass-panelled door can be seen, in full light, a naked woman descending a staircase.

Cover of the Japanese *Surrealist Album*, Tokyo, 1937.

In 1937, the Tokyo review *Vou* wrote that Japanese Surrealism, which had originally made a literary appearance in 1925, was experiencing a fresh impetus in painting as a result of the recent European exhibitions, particularly the one in London. Although the political situation in Japan was extremely unfavourable for the expression of advanced ideas in any field, nevertheless about fifty artists more or less influenced by Surrealism succeeded in exhibiting regularly. During 1937, an issue of the review *Shinzokei* ('New Forms') reproduced drawings, paintings and *collages* by Takimuti, Foujita-Hoheï, Shitakumi, Naïto, Ikemonchi, Shimazu, and Nakana, most of them disciples of Dali.

The writers Tiroux Yamanaka,[1] Shuzo Takiguchi, and Magao Oshita were anxious to give their fellow countrymen some idea of the work being produced by the European surrealists, and, with the help of their French and English friends, they were able to assemble a comprehensive selection of drawings, engravings and photographic reproductions. This material was shown at an exhibition which opened on June 18, 1937 at the Ginza Galleries in Tokyo, with fifty-two artists represented; the show was a great success, both in terms of the number of visitors, and of its effect on the young intellectuals of the Japanese capital. This success was repeated at Osaka, Kyoto and Nagoya, where the exhibition was subsequently shown.

Following this, the review *Mitsue* ('Aquarelle') published a special number, put together by Takiguchi and Yamanaka, under the title *Surrealist Album*: this volume was illustrated by paintings, drawings and engravings, as well as reproductions of surrealist sculpture and objects, and included six inset plates (two in colour) and 125 other examples of the work of forty-one Western surrealists.

The International Surrealist Exhibition in France in 1938 included paintings by several Japanese artists living in France at the time: Okamoto, Suzuki, Shimozato, and Otsuka.

1. Who edited the Tokyo review *Surrealist Exchange*, the first number of which appeared in 1936.

In London, the interest aroused by the 1936 Surrealist Exhibition led to a second exhibition during the following year, at the newly opened London Gallery in Cork Street. This exhibition was devoted exclusively to Objects. On show were constructions from Paris already shown at previous exhibitions, and objects created by the English surrealists themselves, whose ranks had been strengthened since 1936 by the adherence of several more painters and sculptors, including Edith Rimmington, James Cant, F. E. McWilliam, Samuel Haile, Robert Baxter, and Ceri Richards. The catalogue, *Surrealist Objects and Poems*, listed forty-five names and 135 works, printed a number of poems, and included reproductions of objects and *collages* by Baxter, Cant, Norman Dawson, Evans, Howard, and Nash.

Surrealism was also very much in the public eye in that most Parisian and most international of all worlds, that of fashion. Even before 1914, the audacity of Paul Poiret, following on the heels of the cubist and futurist revolutions, and helped by the Ballets Russes' innovations in costume and scenery, had succeeded in throwing Parisian *haute couture* into a sort of creative frenzy. The pre-eminence of Paris couture, as Christian Dior remarked in an article published shortly before his death, in the journal *Arts*, resulted above all from the perfection and taste of its standards of workmanship: Poiret transformed it into a laboratory of constantly evolving and changing shapes. Each season saw the radical alteration of a silhouette which, until then, had remained almost unchanged for decades.

Even so, the vision of Poiret's fashions and those that he influenced until the end of the twenties, glimpsed in any retrospective exhibition of female costume, may well leave one wondering how women could ever have put up with such tinselled style. It goes without saying that women's present manner of dressing will provoke equal astonishment at a later date, and that fashion consists precisely in creating pretty or surprising things that will seem ugly or commonplace the following day. It should be observed, though, that the charm of the '1900 style', for instance, which Poiret destroyed, is by no means wholly anachronistic: those dresses were jewel-boxes, not disguises.

Fashion exists essentially in terms of its own endless disorientation, which is no doubt why it has often fascinated poets. Stéphane Mallarmé

Paul Delvaux : *The Echo*. 1943.

Paul Delvaux: *The Sleeping Town*. 1938.

himself edited a fashion magazine, *La Dernière Mode*, in 1874, writing all the material under various pseudonyms for the eight issues: articles about women's costumes, as well as travel, cookery, jewellery, social activities, and even literature. *Minotaure* no. 6 (1935) gave long extracts from this review, presented by Henry Charpentier. In *Le Poète Assassiné*, Apollinaire devotes the chapter 'Mode' to the idea of transposing Boccioni's futurist manifestoes to the field of women's clothing, proving himself in the process as good a prophet as the Italian painter: 'All the substances of every realm of nature can now enter into the composition of a woman's dress.... Porcelain, sandstone and earthenware have suddenly appeared in sartorial art. These substances are worn as belts, as hat pins, etc... and I have even seen an adorable hand-bag composed entirely of those glass eyes which can be found at oculists.... Slippers are being made of Venice glass and hats of Baccarat crystal. Not to mention the gowns painted in oils, the woollens in bright colours, the gowns curiously stained with ink....' His fashions were twenty or forty years ahead of their time, if not more: 'I have seen a young woman on the boulevard dressed in tiny mirrors that were appliquéd to the fabric. In sunlight the effect was dazzling. It was like a walking gold mine. Later, it began to rain, and the lady looked like a silver mine. Nutshells make pretty pendants, especially if one alternates them with hazel-nuts. Gowns embroidered with coffee-beans, cloves, garlic, onions and bunches of dried grapes will continue to be fashionable for formal wear. Fashion becomes practical, scorns nothing, and ennobles everything. It does for substances what the romantics did for words.'

During the darkest days of the sack-dress of 1925-1928 and the cloche hat, the surrealists' charming women friends were generally indifferent to 'what was being worn', and tended to dress up as 'child-women' with tightly waisted skirts and attractive hooded caps. Fashion began to catch up with this way of dressing and in 1930 rediscovered the 'romantic' style. In the end, Salvador Dali followed high society into the fashion-designers' salons, and in 1935-1936 created a series of eccentric designs for the house of Schiaparelli, including a hat shaped like a shoe, and a flowing evening-dress printed with lobsters disporting themselves between the mayonnaise and the parsley. Much to Dali's regret, Schiaparelli would not allow real mayonnaise to be spread on the gown. He thought up other ideas for prints: bouquets in *trompe-l'œil* printed on a flesh-pink fabric so that they appeared to be fastened to the skin by safety-pins from which a little blood trickled; a design which made the fabric appear dirty and torn, and so on. Eager to emulate these ideas, the manufacturers made enquiries, and Magritte's *Key of Dreams* was soon to be seen faithfully copied (without the artist's knowledge) in minute size on an *haute couture* fabric.

Dali also designed furniture for fashionable decorators, in particular a luxurious 'mouth-couch' which imitated the shape of huge feminine lips in red satin. For the same clients, Giacometti sculpted lamp-stands: hands holding the lamps, for example.

During the 1938 Surrealist Exhibition in Paris, a magazine asked Méret Oppenheim to compose a page of 'surrealist jewellery'; in conjunction with Dominguez, she suggested a number of curious and amusing inventions, such as mother-of-pearl buttons on which were engraved tiny human foot-prints, or a 'bracelet-watch for globe-trotters'

Gown by Schiaparelli, with a printed design by Salvador Dali. 1936.

279

Pablo Picasso: *Women's Heads*. 1938.

pected split levels and angles, recesses with supple contours, some of them shaped like human profiles; display figures whose forms were rudimentary, even coarse, modelled the precious gowns; the statue of a lion was decorated with a mane in bright red fur. The sense of disorientation was obtained by means of an exteriorized, formal novelty, ephemeral but charming.

To conclude the 'chapter of frivolities', it may be noted that in 1935 André Breton's second wife, Jacqueline, probably inaugurated a new style in coiffure by wearing her hair 'à la Fontanges';[2] a fashion that became all the rage a few years later, complicating hair-styling to an extraordinary degree, and reaching its dizziest heights of extravagance in Paris during the German occupation. But, one day in 1936, Dora Maar arrived at the Café de la Place Blanche with her hair dishevelled and flopping down over her face and shoulders, like someone just rescued from a shipwreck. At the surrealists' table everybody—or nearly everybody—exclaimed in admiration. Dora Maar was a young photographer who had come into contact with the surrealists in 1934; afterwards she had met Picasso, and she was already beginning to resemble one of the 'blue period' portraits. It is well-known that before and during the last war, Picasso painted a number of pictures on the theme of the woman-with-hair-hanging-down, a style which had a vogue later among the so-called 'existentialist' ladies. This particular hair-style also encouraged several well-meaning young women to try their luck in variety and cabaret shows, with the assistance of a complaisant microphone.

consisting of a chain of watches giving the right time in the different continents.

In addition to Surrealism's episodic incursions into the kingdom of fashion, certain productions may be mentioned which carried the stamp of a refined elegance and figured quite frequently in the group's exhibitions and reviews. Madame Valentine Hugo contributed to the elaboration of certain 'exquisite corpses' her truly exquisite technique of drawing with coloured crayons on black paper; she also constructed attractive Objects, and André Breton asked her to illustrate a re-edition of Achim von Arnim's *Strange Tales* for which he had written a preface.[1] Several of her delicately-designed 'dream' images appeared in surrealist publications. Madame Léonor Fini, expressing a more precise elegance, painted strange oneiric pictures, while the fashion magazines published her extremely chic drawings and reproduced furniture that she had decorated.

At the 1937 World Exhibition in Paris, the Pavilion of Fashion Designing revealed a markedly surrealist influence. In place of the usual cold vistas of plate-glass typifying such displays, the pavilion's decorators had produced an interior that provided some surprises for the public—unex-

The surrealist exhibitions described above all had an informative character: they grouped various works, allowed comparisons between them, and provided general surveys or balance-sheets of a plastic activity whose preoccupations had become international. But, in Paris, the surrealists had wanted for some time to organize an exhibition that would also be a creative act, breaking radically with the time-honoured concept of works hung on the anonymous walls of galleries, salons, or museums. They dreamed of creating an atmosphere into which the works on display would be integrated, a background as metaphorical as those works and absolutely concrete.

1. Editions des Cahiers Libres, Paris, 1933.

2. A towering head-dress worn by one of Louis XIV's mistresses, Marie de Fontanges.

The opportunity to realize this project presented itself when the Galerie Beaux Arts, in the Faubourg St Honoré, put its spacious premises at the disposal of the group, giving it complete freedom in the arrangement of the rooms. And in January, 1938, an International Exhibition of Surrealism opened in Paris.

The visitor received his first shock in the lobby, where Salvador Dali was showing his *Rainy Taxi*, an old crock inside which an ingenious system of tubing produced a violent downpour that soaked two mannequins, one, with a shark's head, in the driver's seat, the other, a bedraggled blonde in evening dress, seated in the rear among heads of lettuce and chicory over which enormous Burgundy snails were drawing their slimy trails, exhilarated by the deluge.

Once through the lobby, the visitor entered *Surrealist Street*, a long, broad passageway peopled by twenty or so delectable wax models costumed in various unique styles that would certainly have enchanted Guillaume Apollinaire: a tearful one, with fat crystalline tears rolling down her cheeks and her bare shoulders, wearing clay pipes in her hair from which iridescent bubbles emerged (Man Ray); one simply a widow, draped in black veils and trampling upon a male figure sprawled on the ground (Max Ernst); one wearing nothing but a man's jacket with a red electric light-bulb in the breast pocket (Duchamp); one garbed in moss and mushrooms, with a bat's wings for head-covering (Paalen); one a water-nymph enmeshed in a lead-weighted casting-net (Marcel Jean); one brandishing a siphon from which gushed a jet of fabric that enfolded her (Dominguez). Other figures were interpreted by Miró, Arp, Matta, Seligmann, Sonia Mossé, and Espinoza. Dali's mannequin was masked, and adorned with small spoons, the head of Maurice Henry's creation disappeared in a cloud of cotton wool, and Tanguy had burdened his Sleeping Beauty with mysterious spindles. Léo Malet had decorated his lady with various accessories, including a glass globe at stomach-level in which a goldfish darted to and fro: the general effect of this appliance was so suggestive in this particular position that it was finally decided to remove it. But the greatest success was achieved by André Masson who had placed his mannequin's head in a cage, gagged her with a black velvet band, and, where the mouth would have been, set a flower: a pansy ('...pansies, that's for thoughts'). The figure was otherwise unadorned, except for a 'G-string' covered with glass eyes.

All along the passage-way a series of blue enamel plaques spelt out in white letters the names of historic Paris streets: the *Rue de la Vieille Lanterne* in which Gérard de Nerval committed suicide; the *Rue Vivienne* where Lautréamont lived; the *Rue Nicolas Flamel*. There were attractive names, such as the *Porte des Lilas*, *Passage des Panoramas*, and *Rue de la Glacière*: and invented names like *Rue Faible*, *Rue de Tous les Diables*, *Rue de la Transfusion du Sang*, *Rue d'une Perle*, *Rue aux Lèvres*, *Rue Cerise*, and *Rue Albert Tison*, the last being the name of an entirely imaginary person. Nothing could be more real than these appellations, since in Budapest, for instance, there exist a hundred streets with curious names, including a Perfumed Street, a Poet's Street, a Minute Street, a Motor Street, a Tangled Street, a Sunray Street, and so on.

This passage led into the great central hall, arranged by Duchamp in the form of one of the most remarkable object-pictures—on the architectural scale—that Surrealism had ever known. As he had done before in the Dada movement, Marcel Duchamp was playing the decisive role of a 'benevolent technician', and had agreed to supervise the exhibition and provide the basic ideas. He had succeeded in transforming the central hall into a space in which the marvellous coincided—at the level of humour, so to speak—with an essential disorientation, a fantastic metaphor in which the spectator found himself plunged, whether he wanted or not. The room had become an immense grotto, its roof a vault of twelve hundred sacks of coal hanging side by side, its gently undulating floor covered by a thick carpet of dead leaves, and in a fold of the ground a pool glistening with water-lilies and reeds. In the centre of this subterranean glade constituting a synthesis of the inner and outer worlds, on a slight elevation, a position of honour was held by one of those perforated iron braziers still to be seen at that time on the *terrasses* of the Paris cafés, and round which the surrealists had foregathered so often in wintertime. So the brazier represented friendship; while love was represented by four enormous, luxurious beds, glowing under embroidered satin counterpanes, at each corner of the hall.

On each side of the brazier, the tetrahedrons of two revolving doors served as display-boards for graphic works. Since pictures covered what remained of the walls, Duchamp had thought of installing electric 'magic eyes', so that lights would have gone on automatically as soon as the spectator had broken an invisible ray when passing in front of the paintings. The scheme proved too difficult to carry out and had to be abandoned. It was then decided to provide visitors with electric torches so that they could illuminate individually each particular part of the room; but the public soon pocketed the entire stock of torches, and there was no alternative in the end but to instal permanent lighting.

A few hours before the opening, on the evening of January 17, 1938, everything was ready. In the lobby, the rainstorm raged inexorably inside Dali's taxi, in the corridor-street the motionless procession of future fashions paraded, and in the tunnel-forest the brazier glowed under the coal-packed ceiling. Objects appeared in outline, glowed, or moved in the semi-darkness: Duchamp's *Rotary Demi-sphere*, an *Ultra-furniture* designed by Seligmann in which women's legs replaced those of the stool, a *Lightning-conductor-gallows*

International Surrealist Exhibition, Paris, 1938: Mannequin by André Masson.

constructed by Paalen in homage to the eighteenth century German satirical writer G. C. Lichtenberg. The famous *Fur-covered Cup, Saucer and Spoon* were prominently displayed in a show-case. The water of the pool reflected a dressmaker's dummy coloured sea-blue, on which I had painted its skeleton in yellow and brown continents, as though on a globe of the world. And everywhere there were hands: the hand as a symbol of Surrealism industrious and dreaming, hands floating on the fluorescent liquids contained in compartments of a table constructed by Hugnet, *Fire-fly* hands escaping from the sides of a vase (Seligmann), hands that were door-knobs, and the hand outstretched over the silent, revolving record of Dominguez' gramophone, *Never*.

It was then that I saw Duchamp standing at the entrance of the still deserted hall, casting a final eye over his creation. We exchanged a few words and he soon went. He did not appear at the official opening; afterwards, it was learnt that on leaving the gallery he had taken the train for England.

Meanwhile, coffee was beginning to roast behind a screen, permeating the whole premises with 'perfumes of Brazil', while a loud-speaker blared out the German army's parade march. It was a brilliant crowd which thronged the premises—international Paris society in full evening dress, as requested by the invitation cards to the '*vernissage*'. The invitations had also announced that 'the authentic descendant of Frankenstein, the automaton Enigmarelle, constructed in 1900 by the American engineer Ireland, will cross the main hall of the Surrealist Exhibition at half past midnight, in false flesh and false blood.' Paul Eluard, in tails, made the opening speech, and a dancer, Hélène Vanel, interpreted around and inside the pool a dance called *The Unconsummated Act*. Everyone waited for Enigmarelle, but Frankenstein's progeny did not appear.

The entire press spoke of the event. With a very few exceptions, it was an outcry of indignation: sneers, insults, recriminations, expressions of disgust. Naturally, the general public packed the Galerie Beaux Arts throughout the run of the exhibition.

Besides the names of the 'generator-referee' Duchamp, and the 'organizers' Breton and Eluard, the exhibition catalogue's 'credits' nominated as 'assistant' a certain Claude Le Gentil (who, as far as I can remember, was more of an 'attendant' throughout the enterprise), followed by Dali and

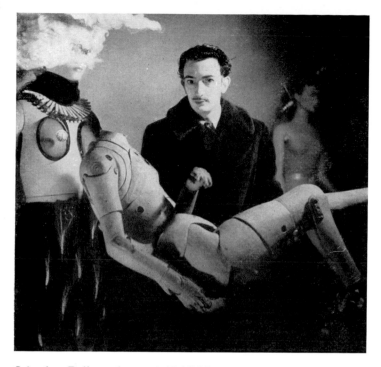

Salvador Dali at the 1938 Exhibition.

Salvador Dali: *Rainy Taxi*.

Mannequin by Man Ray.

Mannequin by Léo Malet.　　　　Mannequin by Max Ernst.　　　　Mannequin by Wolfgang Paalen.

Kurt Seligmann: *Ultra-Furniture*

International Surrealist Exhibition, Paris, 1938: The Pool.

Ernst as 'technical advisers', and Man Ray as 'lighting superintendent'. Paalen's name was attached to the duties 'waters and brushwood'.

To accompany the catalogue, a *Dictionnaire Abrégé du Surréalisme* was compiled by Breton and Eluard. In this poetic lexicon, published by the Galerie Beaux Arts, the names of most of the participants in the movement are mentioned, each with a special description. Among the painters, Arp is baptized 'the dune-eel'; Dali is 'the

Scene from Alfred Jarry's play *Ubu Enchaîné*. Decor by Max Ernst, production by Sylvain Itkine. Paris, 1937.

prince of Catalan intelligence, colossally rich'; Dominguez, 'the dragon-tree of the Canaries'; Ernst, 'the superior of the birds'; Magritte, 'the cuckoo's egg'; Masson, *'l'homme-plume'*; Miró, 'the sardine-tree'; Tanguy, 'the guide from the age of mistletoe druids'. In a supplement, Brauner figured as 'the white rose top-boot', and Seligmann as 'the sheaf of wings'. Among the entries in the *Dictionary*, Chirico's name is followed by quotations from Apollinaire, Dali and Breton. Duchamp is 'the most intelligent and (for many) the most troublesome man of this first part of the twentieth century' (Breton). As for Picasso, he is held to be a painter 'whose work since 1926 has objective qualities in common with Surrealism'. The words *Collage* and *Frottage* are annotated by passages from Max Ernst's *Beyond Painting*, the process of Decalcomania is explained, and so on.

The *Dictionnaire* contains a number of commonly-used words accompanied by examples. Thus, the word *Air* is followed by these quotations: 'In the beautiful black air' (Lautréamont); 'My hunger is bits of black air' (Rimbaud); 'The air of the room is as beautiful as drum-sticks' (Breton). The word *Water*: 'Water is a moist flame' (Heraclitus); 'Close your eyes tight against the forests of blue clocks and violet albumins, stay deaf to the cajolements of tepid water' (Maeterlinck); 'The pure water of her head in your hands' (Benjamin Péret); 'Cold water has naked legs' (Henri Pastoureau); 'In front of a portrait of water lowering its arm in the bathtub' (Pablo Picasso); 'You arise the water unfolds —you lie down the water blossoms' (Paul Eluard). And the word *Glove (gant)*: 'Gloves are worn by *Gantlemen*. The glove is a moulding of a pierced head and serves as a good substitute for the index finger for tickling the new disposition' (Arp). There are also definitions provided by the game of question and answer: *Umbrella* is a bluebird turned black; *Mystery*, the haughty wind in a suburb; *Reason*, a cloud eaten by the moon; *Erotism*, a sumptuous ceremony underground; *Fossil*, a sleep-inducing invention of Leonardo da Vinci's, etc.

The pages of the *Dictionnaire* were abundantly illustrated with vignettes, portraits, ornamental capitals, and decorations of various kinds. Well-known motifs were reproduced, such as Dali's 'soft watch', or the 'surrealist flag'—against a splash of blood, a black swan carrying on its back an anvil topped by the stinking corpse of a common crab (cf *Les Chants de Maldoror*, Chapter VI). The activities of the movement and the work of its adherents were copiously represented with

Matta: *Psychological Morphology 'no. 134'*. 1939.

reproductions of pictures by Duchamp, Chirico, Max Ernst, Man Ray, Masson, Miró, Tanguy, Magritte, Arp, Moore, Giacometti, Dali, Toyen, Styrsky, Penrose, Paalen, Jennings, Seligmann, Dominguez, Shimozato, Suzuki, Otsuka, Espinoza, Remedios, Delvaux, Bjerke-Petersen, Freddie, Thoresen, Nash, Brauner, Marcel Jean, Brignoni, Cornell, Matta, Bellmer, etc; photographs by Man Ray and Ubac; *collages*; objects, group photographs (French, Belgian, English, Czech, Danish); a scene from *L'Age d'Or*; one of Max Ernst's stage-sets for *Ubu Enchaîné*.

In 1933, on the advice of André Breton, I had pointed out to Sylvain Itkine, a young actor who wanted to found an avant-garde theatre, that a production of Alfred Jarry's hitherto unacted play,

Ubu Enchaîné, would present interesting possibilities. Itkine was very taken up with this idea and, despite innumerable obstacles, worked steadily towards its realization. But it was only in November, 1937, that he was finally able to assemble a company and put on a few performances of *Ubu Enchaîné* at the Comédie des Champs-Elysées,

preceded by Jarry's playlet *L'Objet Aimé* (with music specially composed by the actor-composer O'Brady). At my suggestion, he commissioned Max Ernst to design the stage-sets. The framework envisaged by Ernst for Père Ubu's exploits entailed *collage-décors* constructed from parts of old prints, photographically enlarged to life-size, which combined to produce 'period pictures' full of a strange humour.

The theatre programme was supplemented by a brochure paying homage to Jarry, with texts by various surrealists and a series of portraits of Père and Mère Ubu by Picasso, Man Ray, Miró, Magritte, Marcel Jean, Maurice Henry, Paalen and Tanguy. Itkine had also obtained drawings from his fellow actors Roger Blin and Loris, the painter Coutaud, and the cartoonist Jean Effel (who had also designed amusing stage-sets for *L'Objet Aimé*).

A tragic destiny prevented Itkine from fulfilling his theatrical vocation. Towards the end of the second World War, he joined the ranks of the Resistance, fell into the hands of the Gestapo, was found to be carrying a list of enemies due for extermination, and was tortured to death.

Max Ernst had not designed any costumes for *Ubu Enchaîné*, so that these had to be improvised at the last moment. In fact, by the time the production finally opened, Ernst was separated from his first wife, Marie-Berthe, and living in the south of France together with Leonora Carrington, a young Englishwoman whom he had met in London a few months earlier. Leonora Carrington had made paintings and drawings without any formal training until she was nineteen, when she started attending Ozenfant's studio (this artist was giving lessons in London at the time), but her compositions owed nothing to the 'purist' preoccupations of the former director of *L'Esprit Nouveau*. The influence of Max Ernst served only to lead her more surely in the direction of a strange kind of painting: dreams and obsessions tinged with humour, confrontations of semi-hieratic, semi-caricatured personages in a space and among objects outside the confines of rationality—works often assuming the nature of a direct satire on Leonora's own social background, which was English upper middle class (her father, a 'self-made man', was president of the Imperial Chemical Industries combine). Two of Leonora Carrington's paintings

Joan Miró: *La Mère Ubu*. 1937.

Matta: *Here, Sir Fire, Eat*. 1942.

Max Ernst: *The Fascinating Cypress*. 1940.

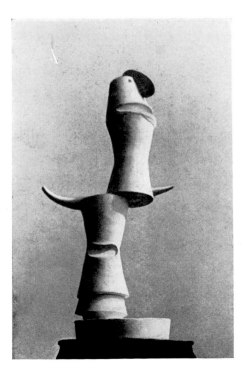

Max Ernst: Drawing. 1938.

Max Ernst: *Oedipus*. 1934.

were on show at the Paris Surrealist Exhibition, *The Silent Assassin*, and *What Shall We Do Tomorrow, Aunt Amelia?* During the same year, the Surrealist Exhibition in Amsterdam showed two more of her pictures, *Lord Candlestick's Meal*, and *Lord Candlestick's Horses*.

Leonora Carrington and Max Ernst went to live in the little village of St Martin-d'Ardèche, in a rustic house which they proceeded to transform according to their fancy. Max Ernst painted frescoes in some of the rooms, and constructed monumental sculptures against the outside walls and along the terrace.

Ernst has always practised sculpture. In 1934-35, the balcony of his studio at the top of a building in the rue des Plantes in Paris displayed curious and impressive compositions such as *Oedipus, Lunar Asparagus* and *Moon-dial*.[1] His sculptures seem always to have imposed themselves on him as architectural necessities, points of coalescence, so to speak, of the surrounding landscape. In 1934, staying with Giacometti in Ticino, he undertook to sculpt a number of the granite boulders, large and small, that dotted the countryside. By the time he had left his friend's house, the garden was peopled with totems bearing magic signs or the outlines of strange beasts cut from their rounded surfaces. At St Martin-d'Ardèche, Ernst created bird-dragon-men in cement on the walls of Leonora Carrington's house, figures which spread their feathered limbs, their claws and beaks, in defensive, menacing or protective attitudes.

During this period he was also painting new Forests: hybrid plant-life proliferating under a green sky, creepers, folioles, clusters of fantastic flowers, like jungles in which *The Joy of Living* and *The Triumph of Love* were exultant.

The last International Surrealist Exhibition before the second World War took place in Holland, at the Robert Gallery of Amsterdam (April, 1938), with contributions from about forty artists. In July of that year, a surrealist group was formed in Chile, named *Mandragora*, and a review of the same name was launched in December. The two artists principally associated with the group's foundation, Braulio Arenas and Jorge Caceres, organized a *Surrealist Exhibition* of their work in Santiago de Chile at the same time; their *collages,*

drawings, paintings, sculptures and objects attracted many visitors.

In the spring of 1938, André Breton returned from Mexico, bringing with him a large collection of objects and pictures, some of which were shown in 1939 at the Galerie Renou et Colle in Paris. They were nearly all naïve or popular works: anonymous nineteenth-century Mexican paintings demonstrating all the splendours of 'naïve consciousness', equally ingenuous altar-pieces, a huge number of popular objects—earthenware, masks, caskets, frames, dolls, money-boxes, whistles, cakes, garments, 'funeral objects' such as the sugar skulls that Mexican children eat—passionate creations in which the instincts of life and death are bound together by a superbly unspoilt plastic feeling. Also on show were surrealistically naïve pictures by Frida Kahlo, wife of the painter Diego Rivera; pre-Columbian objects; and remarkable examples of the work of the Mexican photographer Alvarez Bravo.

Breton also brought back from his visit (described at length in his article entitled 'Mexico' in *Minotaure* no. 12-13) a manifesto, *For an Independent Revolutionary Art*, signed by Rivera and himself; Leon Trotsky, whom he had met in Mexico, helped to formulate its terms. The Mani-

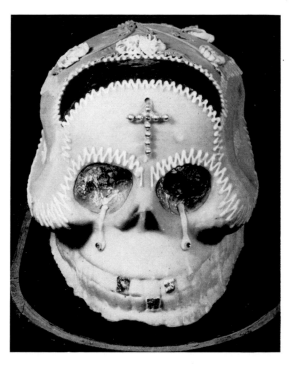

Skull made from sugar: Mexican popular object.

1. *Œdipus* and *Lunar Asparagus* are reproduced in Motherwell: *Max Ernst: Beyond Painting (op. cit.)*

Victor Brauner: *Composition.* 1933.

Victor Brauner: *The Inner Life.* 1939.

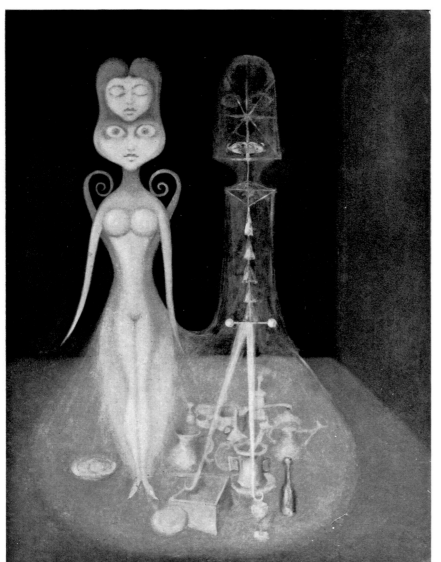

festo supported the thesis of the independence of expression of the revolutionary artist,[1] and demanded the formation of an International Federation of Independent Revolutionary Art. A review in newspaper format, *Clé*, which appeared in 1939 (two issues) in support of this initiative, published the last surrealist tract before the outbreak of war.[2] But, in fact, the I.F.I.R.A. remained a project.

Victor Brauner's four-year stay in Bucharest between 1935 and 1938 had helped to retain an interest in Surrealism among avant-garde circles in the Rumanian capital. In 1936, the Unu Press published *Sadismul Adevaruluui* ('The Sadism of the Marvellous'), a collection of essays by the critic Sacha Pana on Dada and Surrealism. It included a drawing by Brauner which was surrounded by photographs of the members of the surrealist group in Paris.

Brauner returned to Paris during 1938, and, on August 27, was the victim of a serious accident while visiting a friend. During a quarrel to which he was merely a witness, one of the parties to the dispute hurled a glass in a sudden moment of anger: the glass struck him in the face and fatally injured his left eye. An article by Pierre Mabille, 'The Painter's Eye', published in 1939 in *Minotaure* no. 12-13, related and discussed the facts. The paintings by Brauner reproduced in Mabille's article cast a disquieting light upon the secret determining factors of this tragic affair: as far back as 1931, the artist had depicted himself in a self-portrait with one blind eye. Another of his pictures from the same period shows a male figure with his eye pierced by a shaft carrying the letter D—the initial of the name of the person responsible for the accident. And several compositions by Brauner between 1930 and 1938 included motifs suggesting the enucleation of an eye or eyes.

The happening was less accidental than it seemed, in fact, and the premonition derived from obsession; Mabille found in the persistence of the theme a kind of desire on Brauner's part to attain inner vision, a world that can be seen only 'with closed eyes'—such a desire must certainly have

1. For the text, see *Documents Surréalistes*, pp. 372-378.
2. See *Documents Surréalistes*, pp. 389-391.

included a powerful element of masochism, judging by the means of realization proposed in the artist's paintings and the manner in which that desire was actually fulfilled. Mabille emphasized, nevertheless, that it is difficult in our time to account for such facts in the language of traditional science: 'It is clear,' he wrote, 'that psychology, philosophy and moral science are stagnant' in comparison with the physical and mathematical sciences. 'The retrograde desire to keep human interests cooped up inside the framework of an already outmoded Cartesian viewpoint is one of the most profound reasons for the contemporary drama.'

After his accident, Brauner painted pictures differing greatly from his former production; they became, in effect, more 'interior'. Mabille states in the article just quoted that Brauner's father was a dedicated spiritualist and student of magical experiments. Retrospectively, his son 'had been highly critical of these enterprises and their lack of controlling elements. Yet his unconscious mind had retained the memory of the strange atmosphere in which his first years had passed.' It is this peculiar climate which Victor Brauner's period of 'twilights' seems to recall. Ghosts, ectoplasms, it seems, are materialized in the half-light, as in *The Anemone* (1938); or else they are huge faces with staring eyes, their expression showing a deep desire to fascinate, as in *Self-Separation*, *The Departure*, and *Between Day and Night* (reproduced in *Minotaure*, no. 12-13, 1939).

After the tenth issue of *Minotaure* appeared in 1937, its owner Albert Skira parted company from his artistic director, E. Tériade, and set up an editorial committee composed of André Breton, Marcel Duchamp, Paul Eluard, Maurice Heine, and Pierre Mabille; this committee was reduced to three—Breton, Heine, and Mabille—for the final issue, no. 12-13. 'The animal-headed review' published an introductory declaration in that last number in which it announced its intention of 'distinguishing itself fundamentally from any other publication headed by a member of the Institut or a museum curator. It adopts a conception of artistic and intellectual happenings that is ABSOLUTELY OPPOSED TO ALL RETROGRADE IDEAS. As far as this review is concerned, the happenings in question cannot possibly consist in the resurrection of old miniatures and prayer-books, however heavily they may be gilded; nor

can they consist in keeping a day to day illustrated catalogue of a famous painter....'

The allusions were perfectly clear to *Minotaure*'s colleagues, the super-luxurious magazine *Verve*, specializing at the time in medieval and oriental illuminated designs; and *Cahiers d'Art*, faithfully reporting in each quarterly issue the metamorphoses to which Picasso was submitting reality with ruthless mastery. Picasso continued to treat objects and figures according to his usual game of broken mirrors, and some of his latest pictures even seemed to reflect exterior reality in the fragments of *curved* mirrors, thus giving birth to several entirely novel monsters.[1]

But although it was exclusively surrealist, *Minotaure* was not comparable to the fiery

André Masson: Drawing. 1937.

publications that had hitherto served the cause of the movement. This review embodied a field of ideas that had gained in scope and influence what it had lost of its original violence, just as an explosion dissipates its force in the atmosphere it impregnates. It is significant that the *Dictionnaire Abrégé* includes the word *Surrealism* without mentioning the original definition ('pure automatism...' etc), which it replaces by a series of

1. For instance, *Buste de Femme* (1939), *Man with Lollipop* (1938), *Portrait of Miss D. M.* (1939), etc. Cf *A Pablo Picasso* by Paul Eluard (Editions des Trois Collines, Geneva, 1944), pages 128, 147, 161, etc.

commentaries and opinions, some of them aggressive declarations in the old spirit, others proposing vaster or subtler aspirations. For Breton, Surrealism is constantly seeking the *'point de l'esprit'*, the spiritual point of which he speaks in his *Second Manifesto*; for Aragon, it was a 'vice' with the *image* for 'narcotic'; for Eluard it is an instrument of knowledge; for Crevel it was the conflagration of 'Reality's Department Store'; while for the critic Marcel Raymond it is a *'school'* of poets'.

Surrealism had radically altered since its early days when it had been almost exclusively propagated by champions of written poetic expression, to such an extent that the question had even been raised as to whether such a thing as surrealist painting could exist. Now the movement was spreading its influence throughout the world by means of a pictorial language. Most of the newcomers from now on were painters, and Surrealism made itself known primarily through exhibitions, which also kept together—at least in the catalogues—those veterans whose contact with the French group had become less and less frequent. Miró had not attended meetings of the group for years, Max Ernst was seen only very rarely, Arp had never been a regular visitor, Magritte remained in Belgium, Dali was pursuing his personal career quite apart from his former friends. And, as has been mentioned, neither Balthus nor Delvaux ever took any part in the life of the movement, and Clovis Trouille hardly any (none of his work was included in any of the exhibitions discussed in this chapter).

André Masson took part in the 1938 Exhibition, after a ten-year break, but remained outside the group and limited himself to personal contact with a few of its members. *Minotaure* no. 11 (1938) published drawings by Masson tending towards a mythical-philosophic content: *Heraclitus, Construction of a Man, Minotaur's Melancholy*, etc. He designed the cover of no. 12-13, which contained two of his paintings, *The Louis XV Armchair*, and *Metamorphosis of Lovers*; in these the pool with water-lilies and the flower-mouth from the Galerie Beaux Arts reappear.

The painters still paid tribute to Surrealism with the quality of surprise contained in their work, but that did not imply their participation in its other activities, especially on the political level, although such participation would at one time have been almost mandatory. But it is true that outside events were beginning to show proof of an aggressiveness powerful enough to defeat any attempts to master the situation.

In several European countries, the surrealists had been among the first victims of the fascist dictatorships. In Yugoslavia, Surrealism was obliterated, as we have seen. Franco had launched his *putsch* from the Canaries, which meant the immediate dissolution of the surrealist group there: several of the contributors to the *Gaceta de Arte*, including Pérez Minik and Lopez Torres, were shot by the Spanish fascists; Garcia Cabrera was deported to Rio de Oro, but succeeded in escaping, and joined the Republican forces in Catalonia. Oscar Dominguez was in the Canaries at the time of the military uprising, and escaped certain death thanks to a Tenerife prostitute who hid him; the young woman stole for him, from a Portuguese 'client', a passport which Dominguez carefully altered, and with which he was able to return to France. Finally, in Czechoslovakia, the arrival of Hitler's troops obliged all avant-garde artists to suspend their public activities and—as in Denmark—go into concealment, or escape from their country.

Marcel Jean: *Portrait of Mlle L.B.* 1938.

PART THREE
SURREALIST PAINTING AFTER SURREALISM

Yves Tanguy: *The Rapidity of Sleep.* 1945.

Some time in 1935, Matta and a few friends were at Federico Garcia Lorca's house in the Spanish city of Cordova. From where he was sitting on the verandah, Lorca was carrying on a conversation with a friend in a first-floor room who was getting dressed prior to joining them downstairs. 'Federico!' Lorca's friend called through the open window, 'which shirt should I wear? The blue silk one or the white one?' 'Put on the blue shirt!' replied Lorca. 'What about the trousers?' 'Put on your black trousers!' 'And the jacket?' 'Your embroidered jacket!' and so on. The dialogue involving the invisible friend's costume continued between the ground floor and the room upstairs. 'And don't forget your light-brown sombrero!' But when the person in question had finally completed his toilet and appeared at the door, he was bare-headed, dressed in a white shirt and flannel suit like everyone else.

None of these young Spaniards was in the least surprised that their friend had dressed himself in ordinary clothes *as well as* in an imaginary costume. They accepted everyday reality as naturally as they accepted poetic reality. When telling this story, or others of a similar nature, Matta points out that this attitude certainly represents the essential quality of living poetry that lies deep within the Spanish people: an attitude in which the real is not subservient to the imaginary, nor the imaginary to the real, but where real life and the life of the imagination co-exist, being not only similar but, to some extent, interchangeable. Don Quixote and Sancho Panza are really one, and Cervantès only succeeded in dividing this single personality into two by the use of extreme exaggeration, caricaturing the two aspects.

Matta likes to claim that 'nothing has ever happened to him in his whole life.' He views his career as a discoverer, his travels, and his homes in so many countries throughout the world, as a perfectly normal existence. Roberto Matta Echaurren was born on November 11, 1912, in Chiloe in the south of Chile, to an old-established family of European descent, of mixed Spanish, Norman and Catalan blood; the family had several branches in America and Europe, but the French influence had always been preponderant. He first devoted himself to architecture, and acquired a complete training in this field while still very young. At the age of seventeen, he was already engaged in architectural and decorating projects for friends in Santiago de Chile; with such success, indeed, that he soon found himself at the head of a prosperous and time-demanding interior decorating enterprise.

He suddenly decided that he had had enough of this too business-like activity, wound up his affairs, and left for Europe. He was nineteen, and his first stop was Italy where he took notes and made sketches in the museums, studying the methods of composition of the masters. Then he was in Spain, in Yugoslavia, in Russia, and in England where he met René Magritte (who had been persuaded by Mesens to come over to London, and was working there at the home of a patron of the arts). He had not yet started painting. During 1934-1935, he studied with Le Corbusier, and succeeded in astonishing the architect by the originality of his building and furnishing suggestions.

In September, 1937, he met in France a young Englishman, Gordon Onslow-Ford, whose parents had mapped out a naval career for him. The drawings which Matta was just beginning to

compose so intrigued Onslow-Ford that he decided, in his turn, to become a painter, and tried to
persuade his parents how interesting it would be
for them to have an artist for a son instead of a
naval officer. The two young men became close
friends, and shared all their problems together
during the years immediately preceding the second
World War.

Until then, Matta had, as we have seen, had
no contact with artists' circles. Towards the end
of 1937, he began to show his drawings to a few
painters in Paris, to Picasso, and to Salvador Dali,
whom he went to see armed with a letter of introduction given him some time previously by Lorca
—that great poet had died the year before, assassi-
nated by Franco's henchmen. It was Dali who sent

the young artist to Breton. The latter had just
opened a shop on the Rue de Seine specializing in
surrealist art and primitive objects, the whole
enterprise being placed poetically under the aegis
of *Gradiva*, the heroine of Jensen's novel whom
Freud made the subject of a celebrated study.
Breton immediately bought two drawings from
among those that his visitor showed him, and was
vigorous in his encouragement.

In 1938, the review *Minotaure* (no. 11) published
a text by Matta, illustrated by an architectural
drawing, entitled 'Sensitive Mathematics—Architecture of Time', in which the author explained
some of his ideas for the interior lay-out of houses;
he emphasized the necessity of bringing subjective
desires and contradictions into play, as it were,

so that, through a particular organization of living space, it would be possible to provide a sort of sensuous tranquillity in addition to satisfying the usual elementary necessities. Some of his proposals have been adopted by present-day decorators. Matta was already foreseeing and drawing those 'exciting and perfectly-moulded' articles of contemporary furniture which 'unfold from unexpected spaces, yielding, adapting themselves, swelling like a foot-step in water; or a single book reflecting its images from mirror to mirror in an incalculable path that traces a new space, architectural, habitable.' We should also find, he wrote, 'for each of those umbilical cords which put us in touch with other suns, utterly liberated objects that would act as psychoanalytical mirrors of plasticity.'

On being invited to join other surrealist artists in illustrating the proposed re-edition of *Les Chants de Maldoror*, Matta read Lautréamont's work for the first time: it was a discovery of primary importance for him. He immediately recognized an element in the *Chants* that Europeans might never have suspected: the overwhelming presence of the New World's untameable nature. The European countryside can furnish no conception of the essential hostility of the terrain throughout most of America, lands violated but never conquered by modern man, with their catastrophic climates and their vast geography, their crushingly powerful or treacherous plant-life, their goading insects and their venomous reptiles, not to mention the human beings, among whom the 'savages' are not necessarily the most to be feared. Latent or explosive, this atmosphere of menace and ungovernable violence permeates Lautréamont's book from one end to the other.

Matta began to interpret the struggles between man and nature, and between man and his own nature, in his first graphic attempts—drawings in coloured crayon, in a style that was entirely new in surrealist art, containing no true objects, but constituting in themselves objects in full revolution.

In 1938, while staying with Gordon Onslow-Ford at Trévignon, near Concarneau in Brittany, Matta painted his first pictures in oils, six large canvases of which one was reproduced in the final issue of *Minotaure* (no. 12-13, 1939). That same issue also contained a reproduction of one of Oscar Dominguez' 'cosmic' compositions, belonging to the most important period—which Matta admired—of the artist's work. In comparing the two pictures, it is possible to discern a common feeling for original violence: in Dominguez' work, the spheres of torn matter emerging from grey vapours and shreds of ocean seem to carry the immemorial echo of some age-old catastrophe, while Matta's work expresses today's cataclysmic events in the heart of the nebulae and suns of being.

With Matta, as with some other surrealists, invention is derived from a sort of automatism: material accidents, unforeseen combinations and interplay of colours form the physical texture of explosive landscapes out of which meaningful shapes emerge.

Matta, Yves Tanguy and Esteban Francès joined André Breton during the summer of 1939 at Chemillieu (Ain), at an estate which Gordon Onslow-Ford had leased so that he and his friends could spend a holiday together. They all played various surrealist games, worked occasionally, and relaxed a great deal of the time. Kay Sage was staying not far away, in the Château de Bourdeaux, and often played hostess to them. Born in Albany, the capital of New York State, Kay Sage had lived in Europe, and especially in Italy, since childhood. She had always drawn and painted, untaught, having studied only for a few months during 1924 at the Scuola Liberale delle belle Arti in Milan. In 1936,

Kay Sage: *No One Heard Thunder*. 1939.

299

she exhibited some abstract paintings at the Galleria del Milione in that city. After her arrival in Paris in 1937, her work became more evocative. The paintings she showed at the Salon des Surindépendants in 1938 were immediately noticed by Breton, Tanguy, and a mutual friend, the Greek writer Nicolas Calas. Soon afterwards, she met the surrealists, and not long after that she and Yves Tanguy decided to share their lives together. They were only parted by his death in 1955.

September, 1939... and, in Europe, it was war once again. While the surrealists subject to mobilization put on their appropriate uniforms, Yves Tanguy, who had been declared medically unfit by the military authorities, rejoined Kay Sage during December in New York, preceded there by Matta and Onslow-Ford. Max Ernst had remained a German citizen, and his life was filled with complications during the 'phoney war' period.

Leonora Carrington: Drawing. 1939.

The very month of the outbreak of war, he was interned with a hundred or so other German nationals at Largentière, not far from St Martin-d'Ardèche. Leonora Carrington was still able to visit him, and bring him clothes and provisions, but soon afterwards he was transferred to Les Milles camp near Aix-en-Provence, where he was dumped in the company of two thousand other detainees in an old brick-works entirely devoid of hygienic arrangements. He stayed there for three months, and was only freed finally at Christmas, 1939 thanks to Paul Eluard, who pleaded his cause personally with the appropriate minister.

Ernst had met Hans Bellmer at Les Milles camp and, despite the incredible physical conditions, they had both been able to continue expressing themselves graphically by using the process of decalcomania. On his return to St Martin-d'Ardèche, Max Ernst experimented further with this technique, and produced paintings such as *Europe After the Rain*, and *Dream by a Young Girl about a Lake*. *The Stolen Mirror* is a vast landscape which has a great affinity with certain territories in the New World, specifically Arizona with its mountains like stratified stepping-stones, although the artist can hardly have imagined that he would one day be living there.

In May, 1940, at the start of the German offensive, *gendarmes* appeared once more at Leonora Carrington's house and took Max Ernst away as a 'suspect' to an internment camp at Loriol (Drôme), then once again to Les Milles. When the collapse of the French army seemed imminent, the prisoners in Les Milles camp were sent in the direction of Bayonne, then rerouted to Nîmes, where the armistice set them free and Max Ernst was able to return to St Martin-d'Ardèche.

Leonora Carrington was no longer there. During the final phase of the German offensive, an English woman-friend had taken her away by car towards Spain. In a state of complete mental confusion, she had signed an official deed giving away her house to a neighbour, had arrived in Andorra, then in Barcelona, and had finally reached Madrid. She had been so shaken by the series of emotional shocks she had experienced during the preceding months that she underwent a severe psychic crisis, and was committed to a clinic in Santander where she had to remain for several months. In 1943 she told the story of her mental adventure, in an astonishing little book called *En Bas*.[1] Leonora Carrington's tale is clear, precise and at the same time marvellously poetic; it also demonstrates the special lucidity that so-called 'mad' people are capable of attaining, and the incapacity of certain doctors to establish truly sympathetic contact with those entrusted to their care.

1. Reprinted in English translation as 'Down Below' in the review *VVV* No. 4, New York, February, 1944.

After the fall of France in 1940, a great number of painters and writers made their way into the zone that remained unoccupied by the German forces, and led an uncertain existence throughout that summer. Many of them looked towards the United States as a land of plenty and liberty, far from a Europe groaning under the burden of war and dictatorships. A 'Committee of Aid to Intellectuals', organized by individuals and groups in America and supervised in France by Mr William Fry, aimed at securing the departure for the New World of scientists and artists, offering them meanwhile a refuge not far from Marseilles, the Château Air-Bel.

There, to while away the time and keep their minds off an unsettled future, some of the surrealists took up the old 'games' once more, tried to invent new ones, or ressuscitated more classical ones. They had the idea of replacing the four suits in playing-cards by emblems symbolizing Love, Dream, Revolution and Knowledge: flame, star, wheel and key-hole; Père Ubu became the joker of this new 'Tarot de Marseille', and the hierarchy of court cards was changed from King, Queen and Jack to Guardian Spirits, Sirens and Mages: thus, for the red flame of Love, Baudelaire, the Portuguese Nun and Novalis; and for the black star of Dreams, Lautréamont, Alice and Freud.[1]

After countless difficulties and adventures, many refugees succeeded in reaching America. A photograph taken in March, 1942, at the Pierre Matisse Gallery in New York, shows a group of 'artists in exile': Matta, Zadkine, Tanguy, Ernst, Chagall, Léger, Breton, Mondrian, Masson, Ozenfant, Lipchitz, Tchelitchew, Seligmann, and Eugène Berman. Man Ray had returned to America in August, 1940 and was living in California, where he remained until 1951. Marcel Duchamp had been in Arcachon at the time of the French capitulation, but went back to Paris, where a friend who dealt in foodstuff obtained for him a permanent pass for the 'free zone' as a cheese buyer! As may be supposed, Duchamp was quite unconcerned with the official reason for his voyages, but took advantage of his opportunity to travel between Paris and the South of France. In 1942, he decided to return to New York, by way of Casablanca and Lisbon; there, in May, he embar-

ked on a Portuguese steamship which, being a neutral vessel, made a peaceful crossing of an Atlantic Ocean infested by warships and submarines.

In Mexico, the poet Cesar Moro, and Wolfgang Paalen (who had come to live in that country shortly before the war started in Europe) had organized an 'International Surrealist Exhibition' in February, 1940 at the Galeria de Arte Mexicano in Mexico City. This show brought together the work of a large number of painters and sculptors,[1] in addition to works by a few Mexican artists influenced by Surrealism, and *collages*, *frottages*, rayograms, decalcomanias, *fumages*, *encrages*, 'exquisite corpses', pre-Columbian objects, drawings by the insane, photographs, and so on.

During the war, Paalen published a review in Mexico called *Dyn* (six numbers between 1942 and 1944), which included reproductions of his own work and that of other artists living in Mexico, as well as a few painters in the United States. In the first issue, he stated in an introductory note that he 'no longer believed Surrealism capable either of determining the artist's position in the world today, or of formulating objectively art's reason for existence.'

In Marseilles, Wifredo Lam had joined the gathering of surrealists at the Château Air-Bel. This Cuban artist was born in Sagua la Grande, on December 8, 1902; his mother was of mixed African, Indian and European origin, while his father was Chinese, a businessman from Canton who had settled in the island, and whose name, Lam Yam, appears to mean 'the man from the wild cape, watching the blue sky'. Lam's father died in 1926, after a fall, at the age of a hundred and eight, but not before he had resisted for five whole days the effects of his accident and the incantations of the local sorcerers.

His son Wifredo attended courses at the Havana School of Fine Arts for some time, then left for Europe when he was nearly twenty. Spain has

1. The cards were drawn by Frédéric Delanglade from original designs by Brauner, Breton, Dominguez, Jacques Hérold, Wifredo Lam, Jacqueline Breton, and Masson. Sixteen of the cards, with a description of the game by André Breton, were reproduced in *VVV*, No. 4 (pp. 38, 59, 81, 88-90).

1. Bellmer, Brauner, Brignoni, Chirico, Dali, Delvaux, Dominguez, Duchamp (reproductions), Ernst, Espinoza, Onslow-Ford, Francés, Giacometti, Jennings, Frida Kahlo, Kandinsky, Klee, Magritte, Masson, Matta, Miró, Moore, Méret Oppenheim, Penrose, Paalen, Picabia, Picasso, Man Ray, Remedios, Rivera, Seligmann, Eva Sulzer, Tanguy, Ubac.

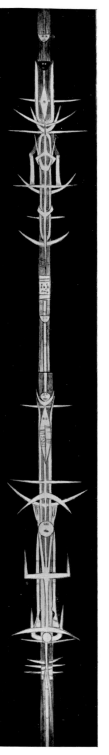

Wifredo Lam: *For the Moon*. 1958.

Wifredo Lam: *The Jungle*. 1943.

always remained a focal point for Cubans, whose country was itself Spanish territory not so long ago, and it was to Madrid that Lam went to study and paint; his contacts there were mostly with the officials of art who reacted indignantly to the sight of his pictures. But, in between return voyages to Cuba, he stayed there until the end of the Spanish Civil War; after the defeat of the Loyalists, he took refuge in France. In Paris, he met Picasso who provided him with constant encouragement, and whose influence is visible in Lam's first Paris compositions. He also became a close friend of Oscar Dominguez. In 1938, the Galerie Pierre organized an exhibition of Wifredo Lam's paintings.

In the spring of 1941, he left Marseilles for Martinique, in a ship crowded with other refugees (including André Breton and his family), under conditions comparable to those of a gang of galley-slaves, in the words of the ethnologist Claude Lévi-Strauss who was also a passenger.[1] From Martinique, where they found André Masson, Lam and his friends went on to Santo Domingo; then Lam left for Cuba, while Breton and Masson went on to New York.

Back on native soil once more, Lam was able to make full use of the artistic experience he had acquired in Paris. His new paintings, such as *L'Ame Extérieure* and *La Chanteuse des Poissons* (1942),[2] embodied ghostlike fetishes. At his first exhibition in New York, at the Pierre Matisse Gallery in 1942, he showed savage gods, painted with long, firm strokes. His second exhibition at the same gallery in 1943 began to synthesize the menacing nature of the New World: tree-trunks and palms assume the shape of armed and hostile symbols. Grey, green, brown and black, the tangled *Jungle* becomes animal; or perhaps it is the human being who is changing into a moving tree with countless eyes. Mythical, living things sprout shoots from which more horned heads spring up like buds.

Since the war, Lam has spent much of his time in Paris, the city where he most prefers to work. On tall, narrow canvases, he creates great white fetishes against a black background, symbolic columns with symmetrical, cruel gestures. Lam's work represents primitive purity and violence, rediscovered in new forms. His signs have the power of the thing signified and of magic spells—a

1. Cf Claude Lévi-Strauss: *Tristes Tropiques* (Plon, Paris, 1955).

2. The latter is reproduced in *VVV*, No. 2-3, New York, 1943 (p. 36).

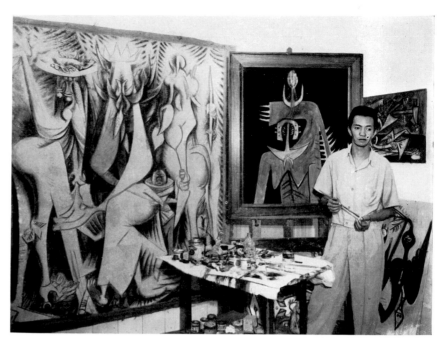

Wifredo Lam in his Havana studio, 1949.

mystery of atavisms and atmospheres whose secret he guards well.

During 1940, many reviews concerned with contemporary literature and the arts disappeared in Europe, and especially in France. This fact no doubt provided the initial impetus for the poet Charles Henri Ford in New York, when he decided to launch a regular bulletin of modern poetry and art, to be called *View*. Its first issue appeared in 1940, and its beginnings were modest, with the first numbers consisting simply of a few unbound sheets. Its existence remained rather precarious, despite its eventual life of seven years. In 1941, the October-November issue of *View* (no. 7-8) was entrusted to Nicolas Calas, who edited a number devoted entirely to Surrealism. It was one of the first indications of the presence of Surrealism in the United States.

The issue contained an interview with André Breton, articles by Seligmann and Calas, the captions from *La Femme 100 Têtes* translated and presented in the form of a long and splendid poem under the title 'The 100 Headless Woman', reproductions of work by Leonora Carrington, Masson, Seligmann, and vignettes by Hayter, Tanguy, Kay Sage, Ernst, Onslow-Ford, Lam, Matta, Dominguez, and Brauner. There was correspondence from abroad: letters from Roger Caillois in Buenos Aires, Suzanne Césaire in Martinique, and Pierre Mabille in Guadeloupe. A delirious letter was printed from the French poet Antonin Artaud, a patient at the time in an asylum in France, in which he pleaded for heroin. From Victor Brau-

go to New York find me an artistic mission (sic) so that I can go there to look around.'

The surrealist number of *View* contained the reproduction of a painting by a most curious figure, Morris Hirshfield. This artist was born in Russian Poland in 1872, came to America at the age of eighteen and worked as a factory-hand in a women's clothing factory. Later he became a manufacturer of boudoir slippers, founding the 'E. Z. Walk Manufacturing Company' in 1902, employing over three hundred people. In 1917, Hirshfield gave up his business due to illness. He had always done a bit of drawing, but his first paintings, including *The Beach Girl* and *The Angora Cat*, date only from 1937.

The images he created were large, carefully painted, naïve, with a sort of magic erotism as their main characteristic. His eternal subject was woman, nearly always naked, sometimes very openly naked like his *Nude at the Window* whose pure, white body looms up against a black background, between the symmetrical folds of half-drawn curtains. Occasionally accompanied by stylized animals, these priestesses of carnal desire have the round faces of the virgins in Russian ikons, the same staring eyes, heavy tresses, and delicately tapering hands and feet—but they also compel attention by their haunting nudity, sometimes unconcealed, sometimes merely suggested.

Hirshfield continued to paint these esoteric-erotic images until his death in 1946. During his lifetime they encountered the usual sarcasm and outcries of indignation. Nevertheless, his paintings were included in the 1942 Surrealist Exhibition in New York, and aroused the interest of dealers and collectors. He also made landscapes inspired by picture postcards; his last painting was an interpretation of a view of the Sacré Cœur on a postcard sent him from Paris by the New York picture-dealer Sidney Janis. The Montmartre edifice —which does, in fact, look rather like an enormous synagogue—appeared in Hirshfield's composition transformed into a Judeo-Byzantine chapel, surrounded by gardens planted with symmetrically-arranged flowers and trees. Hirshfield entitled this work *Parliamentary Buildings.*[2]

Morris Hirshfield: *Two Women in Front of a Mirror.* 1943.

ner came an impassioned message stating: 'I am the birth of the object. I am the end of the object. I am the spectre and the apparition. Everything commences and disappears through me and in me....' Finally a missive, dated January 17, 1941, from Marcel Duchamp (who was still in France at that time) was reproduced in facsimile: it was written on one of the printed forms used in occupied France for correspondence with the 'free zone'. With Duchamp's own words printed here in italics, it runs: '*Mary*[1] *and I* in good health—*hardly* tired...— I am working *on my box which is finished—If you*

1. Mary Reynolds, friend of Duchamp living in Paris, who died in 1955. Her collection of contemporary books and documents, some of them with bindings designed and executed by herself, is now in the library of the Chicago Art Institute, which has published a bibliography compiled by Hugh Edwards, with a foreword by Duchamp: *Surrealism and its Affinities: the Mary Reynolds Collection*, 1956.

2. Reproduced in *View*, Series VII, No. 1.

Wifredo Lam : *The Caribbean Parade.* 1945.

Yves Tanguy: *Real Numbers*. 1946.

With its second series, *View* began to look more like a small magazine, with plentiful illustrations. The first number (April, 1942) was devoted to the work of Max Ernst, the second (May, 1942) to that of Yves Tanguy (and the 'neo-romantic' Pavel Tchelitchew).

Max Ernst had arrived in New York on July 14, 1941. In 1942 he married the American Peggy Guggenheim,[1] but they separated soon afterwards. The first work painted, or rather completed, by Ernst in the United States (he had begun it in France) was entitled *Napoleon in the Desert*. The use of decalcomania, combined sometimes with other techniques,[2] allowed him to create new legends, like *Night and Day* in which the silhouettes of a nocturnal landscape are illuminated in certain places to become separate pictures of rocks; or *Moon over Wellfleet*; or *Summer Night in Arizona*, and so many other images that not only illustrate but also signpost the artist's different homes in the United States. One of these decalcomania-paintings shows cliffs towering high above a deep lake, like the façades of a living palace in which the fascinating window of a single ominous eye is opening: this is *The Eye of Silence* (1944), a landscape full of frenzied existence, and swathed in the oppressive atmosphere of Böcklin's *Island of the Dead*, the raw rock seeming to attain the sensitivity of the most delicate organs. Ernst has endowed these brilliant stains with a definitive meaning, surrounding them with bright or dark shores, marking out a horizon, creating planets that shine down on them, transforming them into leaves, forests, personages, sentient rocks. These anonymous surfaces permitting all dreams become the sites and forms of a single dream, his own, that blends all the others.

The issue of *View* devoted to Max Ernst reprinted the catalogue of his exhibition at the Valentine Gallery in March-April, 1942, where some thirty of his pictures dating from 1937 to 1942 were shown; it also contained a portrait of Ernst by Leonora Carrington, together with her text, 'The Superior of the Birds', another portrait by Bellmer, a laudatory article by Joseph Cornell entitled

Dorothea Tanning: *Profanation of the Host.* 1943.

'Story Without Words', a photograph of Ernst surrounded by his collection of American fetishes, and finally some 'souvenirs' by the artist which were later reprinted in Robert Motherwell's *Max Ernst: Beyond Painting*.[3]

At the end of 1940, while assembling works by women painters for a proposed show which he had been asked to organize at the Art of This Century gallery, Max Ernst met Dorothea Tanning.

Max Ernst: Sand drawing, Lake Pontchartrain (New Orleans). 1941.

1. Peggy Guggenheim had succeeded in getting her important collection of modern painting transferred in 1942 from France to the United States, where it formed the nucleus of her gallery, Art of This Century. The pictures are now housed in Venice, the owner's present home.

2. For example, *oscillation*, which produces an interlacing of lines by means of a funnel filled with paint and swung from a cord over the canvas (for instance, *The Crazy Planet*).

3. *Op. cit.*

Max Ernst: *The Eye of Silence*. 1944.

Julien Levy had come across her paintings the previous year, had been impressed by them and shown her work in his gallery. She was born in the small town of Galesburg, near Chicago, and cherished two ambitions from childhood, both of which she eventually achieved: to be a painter,

Dorothea Tanning and Max Ernst, Arizona, 1948.

and to go to Paris. So she started off by painting, despite her family's lack of enthusiasm for the idea, but spent only a few hours in the art school classes. After a period in New Orleans she came to New York in 1935 and had her first introduction there to the work of the surrealists, largely through the great 1936 Exhibition at the Museum of Modern Art. Her paintings were already illustrating scenes containing unexpected pictorial metaphors.

At the beginning of the war she got to know most of the surrealists living in America, through Julien Levy. And after meeting Max Ernst, she shared his existence. They were married in 1946 in Los Angeles, and at the same time and place Man Ray married Juliette Browner: the two couples were witnesses at each other's wedding. In 1945,

Max Ernst and Dorothea Tanning were at Great River, Long Island, not far from New York; here, in a garage turned into a studio, Ernst spent the summer constructing sculptures, hieratic figures evoking chessmen: *Moon Mad, The King Playing with the Queen, White Queen, An Anxious Friend.*

Then the couple went to live in Sedona, Arizona, a hamlet of about fifty inhabitants which the

Max Ernst: *An Anxious Friend.* 1944.

Kay Sage: *Tomorrow is Never.* 1955.

Kay Sage: Drawing. 1943.

presence of the Ernsts helped to transform eventually into something like a small town, as a result of the other artists and the visitors they attracted to the spot. When they first arrived there, they were surrounded by an almost complete solitude, with the magnificent stratified hills dominating their ranch, and all around them the desert and its strange inhabitants, such as the 'secretary-bird', and the Gila monster *(Heloderma suspectum)*, a large lizard, sluggish and dangerous, which never loosens the grip of its jaws once they have fastened on a prey or adversary.

The art of Dorothea Tanning now began to depict suites of rooms haunted by little girls in rags, seemingly turned into demons by their journey 'through the looking glass', ripping wallpaper into shreds along corridors with doors ajar (for instance, *Children's Games*, 1942),[1] while elsewhere an enormous sunflower lies in wait on the landing (*Eine Kleine Nachtmusik*, 1944), like the giant

1. Reproduced in *VVV*, No. 2-3 (p. 106).

knight's armour-clad foot in the great court of the castle of Otranto.

In the garden of the house at Sedona, Max Ernst constructed a group of large sculptures in cement, completed in 1948 and called *Capricorn*: against a backcloth of the surrounding countryside, stand two figures, male and female, Bull and Moon.

In 1941, Yves Tanguy and Kay Sage set up house in Woodbury, in a part of Connecticut that became a popular retreat for artists and writers during the last war. Their home was one of those old villas that one can find round each bend of the road in the countryside north-east of New York City. Europeans who visit this region are sometimes struck by the contrast between these immaculate, white-painted wooden houses, looking as if they had been put together from the pieces of a toy construction kit, but furnished inside with labour-saving gadgets still undreamt of on the other side

310

of the Atlantic—and the surrounding natural environment, deserted by the first colonists before they had civilized it, where woods cluttered with dead trees are encroaching once more on the abandoned sites.

The extraordinary kindness of a more than hospitable race diminishes to a great extent the feeling of strangeness experienced by someone arriving there for the first time. But neither voyages, landscapes, nor climates, however extreme, could impose their character on the profound art of Yves Tanguy. It is, rather, the general atmosphere, a different everyday life, that leaves certain marks on the scenes that his paint-brush created in America. His paintings began to depict—always on the same lustrous, milky shore—forms that had become more precise and glossy, that arranged themselves into complex pieces of apparatus which seemed to be distilling delicious liqueurs whose lively colours sometimes tinted a retort or a crucible. These objects had grown larger, too, as if the artist had approached closer to the tiny specks that had once dotted sparsely the infinite stretches of his inner world.

For what radio receivers was this geometric scaffolding of rods and spheres designed *(Slowly Toward the North*, 1942)? What is the unknown substance composing this blue liquid that fills all these white saucers, and that is boiling under the control of a weird gadget on a table with articulated supports (*Indefinite Divisibility*, 1942)? *The Closing Days* (1944) contains great plaques of warm, pliable material whose colourings seem to be reacting to new lights.... *Closed Sea, Wide World* (1944).[1]

In America, Kay Sage's art also assumed fresh qualities, revealing a certain hallucinatory sense of architecture. Ancestors of hers were among the original colonists of New England, and it seems that atavistic echoes appear in her visions of cities yet to be born and already abandoned, whose tall scaffoldings seem to have been erected on some distant planet by vanished discoverers.

Her nostalgic paintings represent ghost-cities, like those hallucinating towns that still exist today, in Nevada for instance, deserted for more than half a century and still intact with their lofts, their farms, their bars, some houses still half built: life suddenly vanished from them one day when the

1. These four paintings are reproduced in James Thrall Soby's monograph *Yves Tanguy* (Museum of Modern Art, New York, 1955).

Kay Sage and Yves Tanguy, 1954.

precious lodes of metal in the surrounding mountains became exhausted, and the adventurers packed up and left all together for other Eldorados. Even peaceful Connecticut experienced more than one such exodus, when the fertile lands of the West or the Californian placers beckoned, and the

Dorothea Tanning: *Eine Kleine Nachtmusik.* 1946.

tracks and foundations of abandoned villages may still be found on some hillside now covered with undergrowth.

Although it has changed its nature, Chirico's sense of menace remains visible in Kay Sage's work, in the mystery of perspectives. *An Island in the Night* depicts an unfinished, uninhabited town, its walls and statues still veiled behind cloths torn by the wind, for its future citizens have travelled on further, towards new lands—perhaps even *Three Thousand Miles to the Starting Point*.

Kay Sage creates her sharp, disquieting landscapes with light rather than colour, the pure, dense light of a land of pioneers.

In June, 1942, in New York, the surrealists published the first issue of a review of poetry, the plastic arts, anthropology, sociology and psychology (an American *Minotaure* no less luxurious than its French predecessor) entitled *VVV*: the 'V for Victory' that had become the constant radio theme of an embattled and stubborn Britain, but tripled in a new abbreviation which was intended to signify, according to the explanations given on the first page of the review, 'victory over the forces of aggression—V over that which tends to perpetuate the enslavement of man by man—V again over all that is opposed to the emancipation of the spirit'; or again, a triple 'view': 'the View around us—the View inside us' and their synthesis which 'takes account of the myth in process of formation beneath the Veil of happenings'.

After an introductory note by the writer Lionel Abel, 'It is Time to Pick the Iron Rose', this first number, under a cover composed by Max Ernst, presented various studies: 'Indian Cosmetics', on the Kaduveo Indians of Brazil (Claude Lévi-Strauss); 'The Evil Eye', on magic (Kurt Seligmann); 'Some Testimonial Drawings of Dream Images' (F. Kiesler); a note on the strange compositions of the seventeenth-century German scientist and polymath Athanasius Kircher; and on modern art, Robert Motherwell's essay 'Mondrian and Chirico'.[1] There was also the inevitable commentary on Lautréamont's sewing-machine and umbrella, Harold Rosenberg's 'Life and Death of the Amorous Umbrella'; a translation of a fragment from Jarry's *Guignol* by Edouard Roditi; an early text by Arthur Cravan, poems in English and French, and reproductions of works by Chirico, Ernst, Masson, Matta, Picasso, Seligmann, Tanguy, Hare, Onslow-Ford, etc. Finally, printed in French as well as English, André Breton's 'Prolegomena to a Third Manifesto of Surrealism or Else' proposed, in the context of a lengthy dissertation, a

Marcel Duchamp's studio in New York.

1. *Op. cit.*

myth of 'The Great Invisibles', restating the well-known hypothesis of the existence of beings to whom we stand in the same relationship as the atoms of which we are composed stand to ourselves, beings which would, basically, direct our individual and social evolution.

This same year, 1942, from October 19 to November 17, a Surrealist Exhibition was organized in aid of French children and prisoners, on the premises of the Coordinating Council of French Relief Societies, at 451 Madison Avenue, New York. The contributing artists were either living in the United States or other countries in the New World, or else, though still in Europe, were represented in American collections: they included Ernst, Duchamp, Tanguy, Magritte, Arp, Onslow-Ford, Matta, Seligmann, Chagall, Giacometti, Frida Kahlo, Lam, Delvaux, Francès, Chirico, Méret Oppenheim, Breton, Miró, Klee, Leonora Carrington, Masson, Moore, Picasso, Oelze, Brauner, Brignoni, Bellmer, Dominguez, Remedios, and the Americans John Goodwin, Jimmy Ernst, Ralph Nelson, Lawrence Vail, Robert Loughlin, William Baziotes, Hedda Sterne, Kay Sage, Frederick Kiesler, Barbara Reis, Robert Motherwell, David Hare, Morris Hirshfield, Alexander Calder.

The show was to be held in the living-rooms of the Reid Mansion, which were designed in the best of bad taste, with nineteenth-century wooden panelling and gaudily painted ceilings. Marcel Duchamp was entrusted with their preparation, and proceeded to mask the antiquated decorations with an immense 'spider's web' made of miles of white twine stretched across the rooms, an aerial labyrinth criss-crossing at every angle and, ironically, covering the old-fashioned decor and the modern painting equally with its network of tangled cords.

The catalogue of the exhibition was called 'First Papers of Surrealism' (suggesting an immigrant's first naturalization papers). The front cover of this booklet, devised by Duchamp, represented a crumbling wall pierced by five bullet-holes (the paper actually has five holes drilled through it at the places showing the impact of the bullets); the back cover reproduced the greatly enlarged photograph of a slab of Gruyère cheese:

'*Here then for my fast is a piece of Gruyère*'
(Apollinaire).

Duchamp's humour did not stop there. To overcome the difficulty, due to the circumstances of the time, of publishing portraits of many of the exhibitors, he had suggested using the system of 'compensation-portraits'. Thus, the catalogue reproduced approximations of the real features of certain painters, selected from among thousands of anonymous documents. Duchamp himself became Rrose Sélavy with the face of an emaciated woman; Magritte became an ageing explorer in a solar topee; Picasso, two heads photographed together, looking in opposite directions; Brauner, a suspicious-looking painter armed with his maulstick. Chirico was transformed into a classical sculpted profile, Max Ernst into a prophet with a long snow-white beard, Masson into an Eskimo, Lam into a grimacing savage, and so on.

To provide some balance to so much metaphoric sarcasm, a Foreword by Sidney Janis declared that 'Surrealism from its inception, became and has ever since remained the cardinal germinating source for many of the most gifted and far-seeing artists on the international scene.' Further on, a text by Robert Allerton Parker discussed the 'Explorers of the Pluriverse',[1] his theme being that 'America has produced pioneers of the inward realm no less than of distant horizons'; the author mentions Cotton Mather's book *Wonders of the Invisible World*, Jonathan Edwards' famous eighteenth-century sermon 'Sinners in the Hands of an Angry God', and the folk-lore and folk-art of cults sponsored by prophets and messiahs from Mother Ann Lee and Joseph Smith to Father Divine. Poe is a superb example, says Parker, of 'marginal' consciousness, as also are Herman Melville, and Benjamin Paul Blood whose work was saved from oblivion by William James. He emphasizes the importance of Charles Fort (died 1932), who used his collection of newspaper clippings, by a kind of literary *collage* and *montage*, to provide the basis of his books about a highly unpredictable universe; the painters Alfred Ryder and Louis Eilshemius are cited as eccentric craftsmen (Marcel Duchamp had been an admirer of Eilshemius since 1915); and, finally, Clark Ashton Smith is mentioned as being a powerfully imaginative science-fiction writer.

Further on in the catalogue, Breton reverted to his favourite theme, and 'staged' the myths of the Golden Age, Orpheus, original sin, Icarus, the Philosopher's Stone, the Graal, artificial men, interplanetary communication, the Messiah, putting the King to death, the Twin Souls (the Androgyne), Science Triumphant, the Myth of Rimbaud, the

1. 'Pluriverse': a word coined by Blood, whose book of that title was published in 1920, the year after his death.

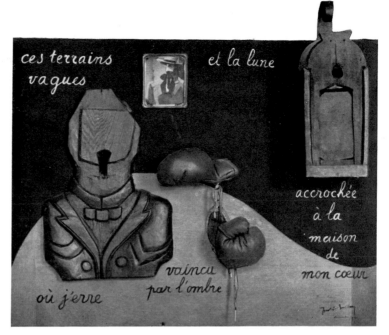

André Breton: *Object*. 1941.

Superman, and, finally, his own 'Great Invisibles', illustrating each legend with old paintings and engravings, works by surrealists, and poetic and literary quotations.

This was followed in the catalogue by two letters from abroad, one of which was from Henri Matisse to his son Pierre; and lastly, reproductions of a mobile by Calder and pictures by Leonora Carrington, Brauner, Hirshfield, Miró, Seligmann, Chirico, Duchamp, Matta, Ernst, Tanguy, Masson, Kay Sage, Lam, Oelze, Motherwell, Onslow-Ford.

View no. 4 (second series, January, 1943) was entitled *Americana Fantastica* and brought together a large number of strange documents in the spirit of Max Ernst's *collages*: old engravings, photographs, etc. The cover was designed by Joseph Cornell who, in the same issue, gave an account of the history of a sort of pagoda, a 'Chinese-style' tower erected in France during the eighteenth century and apparently transported later on to New Jersey to satisfy the whim of a small girl. The review also printed reproductions of his objects *Spent Meteor*, and *De Medici Slot Machine*.

313

Born in New York in 1904, Joseph Cornell was twenty-six when he first saw Max Ernst's album, *La Femme 100 Têtes*, and perhaps its plates helped him to define more closely a whole world of poetic symbols. In any case, it was soon after this encounter that Cornell, though hitherto out of touch with the artistic movement, showed his own first efforts at *collage* to Julien Levy, who included them in an exhibition of works by the surrealists in January, 1932. In 1933, he wrote the scenario of a 'stereoscopic' film, *Monsieur Phot*.

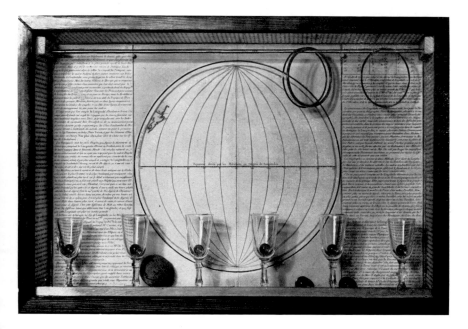

Joseph Cornell: Object-Box. 1950.

The 1936 exhibition at the Museum of Modern Art included a photograph by George Platt Lynes of a curious composition of objects by Cornell, called *Soap Bubble Set*.[1] The artist's first one-man show was held at Julien Levy's in December, 1939, and he took part in another surrealist exhibition at the same gallery in February, 1940.

However, Cornell refuses to be associated with Surrealism. Although he met most of the painters and writers representing the movement who were in the United States during the war, he has resolutely remained isolated in his work. Nevertheless, his creations quite visibly share the same atmosphere as the work of the surrealists; in the field of objects, they are a personal extension and an enlargement of it—Cornell's ideas have achieved concrete

1. Reproduced in *Fantastic Art, Dada, Surrealism* (p. 155).

expression in the fabrication of glass-panelled boxes, each of which encloses within its transparent walls a precise and singular dream.

The starting point for some of the series of image-objects which he elaborates is invariably a long-meditated and engrossing basic idea. In the house on Utopia Parkway, in the Flushing district of New York, that has been his home for many years, Joseph Cornell seems not to notice the roar of aircraft using the nearby airport of La Guardia as he talks to his occasional visitors, with a kind of reticent passion, about the many people in America who kept pigeons thirty years ago, now grown so few that no one even seems to know any longer what a dove-cote is. So he has built up a large collection of documents dealing with these abodes and their winged guests: photographs from magazines, postcards, naïvely symbolic engravings, zoological and architectural studies, all kinds of associative images—and from this gestation have resulted several 'boxes' in which white balls roll along strips of wood placed one above the other, in front of circular openings. Some of these glass dove-cotes give a strange impression of depth, due to a simple but cunning play of mirrors; the sense of mystery derives from the clarity and absolute bareness of the symbol, qualities that raise questions impossible to put into words.

In the same way, a prolonged meditation preceded the artist's conception embodying the photograph of a Renaissance portrait: in the *De Medici Slot Machine*, a rectangular compartment contains the image of this adolescent from a previous century, framed by small objects whose evocative power in these particular surroundings is not lessened by the fact of their being contemporary products. There are also boxes in which the 'backcloth' consists of a view of the constellation of Andromeda, or an ancient engraving representing the solar system, or an advertisement or other text from some old French newspaper (Cornell's knowledge of French is imperfect, but he makes use of captions, press-cuttings and phrases in the French language with astonishing accuracy as far as syntax and meaning is concerned). Balls, flasks, glasses containing blue marbles all become symbols when brought face to face on tiny shelves, as in the windows of some shop dealing in unknown goods. These are surrealist habitual objects, sleep-inducing potions, as too are his rows of little bottles like those in chemists' shops, offering ironically—for what magical cure?—their diffe-

International Surrealist Exhibition, New York, 1942. Twine by Marcel Duchamp.

Compensation—portraits.

Duchamp.   Picasso.   Matta.   Chirico.

Yves Tanguy : *Indefinite Divisibility*. 1942.

rent panaceas: twigs, lead shot, feathers, gravel, cotton-wool....

Cornell has also designed narrow glass cases containing several levels along which streams of black or light-brown sand are running in stratifications, carrying with them a few commonplace objects such as metal rings or pebbles. These creations are neither facile nor simply pretty; on the contrary, they possess a real and severe beauty that is not in the least monotonous. Like the fluid in a photographer's developing-tray, the flowing sands 'develop' images that are exact, changing, and new.

His 'crystal cages', guardians of clear, urgent dreams, are made in the image of a solitary man who would like to be unapproachable and is yet tormented by a desire to communicate with his fellow men. Between his hands, small worlds spring up unceasingly, full of reality and life.

Launched in October, 1942, *VVV* seems to have been intended originally as a monthly review (a second number was announced for October, with a cover by Chagall), but in fact only two further issues

Matta: Cover for *VVV*, no. 4, February, 1944.

were published, in the form of substantial annuals. Number 2-3 was designated an *Almanac for 1943*, and the fourth and last issue appeared in 1944, with a cover by Matta. The *Almanac*'s cover, designed by Marcel Duchamp, is an old (but topical) engraving, representing an apocalyptic knight carrying scythe and hour-glass, astride a globe of the world; the figure's jerkin has been transformed into an American coat of arms, with stars and stripes. This double issue of *VVV* also contained the '*réplique 1943*' of a picture-puzzle by Duchamp, a nursemaid standing near a wistful-looking lion in a cage: '*Nous nous cajolions*'.[1] No. 4 reproduced the same author's *Allégorie de Genre*, in which a profile of George Washington is cut out of an outline map of the United States, the territory of the Union and its founder's features being represented by the same piece of bandage-gauze sprinkled with golden stars and striped by smeared red lines.[2]

Myths, divinations, revelations provided much

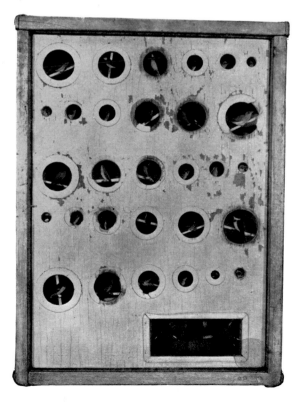

1. A pun on '*Nounou cage aux lions.*'

2. Duchamp had originally devised this *montage* in response to a request by *Vogue* for a magazine cover. But they had turned it down.

Joseph Cornell: *Forgotten Game*. 1950.

of the substance for *VVV*. No. 2-3, for example, included William Seabrook's account of a shared ecstatic experience, 'The Door Swung Inwards'; a 'Prognostication by Paracelsus' annotated by Kurt Seligmann; Benjamin Paul Blood's pamphlet 'The Anaesthetic Revelation'. An article by Robert Allerton Parker, 'Such Pulp as Dreams are Made on', discussed Clark Ashton Smith (already mentioned in *First Papers of Surrealism*) and another science-fiction writer, H. P. Lovecraft, little known in his lifetime, who was obsessed by the idea of a still-active prehistoric malevolence. The painter G. Kamrowski contributed a 'Panorama-graph' to the same issue, a two-page historical-mythological *montage* which he entitled 'Humans'. In No. 4, a letter from Robert Lebel gave a rather sceptical opinion on the possibility of creating new myths: '...To try and create a new myth is rather like establishing the "myth of those without myths", or the "clan of those without a clan", since the individuals it is proposed to bring together are precisely those who have found that none of the public forms of collective activity measure up to their standards.'

It was left to Frederick Kiesler to introduce an experimental note, with his 'Twin-Touch-Test': the idea was to place one's hands on either side of a wire screen let into the back cover of the *Almanac*, fingers and palms in close contact, run both hands simultaneously down, repeatedly, and describe whether it proved to be an unusual feeling of touch.

Kiesler is an architect of Austrian origin, whose avant-garde enterprises during the early twenties in Europe include set-designs for Karel Capek's film, *RUR* (1922); 'moving scenery' for Eugene O'Neill's *Emperor Jones* (Berlin, 1923); the design of a pioneer 'theatre in the round' (Vienna, 1924); and the model of an 'aerial town' at the 1925 Paris Exhibition. *VVV*, no. 4 reproduced a photo-montage that included a 'spheroid model' of his 1924 'Endless House' (shown at the 1926 New York International Exhibition) and a view of his 1934 project, the 'Space-House'. The *Almanac* had previously published his thesis on 'Design-Correlation', accompanied by two diagrams with swivelling cut-outs that explain the principles behind his various constructional designs in the galleries assigned respectively to abstract and surrealist art at Art of This Century. Three photographs show views of the galleries.

The *Almanac* also printed a 'Letter from Chile' in the form of a retrospective calendar of the activities in that country, since 1938, of the *Mandragora* surrealist group.

Among the many literary and art reviews and publications that sprang up in the United States during the last war, it is certainly *View* which—although never in any way an 'official' organ of the movement—provides the most striking evidence of the gradual penetration of American intellectual life by the ideas and themes of Surrealism.

With its third series (1943), *View* became a full-scale magazine. It published translations of two extracts from Chirico's *Hebdomeros* (Series IV, Nos 3 and 4) and three instalments of Raymond Roussel's *Impressions d'Afrique* (III: 4, IV: 1, IV: 2), as well as of texts by the thirteenth-century English bishop Robert Grosseteste (IV: 2), Pico della Mirandola (IV: 3, IV: 4), and Bluet d'Achères, nicknamed the 'Comte de Permission', court jester to Henri IV of France (V: 5). The pages of the review were illustrated by reproductions of the work of surrealist painters and, more frequently, surrealistically-inclined, 'neo-romantic' or naïve painters. Duchamp, Man Ray, Lam, Hirshfield, Magritte, Masson, Seligmann, Calder and Francès were among those who designed covers for *View*. Man Ray's thesis, 'Photography is not an Art', appeared in Series III, no 3, and his surrealist fantasy, 'Ruth Roses and Revolvers', in Series IV, no 4; while other artists, including S. W. Hayter and André Masson, contributed articles to various numbers. Erudite studies by such writers as Nicolas Calas, Lionel Abel, Denis de Rougemont, Sidney Janis, Robert Melville, James Johnson Sweeney, Meyer Schapiro, Parker Tyler (associate editor of *View*), Kurt Seligmann, and Charles Glenn Wallis were a regular feature. But the review also gave considerable space to American and French poets, published poems in primitive style, the writings and drawings of children, naïves, and autodidacts, and, in its 'Children's Pages', sought out manifestations of the particular quality of freshness inherent in extreme youth. An article by Edouard Roditi on the *trompe-l'œil* still-lives by William Harnett describes the artist as a 'nineteenth-century American necromantic', and an account is given of the strange allegories in paint by Florine Stettheimer, who died in 1945 (V: 3; for reproductions of this artist's work see also IV: 3, V: 1 and VII: 2). Each issue contained critical reviews of current literature, art, and music.

The October, 1945 issue (V: 3) detailed the

creative ingenuity of an American conscientious objector, an artist who declared himself unconcerned by politics or religion, and was in prison for refusing to serve in the armed forces because it was an activity that 'had nothing to do with painting'; there is a description of the methods he used to construct objects from porridge or newspaper while in prison, and the various technical innovations that enabled him to shape and paint these objects.

The review did not escape the dead hand of censorship, either. Its December, 1943 issue (III: 4) ran into trouble because of some of its illustrations—a pen and ink drawing by Picasso of one of his Minotaurs, Michelangelo's *Ganymede*, and three inoffensive naked women by the surrealist-influenced Leon Kelly—all of which were doubtless considered 'obscene' by the postal authorities, who decreed that the number in question might not be mailed to bookstores or subscribers in unsealed envelopes; the ruling was soon reversed as a result of concerted protests by distinguished individuals.

The March, 1945 issue of *View* (V: I) was entirely devoted to Marcel Duchamp. It served both to cast some light on the unique position of the author of *The Bride Stripped Bare by her Bachelors, Even* in contemporary poetic thought, and to demonstrate the ever-growing magnetism that his personality exercised in America. The cover shows a wine bottle (whose label is really Duchamp's Service Record sheet) floating in the immensity of a starry sky, and a cloud of smoke rising from its neck.[1] On the back cover, a statement signed by Duchamp asserts: '*Quand la fumée de tabac sent aussi de la bouche qui l'exhale, les deux odeurs s'épousent par infra-mince.*' The number opened with a poem of tribute to Duchamp by Charles Henri Ford, 'Flag of Ecstasy', followed by Breton's 'Lighthouse of the Bride', Gabrielle Buffet's 'Magic Circles',

1. On the contents page, a note by Peter Lindamood, 'I Cover the Cover', describes in detail the creation of this image by Marcel Duchamp.

Alexander Calder's studio, 1958.

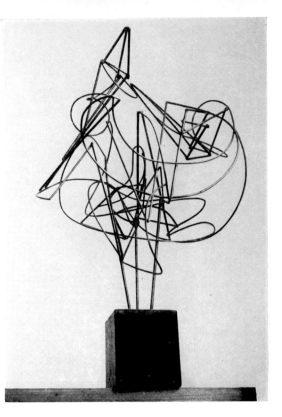

Isabelle Waldberg:
The Sextant. 1954.

David Hare: *Thirsty Man.* 1946.

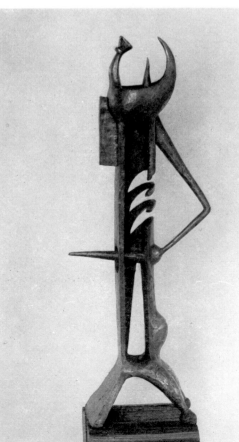

Robert Desnos' word-plays about Rrose Sélavy, studies by James Thrall Soby, Harriet and Sidney Janis, and Nicolas Calas, and Kiesler's 'Triptych' (a *photo-montage* with cut-out flaps) entitled '*Les Larves d'Imagie d'Henri Robert Marcel Duchamp*'. Texts by Man Ray, Julien Levy, Robert Allerton Parker, Mina Loy, and Henrie Waste (pseudonym of Effie Stettheimer, sister of the painter Florine Stettheimer) were assembled under the general title of 'Duchampiana', while Leon Kochnitzky discussed 'Marcel Duchamp and the Futurists'.

Birds:

In his Connecticut farm, Alexander Calder raises the swaying, murmuring throng of his Mobiles. His barn-studio has been turned into an incredible jumble of sheets of metal, boxes, paint-pots, papers, letters, drawings, tools, trestles, work-benches, ropes, cigar-boxes, iron rods... over which hovers the circular, grave, trembling flight of the metallic birds of prey that are suspended there, soaring, wheeling, borne along by the lightest breath of wind crossing the great cage whose only bars are those in its windows.

Towards the end of the war, birds of a different kind were to be seen in America: they came from Spain, where Miró was living, and they were the flocks of geometrically-shaped birds that darted across the surface of his recent paintings. Their exhibition at the Pierre Matisse gallery evoked a wave of interest and admiration: *Women and Birds Under the Moon*, *The Rosy Twilight Caresses the Sex of Women and Birds*, *Women and Birds in the Night*... birds, and stars, leaving the traces of their passage in the picture's atmosphere, like the rosary of human motion seen in a chronogram.

Lastly, the invisible birds of Isabelle Waldberg are aerial sculptures using rods of willow or metal: the swallow has built its cage with the trajectories of its flight.[1]

During 1941, and afterwards, Enrico Donati painted clouds coloured deep blue or Adriatic green, from which brilliant shapes with shifting hues burst forth. In these celebrations, the night is filled with sparkle and glitter, lit up by the glow of ships on fire, and the exploding spheres and trains of fast-burning powder have all the charm of rockets

1. See *VVV*, no. 4.

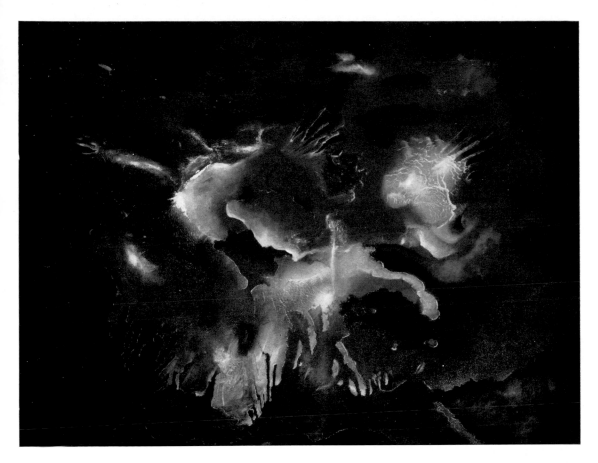

Enrico Donati: *Bolero*. 1943.

'climbing to the top of their own summits and leaning over to look down'. The chance effects of pigment or brush are illuminated by meanings that vanish in the moment they are stated, a firework display of possibilities: *Le Philtre, Nocturne, Baptism of the Birch-tree, Conception of Venus*, etc.[1]

In preparation for the launching of the American edition of André Breton's *Le Surréalisme et La Peinture*,[2] Donati and Marcel Duchamp arranged a special window display at the bookshop owned by the publisher, Brentano, on Fifth Avenue in New York. The display included among its other features a reconstruction of the 'shoe-feet' in Magritte's

picture *The Red Model* (which was reproduced on the cover of Breton's book), and was a centre of shocked and fascinated attention for the passers-by. Brentano's decided that this window-dressing had better be removed, whereupon all the objects were dismantled and re-erected in the window of the neighbouring Gotham Book Mart on Forty-seventh Street.

Estebal Francès covered large canvases with symbol-shapes, kaleidoscopic views of stars, pyramids, spangles, and stones: *The Bull in the Window, Membranes of Space, El Humo....* Kurt Seligmann used bold strokes to paint his human figures enveloped in an aura of tormented medievalism; as we

1. Reproduced in *View* (VI: 1), in *VVV*, no. 4, and in *Le Surréalisme et la Peinture* (with an essay on the artist).

2. This new edition contained the texts of the original French edition, augmented by the 1941 preface to Peggy Guggenheim's catalogue *Art of this Century*, introductory essays from reviews such as *Minotaure* and *View*, and various catalogue prefaces. A Preface presents the original texts as being 'unretouched', although they have in fact undergone certain modifications, including the suppression of

insulting references to the American collector Dr Barnes, and of some unkind remarks about Chagall, and the elimination of the entire long note in which Breton discusses scathingly the idea of God, ending with the words 'God is a swine' (this note can be found in the translation of extracts from *Le Surréalisme et la Peinture* published as a booklet under the title *What is Surrealism?* by Faber & Faber, London, 1936).

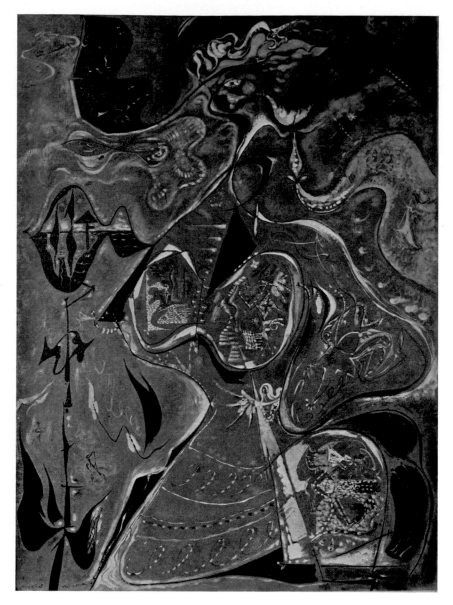

in 1944 and was married, for some years, to David Hare who was officially the Editor in Chief of *VVV*.

About 1941, Hare made his first 'heatages', (a process also utilized by Raoul Ubac),[2] consisting in heating and, in places, melting the gelatine of a photographic negative after development, which can change women's bodies, for instance, into birds of paradise, savage gods, or braziers *(The Retroactive Wish as a Reality, Hidden Fundamental*, etc).[3] Later, Hare devoted himself to sculpture, grouping menacing figures and tense, rounded forms *(Egyptian Golem, The Taxidermist...*).

Man Ray was teaching photography and painting —in a most unpedagogic manner—in a Los Angeles college. He concerned himself during this period with creating objects: *Palettable* (1941), *Artificial Florist* (1943), *Silent Harp* (1944)....

As for André Masson, he did not budge from his Connecticut home throughout the war, and painted *Indian Summers*, and *Iroquois Landscapes* in the typical browns, reds, blacks and whites of American Indian art, as well as pictures like the *Belle Italienne*. *VVV* published several of his philosophical-allegorical drawings.

Salvador Dali's productions are not included among the activities enumerated in this chapter. Dali had long been completely separated from the surrealists, and was pursuing a career in which he achieved brilliant results, especially in the field of commercial art.[4] As is well known, he subsequently undertook the conquest of the religious art market with equal success. A visitor to the Washington National Gallery, which hitherto contained only masterpieces, or to the New York Metropolitan Museum, who is not imbued with the ardent Catholic faith professed today by the author of *The Profanation of the Host*, may well wonder why these institutions should have found space for Dali's *Last Supper* or his *Crucifixion*. However, I have a feeling that even a true believer must feel some embarrassment in the presence of these gigantic, cheaply-coloured conundrums.

André Masson: *La Belle Italienne*. 1943.

have already seen, he had contributed several essays on magic to *VVV* and *View*.[1] The Brazilian sculptress Maria's specific contributions to surrealism were bronzes consisting of interlaced forms like lianas in virgin forests. Jacqueline Lamba-Breton painted dream-like pictures, full of scintillating apparitions. She became separated from Breton

After spending some time in New York, Leonora Carrington left for Mexico and made her home in that country. The account of her Spanish exper-

1. His book, *The Mirror of Magic*, appeared in 1948, (Pantheon Books, New York).

2. See below, pp. 335.

3. See *VVV*, no. 1, and *First Papers of Surrealism*.

4. See, for example, the back cover of *View*, III, 4 (1943) for one of the many advertisements drawn by Dali.

iences, *Down Below*, was published in *VVV*, as were her stories *Waiting*, and *The Seventh Horse*, in which the fantastic weaves its webs of terror and desire around the actions of everyday life—eating, walking, sleeping. Her paintings at that time were imaginative continuations of her stories, and her stories became descriptions of her paintings: reality and its transformations, and displacements of situation, appearance, and proportion create a dramatic and humorous atmosphere.[1]

During 1946-1947, the Loew-Lewin film company sponsored a competition for the execution of a picture representing *The Temptation of Saint Anthony*; the winning composition was to be featured in a film inspired by Maupassant's story *The Private Affairs of Bel Ami*. Eleven painters took part in the contest: Ivan Le Lorraine Albright, Eugene Berman, Leonora Carrington, Salvador Dali, Paul Delvaux, Max Ernst, Louis Guglielmi, Horace Pippin, Abraham Rattner, Stanley Spencer, and Dorothea Tanning. The jury, composed of Alfred H. Barr Jr, Marcel Duchamp and Sidney Janis, awarded the prize to Max Ernst's picture. The participating artists were invited to comment on their own contributions for the catalogue of the exhibition which followed the competition.[2] This is what Leonora Carrington wrote about her own composition:

'The picture seems pretty clear to me, being a more or less literal rendering of St Anthony complete with pig, desert and temptation. Naturally one could ask why the venerable holy man has three heads—to which one could always reply, why not?

'You will notice the veteran's suit to be whitish and of an umbrellaoid form which would lead one to believe that the original colour had been washed or bleached out by the vagaries of the weather or that the monkish apparel had been cleverly constructed out of used mummy wrappings in umbrella or sunshade form as a protection from sand storms and sun, practical for someone leading an open air life and given to contemplation (as Egyptologists apparently didn't exist in those days, mummy wrappings were no doubt to be gathered like blackberries and therefore to one of an economical

and modest turn of mind they would provide a durable and apt clothing for the desert).

'The Saint's traditional pet pig who lies across the nether half of the picture and reviews the observer out of its kindly blue eye is adequately accounted for in the myth of St Anthony, and likewise the continually flowing water and the ravine.

'The bald-headed girl in the red dress combines female charm and the delights of the table—you

Leonora Carrington: *The Temptation of Saint Anthony*. 1946.

1. Her paintings from 1942 include *A l'Auberge du Cheval d'Aube*, *The Hunt*, *The Oval Lady*, etc.

2. For his part, Marcel Duchamp wrote, on the subject of his participation in the jury: 'Jurors are always apt to be wrong. The only argument in favour of this jury is that the three differed in their selection of the first, second, and third prizes, showing how close the decision was. But even the conviction of having been fair does not change my doubts on the right to judge at all.'

will notice that she is engaged in making an unctuous broth of (let us say) lobsters, mushrooms, fat turtle, spring chicken, ripe tomatoes, gorgonzola cheese, milk chocolate, onions and tinned peaches. The mixture of these ingredients has overflowed and taken on a greenish and sickly hue to the fevered vision of St Anthony, whose daily meal consists of withered grass and tepid water with an occasional locust by way of an orgy.

'On the right, the Queen of Sheba and her attendants emerge in ever-decreasing circles out of a subterranean landscape towards the hermit. Their intention is ambiguous, their progress spiral.

'And last to the ram with the earthenware jar one could only quote the words of Friar Bacon's brazen head: Time was—Time is—Time is past. I was always pleased with the simple idiocy of these words.'

In connection with the hermit's broth, I cannot resist the temptation to set down one of the cooking recipes invented by Leonora Carrington, who is the creator of a whole number of surrealist dishes —some of her guests in New York have retained a lasting memory of a 'hare with oysters' that she once served. Here, then, is her method of preparing Stuffed Beef in Sherry Wine, in which the oyster again plays an interesting part.[1]

'Take a large slab of beef and whack it heartily until it is tender; massage it gently with the following mixture: one spud garlic chopped very fine, onion ditto, parsley ditto, powdered thyme, nutmeg and very little allspice; let these penetrate for five hours. (Also add mace, marjoram, basil.)

'Take three onions chopped fine, half a pound of mushrooms ditto, one pound of sausage meat, a few ounces of marrow, chopped fine, burnt-brown bacon fat. Chopped parsley, blade of mace, breadcrumbs steeped in Porto or Madeira, twelve oysters, nutmeg, cream, lemon juice, chopped almonds and ketchup.

'Line your slab of beef with bacon and roll the above force meat into it, securing with string and skewers. Now stew very gently for three hours in sherry, finally adding a dash of vinegar. When almost cooked, brown the top in oven, meanwhile decreasing the juice. Add as much sherry as needed, more cream, oysters, whole, and mushrooms.

'Serve in big dish surrounded with sherry and oyster sauce (cream may be added at last moment).'

Leonora Carrington, 1946.

1. See *VVV*, no. 2-3.

Ever since Plato, it has been repeated that Art and Science differ in one respect, which is that Art seeks Beauty, while Science is concerned with Truth. But if one attempts to interpret these definitions concretely, it becomes apparent that the two activities intersect at several points. The plastic arts 'represent' the world, at several levels: an external representation which can be considered an almost scientific operation, and a representation of the structural relationships between physical objects which is, to an even greater extent, close to the task of science; and art is complicated by many additional tendencies.

Matta's 1938 series of 'psychological morphologies' were already phenomenologies showing inner experience in an inorganic material form. At the beginning of his stay in the United States, his pictures began to reveal an increased interest in what may be called the geological aspect of reality. Matta began to describe the phenomena of every province of nature in physical terms. 'What does it Matta,' he remarked with wry humour at the time, 'that Matter is as mad as a hatta?' A pure, almost fluorescent colour streams in light or deep streaks, forming clouds in which the glowing fire of the first crystals and of precious stones bursts out (*The Earth is a Man*, 1942; *Elminonde*, 1943...).

Here, the optical phenomenon is also an optical sensation. The sensations of colour in Matta's work resemble phosphenes, those luminous efflorescences that can be perceived when one closes one's eyes. As for Chirico, what counts for Matta is what he sees 'with his eyes closed', but he transcribes it directly, taking it as a phenomenon. The eye, and with it the entire system of the optic sense, detaches the phenomenon from its conditions of realization and from its antecedents, isolates it, retains it after it has vanished; and it can equally well see its own sensations, which it is approaching at that stage by what may be called *Inscape*—following the title of one of Matta's first paintings (1939)— if we take 'inscape' to signify an escape *inwards*, a 'self-invasion'.

Then, in *Le Vertige d'Eros* and other works from 1944 (*To Escape the Absolute*, for example), the luminous matter crossed by concentric vibrations begins to divide into something like partitions, forming solid parvises and half-skeletal, half-organic objects. 'My main preoccupation,' Matta has stated, 'through the period of *Le Vertige d'Eros* was looking into myself. Suddenly I realized that, while trying to do this I was *being with* a horrible

Matta: *Elminonde*. 1943.

crisis in society[1]. My vision of myself was becoming blind for not being made one with people around me, and I sought to create a new morphology of others within my own field of consciousness.'[2] In this manner, extraversion becomes a function of intraversion. In a homage to Marcel Duchamp entitled *The Bachelors Forty Years Afterwards* (1942), large empty segments of the canvas repulse the flow of bright lava and are crossed by forms resembling tools or gear-mechanisms—machines, in fact. Matta is resuming the game for which Duchamp had once inscribed the complex and essential rules on his

Matta: *The Glazer's Achievement.* 1947.

great transparent picture, *The Bride Stripped Bare by Her Bachelors, Even.* The clamorous walls become vitrified, matter transforms itself into every variety of *glass.* And there emerges *Le Vitreur*[3] (1944).

In 1945, the Julien Levy Gallery held an exhibition based on the theme of the Game of Chess, in which Max Ernst, Man Ray, Tanguy, Duchamp and many others took part; for this show Matta made a drawing which became the starting point for his painting *The Heart Players.* Here, the game contained a new piece, the *Matto* (Italian for 'fool', and also the *Mat* or Fool of the Tarot) whose role was to incarnate the irrational. According to the artist, the Matto did not follow fixed rules but tended to make them up as he went along; he also had the power to destroy the game.

Matta's pictures had become Labyrinths of Glass, with walls opening out, like a complex system of baffle-plates, towards an infinity of directions. The inhabitants of these scaffoldings of girders, bars, transparent plates, and 'psychological compartments' with contradictory perspectives, designed and built with consummate art, seem always able to escape, but the same obstacles rear up again a little further on, and no one can ever really find his way out of the construction (typified by *The Pilgrim of Doubt*, 1946).

Man possesses individuality, and is therefore separated from the rest of the world: in fact, he is 'his own prisoner', as has been said of Yves Tanguy, whom Matta acknowledges to be—with Marcel Duchamp—one of the main influences in his work. According to Sir Arthur Eddington, man lives in an absolutely empty desert, and when, after long voyages of exploration, he finally encounters vestiges of a being similar to himself, then he has simply stumbled upon his own tracks. This could provide a good description of Tanguy's painting, but with Matta there is an added phenomenon of magical transformation, as studied and practised by the hunters among primitive peoples: in order to kill an antelope in the chase, the pursuer had to assume its appearance (as is clearly shown in early cave-drawings), but if he was tracking any other prey he had to abstain even from eating the flesh of the antelope, otherwise the game would turn into an antelope and escape. To find his own image once again, the hunter had also to become *the other.*

1. *Être avec* ('To Be With') is the title of a 1946 painting by Matta.

2. Statement quoted in William Rubin's preface to the catalogue of Matta's exhibition at the Museum of Modern Art, New York, September-October, 1957.

3. This picture no longer exists. A detail from it is reproduced in the American edition of *Le Surréalisme et la Peinture.*

The western route out of Manhattan tunnels under the Hudson River, and surfaces in New Jersey as a highway perched on stilts, a viaduct straddling endless marshy vistas pitted with islands of automobile graveyards and scrap-iron dumps. With helicopters growling overhead and roadside signs announcing ominously that speed is checked by radar, the rainbow-hued chariots whizz along the eight-track surface in a two-way stream, as the road leads on past the tubular cathedrals of oil refineries, with plumes of smoky flame licking the spires of slender chimneys, until they disappear finally behind screens of haze on the horizon. Then the highway passes Newark's huge airport on one side and, on the other, docks with white, red and black cargo-ships imprisoned among forests of cranes; afterwards, more factories, all brand-new, laid out in clean patches cut from the surrounding scrub. The urgent messages 'Top Speed 60 mph' at intervals along the route seem like repetitive psychic mechanisms which these metallic insects obey more readily than they do the menacing radar-spy, since it is they, really, who are giving themselves these orders.

And where are the human beings in this 'world of the future'? At the end of his voyage, the traveller can arrive at a hotel where not one employee is visible; automatic glass doors will open up to allow him to pass through to a reception desk where a solitary clerk will assign him a room, while apologizing for his own unavoidable presence. Soon, says the clerk, reassuringly, even he will be replaced by a machine.

Human beings have become invisible in the cages they have constructed to enlarge their labyrinth. One cannot help thinking of Piranesi's *Prisons*, with their viaduct-stairways mounting endlessly towards unapproachable summits. On each landing of this vertiginous spiral there are human beings, growing ever smaller....

Matta's creatures demonstrate in the most modern way possible their human desire for transformation and struggle, especially in such huge

anguished compositions as *L'Espace et le Je* (1944), *Être Avec* (1946), *Les Avœugles* (1947), *Every Man a King* (1947). These vitrified, tentacular beings, these cyclopean and Argus-like creatures which see perfumes and gravitation, these erotic, vengeful insects which touch light and shadow, which hear wave-lengths, hunters of stars and seekers of buried treasure, beings that are at once telescope and microscope, speedometer and astro-computer—they are their own prey. These Invisibles are mankind.

Matta's lucidity and humour show the images of the representatives of the *mechanical kingdom* in great mirrors, and so it is understandable that a lot of people have tried to forget these paintings by claiming that their content is mere science-fiction. There is, without question, a link between Matta's art and science-fiction: but it is the kind of link which gives an idea of the *distance*

Matta: *Composition.* 1945.

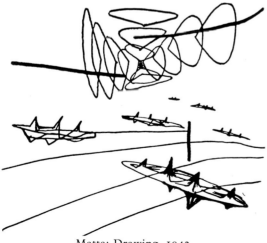

Matta: Drawing. 1943.

Matta: *The Prophetor.*
1954.

between a literature based usually on scientific amateurism, and poetry. His myths do not develop in the reassuring depths of interplanetary space; they conjure up the world of today, with its towns beneath towns, and its ever-changing skies. In the pictures of his American period, Matta gave shape to the inner thought—*the unconscious consciousness,* so to speak—of a civilization which has found its most extreme expression in the United States. He never yields to a facile romanticism of machines, nor does he follow the equally sterile course of condemning science: his work is a struggle to understand what is happening around us—and to make it understood.

Arshile Gorky was born in Tiflis, Russia, of Armenian parents, and came to the United States while he was still very young. Until 1942 he had only painted talented imitations of Picasso and Miró. But the arrival of artists from Europe at the beginning of the second World War opened up new horizons for him. He developed a very close relationship with Matta, who gave him the example of a greater freedom in the treatment of forms and in the use of pigment. Gorky also became a great admirer of André Breton, who could hardly fail to appreciate this devotion. The final text in Breton's 1945 edition of *Le Surréalisme et la Peinture* is devoted to Gorky, whom the author describes as 'a man who treats nature like a cryptogram upon which the painter's previous tangible imprints have just left their *stencil*.' This artist did indeed compose his paintings by transposing a natural scene, but one has the impression that with him the images so obtained divulge a disordered rather than a mysterious nature, expressing survivals rather than geneses, and, even, holocausts rather than creations. The critic Parker Tyler, writing in *View* (V:1, March, 1945), comments that the picture *The Liver is the Coxcomb* 'is apparently the successfully deceptive dismemberment of a rooster, but the canvas is so large that the butchery seems to have taken place in Grand Central Station.'

The signs which Gorky's 'stencil' produces here

are those of a threatening catastrophe. Objects and sensations tumble headlong. His own description of the various items in this painting (which is generally considered to be his masterpiece) allows one to detect a common denominator: 'the song of a cardinal, liver, mirrors that have not caught reflection, the aggressively heraldic branches, the saliva of the hungry man whose face is painted with white chalk...' surely constitute the vision of a *shipwreck*, the chaos prevailing in the tilting saloons of a sinking ship that is being inexorably drawn down to the nothingness of the ocean's bed.

Gorky's unhappy, passionate life ended in a succession of tragedies: a fire destroyed many of his paintings, an automobile accident fractured the vertebrae of his neck, and he became deeply involved in unhappy emotional relationships. He had developed cancer, and, in 1948, in face of these accumulated tribulations he put an end to his life.

In 1946, the *Bulletin of the Museum of Modern Art* (vol. XIII, no. 4-5, New York) published a series of interviews in which James Johnson Sweeney questioned some of the European artists who had lived in the United States during the second World War: Masson, Ozenfant, Seligmann, Léger, Ernst, Duchamp, Tanguy, Lipchitz, Hélion, Chagall, and Mondrian. Most of the artists consulted spoke mainly of themselves, but some of the statements cast light upon the circumstances in which the artistic movement evolved in America, and the essential differences between this activity and the conditions prevailing in other times and places.

'During my first months in New York,' said Max Ernst, 'there were many Paris painters here. At first the surrealist groups seemed to have a real strength; but little by little they began to break up. It was hard to see one another in New York. The café life was lacking.' In the immense American metropolis, the artists quite often lived at considerable distances from each other. As Ernst said: 'Here you would have to phone and make an appointment in advance. And the pleasure of a meeting had worn off before it took place.'

Tanguy agreed with this assessment: 'It is rather hard to be without cafés. It is such a wonderful thing in Europe—and particularly in Paris—to be able to stroll about leisurely and meet one's friends informally.' And Seligmann, too, declared that 'the unconquerable American space has scattered the group of Europeans who were accustomed to meet regularly in Parisian cafés. Many were forced or preferred to live in the country. The exchange of ideas grew rare.'

'As a result,' concluded Max Ernst, 'we had artists in New York, but no art. Art is not produced by one artist, but by several. It is to a great degree a product of their exchange of ideas one with another.'

Marcel Duchamp made the point that life among the artists in New York was quite different during the first World War: there was much more cohesion, and the activities of the avant-garde were limited to a relatively small group—'nothing was done very publicly'.

But things had changed. The bombs had been prepared during the pre-dadaist period; now that the atmosphere was thoroughly impregnated with the grandeur of their explosions, the visiting artists brought with them across the Atlantic Ocean not only their gifts of invention, but also the message of a quarter century of practical achievement. Certainly, the existence or absence of cafés in New York could hardly alter the situation: the work of these artists who had come from Europe was, to some extent, achieving an autonomous development.

Nevertheless, the atmosphere of the Paris café was at least partially provided in New York, from

Arshile Gorky: *The Liver is the Coxcomb*. 1944.

329

1943 onwards, by 'The Club', a meeting place for artists (plus a few select poets and art critics) which opened up originally on Eighth Street in Greenwich Village. There, David Hare, Willem de Kooning and a number of others joined the artist-writer-critic (and admirer of Max Ernst) Robert Motherwell. Arshile Gorky's work was followed with interest by this group, which seems to have initiated the 'abstract expressionist' manner in painting.

The film *Dreams That Money Can Buy* was produced in New York in 1944 by Hans Richter. It comprised six fantastic visions that alternated dream, song and narrative. Max Ernst's contribution was 'Desire',

a sequence inspired by the *collages* of *La Femme 100 Têtes*, in which Ernst himself and Julien Levy played leading roles. Fernand Léger's sequence, entitled 'The Girl with the Prefabricated Heart',

was an idyll between store-window display models. Man Ray's 'Ruth Roses and Revolvers' included a scene in a cinema, where the audience mimicked all the actions of the actors on the screen. Marcel Duchamp presented the swirling vortices of his Optical Discs, and a procession of naked women on a staircase. Calder demonstrated the elegance of his mobiles in a 'Ballet', and the agility of his animated figures in his celebrated 'Circus'. And, lastly, Richter himself provided the link between the various sequences with 'Narcissus', the story of a poet who sells his dreams to all takers.

Hans Richter had originally been a cubist painter and then, during the first World War, a member of the Dada group in Switzerland, where he had met the Swedish painter Viki Eggeling in 1918. Eggeling's 'Rolls'—long bands of paper covered by the successive variations of an abstract design (*Vertical-horizontal*, 1919; *Diagonal Symphony*, 1920) —led Richter to compose similar Rolls himself, and then to make films in which, for the first time, abstract forms became animated: *Rhythm 21* (1921), *Rhythm 23*, and *Rhythm 25*. In *Les Yeux sur le Plat* (1926) he introduced a poetic-humorous note, which he sustained in *Chapeaux Vol au Vent*, made the following year with sub-titles by Robert Desnos. From 1926 to 1930, Richter directed the avant-garde Berlin review 'G'. In Zurich in 1939, he was working on a production of the adventures of the legendary Baron Münchhausen, with the collaboration of Jacques Prévert, J. B. Brunius and Maurice Henry; but this project was interrupted by the war.

During 1956-1957, Richter completed a further 'film-poem' (made in America and in Europe) called *8 × 8*—eight games of chess, some fantastic, some poetic, in which the chief parts were played by the author's friends: Arp, Duchamp, Tanguy, Julien Levy, Huelsenbeck, Calder, Jacqueline Matisse, Ernst, Dorothea Tanning, Kiesler, etc, not to mention M. Jean Cocteau. Richter extracted two short documentaries from this film: *Dadascope*, poems or declarations read by Raoul Haussmann, Huelsenbeck, Arp, Schwitters, and Duchamp; and a second short film featuring Duchamp (together with the American chess champion Larry Evans) called *Passionate Pastime*, relating in images the history of that ancient game which is supposed to have been invented by the rajahs of India long ago so that their disputes might be settled without going to war.

Marcel Duchamp, Max Ernst and Hans Richter, 1953.

A scene from Hans Richter's film, *8×8*, 1957.

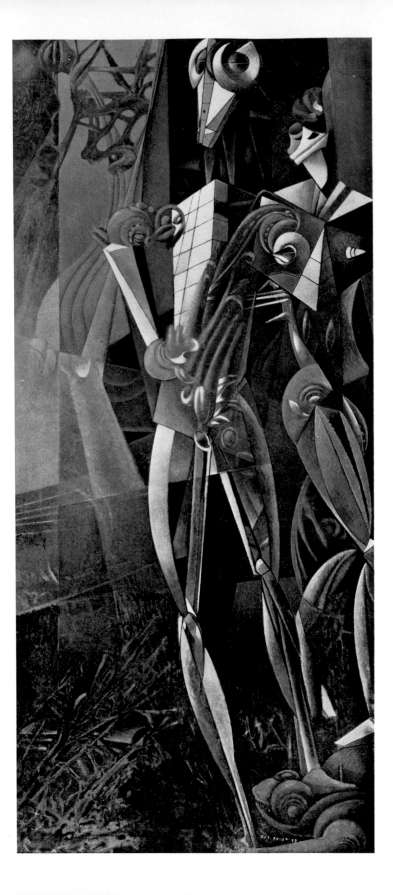

Max Ernst: *Chemical Nuptials*. 1948.

In 1940, Picasso was one of the very few artists who stayed in Paris when the German troops marched in. He worked throughout the war in his studio in the rue des Grands-Augustins, giving free expression to his usual playfulness and inventiveness, and creating some splendid sculpture-objects, including a Minotaur's head fabricated from a bicycle saddle and handle-bars, cast in bronze. He even amused himself by writing a play, *Desire Caught by the Tail*.[1]

Living in the south of France, Picabia, the 'anti-artist' *par excellence*, also continued to be playful in his own very special manner. Since his financial situation was at last beginning to show the strain resulting from a long, extravagantly careless life, he did not hesitate to turn out a series of paintings for a dealer in North Africa whose clientèle consisted mainly of sheiks and wealthy colonists: the resulting pictures of provocatively undressed girls, in the worst possible taste, demonstrated his usual virtuosity with a kind of careless ease, and must have afforded a good deal of amusement to this impenitent dadaist.

Among the other painters who remained in France, Hans Bellmer led a more or less clandestine existence in the south, painting portraits for a living. Oscar Dominguez had returned to Paris, but his inspiration was becoming increasingly remote from all his previous modes of expression: his paintings were now directly inspired by the more superficial aspects of Chirico's early work, and, following that artist's technique, Dominguez depicted objects with sharply defined outlines standing out against green skies. His combinations of image and idea were sometimes both striking and new (for instance his composition *The Pirate*), and he exhibited these pictures in 1943 at the Galerie Louis Carré; but the influence of Chirico sometimes involved him in mimicry, and even in outright deception.

Victor Brauner had taken refuge in a small village in the Alps, and the technique he evolved at that time resulted directly from war-time shortages: with oil paints unobtainable, he created paintings in wax, spreading a thin base of melted candle-grease on canvas or cardboard, and engraving on this surface a design accentuated afterwards by means of smoke-black, the shapes themselves being coloured by lightly glazed hues. More cabbalistic than kabalist, and revealing (with an irony that was perhaps involuntary) the 'spiritualistic' memories of his childhood, Brauner's *wax paintings* borrow their themes from alchemy, from the tarot, from Egyptian designs, and from the codices of ancient Mexico. They also contain an element of anguish and of personal desires: the profile with fixed stare and a bitter expression which reappears so often in Brauner's waxes is always a self-portrait.

Jean Arp and Sophie Taeuber had gone to Grasse, in the South of France, to live with Jeannine Buffet (the daughter of Picabia and Gabrielle Buffet-Picabia). Increasingly worried by the fate of all the works he had had to leave behind in his house at Meudon (in the occupied zone), Arp decided to go and see for himself if all was well. This decision involved him, as one might suspect, in a superbly laughable adventure at the demarcation line of the German occupation zone: some 'guides' who had

1. An English version, illustrated by the author, was published by Rider, New York, 1950.

Jean Arp: *Mediterranean Relief*. 1941.

a fire in a hearth with a badly-drawing chimney. When her companion came in a few hours later, he found her lying inert on her bed, asphyxiated. Some years before, in June, 1939, Sophie had recorded the following dream while staying in Ascona, in the Swiss canton of Ticino: 'Last night I dreamt that I was on a beach. At one moment it was the sun-drenched sands of Ascona, the next moment it was the rocky ravines of the Val Bavona. I heard the voices of my friends grow fainter and fainter. I was alone on the beach, and, while the night fell, my index finger wrote the word "happy" on the sand, as though it had been impelled by an outside force. While tracing the letters, I saw the word sink into the stone. A muffled, whispering noise made me look up. It was a great slab of rock which had broken loose and was poised ominously above me. And the thought flashed into my mind that if it crushed me that very moment, all that would be left of me would be the single word "happy".'

made it their business to help illegal travellers across this dangerous border, mistook him for a local Resistance chief known as 'Jean' and, to his utter bewilderment, bundled him into the boot of a car and smuggled him safely into occupied territory! When he arrived eventually in Meudon, Arp was able to reassure himself that nothing had been touched and then returned south without further incident.

In 1942 he managed to reach Switzerland with his wife. While guests of the painter Max Bill in Zurich, Sophie tried, one winter's evening, to light

A few young people attempted to redevelop a surrealist activity in Paris during the last war. Noël Arnaud, J. F. Chabrun, and some other poets and writers, together with the painters Jacques Hérold, Aline Gagnaire, Manuel, etc, founded the 'Éditions de la Main à Plume'.[1] The only members of this group who had participated in surrealist activities before the war were Adolphe Acker (who wrote articles under the pen-names Chancel and Champ during the German occupation), Hérold and Robert Rius (who later joined the ranks of the Resistance, was captured by the Germans and shot). Several little reviews were produced: in 1941, *La Main à Plume* (a collection of texts whose authors remained anonymous), followed by *Géographie Nocturne, Transfusion du Verbe*; in 1942, *La Conquête du Monde par l'Image*; in 1943, *Le Surréalisme Encore et Toujours*. These publications repeated the tone and the themes of pre-war Surrealism, printing dream narratives, collective poems, analogical analyses of poems, and so on. In an article entitled 'The Keys to the Shooting Range', Léo Malet described his procedures of *décollage* (unsticking) of posters (mentioned already in 1938 in the *Dictionnaire Abrégé du Surréalisme*), and *reflection-objects*.[2] Under the title 'The

1. Cf. Rimbaud: '*La main à plume vaut la main à charrue*' ('the plough is not mightier than the pen').

2. See above, p. 252.

Petrification of Time', Dominguez explained his theory of *lithochronic objects*.[1] Raoul Ubac, in a 'Note on Movement and the Eye', spoke of Marey's chronograms. There were reproductions of work by Delvaux, Magritte, Picasso (his bicycle-minotaur figure appeared on the cover of *La Conquête du Monde par l'Image*), Dominguez (his 1939 composition *L'Estocade Lithochronique*), Maurice Henry, Arp, and Ubac (*La Nébuleuse*, one of the first photographs made from a 'heated' negative, in 1939).

In 1943, in *Le Surréalisme Encore et Toujours*, vignettes and illustrations (for instance, a 'collective drawing' executed by Brauner, Breton, Lam and Hérold), recalled some of the 'games' played in 1940 in Marseilles, and the work of artists who had emigrated or were otherwise absent from France (Ernst, Miró, Tanguy, Brauner).

A leaflet headed *Informations Surréalistes*, printed by '*La Main à Plume*', announced in 1944 a special number on the Object, but it was overtaken by events: the landing by the Anglo-American forces in Normandy demonstrated that, for the time being, 'the sword was mightier than the pen'.

In London, the English surrealist group held meetings throughout the war, at first each Wednesday evening at the Barcelona Restaurant in Soho's Beak Street, then later in a succession of Soho pubs. These meetings were attended by a group of painters, Robert Baxter, Emmy Bridgewater, John Banting, Antonio Pedro, Edith Rimmington, and, occasionally, Lucien Freud, and Peter Rose Pulham; the surrealist painter Conroy Maddox was in Birmingham throughout the war (as was the critic Robert Melville) and so was rarely seen. The poets and writers who came regularly included J. B. Brunius, E.L.T. Mesens, Simon Watson Taylor, Serge Ninn, and the Turkish poet Feyyaz Fergar; later the anarchist cartoonist Philip Sansom and the jazz singer George Melly appeared at these rendezvous. 'Exquisite corpses' and multilingual collective poems were enthusiastically composed on these occasions, and politics were a constant topic of discussion. In March, 1944, Mesens and Brunius published a tract, *Idolatry and Confusion*, directed against the kind of French war-time literature (Aragon, Eluard,

Vercors) which *Le Surréalisme Encore et Toujours* had also condemned in Paris. In November, 1944, the pamphlet *Message from Nowhere*, edited and published by Mesens from his London Gallery, paid tribute to Alfred Jarry, and included translations of *La Chanson du Décervelage* ('The Song of Debraining') and an extract from *Les Minutes de Sable Mémorial*.

Mesens had established himself in London in 1938, taking over the direction of the London Gallery, which closed its doors in 1940 and re-

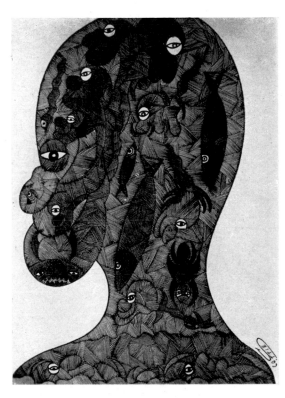

Scottie Wilson: *Handmade Pen Drawing*. 1944.

opened them between 1946 and 1951. He published a combined review-catalogue originally entitled *London Gallery Bulletin*, and then simply *London Bulletin*: its final triple issue (No. 18-20) appeared in June, 1940, with a reproduction of Chirico's 1916 painting *The War* on the front cover. This review had provided a very thorough coverage of Surrealism in terms of painting and sculpture, between 1938 and 1940. Mesens was largely responsible for organizing the 'Surrealism Today' exhibition at the Zwemmer Gallery, in London (June, 1940), a surrealist exhibition at the Oxford University Art Society (Autumn, 1940), and a series of art-shows

1. First discussed by André Breton in his article 'Concerning the Most Recent Tendencies in Surrealist Painting', in *Minotaure* no. 12-13 (1939), reprinted in the American edition of *Le Surréalisme et la Peinture*.

combined with lectures (December, 1940 - January, 1941), arranged by the art department of Dartington Hall School (in the south-western county of Devonshire) to trace the development of Fauvism, Cubism, Dadaism, and Surrealism.

In October, 1945, the exhibition on the theme of 'Surrealist Diversity' at the Arcade Gallery in London brought together work by most of the surrealist artists scattered throughout the world. And this same gallery presented for the first time the images created by 'Scottie' Wilson.

Mesens wrote a preface to the catalogue of this exhibition which included a short account of the artist's life. Wilson was born in Glasgow in 1890, and emigrated to Canada, where he opened up a second-hand furniture shop. His commercial enterprises were far from successful, but these mundane matters did not worry Scottie unduly, and he simply withdrew to his back office to compose his extraordinary drawings. Scottie used

thousands of closely spaced, patiently aligned pen-strokes to elaborate precisely defined, delicately coloured forms in which, according to Mesens, he was able to discover 'the memory of a Glasgow fountain, the vestiges of the North American Indians' totems, and the spirit of flowers and fishes'. Perhaps the failure of his own relationship with modern civilization gave him an instinctive sympathy for the virgin territories of the New World, and the testimony of the primitive peoples who described their universe in their art must have inspired this artist-magician to create what he himself has termed a 'life's dream'. In his empty shop in Toronto, and later on in England, Scottie Wilson really did blend dream and life in the strange compositions he has always filled with the pure essence of primitive conjurations.

In July, 1946, Simon Watson Taylor published *Free Unions - Unions Libres*, a review-anthology containing material assembled during the last years of the war. Various texts, by J. B. Brunius, Benjamin Péret, Watson Taylor, and Conroy Maddox, together with critical notes, quotations, and translations, reaffirmed the surrealist position against wars, moral systems and religions. Jarry was given pride of place, once again, with some scenes from *Ubu Roi*, and Sade was represented by a translation of the political harangue '*Français, encore un effort si vous voulez être républicains*' which forms part of that author's book *La Philosophie dans le Boudoir*. The volume also included a number of poems, and reproductions of *collages*, drawings, and paintings by members of the English surrealist group.

International Surrealist Exhibition, Paris, 1947. The Hall of Superstitions.

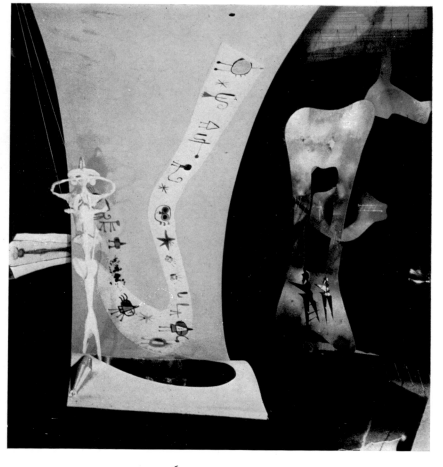

As soon as the war was over, other attempts were made to regroup the forces of Surrealism. Several painters, including Dominguez, Delanglade, Fernandez, Marcel Jean and Maurice Henry, undertook, in December, 1945, to execute a 'collective fresco' which covered the walls of the faculty hall of the Saint Anne psychiatric centre in Paris with its intermingled images.[1] At the same time, in Brussels, a Surrealist Exhibition brought together pictures, objects, drawings, photographs, and writings by Arp, Brauner, Chirico, Dominguez, Ernst, Gagnaire, Hérold, Marcel Jean, Klee, Magritte,

1. Reproduced in 'Art', a special number of the review *L'Architecture d'Aujourd'hui*, Paris, 1946. This fresco replaced one done by Delanglade which was effaced by order of the German authorities during the war.

Matta: *The Angry One*. 1958.

Yves Tanguy: *Multiplication of the Arcs.* 1954.

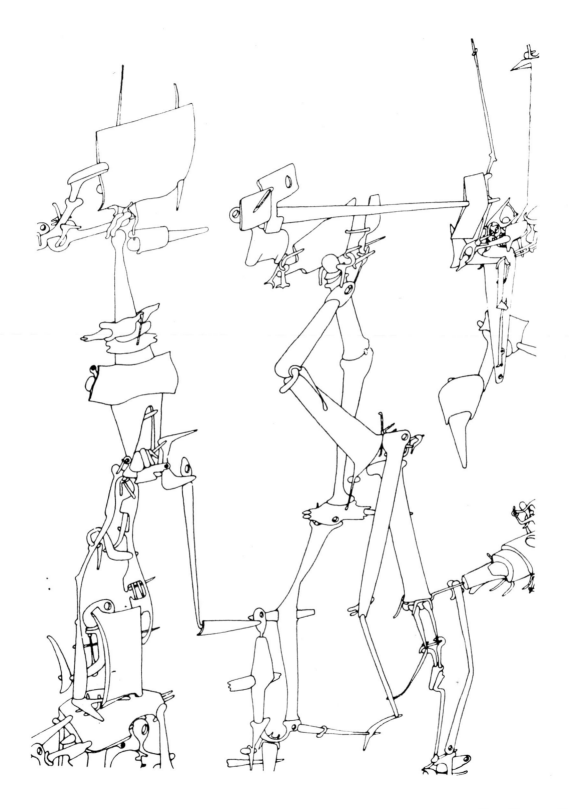

Yves Tanguy: Drawing. 1949.

Yves Tanguy : *Where Are You?* 1954.

Malet, Mariën, Nougé, Savinio, Scutenaire, Ubac, and many others. But the most ambitious effort was to be the International Exhibition that took place in Paris, at the Galerie Maeght, during the summer of 1947.

While returning from America at the end of 1945, André Breton had stopped off briefly in Haiti, at

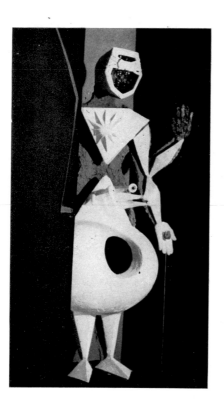

the invitation of Pierre Mabille who was at that time the French cultural attaché to the government of this island republic. Breton was as seduced by the exotic character of Haiti as he had been previously by Tenerife and Mexico. In a letter to Enrico Donati, he enumerated the past and present attractions of the island: 'cactuses, coconut palms, mangroves, rubber trees, banana plants, avocados, sand-box trees, bread-trees, traveller's trees, bagahondas, madrepores, sea-fans, coffer-fishes, moon-fishes, egrets, herons, carpenter-bees, the Assotor-drums, the spilt blood of black pigs, voodoo charms, petaloid hatchets, Ogoun Ferraille and Erzulie Freda-Dahomey, General Toussaint-Louverture and the Emperors Dessalines and Christophe....'[1] Breton also had the opportunity, while there, to

see the pictures that a group of plain island folk—carpenters, servants, peasants—had been painting for some time under the leadership of Philomé Obin and Hector Hippolyte (the latter a Voodoo priest), and with the encouragement and support of the American Dewitt Peters who had created a 'Haiti Art Centre' for their benefit.[2] And finally, he had been able to attend ceremonies of the Voodoo cult, and had been greatly attracted by their mixture of magic and mysticism, of legend and religion, and by their blend of will and acceptance—a will to transform the world of everyday appearances and a desire to surrender reality to 'superior' powers.

When the Galerie Maeght proposed the organization of a surrealist exhibition, Breton thought it would be appropriate to accentuate mythical themes and it was decided to transform the premises by means of appropriate decorations, as had been done in 1938 at the Galerie Beaux Arts. A 'place of initiation' was envisaged, in which the visitor would have to traverse the stages necessary to acquire Knowledge—or, more exactly, would have to follow a kind of 'spiritual progression', commencing with the climbing of twenty-one steps 'shaped like the spines of books inscribed with twenty-one titles corresponding in significance to the twenty-one major arcana of the Tarot', explained the letter of invitation which was sent out to a select list of future participants. After this, one was to pass into a 'hall of Superstitions', and then into a further room in which it was raining perpetually. After these purifications, the visitor explored a 'Labyrinth' composed of twelve recesses with a 'cultic atmosphere' emanating from 'objects of an intercessory character' and from 'propitiatory offerings' deposited at the foot of altars set up 'on the pattern of pagan cults' (in other words, the Voodoo cult) and dedicated 'to a being, a category of beings, or an object capable of being endowed with a mythical life'.[3]

1. Text reproduced in facsimile in the catalogue of the Donati exhibition, Galerie André Weil, Paris, May, 1949.

2. Some paintings by Hector Hippolyte were included in the 1947 International Surrealist Exhibition in Paris. An exhibition of 'Painters of Haiti' took place in Europe in 1950, opening at Amsterdam's Stedelijk Museum, and showing subsequently in Paris, London, Munich, Brussels and Berne.

3. These objects or beings were: 1) the 'Worldly Tiger', after a story by Jean Ferry about an imaginary animal-training act; 2) 'La Chevelure de Falmer', described in Les Chants de Maldoror (last strophe of Song IV); 3) the Gila monster (mentioned above, p. 310); 4) Jeanne Sabrenas, the cantinière in Jarry's novel La Dragonne; 5) Léonie Aubois d'Ashby, from Rimbaud's poem Devotion; 6) the Secretary-Bird, 'dear to Max Ernst' according to the letter of invitation; 7) the Condylura 'or Star-nosed Mole of medie-

Jacques Hérold: Altar for the 'Great Invisibles.'

Wifredo Lam: Altar for *'La Chevelure de Falmer'*.

Matta and Frederick Kiesler at the 1947 Surrealist Exhibition.

In addition a 'kitchen' had been planned, in which, after all his trials, the newly initiated visitor would have found material reward in the form of surrealist dishes: but this project was not carried out. Another unrealized idea was to show the work of 'surrealists despite themselves': precursors such as Bosch, Arcimboldo, Blake, Rousseau, etc, together with 'those who had ceased to gravitate in the movement's orbit'; Chirico, Picasso, Masson, Dali, Paalen, Magritte[2] and Dominguez were among those included in this second category.

Marcel Duchamp was staying in France at the beginning of 1947, and had agreed to make some suggestions. He imagined the hall of Superstitions as a white grotto and proposed that the effect should be produced by stretching an immaculate fabric on some suitable framework; he also drew up plans for the Labyrinth, and for the Rain hall, in which he recommended that a billiard table should be installed—one of the rare notes of deliberate humour in the exhibition. Then Duchamp returned to America, and Frederick Kiesler arrived from New York to supervise the construction work, a task in which he was aided by an extraordinarily ingenious craftsman who could tackle anything, and was known only by the lamentable nickname 'Zigoto'. Despite the penury of material means which was still to be felt in Paris at that time, Zigoto succeeded in getting into shape and coaxing into action the exhibition's constructions and machinery (during the course of these labours, a badly-adjusted circular saw removed three of the poor fellow's fingers).

Kiesler also had the almost impossible task of

val authors'; 8) Duchamp's 'Gravity Manager' (see above, Chapter Four); 9) Brauner's object, the 'Wolf-table'—an elegant little table furnished with a tail and a miniature wolf's head; 10) Raymond Roussel; 11) Breton's 'Great Invisibles'; 12) the window of 'Magna sed Apta' from George du Maurier's novel *Peter Ibbetson* (the American film of this novel, made in 1935, had greatly impressed the Surrealists).—These myths of the future were each assigned a particular sign of the Zodiac. Breton had wanted to include, as well, the *Invisible Object* (see p. 228), but despite repeated requests to Giacometti, the latter refused his co-operation. In fact, a thirteenth altar was added to the twelve others, devoted to objects created by the alchemist-artist Maurice Baskine (who had made engravings for the de luxe copies of the second edition of André Breton's *Arcane 17*).

The altars were erected by: M. Baskine, F. Bouvet, V. Brauner, A. Breton, F. Delanglade, J. Heisler, J. Hérold, W. Lam, Matta, Seigle, J. Serpan, C. Tarnaud, Toyen.

2. Since the end of the war, Magritte had been painting pictures in the 'impressionist' manner. After a few years of these exercises, for which he showed as little aptitude as did Chirico, he abandoned what he now refers to, it seems, as his *'époque maudite'*, and reverted to his technique of pictorial object-lessons.

arranging in a relatively small space, made even smaller by so many symbolic presences, the pictures which were streaming in from Paris, from the whole of Europe and from both Americas: there were surrealist paintings, and abstract, would-be surrealist, non-figurative symbolic, and vaguely esoteric efforts, some of enormous size. They were accommodated somehow or other, in the Labyrinth, in the Rain hall, in a bookshop which had taken the place of the 'kitchen', in the entrance-lobby, on the landings and staircases, and in the gallery owner's private office which was transformed into an additional exhibition room. The catalogue named eighty-seven participating artists, but even this list was incomplete. Twenty-four countries were represented.

At the *vernissage* (July, 1947), the crowd underwent such a barrage of exploding flashbulbs that Jacques Prévert, who was at the function, commented that anyone would think the photographers were photographing each other. At the top of the staircase of sacred books, swept by the rays from the revolving lamp of a small light-house, the hall of Superstitions designed by Kiesler in the shape of an egg (the idea of a white grotto had been abandoned) contained the pictures sent by those surrealists still in America. One of Max Ernst's most beautiful paintings, *Euclid*,[1] appeared—or rather, disappeared—behind a window cut out of the great green canvas stretched around the room. Kiesler's *Totem of Religions* stood next to Duchamp's object-photograph *Le Rayon Vert*. The visitor passed under a *Scaffolding* by Tanguy—a blue-grey panel, a gently-contoured form hanging from the ceiling—and before various symbols and objects, paintings and sculptures: from Miró a *Cascade*, from Matta a *Whist*, from Ernst a *Black Lake*, a *Vampire* from de Diego, an *Anguish-Man* from Hare, and, from Donati, *The Evil Eye*.

I can still recall, in the Labyrinth, the impressive fetish created from the sketches sent by Lam from Cuba for the '*Chevelure de Falmer*'; and the altar, veiled by a green net starred with flies, conceived by Breton for Rimbaud's poem *Devotion*. The Czech artist Jindrich Heisler had built, for the altar of Jarry's *La Dragonne*, a weathercock which was supposed to spin round through the action of white mice racing around a wheel-cage: but this mechanism soon became blocked by the little creatures' droppings. Jacques Hérold had represented the Great

Invisibles as an enormous Père Ubu in plaster in whose *gidouille*[2] the curious could see their features distorted by a concave mirror. The structure dedicated to Raymond Roussel contained a small electric bell, installed there by Matta, and emitting a continuous, quavering note which, he said, represented 'intellectual light'. Brauner's *Wolf-table* was luxuriantly draped with veils of white muslin, like the cradle of a royal baby. The magician Baskine's *Bag of Tricks*, in 'phantasophal' matter, was petrified in its recess. But many of the other altars really seemed to foreshadow the outfits in the 'Do it Yourself Voodoo Kits' which some astute businessmen in the United States were soon to market, for the initiation of youth, as 'the most weird gift sensation of all time'.

The rain poured down steadily on to banks of artificial grass, and the billiard players were condemned to inaction, since the public had —of course— pocketed the balls.

Were fragments of complex symbolic structures such as Duchamp's 'Gravity Manager' or Lautréamont's '*Chevelure de Falmer*', or zoological curiosities such as the Gila monster or the secretary-bird, capable of becoming myths? And what, indeed, linked the hagiographic data presented by Surrealism in 1947? The catalogue-anthology *Le Surréalisme en 1947*, published by the Galerie Maeght with contributions by more than thirty authors, brought varied answers to these questions, and to several others which the visitors may have asked themselves. In the preface, writing about the future of the myths in question, André Breton remained expectant; but Victor Brauner drew the logical consequence from his accession to the divinities of the Labyrinth and proclaimed his *Autocoronation* signed Rotcivus Renuarb, 'Grand Master of permanent Exile, Sole Commander of catapulted Space, First hemispheric Shereef, Grand Militant of psychopathology', etc, while one of his colleagues on this new Olympus, Jean Ferry, in an *Employee's Dialogue*, showed an irony concerning 'candidates for the job of *poète maudit*' which contrasted with the violence of a *Declaration* by the English Surrealist Group. An essay by Georges Bataille entitled *The Absence of Myth* declared that 'myth and the possibility of myth are vanishing: all that remains is

Marcel Jean: *Surrealist Escutcheons*. 1950.

Marcel Duchamp: Or and vert chequé; two crowns over all, a chess queen argent and a chess king sable per fess.

Giorgio de Chirico: Argent, a base vert; a sun azure couped quarterly issuant from the sinister corner.

---

1. Reproduced in Motherwell, *Max Ernst: Beyond Painting* (*op. cit.*)

2. Jarry's invented name for Ubu's spiral-outlined protuberant stomach.

Yves Tanguy: Azure; a sphere or.

Max Ernst: Gules and argent quartered; a female figure decollated unhabited proper upon charges, in 1 a grass-hopper or, in 2 an annulet gules, in 3 a leaf gules, and in 4 a chimera or.

Wifredo Lam: Sable; in a lozenge or, a three-headed pheon carnation, two in pale at the base, one in chief embowed.

an immense void, loved and miserable', and Robert Lebel stated, without illusions, that 'the venal value is the one objective sign for a work of art of its sacred status'.

Other articles took liberty as their theme (Arpad Mezei, Nicolas Calas, J.B. Brunius, Pierre Mabille, Ferdinand Alquié), perhaps because liberty was becoming, just then, one of the myths whose cult was the most neglected of all in this planet. Henri Pastoureau declared himself *For a Major Offensive against Christian Civilization*; Maurice Nadeau dealt with *Sade and Permanent Insurrection*; Julien Gracq recounted *A Nightmare*; Jean Arp evoked his vanished companion, Sophie Taeuber, in *The World of Memory and Dream*; Aimé Césaire was represented by a poem, *Midday-knives*; Mezei and I submitted some reflections on *Lautréamont and the Occult World*; in *Landscapes* the American writer Henry Miller related his journeys in France; Jacques Hérold's interest had been absorbed by *The Obedient Egg, the Disobedient Egg*, etc. *The Nocturnal Sand*, a text signed by Gherasim Luca, Gellu Naum, Paul Paun, Virgil Teodorescou and Trost, marked the renewal of surrealist activity in Rumania. (In Bucharest, Luca had published a *First Non-Oedipean Manifesto*, and Luca and Trost together *Dialectic of Dialectics*; they had already exhibited their 'coloured graphies, cubomanias and objects' in the Rumanian capital in January, 1945.)[1] The catalogue also contained an amusing *Plan for a World Exhibition* by André Frédérique, and some disrespectful suggestions which Benjamin Péret had sent from Mexico, where he was still living, concerning 'votive objects' and 'nourishment' for altars (one can only regret that these ideas were not taken up). And Marcel Duchamp had decorated the covers of the anthology's de luxe edition with a woman's breast in sponge rubber, having hand-coloured all 999 copies himself, while

in New York, with the help of Enrico Donati.

The publication contained a large number of reproductions. In the de luxe edition, additional engravings and lithographs were inserted.[1]

The 1947 exhibition was, in general, greeted with less passion—for or against—than its 1938 predecessor, but it still aroused huge curiosity, and for several months an absolute mob of young people jammed the cafés which André Breton had begun to patronize once again. Breton thought it possible to direct these juvenile whims towards more significant tasks; he attempted to revive the 'Bureau of Surrealist Researches' of 1925, at the Galerie Nina Dausset in the rue du Dragon in Paris, under the new name of *Surrealist Solution*. The experiment finally reduced itself to a few exhibitions, one of which showed early 'exquisite corpses'. In 1948, five numbers of a typed and drawn sheet called *Néon* appeared. In March-April, 1950, the review *La Nef* published a special issue entitled *Surrealist Almanach of the Half-Century*, which was largely retrospective. In 1952, André Breton still had occasion to preface an Exhibition of 'Surrealist Painting in Europe', organized at the Saarbrucken Museum by the painter Edgar Jené,[2] which brought together mostly old work by twenty painters and sculptors: Arp, Bellmer, Brauner, Delvaux, Dominguez, Dali, Donati, Ernst, Hérold, Marcel Jean, Jené, Magritte, Masson, Miró, Man Ray, Paalen, Tanguy, Seligmann, Toyen, and Isabelle Waldberg, and also a few artists 'with surrealist tendencies'. But there was hardly a single exhibitor who was still in contact with the writer of the preface.

'Movements,' Marcel Duchamp has said (in the *Catalogue of the Collection of the Société Anonyme*), 'begin as a group formation and end with the scattering of individuals.' Breton's efforts to prolong the life of a group of which he had been the marvellous 'agent' when surrounded by brilliant individuals, have given extremely disappointing results now that all his erstwhile friends have left him. On the

1. During 1944 and 1945, the Éditions de l'Oubli in Bucharest had published, also in French: Trost's *Vision in the Crystal* and *The Navigable Profile*, and Luca's *Quantitatively Loved* and *The Passive Vampire*, all illustrated by their authors. Political developments in Rumania interrupted these researches in 1948. Luca and Trost were able to reach France—while one of Brauner's brothers (a student of music and folklore) was arrested in 1950 and disappeared without a trace. In Czechoslovakia, too, events began to take a sometimes tragic turn for the writers and painters. Toyen and Heisler had arrived in Paris in 1946; but their friend, the writer Karel Teige, and his wife both committed suicide in 1950 when the police came to arrest him. It is known that another Czech writer, Zavis Kalandra (who had been one of the most gifted defenders of Surrealism before the war, while a member of the Czech Communist Party), was executed in 1949, despite the protests of a great many Western intellectuals.

1. By Miró, Hare, Calder, Arp, Maria, Capacci, Kay Sage, Lam, Brauner, Dorothea Tanning, Jacqueline Lamba, Tanguy, Bellmer, Elisabeth Van Damme, Donati, Marcel Jean, Hérold, Ernst, de Diego, Toyen, Matta.

2. Jené had published, in Austria, in 1950, *Surrealistische Publikationen*, announced as 'the avant-garde's first pronouncements in the German language on intellectual and social questions', with the co-operation of Paris poets and artists. Jené exhibited his own work at the Galerie Nina Dausset in Paris in 1948.

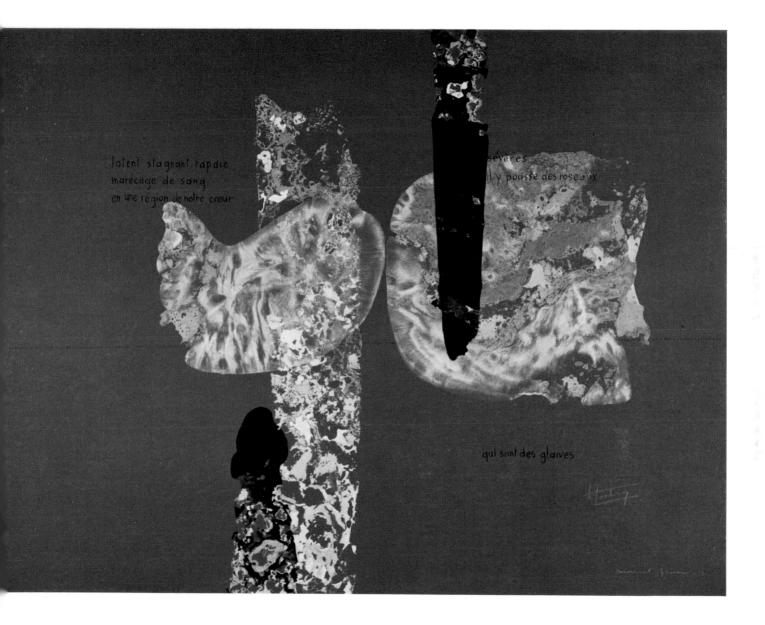

latent stagnant rapace
marécage de sang
en une région de notre cœur

sévères
il y pousse des roseaux

qui sont des glaives

Marcel Jean and Henri Pastoureau: *Poem-Flottage.* 1956.

Victor Brauner: *Composition in Wax.* 1945.

credit side of reviews like *Médium* (twelve numbers between 1952 and 1955) and *Le Surréalisme Même* (several numbers since 1956), which André Breton has directed during these last ten years, can be placed a few contributions by early adherents of the movement[1] or by occasional collaborators; on the debit side can be placed a number of platitudes and repetitions, presented sometimes as discoveries....

Since the end of the second World War, surrealist techniques have been used by many new painters solely for their visual interest, and we have witnessed the very opposite to a renewal of the metaphoric image: a counter-attack by sensual painting. A manner appeared, rather than a style, and an art of fantasy, not imagination. I refer to the phenomenon generally known as *Tachisme* (whatever its numerous offshoots may call themselves), a label covering the most diverse intentions: some painters use concrete elements as a point of departure and end up with a blob *(tache)* or with a stroke, a slash, a smear. Most of them use a blob as a point of departure—and go nowhere. In the United States, the critics make distinctions between various schools: 'action painting', 'abstract expressionism', 'tachism', 'molecular style', etc; and in Europe, other designations have been invented, such as '*signifiants de l'informel*', '*art Autre*', and '*arte nucleare*'.

It seems, indeed, to have been in the United States during the forties that painters first systematically proposed as pictures—a triumph for pure automatism!—'natural products manufactured in series': blobs and stains, the effects obtained by different processes, uninterpreted 'old walls', etc. Surrealist painting's departure points had become arrival points, inspiration went no further than 'the means of forcing inspiration', and the objective methods of Surrealism were reduced to a subjective automatism.[2]

Although its first American practitioners remained more or less unknown in Europe for a long time, this type of painting spread like an epidemic through museums, galleries and collections, and promptly conquered the world of fashion: costumes appeared streaked with ink, as suggested by Apollinaire, or marble-veined, like the café tables of days gone by, and for a few seasons were as *tachiste* as the canvases hanging on the walls of the collectors of fashionable art.

One of the captions of *La Femme 100 Têtes* had already announced, in 1930, 'Rubbish Heap, or one port of call is as good as another'. At the beginning of this history, we have seen how Picasso, Schwitters, and others, found the means of new creative work in 'rubbish heaps'. After the war Picasso continued to use objects from scrap-iron dumps[3] as basic elements in his sculptures, and constructed figures of goats and owls out of bits of motors and machines. When Max Ernst recently made use of a *tachiste* technique, revealing once again, at this stage of his long career, a hitherto unknown facet of his art, he was no more content than he had ever been to exploit simply the beauties of natural accident. His exhibition at the Galerie Creuzevault in Paris, in 1958, showed the possibilities of processes in painting, for those able to go beyond the process and beyond painting.[4]

'At the conjunction (beneficent?) of two monuments, one dedicated to Leonardo da Vinci (or any other divinity), the other to W.C. Fields (or to his frivolous turtle-dove), the kings (if any are left) are playing with their queens. A laugh echoes across the centuries, and the flock of gulls continues to hover around the heart of winter.' Among the works on show were to be seen a 1939 'Forest' (entitled *A Slight Calm*) executed by means of the 'windscreen-wiper' technique, which other painters made use of, later on, to botch up their *tachiste* compositions, and which Ernst has recently taken up anew—for instance, in a *Sign for a School*

Jean Arp: Azure; a pall argent indented, dexter a butterfly sable.

Joan Miró: Or; in a gyron gules sinister, an eye azure.

Man Ray: Or and sable twenty-two costs; over all a gurge or.

thought of cutting up the immense surfaces obtained in this manner, and selling them by the yard). There is no doubting his sincerity, however, and this pioneer of 'action painting' found himself before long in an impasse. During 1954 he made several fruitless attempts to return to a figurative esthetic; then he stopped painting altogether, and his death in August, 1956, in an automobile accident was generally considered to have been suicide.

1. The cover of No. 1 of *Le Surréalisme Même* reproduced Marcel Duchamp's 1951 object *Feuille de Vigne Femelle*.

2. For example, the 'dripping' technique which the American Jackson Pollock began to use in 1946 is nothing more than Max Ernst's process of *oscillation* (see p. 307), done 'by hand'. Pollock traced arabesques of colour on his canvas, substituting for his brush a Duco paint-can with a hole drilled through its bottom; in this way he created 'pictures' which he entitled *Number One, Number Two, Number Three,... Number Twelve,... Number Thirty-two...* (he even

3. There is a striking resemblance, sometimes, between these scrap-heaps and certain *tachiste* paintings.

4. Max Ernst is now back in France, and lives most of the year in a little village in Touraine, together with Dorothea Tanning, whose always curious imagination is coloured today by fresh fires.

Max Ernst: *Sign for a School of Gulls.* 1958.

of Gulls, a canvas whose surface is scarcely brushed by the fluttering wings of a thousand white birds soaring in a newborn light. The title here is not just a random metaphor embellishing arbitrarily the effects of impasto and smudging; it takes the spectator into the heart of the essential meanings of an authentic mythology. Signs 'for a school of imponderables—three young dionysaphrodites—four crystalline temperaments—a school of gulls—the dark gods—the parricidal butterflies—another beautiful morning—the rules of the game—a little nocturnal enchantment and—for Alice's friends.' The pictorial matter is extremely tenuous, but it has effects of depth, and is peopled by real images suggested by almost invisible but indispensable retouching.

'At the conjunction of two signs, one for a school of herrings and the other for a school of crystals, thirty-three little girls leave to chase a white butterfly, the blind dance the night away, the princes sleep badly, and the noble crow has the floor.'[1] For Max Ernst, one port of call is as good as another; it is voyage and invention which remain his passion, always.

1. Quotations from a text by Max Ernst in the catalogue of his exhibition.

348

In September, 1948, the Copley Galleries opened their doors in Hollywood, California, with a show of Magritte's work, followed by that of Cornell, Matta, Tanguy, Max Ernst, and Man Ray. The day of the private view of Ernst's exhibition, it was snowing: a phenomenon so rare in the region of Los Angeles that the invitation-holders spent more time watching the snow fall than studying the paintings! Eventually, the Californian public's more or less glacial welcome to the Copley Galleries obliged them to close their doors again in February, 1949.

Since then, William Copley has shown his own work in Paris, in 1953, 1955 and 1959. The opening of his first exhibition (at the Galerie Nina Dausset) was heralded in the Saint Germain des Prés district by gay balloon-advertisements, and instead of cocktails the gallery distributed candy wrapped inside this little poem by Marcel Duchamp: 'A guest + ahost = a ghost'. Copley's painting is humorous, violent and engaging, and his series of 'automobiles' (*L'Après-midi d'un Chauffeur, Liberation on the Grass*, 1955) have offered new and ingenious combinations of 'pictures within a picture'.

In Catalonia, where Joan Miró lives, a whole world of effective signs is constantly renewed; at the opposite pole of surrealist art, Magritte has found once more the pure expression of his baffling problems; Lam's menacing beings acquire an ever greater precision; Hans Bellmer has shown, in his *Anatomie de l'Image*,[1] some magnificent examples of the 'experimental miracles' which Surrealism is capable of performing; Victor Brauner continues to explore the most diverse territory (with constantly changing techniques and means) and extracts from it his own personal magic; Jacques Hérold follows his search of the crystal with that of plain stones; *collages* and their infinite resources continue to fascinate E.L.T. Mesens in London, as well as Kay Sage in the United States; I myself, not long ago, suggested the process of *flottage* as a new 'means of forcing inspiration';[2] Leonora Carrington, in Mexico, has not ceased to send us stories, pictures, and objects whose intensity of humour

1. Éditions du Terrain Vague, Paris, 1957.

2. These *flottage* pictures of mine, illustrated with poems by Henri Pastoureau, were shown in 1956 at the Galerie du Terrain Vague. The process consists in 'floating' oil-paints, diluted with spirit, on water and transplanting onto canvas or paper the outlines and forms created in this manner.

remains as strong as ever; in the United States, Cornell's glass cages are flourishing as never before; many others, too, are pursuing their researches, and before closing this study I shall have occasion to revert to the more recent activity of some painters whose work has already been discussed at length in these pages.

In Chicago, H. C. Westermann creates evocative objects with great technical perfection; in Europe, the Danish painter Thomas Arnel gives new life to the charms of the multiple image. In 1952, the *Imaginisterne* Exhibition in Gothenburg (Sweden) took place under the aegis of Surrealism (Brauner, Lam, Max Walter Svanberg, C. O. Hultén, Gösta Kriland, Karl Henning Pedersen, Anders Oesterlin). More recent collective exhibitions devoted to Surrealism include those organized by the Spanish painter E. F. Granell in Puerto Rico in 1956 (University of Puerto Rico Exhibition Hall: sixteen Puerto Rican painters as well as Granell, with a catalogue preface by André Breton), and by Julien Levy in Houston, Texas in 1958. The latter exhibition was presented at the Houston Contemporary Arts Museum, entitled 'The Disquieting Muse:

William Copley: *L'Après-midi d'un Chauffeur*. 1955.

349

Surrealism' and with a written introduction by Julien Levy; the contemporary section, under the heading 'Surrealism and Related Works: Twentieth Century', comprised paintings by Bellmer, Brauner, Leonora Carrington, Cornell, Dali, Chirico, Delvaux, Duchamp, Ernst, Luis Fernandez, Gorky, Reny Lohner, Magritte, Man Ray, Masson, Matta, Miró, Walter Murch, Picabia, Kay Sage, Seligmann, Tanguy, Dorothea Tanning. Finally, there have been a great number of exhibitions and retrospectives of *Fantastic Art* during the last few years in Europe, which have really all been exhibitions of pre-surrealist, surrealist, and quasi-surrealist painting, with the 1936 *Fantastic Art, Dada and Surrealism* show at the New York Museum of Modern Art as their prototype. The twenty-seventh Venice Biennale of painting in 1954 was dedicated to the theme of the Fantastic; the prize-winners that year were Max Ernst (painting), Jean Arp (sculpture) and Joan Miró (engraving).

The same spirit illuminated the *Compagnie de l'Art Brut*, founded by the art critic Michel Tapié and the painter Jean Dubuffet, which put on show between 1949 and 1950 (first at the Galerie Drouin, in Paris, and later, on the premises of the Paris publisher Gallimard) a great number of works which, before Surrealism, would have remained in the 'reserved sections' of psychopathological collections. Among all the exhibitors, one may mention these few 'explorers of the pluriverse': Aloyse, and his violently erotic compositions; Heinrich Anton's inscribed images; the naïve painter A. Benquet; Scottie Wilson, who has already been mentioned in this book; Crépin, another painter-medium, whose symmetrical fetishes are painstakingly stippled with iridescent colours, and who died (on November 10, 1948) as he himself had predicted, while putting the finishing touches to the last of a series of forty-five 'marvellous pictures'; Miguel H. (Hernandez), a Spanish anarchist-mystic; the astonishing Adolf Wölffli, who spent the thirty years during which he was incarcerated in a Swiss asylum composing, tirelessly and mechanically, thousands of drawings in a style blending unity with variety, and with a strictness of composition which exalts their symbolic power; Gironella and his cork sculptures; Krizek's rough, expressive stones; and many others.[1] These were all either craftsmen, naïves, obsessed or delirious people, for whom, in any case, art was an absolute necessity, the pure poetic expression of their ego.

Meanwhile, the process of integration of many surrealist discoveries continued apace. There are very few painters who do not owe something to the more or less direct influence of the surrealists' researches (I am not, of course, speaking of those who choose to re-hash Dali's repetitive obsessions or make insipid imitations of Ernst or Magritte). In France, art magazines have appeared which seem mere vulgarizations of *Minotaure*, while other para-surrealist reviews specialize in anecdotic and unusual research; studies and essays keep the light of discussion focussed upon a past which is still close to us, or more distant, but always living; a few monographs on painters have appeared (principally in the United States);[2] a recently published book by André Breton, *L'Art Magique*, resumes one of Surrealism's favourite themes; while shop-windows, posters, typography, interior decoration, theatre decor, fashion and the cinema continue to make frequent use of ideas originally formulated by Surrealism, and mingle them inextricably into the pattern of everyday life.

Now we are in the world of today, and this *History* is drawing to a close. Since I started writing this book, it has become far more historic, in a sense, than I would have wished: death has interrupted the explorations of a few of the voyagers whose adventures have been described earlier on.

Yves Tanguy died suddenly at his home in Woodbury, Connecticut, on January 15, 1955; he was just fifty-five years old. This unexpected catastrophe seems almost to have been presaged by his last works. *Multiplication of the Arcs*, painted in 1954, provides a kind of summit to his art, and gives it, literally, its most complete expression: the immense plain, in which the horizon is clearly divided from the opalescent sky, has become entirely covered by the jostling, pressing throng of objects. There is no longer any room for new arrivals.

In his monograph on Tanguy, published shortly after the artist's death, James Thrall Soby wrote: 'I saw Tanguy several times when the *Multiplication* was in progress. He worked on the picture like

1. The Catalogue of the Exhibition of *Art Brut* at the Galerie Drouin in October, 1949 lists about fifty artists and two hundred works.

2. In France, three books to be noted appeared during 1958-1959: Robert Lebel's *Marcel Duchamp* (since published in English in the United States and England), Patrick Waldberg's *Max Ernst* (J. J. Pauvert, Paris), and *Marchand du Sel, écrits de Marcel Duchamp*, edited by Michel Sanouillet (Le Terrain Vague, Paris).

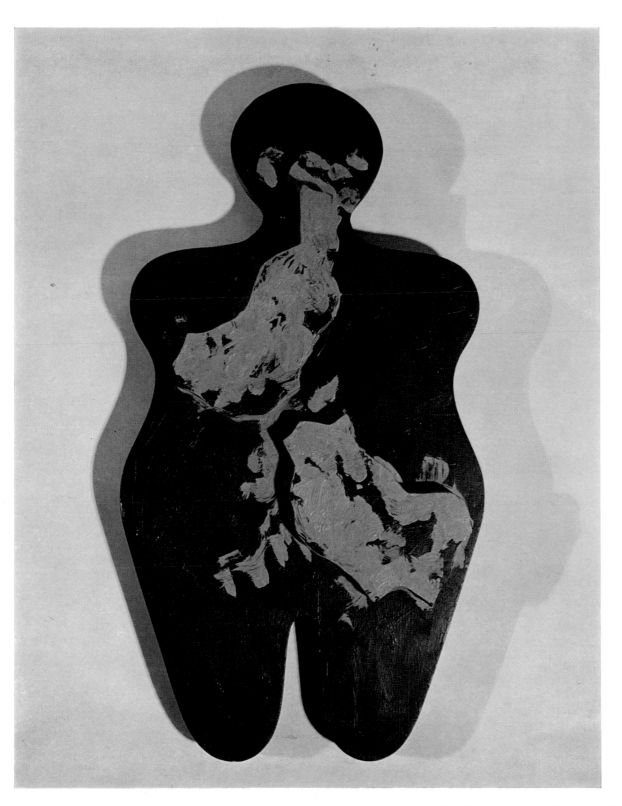

Jean Arp : *Symmetrical Form with the Flakes of Chance.* 1955.

Marcel Duchamp at the age of 85 (photograph taken in 1947).

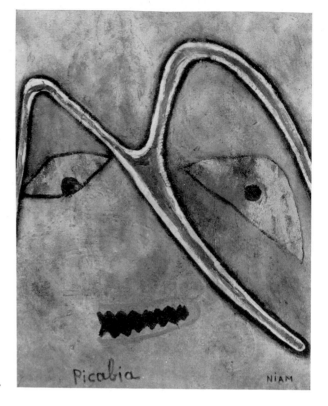

Francis Picabia: *Niam*. 1948.

Man Ray: *La rue Férou*. 1952.

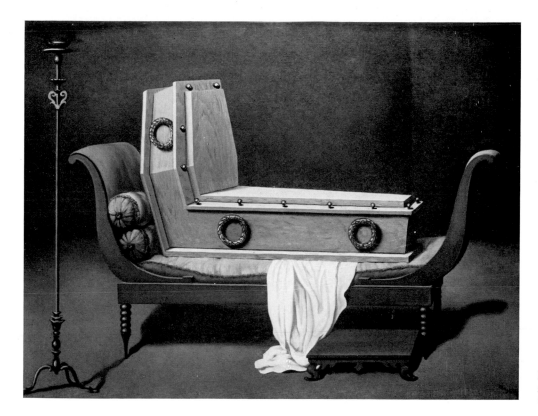

René Magritte: *Perspective of David's Madame Récamier.* 1951.

Crépin: *Marvellous Picture.* 1942.

E.L.T. Mesens: *Theatre or Plain Man.* 1957.

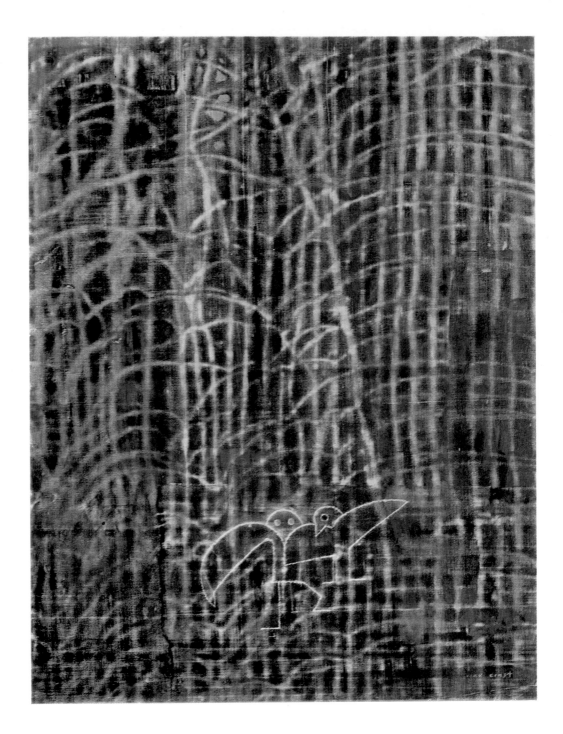

Max Ernst : *The Mysteries of Love*. 1955.

one possessed, hurrying back to his studio after a brief lunch, whereas ordinarily he would have sat for hours, talking about literature and pictures (though never about his own, unless stubbornly pressed) and the state of the world of art, with its chronic feuds and armistices, its developments and counter-developments. Clearly he sensed that the *Multiplication* was to be the summary of lifelong aims and preoccupations.'

But his last painting of all, entitled *Imaginary Numbers*, is a great, tragic vision, dark and seemingly discoloured, with whitish cliffs rearing like livid, anguished objects, over a black sea.

In two books of poems that Kay Sage wrote directly in French, not long ago,[1] those who knew Yves Tanguy can rediscover his own particular language, his nonchalant, sarcastic personality, to which Kay Sage has added the exhilaration of rhythm assonance, and meaning.

> *Au jour le jour, au plat du jour,*
> *un p'tit pâté chouette,*
> *la vie c'est ça, c'est ça tout court,*
> *un cheval, une alouette.*

Such is the 'Menu' proposed by Kay Sage, who says that, for her, 'there is absolutely no conflict between these two forms of expression, painting and writing, nor do they have any connection.' They simply replace each other. 'I have always painted and I have always written,' she adds, 'but never at the same time.' Her little book may be considered as poetry for children or stories for adults, 'light poetry' which is far from being simply light, and, in addition, a linguistic triumph for a writer for whom French is an acquired language. She is equally capable of handling the dangers of a desperate, subtle 'nonsense' in her native tongue[2] — and even in Italian (a few years ago she published some children's poems, illustrated by herself, in Italian, called *Piove in Giardino*). For an explanation of this curious gift, one cannot do better than quote her own words:

> English, French, Italian,
> I can write in all of these,
> but, at best, they are translations:
> I think in Chinese.

1. *Demain Monsieur Silber*, Seghers, Paris, 1957. And *Faut Dire c'qui est*, Debresse, Paris, 1959.

2. *The More I Wonder*, poems (Bookman Associates, New York, 1957).

Some time in 1956, Oscar Dominguez told me of his childhood:

'My father was a wealthy planter in the Canary Islands. Before I was born—my mother had already given him two daughters—he became infatuated with a woman living in a plantation adjoining his own. This beautiful Spanish girl became his mistress, and sometimes visited him in his own home, which my mother accepted in

Wifredo Lam: Drawing. 1958.

silence. One day, when all three were taking coffee together, my mother detected a strange taste in the coffee she had begun to sip; she refrained from drinking it, and managed to collect the cups herself and carry them into the kitchen. There she emptied the contents of her own cup into a small bottle, and had it analyzed: the drink contained poison.

'She showed the results of the analysis to my father. He was so overcome by this revelation—it

355

seems that his mistress must have surreptitiously slipped a drug into my mother's coffee—that he left Tenerife at once and went to live alone in Barcelona, leaving the supervision of his estates to subordinates. His absence lasted several years, until the day that he wrote to his wife, telling her that he wanted to come back and asking her to forgive him. She forgave him, because despite everything she loved my father deeply, and I was born of this reconciliation.

'A year after I was born, my mother became pregnant once more. During her pregnancy, she contracted a kind of puerperal fever for which doctors could do very little, at that time. Seeing that she had not long to live, she asked my father from her death-bed to promise her one thing. "I want our son, the child of our reconciliation," she said, "to be happy always and have no sorrows. Swear to me that this child will never have cause to weep." My father swore. And since the age of one, each time I expressed a wish, or simply made a grimace, I had the whole household at my feet ready to fulfil my every whim and save me shedding a single tear.

'When I grew up, my father sent me to Paris to supervise the importation into France of his fruits and vegetables. In fact, I spent most of my time having parties. I used sometimes to arrive in the Paris market-district at five in the morning, still in evening dress after having just left a night-club. In the buyers' offices I pocketed the profits from my father's bananas. He never said a word.

'My father was a man of many talents. He was an agricultural expert, an engineer, an architect, a painter, a mechanic. It was he who taught me to paint. And he kept the promise that he had made my mother. For me, the party never ended: everything was done to prevent my tears.'

After the war, Dominguez' 'cosmic' period was merely a memory. It seemed that this kind of attrition of will-power which had marked his childhood, was extending itself into his life and art. He held several exhibitions, jumping from one style to another, and occasionally resuming his process of interpreted decalcomania; he still made some fine discoveries, like the series of 'paintings on felt', for example; he produced remarkable tapestry-designs. He also wrote a humorous and poetic little book, *Les Deux qui se Croisent*.[1] But his talents and gifts no longer showed any profound evolution. In addition, many of his new acquaintances treated him as an entertainer even more than as a spoilt child, and he became aware of this depressing role: in his last exhibition, in December, 1957, one of his canvases was entitled *The Clown*, and could have been a self-portrait. Dominguez had confided to a few of his friends that he was counting on this exhibition to pay accumulated debts and get away to Mexico. But the pictures remained unsold. Was this setback decisive, or was there a deeper feeling of a lack of purpose in his career and in his very existence? Oscar Dominguez put an end to his life during the night of December 31, 1957.

A painter's final picture.... The one that Francis Picabia painted shortly before he died on November 30, 1953, after a long and painful illness, represents a precise but undefinable form, swathed in bandages: it brings to mind the way in which new-born babies were once swaddled, or the dead on their last journey, to the tomb.

A great retrospective exhibition of Picabia's work had taken place in Paris, in March, 1949, at the Galerie René Drouin, bringing together 136 pictures, from an 1897 *Landscape* to a 1949 *Declaration of Love*. The catalogue, in newspaper format, was called *491*, contained tributes from Picabia's friends, and examples of paintings from each one of the artist's different periods: the impressionist *Port-de-Bouc* of 1905, the orphist *Procession in Seville* of 1912, the dadaist *Amorous Procession* of 1917, the 1920 painting with objects *The Beautiful Pork-butcher*; *Carnival* (1923) from his period of monsters; a Transparence, *Pink Animal* (1927); the classical *Bed of Water* (1935), the flower-bedecked figures of *Summer* (1938), the abstract *Black Eye* (1948), etc. And *491* also reproduced his celebrated maxims: 'The devil follows me day and night because he is afraid of being alone. — Knowledge is an old error thinking about its youth. — Mystical explanations are the most superficial of all. — It is raining, and I am thinking of the poor people for whom it is not raining.'

The special number of *View* devoted to Marcel Duchamp in 1945 had published two photographs of the author of *Nude Descending a Staircase*: one, by Stieglitz, showing him in 1922, when he was

1. Published in the collection 'L'Age d'Or' (Fontaine, Paris, 1946).

thirty-five, the other taken in 1972, when he will be eighty-five. Which proves that, in 1960, Duchamp is still full of life. He is an American citizen now, and until recently lived in the apartment in New York that had belonged to Max Ernst during the war, in which a strange armchair with an enormous back still evoked the passage of the 'Superior of the Birds'. Duchamp married not long ago, and his present home contains a whole galaxy of chess-boards with their endlessly changing constellations of pieces—for his wife is also a talented chess-player. Here and there a readymade presents itself with an ironic and calm insistence to the attention of the visitor: the *Feuille de Vigne Femelle*, for example, or a 'lock-spoon', or again, that indispensably useless object, a faucet attached to a mantelpiece.

There seems to be something almost miraculous about Duchamp's destiny. Here is a painter who has become a reference-point in any consideration of the modern movement in art, and who has not touched a paint-brush for forty years; a man of great personality who has affixed his signature to the anonymous readymade; a famous man who has made absolutely no effort to acquire his fame, and whose Glass of *The Bride Stripped Bare by Her Bachelors, Even* is today, with Picasso's *Guernica*, one of the most treasured possessions of the Philadelphia Museum of Modern Art, where two rooms are devoted entirely to his other works. — But there are no miracles in chess, just intuition and science, and a real spirit of graciousness, for even the best player may lose. As if he were watching a game in progress, in which a thousand antagonistic or allied forces, active or potential, are poised, Duchamp has never let his attention wander from the intellectual movement, or rather, from the politics of this movement. If the game in progress interests him, and if his intervention is solicited, whether it is a matter of grave problems or of every-day proceedings, he is always in a position to indicate the move to make—usually the winning move.

Since 1949, Man Ray has made his home in Paris once more. He has perfected a new and superior process of developing photographic colour-prints. He continues to paint, and to construct objects. His huge studio is enlarged—inside—by a whole world of apparatus and paintings. Replicas of the 1919 *Lampshade* revolve slowly near a 'loud-speaker picture' which can broadcast music.

Jean Arp, 1956.

In Meudon, Jean Arp's studio has also grown in size, containing the embryos and the successive stages of the beings brought to life by his poet's fingers. But the adult bodies which peopled the garden only stay there a short time nowadays—they are whisked away so quickly by collectors, and the directors of foreign museums. The main quadrangle of the University of Caracas, in Venezuela, contains a *Shepherd of the Clouds*, nearly twelve feet high, which is a giant copy in bronze of a tiny statue, a *Little Imp*, of which there is another medium-sized example in Switzerland.

The repertory of magic spells includes the words, used by Simon Magus, 'which could be read from right to left or from left to right', and also a figure like a circle in which the beginning is identical with the end. The prodigies they raise are proof against disenchantment. In opposition to those philosophical charts in which identity is interior and difference exterior, the chart of magic shows that outwardly similar things are essentially different inwardly. Arp's objects are basically and originally hybrid, but their relationships are governed by

Matta: *The Labiability of the Known.* 1958.

general laws of identification and assimilation. They reach us on the wave-length of a cyclical time in which the future rejoins the past, in which contradiction recreates identity; and their confrontation enhances their subtle and prodigious variety.

Matta left the United States in 1949, and lived in Italy for some years thereafter. His machine-people became more and more integrated into their own atmosphere. The 1953 *Encirclers*, vitrified monsters surrounded by the trajectories of explosions, are themselves 'encircled'. His most recent paintings describe *Polymorphic Conflicts* (the title of Matta's exhibition at the Galerie du Dragon, Paris, in June, 1958). Upon canvases as grey as dreams, in which colour only appears as in dreams, in isolated, violent smudges, and where forms as precise as blueprints emerge from the magnetic mists only to vanish again behind them, the anthropomorphic beings seem to have developed into chains of conflicts. Here, the machine is no longer

a picturesque assemblage from which one can reconstruct known appearances by exterior analogy, by simply reconnecting its unusable broken components. It is a new being, in a constant state of birth, yet exact and efficient, with its frantically taut rods and blades, its quivering multiple transmission-belts and its levers, all materializing our passions' fields of power: witness *Venir S'Apparaître à Soi* (1957).

From the first *Psychological Morphologies* to the 1958 *Knot of Conflicts*, Matta's paintings reveal a struggle of the conscience whose ultimate resolution is still far away. For Matta, the game is never won; his work is an uninterrupted synthesis between the world and himself, an increasingly taut expression of a living, concrete poetry.

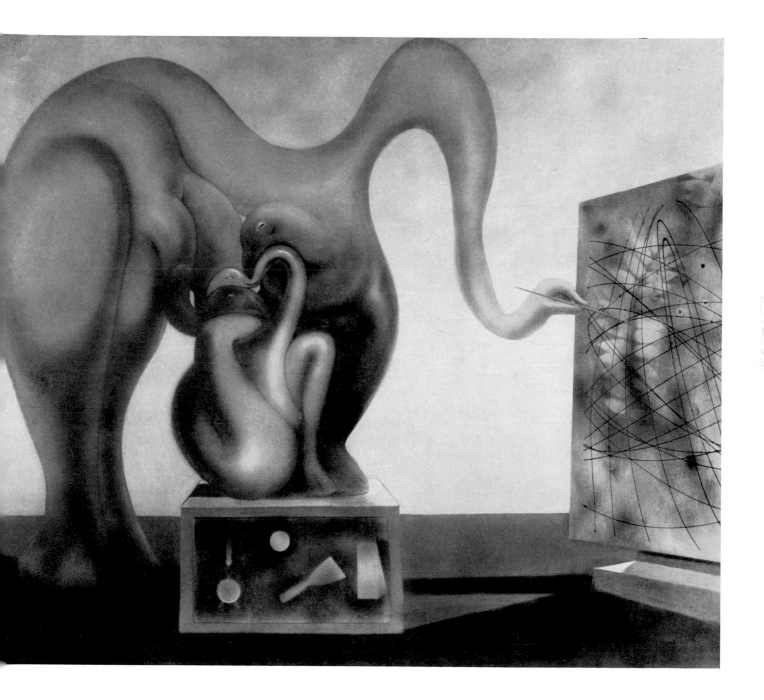

Max Ernst: *Surrealism and Painting.* 1947.

Joan Miró : *The Ladders in Wheels of Fire Cross the Azure*. 1953.

I am tempted to conclude this book in the manner of the long-vanished author of the *Romance of the Round Table*: 'I give thanks that I have had the leisure to finish the rich enterprise that I have undertaken: for I have laboured inquiringly to bring it to an end, and I have completed a lengthy work. Now that it is done, I shall rest a little, and indulge in some diversions.' But the actuality of Surrealism does not allow any such detachment—and, then, does the adventure undertaken by these painters follow that of the Arthurian legend in its hope of discovering some Grail, of drawing near to a higher truth, a supreme spiritual point, or is it not rather the simultaneous and endless creation and exploration of a Labyrinth, that mysterious place in which the most erudite scholars (if one is to believe the ancient stories) have never met anyone but themselves?

The surrealist adventure constitutes, in truth, a cosmology, but a special kind of cosmology: that of a labyrinthine world, with a structure which is difficult to determine, and whose guiding principles are not very easy to define; it resembles the garden in *Through the Looking Glass*, a chessboard ceaselessly developing new squares, its paths returning ceaselessly to their point of departure, as if by the phenomenon of 'curvature of space'.

But this cosmos is a human achievement, which means that the surrealist style contains psychological components. In the maze, the explorer 'meets himself.' His environment imposes its discontinuous nature upon him, transforming him into a hybrid personality, animal-man, plant-man, object-man, plant-animal.... With its infinite capacity for adaptation and change, Minotaur's abode imprisons the architect-explorer, and that is why to encounter the hybrid and dangerous Minotaur in the Labyrinth is also to meet oneself.

Theseus, the very type of the pure, simple, static and continuous man, would wish to set limits to this infinity, to attempt 'a throw of the dice', as Mallarmé has said: in other words, to achieve a stable, definitive form. This decision affects the very nature of time: the Theseus-like man belongs to the past, the labyrinthian individual to the future, to potentiality.

The existence of Surrealism includes these two contradictory factors. What it *accomplishes* is a *future*. In the time of Dada, the first tentative shapes engraved by Arp, or the readymades nominated by Duchamp, were already perfect constructions in their respective fields—and situated in the future. As for Chirico's absolutely precise images, they have had countless descendants. The psychic unconscious is wedded to the primordial level of pure dynamism directed towards the future, while the conscious is the organ of perfection, and dependent upon the past: the transformations born of the meeting of irreconcilable elements typifies the art of Max Ernst and, after him, of other painters as well; together with the art of formless forms, of Tanguy's flawless, veiled beings; while Magritte brings us to the very edge of the abyss of hybrid perfection....

Picasso can never remain entirely in the auroral world of creation—he has constantly to return to the Theseus-like existence of the classics of every age. Picabia created, and then destroyed his creations—by means of innovations impregnated with humour. Miró exercises the magic power of transformation possessed by children and primitive peoples. Matta is the architect of the modern labyrinth, which is entirely dynamic and expands through the contradictions he conceals.

The greatness of surrealist painting lies in its passion for discovery, in its appeal to the Marvellous, in its exact, legible, mysterious content. The Labyrinth builds itself from the inside, but it can become as limitless as our need for liberty.

Paris, 1948-1959.

Max Ernst: Drawing. 1950.

LIST OF ILLUSTRATIONS AND INDEX

CONTENTS

LIST OF ILLUSTRATIONS

36 Marcel Duchamp: *Assisted Readymade with Hidden Noise*. 1916. 5 × 5 × 5". Philadelphia Museum of Art (Arensberg Collection).

37 Marcel Duchamp: *Fountain*. 1917. Readymade: urinal turned upside down. 24" high. Original lost, replica (1950), coll. Sidney Janis, New York. Photo Stieglitz, reproduced in *The Blind Man*, no. 2, New York, May, 1917.

42 Giorgio de Chirico: *Self Portrait*. 1913. Oil on canvas. 32 × 21 1/4". Coll. Richard S. Zeisler, New York.

44 Giorgio de Chirico: *The Anxious Voyage*. 1913. Oil on canvas. 29 1/2 × 42". Museum of Modern Art, New York.

44 Giorgio de Chirico: *The Fête Day*. 1914. Oil on canvas. 31 3/4 × 25 1/2". Coll. Mr and Mrs Morton G. Neumann, Chicago.

45 Giorgio de Chirico: *Portrait of Guillaume Apollinaire*. 1918. Charcoal on paper. 23 1/2 × 21 1/4". Coll. Mr and Mrs William Copley, Paris. Photo Michel Waldberg.

45 Giorgio de Chirico: *The Uncertainty of the Poet*. 1913. Oil on canvas. 41 1/2 × 37". Coll. Roland Penrose, London.

48 Giorgio de Chirico: *The Disquieting Muses*. 1917. Oil on canvas. 38 1/4 × 26". The Gianni Mattioli Foundation, Milan.

48 The Castello Estense in Ferrara.

49 Giorgio de Chirico: *The Duo*. 1915. Oil on canvas. 31 × 22 3/4". Coll. James Thrall Soby, New Canaan, Connecticut.

50 Giorgio de Chirico: *The Melancholy of Departure*. 1916. Oil on canvas. 20 1/2 × 14 1/4". Coll. Roland Penrose, London.

52 Giorgio de Chirico: *The Rose Tower*. 1913. Oil on canvas. 29 1/2 × 39 1/2". Coll. Miss Peggy Guggenheim, Venice.

54 Giorgio de Chirico: *Joy*. 1913. Pencil drawing. 6 1/2 × 8 1/2". Coll. Roland Penrose, London.

55 Giorgio de Chirico: *Metaphysical Interior*. 1917. Oil on canvas. Coll. Barnet Hodes, Chicago.

56 *Was ist Dada? (What is Dada?)*. From the review *Der Dada*, no. 2, Berlin, 1919.

57 Francis Picabia: *Francis by Picabia*. Drawing. 1920. Reproduced in *Francis Picabia* by Marie de la Hire, catalogue of the exhibition of this artist's work at the Galerie La Cible, Paris, 1920.

58 Marcel Duchamp: *Tu m'*. 1918. Oil, graphite, enamelled hand, safety pins, bottle-brush, on canvas. 27 1/2 × 122 3/4". Yale University Art Gallery (Société Anonyme Collection).

59 Man Ray: *Dream*. 1912. Oil on canvas 9 1/2 × 8". Coll. Mme Tchernia, Paris.

60 Man Ray in New York, 1918.

60 Man Ray: *Revolving Doors*. 1916-1917. *Collage* of transparent coloured papers. Plate no. 8 (of ten), from a stencil reproduction.

62 Guillaume Apollinaire: *L'Antitradition Futuriste*. 1913. First page of this manifesto.

62 Recto and verso of the handbill announcing the opening of the 'Grand Dada Season' and Max Ernst's first Paris exhibition, 1921. Bibliothèque Sainte-Geneviève (Jacques Doucet Fund), Paris.

62 Marcel Duchamp: *Apolinère Enameled*. 1916-1917. Corrected readymade: zinc plate (advertisement for Sapolin Enamel) amended and signed. 9 1/4 × 13 1/4". Philadelphia Museum of Art (Arensberg Collection).

63 The review *291*: Cover for no. 5-6, by Francis Picabia. New York, July-August, 1915.

63 The review *391*: Cover for no. 1, by Francis Picabia. Barcelona, January, 1917.

63 The review *391*: Cover for no. 8, by Francis Picabia. Zurich, January, 1918.

63 Three of the Dadaists in Weimar, 1922: Hans Richter, Tristan Tzara, Jean (Hans) Arp.

64 Man Ray: *Seguidilla*. 1919. Airbrush on cardboard. 25 1/2 × 19 3/4". Coll. E. L. T. Mesens, London.

64 Man Ray: *Lampshade*. 1919. Object.

65 The Spiegelgasse, Zurich. Photograph reproduced in the volume *Dada* (Verlag der Arche, Zurich, 1957).

66 Sophie Taeuber and Jean Arp, with Sophie Taeuber's marionettes, Zurich, 1918. Photograph from *Dada* (Zurich, 1957).

67 Jean Arp: Wood engraving illustrating a collection of poems by R. Huelsenbeck, *Phantastische Gebete* (Collection Dada, Zurich, 1916).

68 Jean Arp: *According to the Laws of Chance*. Wood engraving after a *papier collé* of 1917.

68 Jean Arp: Wood engraving illustrating Tristan Tzara's book *Cinéma Calendrier du Cœur Abstrait Maisons*. 1920.

69 Jean Arp: *Tears of Enak*. 1917. Oil, wood.

70 Max Ernst: Cover for *Die Schammade*, or *Dadameter*, Cologne, 1920. *Collage*.

70 John Heartfield: Cover for *Der Dada*, no. 3, Berlin, 1920. *Photomontage*.

70 Raoul Haussmann: *Tatlin at Home*. Berlin, 1920. *Photomontage*. Coll. Hannah Höch, Berlin.

70 Francis Picabia: *The Holy Virgin*. From the review *391*, no. 12, Paris, March, 1920.

71 Francis Picabia: *Portrait of Louis Vauxcelles*. 1917. Drawing. Coll. Man Ray, Paris. Photo Michel Waldberg.

71 Page from the review *New York Dada*, New York, 1921.

71 Francis Picabia: *Natures Mortes : Portrait of Cézanne, Portrait of Rembrandt, Portrait of Renoir*. Reproduced in the review *Cannibale*, no. 1, Paris, March, 1920.

71 Man Ray: Cover design for the review *Littérature*, new series, nos. 1, 2 and 3, Paris, 1922.

73 Max Ernst: *The Hat Makes the Man (the Tailor is the Style)*. 1920. *Collage*. 14×18". Museum of Modern Art, New York.

76 Max Ernst: Dada drawing. Coll. Robert Valançay, Paris.

76 Max Ernst: Two drawings, reproduced in *Littérature*, new series, no. 11-12, Paris, October, 1923.

77 Max Ernst: *Trophy, Hypertrophied*. 1919. *Collage*. 16 1/2×11". Coll. Mr and Mrs Morton G. Neumann, Chicago.

78 Max Ernst: *The Enigma of Central Europe*. 1920. *Collage*. 5 1/8×9 7/8". Coll. Mlle Betty Barman, Brussels.

79 Max Ernst: Plate 7 (of eight) of *Fiat Modes, Pereat Ars* ('Let modes exist, down with art'). Cologne, 1919. Lithograph.

84 Man Ray: Rayogram. 1921. 10 1/4×7 3/4". Reproduced in the album *Man Ray, Photographs 1920-1934*, Random House, New York, and *Cahiers d'Art*, Paris, 1933.

85 Max Ernst: *The Elephant of Celebes*. 1921. Oil on canvas. 49 1/4×42". Coll. Roland Penrose, London.

86 Francis Picabia: *M'amenez-y*. 1918. Portrait in castor oil. Private collection, Paris.

87 Max Ernst: *The Preparation of Glue from Bones*. 1921. *Collage*. Reproduced in *Dada Intirol Augrandair Dersängerkrieg* (the title is printed with alternate lines inverted, to read: '*Dada Au Grand Air / Der Sänger Krieg in Tirol*'), dated '16 September 1886-1921'.

88 Max Ernst: *Collage* for *Répétitions*, poems by Paul Eluard (Au Sans Pareil, Paris, 1922).

89 Francis Picabia: Cover for *Littérature*, new series, no. 4, Paris, September, 1922.

89 Francis Picabia: Cover for *Littérature*, new series, no. 10, Paris, May, 1923.

90 Pablo Picasso: *The Married Couple*. Oil on canvas. Photo Man Ray.

91 Francis Picabia: *Entr'acte*. Scene taken from the film: the funeral procession crossing Luna Park fairgrounds, Paris (the hearse is a garbage-cart drawn by a camel).

91 The Villa des Arts in the Montmartre district of Paris, where Picabia lived during the early twenties. The house belonged to Mme de La Hire; it was here, also, during this period, that a surrealist session of 'sleeps' took place.

93 Kurt Schwitters: Two views of the interior of the *Merzbau* in Hanover, before its destruction by aerial bombardments during the second World War. Photo Landesgalerie, Hanover.

94 Man Ray: *Portrait of Rrose Sélavy*. 1923. Coll. Mr and Mrs William Copley, Paris.

95 Marcel Duchamp: A few notes from the 1934 'Green Box' of *The Bride Stripped Bare by her Bachelors, Even*, arranged on the cover of the Box. Photo Bonhottal.

96 Marcel Duchamp: A few notes from the 'Green Box' of *The Bride Stripped Bare by her Bachelors, Even*. Photo Bonhottal.

100 Marcel Duchamp: *The King and Queen Surrounded by Swift Nudes*. 1912. Oil on canvas. 45 1/4×50 1/2". Philadelphia Museum of Art (Arensberg Collection).

102-103. Marcel Duchamp: *Chocolate Grinder, Glider (Containing a Water Mill), Malic Moulds* (with their 'capillary tubes'), *Oculist Witnesses*. Sketches executed by Marcel Jean from reproductions.

108 Marcel Duchamp: *Chocolate Grinder*. Detail from *The Bride Stripped Bare by her Bachelors, Even*. Philadelphia Museum of Art (Arensberg Collection). Photo Marcel Jean.

109 Marcel Duchamp: *The Bride Stripped Bare by her Bachelors, Even*. Upper panel of the Glass. Photo Marcel Jean (the numbers were added on the photographic print).

109 Marcel Duchamp: *The Bride Stripped Bare by her Bachelors, Even*. Lower panel of the Glass. Photo Marcel Jean (the numbers were added on the photographic print).

111 Marcel Duchamp: *The Bride Stripped Bare by her Bachelors, Even*. Rear surface of the Glass (area of the Grinder and the Sieves) showing the inscriptions: LA MARIÉE MISE A NU PAR / SES CÉLIBATAIRES, MÊME / MARCEL DUCHAMP / 1915-1923 / - *inachevé* / - *cassé* 1931 / - *réparé* 1936. Photo Marcel Jean.

112 Marcel Duchamp: *50 cc. of Paris Air*. 1919. Readymade: glass flask, sealed in Paris; on a printed label the words *Serum physiologique*. The model reproduced has been broken and mended. On a replica executed by Duchamp in 1949 a handwritten label bears the words *50 cc. Air de Paris Réplique type 1949 R.S.* Philadelphia Museum of Art (Arensberg Collection).

112 Marcel Duchamp: *Rotary Demi-sphere (Precision Optics)*. 1925. 59" high. Coll. Mme H. P. Roché, Paris. The convex glass covering the spirals is now cracked. Photo Man Ray.

114 Marcel Duchamp playing chess at the home of Man Ray, 1925. Chess-board and pieces designed by Man Ray.

115 Sonia Mossé: Mannequin. International Surrealist Exhibition, Paris, 1938. Photo Raoul Ubac. Sonia Mossé died in a German concentration camp during the second World War.

116 Man Ray: *The Enigma of Isidore Ducasse*. 1920. Object.

120 Max Ernst: *The Origin of the Clock*. 1925. *Frottage*. Photo Galerie Berggruen, Paris. Version of the *frottage* bearing the same title reproduced in the album *Histoire Naturelle*.

122 Dédé Sunbeam: Drawing. Reproduced in the review *La Révolution Surréaliste*, no. 7, Paris, June, 1926.

122 Pablo Picasso: Drawing. Reproduced in the review *La Révolution Surréaliste*, no. 2, Paris, January, 1925.

125 André Breton, c. 1925. Photo Henri Manuel.

127 Max Ernst, c. 1930. Photo Man Ray.

128 Max Ernst: *Shell-Flowers*. 1927. Oil on canvas.

130 Max Ernst: *The Virgin Spanking the Infant Jesus before Three Witnesses: A.B., P.E., and the Artist*. 1928. Oil on canvas. 77 × 45". Private collection, Brussels.

131 Max Ernst: *Monument to the Birds*. 1927. Oil on canvas. 65 × 51". Private collection, Paris. Photo Roche - Éditions du Seuil.

132 Max Ernst: *Two Children are Menaced by a Nightingale*. 1924. Oil on wood with wood construction. 18 × 13". Museum of Modern Art, New York.

133 Max Ernst: *The Night of Love*. 1927. Oil on canvas. Private collection, Paris.

133 Versailles. Photograph reproduced in the review *La Révolution Surréaliste*, no. 7, Paris, June, 1926.

133 *Maison-attentat*. Photograph reproduced in the review *La Révolution Surréaliste*, no. 12, Paris, December, 1929.

137 Giorgio de Chirico: *The Poet and His Muse*. 1921. Oil on canvas. 35 1/4 × 28 1/2". Philadelphia Museum of Art (Arensberg Collection).

139 Man Ray: Scene from the film *L'Étoile de Mer*. 1927.

141 Cover of the catalogue for the opening exhibition of the Galerie Surréaliste, Paris, 1926.

142 The Galerie Surréaliste, rue Jacques-Callot, Paris, 1926.

142 André Masson: Drawing. Reproduced in the review *La Révolution Surréaliste*, no. 3, Paris, April, 1925.

143 André Masson: *The Bird Hunt*. 1926. Oil on canvas. 29 × 20". Private collection, Paris. Photo Roche - Éditions du Seuil.

144 Francis Picabia, 1928.

145 Francis Picabia: *Woman with Monocle*. 1924. Oil on cardboard. 41 × 29 1/2". Coll. Mme Simone Collinet, Paris. Photo Ivan Bettex.

146 Francis Picabia: *The Shadow*. 1928. Oil and cellophane on cardboard. 58 × 54".

147 Paul Klee: *Ballet Group*, or *The Family*. 1923. Water-colour. 7 × 7 1/2". Photo Giraudon.

148 Paul Klee: *W. Group*. 1930. Drawing.

148 Paul Klee: *Dance of Horror*. Pen drawing. 17 × 12 1/2". Photo Galerie Berggruen, Paris.

149 Pierre Roy: *Metric System*. 1930. Oil on canvas. 57 1/2 × 38 1/2". Philadelphia Museum of Art (Arensberg Collection).

150 Emile Savitry: *The Meeting*. 1928. Oil on canvas.

150 Georges Malkine: *Ecstasy*. Drawing. Reproduced in the review *La Révolution Surréaliste*, no. 7, Paris, June, 1926.

152 Joan Miró: *Head of a Woman*. 1938. Oil on canvas. 21 5/8 × 18". Coll. Pierre Matisse Gallery, New York.

154 Joan Miró, c. 1930. Photo Man Ray.

154 Joan Miró: *The Farmer's Wife*. 1922-1923. Oil on canvas. 25 1/2 × 31 3/4". Coll. Mrs Marcel Duchamp, New York.

155 Joan Miró: *Catalan Landscape (The Hunter)*. 1923-1924. Oil on canvas. 39 1/2 × 25 1/2". Museum of Modern Art, New York.

156 Joan Miró: Charcoal drawing with *collages*. 1933. Coll. Mr and Mrs Morton G. Neumann, Chicago.

157 Joan Miró: *Composition*. 1931. Oil on canvas.

157 Joan Miró: *Composition*. 1935. Oil on canvas. Private collection. Paris.

158 Joan Miró: Object. 1936. Wood, stuffed parrot, etc. 33 1/4" high. Coll. Pierre Matisse Gallery, New York.

158 Joan Miró: *Rope and Personnages*. 1935. Oil on cardboard with coil of rope. 30 × 42". Coll. Mr and Mrs Morton G. Neumann, Chicago.

158 Joan Miró: *Spanish Dancer*. 1928. Collage. 21 × 39". Coll. Mr and Mrs Morton G. Neumann, Chicago.

159 Joan Miró: *Nocturne*, 1938. Oil on canvas. 29 × 22". Private collection, New York.

161 Jacques Prévert and Yves Tanguy at the Lunéville barracks, France, 1921. All the photographs on pages 161 and 163 were communicated by Marcel Duhamel.

161 Marcel Duhamel, 1926.

161 Jacques Prévert in front of the house in the rue du Château, Paris, 1925.

161 Yves Tanguy, 1925.

162 Yves Tanguy: *La rue de la Santé*. 1925. Oil on canvas. 19 1/4 × 24". Coll. Marcel Duhamel, Paris. Photo Alex Darrow.

163 In the 'Prieuré' home of Yves Tanguy's mother in Locronan. In striped jerseys, from left to right: Marcel Duhamel, Pierre Prévert, Yves Tanguy. 1927.

163 Marriage of Yves Tanguy, at the *mairie* of the 14th arrondissement in Paris. From left to right: Yves Tanguy, Jeannette Tanguy, Marcel Duhamel, Jacques Prévert. 1927.

163 Yves Tanguy, 1927.

163 Inside the house in the rue du Château, 1925.

165 Yves Tanguy: *Water-table*. 1929. Oil on canvas. 34 × 41". Coll. J. B. Urvater, Brussels. Photo Alex Darrow.

168 Yves Tanguy at the Ile de Sein, about 1930, aboard the ship *Zenith* which was running a service at that time between the port of Audierne and the island.

170 Yves Tanguy: *Ennui and Tranquillity*. 1938. Oil on canvas. 56×44". Coll. Mrs Leon Falk, Pittsburgh. Photo Raoul Ubac.

171 Yves Tanguy: *The Glance of Amber*. 1929. Oil on canvas. 39×31 1/2". Coll. Mrs Sybil Mesens, London.

172 Yves Tanguy: *Your Tapers Taper (Tes Bougies Bougent)*. 1929. Oil on canvas. 36×29". Coll. Mr and Mrs Morton G. Neumann, Chicago.

173 Yves Tanguy: Gouache. 1936. 3 1/4×9 3/8". Private collection, Paris.

173 Yves Tanguy: Drawing for *Cri de la Méduse*, poems by Henri Pastoureau (Jeanne Bucher, Paris, 1937).

174 'Exquisite Corpses.' Top left and top right: reproduced in the review *La Révolution Surréaliste*, no. 9-10, Paris, October, 1927. Bottom left: c. 1930. Coll. Mr and Mrs Morton G. Neumann, Chicago. Bottom right: 1939. Coll. E. L. T. Mesens, London.

175 Jean Arp: *Head and Bow-ties*. 1929. Painted wood relief. Coll. Dotremont, Brussels.

176 René Magritte: *Perpetual Motion*. 1934. Oil on canvas. 21 1/4×28 1/2". Coll. E. L. T. Mesens, London.

177 René Magritte: *The Migrant Angel*. 1926. Oil on canvas. Coll. Mr and Mrs William Copley, Paris. Photo Michel Waldberg.

178 Magritte, Georgette Magritte and Mesens, at René Magritte's Home, Brussels, 1922.

179 René Magritte: *The Human Condition*. 1934. Oil on canvas. 39 1/4×31 1/2". Coll. Claude Spaak, Paris. Photo Roche - Éditions du Seuil. Several replicas of this 1934 composition exist.

181 Texts and drawing by René Magritte.

184 René Magritte: *The Annunciation*. 1929. Oil on canvas. 45×56 3/4". Coll. E. L. T. Mesens, London.

185 René Magritte: *The Storm*. 1933. Oil on canvas. 20×25". Coll. Kay Sage Tanguy, Woodbury, Connecticut. Photo Alex Darrow.

186 René Magritte: *Threatening Weather*. 1928. Oil on canvas. 21 1/2×28 3/4". Coll. Roland Penrose, London.

188 Pablo Picasso: Drawing. 1928. Reproduced in the review *Cahiers d'Art*, no. 8-9, Paris, 1929.

190 Escutcheon displayed on the covers of the review *Le Surréalisme au Service de la Révolution*.

190 Man Ray: Photographic self-portrait. Reproduced in the album *Man Ray, Photographs 1920-1934*.

192 Man Ray: *Primacy of Matter over Mind*. 1931. Solarized photograph.

193 Jean Arp: *Papier déchiré*. 1937. 11 1/4×12 3/4". Philadelphia Museum of Art (Gallatin collection).

193 Shelves in Jean Arp's studio at Meudon, France. 1959. Photo Marcel Jean.

194 Jean Arp: *Head of an Imp*. 1930. Plaster. 19 3/4" high.

195 Jean Arp: *First papier déchiré*. 1932. 17 1/4×14 3/4". Photo Hervochon.

196 Maurice Henry: Drawing, reproduced in *Maurice Henry's Kopfkissenbuch* (Diogenes Verlag, Zurich, 1957).

196 Maurice Henry: *When One is Sleepy*. 1933. Drawing.

197 Max Ernst: 'There remains then he who speculates upon the vanity of the dead, the spectre of repopulation.' Beginning of Chapter Eight of *La Femme 100 Têtes* (Éditions du Carrefour, Paris, 1929).

198 Marcel Jean: Engraving (on cut-out copper) for the album *Mourir pour la Patrie*, by André and Marcel Jean (Éditions des Cahiers d'Art, Paris, 1935). 13 1/4×10".

199 Max Ernst: *Two Young Girls on a Trip*. 1928. Collage. 4×6 1/4". Coll. Mme Simone Collinet, Paris.

200 Salvador Dali: *Illumined Pleasures*. 1929. Oil on panel. 9 3/8×13 5/8". Coll. Sidney Janis, New York.

202 Salvador Dali: *Accomodations of Desire*. 1929. Oil on panel. 8 5/8×13 3/4". Coll. Wright Ludington, U.S.A.

203 Salvador Dali: *Landscape*. 1931. Oil on canvas. Coll. Mr and Mrs William Copley, Paris.

205 Salvador Dali: *Birth of Liquid Desires*. 1932. Oil. 43 1/2×37". Coll. Miss Peggy Guggenheim, Venice.

206 Luis Buñuel and Salvador Dali: Scene from the film *Un Chien Andalou*. 1929.

206 The Café Cyrano, in the Place Blanche, Montmartre, Paris, where the surrealists met around 1930. View taken in 1959.

209 Salvador Dali: *Millet's Angelus*. Drawing for the catalogue of his exhibition at the Galerie Jacques Bonjean, Paris, June-July, 1934.

210 *Art nouveau* bust. Reproduced as an illustration to the article by Salvador Dali on *art nouveau* in the review *Minotaure*, no. 3-4, Paris, 1933. Photo Brassaï.

211 Antonio Gaudi: *La Sagrada Familia* (the Church of the Holy Family) in Barcelona. Photo Brassaï.

213 Antonio Gaudi: A chimney of an apartment-house, Paseo de Gracia, Barcelona. Photo Brassaï.

215 The *Facteur* Cheval: his Dream Palace at Hauterives (Drôme), France. Photo Denise Bellon.

215 The *Facteur* Cheval: Detail of his tomb at Hauterives. Photo Denise Bellon.

216 Luis Buñuel and Salvador Dali: Scene from the film *L'Age d'Or*. 1930. Skeletons of archbishops lying on rocks by the sea. Coll. French Cinémathèque.

217 Salvador Dali: Paranoiac Face. This is simply the photograph of an African scene which, when placed on end, represents a human face. Reproduced in the review *Le Surréalisme au*

Service de la Révolution, no. 3, Paris, 1931, with a commentary by Dali. He also painted a picture based on this photograph (*Paranoiac Face*, 1935).

217 Salvador Dali: *Hysterical and Aerodynamic Feminine Nude*. 1934. Plaster. 30" long.

218 Salvador Dali: Drawing. Taken from the *Dictionnaire Abrégé du Surréalisme* (Galerie Beaux-Arts, Paris, 1938), in which it illustrates the word *Crutch*, accompanied by the following definition by Dali: 'Wooden support deriving from Cartesian philosophy. Generally used to serve as a prop for the tenderness of soft structures.'

220 The studios in the rue Fontaine, overlooking the boulevard de Clichy. Until 1948, André Breton's studio was on the top floor, at the right in the photograph. View taken in 1959.

221 Salvador Dali: *Meditation on the Harp*. 1933. Oil on canvas.

225 Clovis Trouille: *My Burial Vault*. 1947 Oil on canvas. 29 × 24". Owned by the artist.

226 Alberto Giacometti: *The Hour of Traces*. 1930. Plaster. Photographed in the artist's studio by Brassaï.

228 Alberto Giacometti: *The Palace at 4 A. M.* 1932-1933. Construction in wood, glass, wire, string. 28 1/4 × 15 3/4", 25" high. Museum of Modern Art, New York.

229 Alberto Giacometti: Drawing. Taken from an invitation card to an exhibition of paintings, sculptures, and drawings by the artist at the Galerie Maeght, Paris, June, 1951.

229 Alberto Giacometti: *The Invisible Object*. Bronze, after the plaster of 1934. Photographed in the artist's studio by Brassaï.

230 Yves Tanguy: Drawings and texts reproduced from the review *Le Surréalisme au Service de la Révolution*, no. 3, Paris, December, 1931.

231 Joan Miró: Drawing from 'The Legend of the Minotaur,' a series reproduced in the review *Minotaure*, no. 3-4, Paris, December, 1933.

232 Postcard. From the collection owned by Paul Eluard. Reproduced in the review *Minotaure*, no. 3-4, Paris, December, 1933.

233 Salvador Dali: Cover for the review *Minotaure*, no. 8, Paris, June, 1936.

235 J. de Momper: *Landscape-Head*. Eighteenth century. 20 1/2 × 15 1/2". Coll. Robert Lebel, Paris.

236 Pablo Picasso: *Object*. 1933. Photo Brassaï.

237 Victor Brauner, c. 1935.

237 The rue du Moulin-Vert, Paris. On the left, is the house in which Tanguy, Giacometti, and Brauner lived in 1933. View taken in 1959.

237 The Café de la Place Blanche. View taken in 1959.

238 Victor Brauner: *Kabiline in Movement*. 1937. Oil on canvas. Photo Denise Bellon.

238 Victor Brauner: *Composition*. 1937. Photo Raoul Ubac.

240 Hans Bellmer: *The Doll*. 1934.

241 René Magritte: Cover for the review *Minotaure*, no. 10, Paris, December, 1937.

242 Wolfgang Paalen: *Fumage*. 1938. 7 1/8 × 10 5/8". Reproduced on the cover of the catalogue of the artist's exhibition at the Galerie Renou et Colle, Paris, 1938. Coll. Mme Geo Dupin, Paris.

242 Kurt Seligmann: *End of the Automobile*. 1938. Drawing.

243 Balthus: *Two Young Girls*. 1949. Oil on canvas. Coll. Allan Frumkin Gallery, Chicago.

244 Max Ernst: *Garden Airplane Trap*. 1936. Oil on canvas. 32 × 25 3/8". Coll. Miss Peggy Guggenheim, Venice.

245 Oscar Dominguez: *Exact Sensibility*. 1935. Object-Painting. About 64" high. Only the painting still exists. Private collection, Paris.

246 Oscar Dominguez: *Arrivée de la Belle Epoque*. 1936. Object. 20" high. Private collection, Paris.

247 In the author's studio, 1936. Marcel Jean with Oscar Dominguez, who had just completed his object *Opening*.

248 Photograph by Man Ray, gown by Lucien Lelong, wheelbarrow by Oscar Dominguez. 1937. Another version of this photograph was published in the review *Minotaure*, no. 10, Paris, 1937.

249 Serge Brignoni: Interpreted *objets trouvés*. 1936. Two bricks worn away and rounded by the sea.

249 Bismuth crystals. Photo Man Ray.

249 Natural object. Photo Raoul Ubac.

249 *Bird-man* from Easter Island. Wood. 6" high. Coll. Charles Ratton, Paris.

250 Marcel Jean: *The Spectre of the Gardenia*. 1936. Plaster head covered with velvet, eyes of zip-fasteners. 10" high. Reproduced here on stamps.

250 Perturbed object. A wine-glass found after the eruption of Mont Pelé in Martinique.

250 Mathematical object: 'Enneper's surface of negative constant curve, the differential coefficient of the pseudo-sphere.' Photo Man Ray. Another photograph of this object is reproduced in the review *Cahiers d'Art*, no. 1-2, Paris, 1936.

251 Man Ray: *Object for Destruction*. Drawing of the object constructed in 1932.

252 Man Ray: *Cadeau*. 1936 replica of the object constructed in 1922.

253 Marcel Duchamp: *Rotoreliefs*. 1935. A few of the 'Optical Discs.' Photo Michel Waldberg.

254 Méret Oppenheim: *Fur-covered Cup, Saucer and Spoon*. 1936. Photo Man Ray.

255 Max Ernst: *Une Semaine de Bonté*. 1934. *Collage* from Part Two: Monday - element, Water; example, water.

256 Max Ernst: *Une Semaine de Bonté*. 1934. *Collage* from Part One: Sunday - element, Mud; example, the Lion of Belfort.

258 International Surrealist Exhibition, Galerie Beaux-Arts, Paris, 1938. View of the central hall in process of being arranged. In the foreground, Oscar Dominguez' object *Never*. In the background, the brazier. The ceiling is covered with sacks of coal. A few of the pictures can be seen. Photo Denise Bellon.

260 Salvador Dali: *Turbulent Cover*. 1935. Gouache 15 × 11 1/2". Preliminary design for the cover of the catalogue of his exhibition in New York. Coll. Mr and Mrs William Copley, Paris. Photo Michel Waldberg.

261 Salvador Dali: *Shirley Temple*. 1939. Pastel, gouache, *collage*. 29 5/8 × 43 1/2". Coll. Foret, Paris. Photo Almasy.

262 Wilhelm Freddie: *War Memorial*. 1936. Oil on canvas. This picture was seized by the British customs authorities in 1936, and in 1937 was confiscated by the Danish police, who placed it in the Copenhagen Criminological Museum. Coll. Criminological Museum, Copenhagen.

263 Jindrich Styrsky: Drawing. 1934.

264 Cover of the catalogue for the Surrealist Exhibition in Tenerife. 1935.

265 Oscar Dominguez: Decalcomania without object. Reproduced in the review *Minotaure*, no. 8, Paris, June, 1936.

267 Oscar Dominguez: *Lancelot 28° 33'*. 1939. Oil on canvas. 29 × 39 1/2".

269 Oscar Dominguez: *Nostalgia of Space*. 1939. Oil on canvas. 27 5/8 × 35 1/2". Museum of Modern Art, New York.

270 International Surrealist Exhibition, London, 1936. The flower-headed woman in Trafalgar Square. Photo Keystone.

271 Raoul Ubac: *Fossil of the Paris Stock Exchange*. 1937. Photorelief.

271 Humphrey Jennings: *A Woman*. 1934. Oil on canvas.

272 Roland Penrose: *Captain Cook's Last Voyage*. 1936. Object.

276 Cover of the Japanese Surrealist Album. Tokyo, 1937. The background is composed of a picture by Max Ernst.

278 Paul Delvaux: *The Sleeping Town*. 1938. Oil on canvas. 53 1/4 × 57 1/8". Coll. Robert Giron, Brussels.

279 Gown created by Schiaparelli, fabric with a print by Salvador Dali. 1936. Photograph from *Vogue* Magazine.

280 Pablo Picasso: *Women's Heads*. 1938. Drawings reproduced in *Pablo Picasso*, by Paul Eluard (Éditions des Trois Collines, Geneva & Paris, 1944).

282 André Masson: Head of the mannequin presented by the artist at the International Surrealist Exhibition, Galerie Beaux-Arts, Paris, 1938. Photo Denise Bellon.

283 Salvador Dali at the Galerie Beaux-Arts, holding the articulated mannequin which was to be placed by Max Ernst at the feet of his 'Widow' (see photo, p. 284). On the left, the mannequin created by Maurice Henry; in the background, the mannequin by Man Ray. Photo Denise Bellon.

283 Salvador Dali: *Rainy Taxi*. International Surrealist Exhibition, Galerie Beaux-Arts, Paris, 1938. Photo Denise Bellon.

283 Man Ray: Head of the mannequin presented by the artist at the International Surrealist Exhibition, 1938.

284 Léo Malet: Mannequin. International Surrealist Exhibition, 1938. In the background, the mannequin by Dominguez. Photo Man Ray.

284 Max Ernst: 'The Widow,' the mannequin presented by the artist at the International Surrealist Exhibition, 1938. In the background, the mannequin by Sonia Mossé. Photo Denise Bellon.

284 Wolfgang Paalen: Mannequin. International Surrealist Exhibition, 1938. Photo Denise Bellon.

284 Kurt Seligmann: *Ultra-Furniture*. 1938.

285 International Surrealist Exhibition, Galerie Beaux-Arts, Paris, 1938. The Pool. Behind the Pool, one of the four beds. On the right, *The Horoscope*, object by Marcel Jean. In the background, from left to right, pictures by André Masson, Roland Penrose, Wolfgang Paalen. Photo Denise Bellon.

286 *Ubu Enchaîné*, by Alfred Jarry. Photograph of the production at the Comédie des Champs-Elysées theatre, Paris, in November, 1937: Act Five, Scene Six, the Sultan Soliman-the-Magnificent with his Vizir. Production by Sylvain Itkine, decor by Max Ernst.

287 Matta: *Psychological Morphology 'no. 104.'* 1939. Oil on canvas. Coll. Gordon Onslow-Ford, U.S.A.

289 Joan Miró: *Portrait of Mère Ubu*. One of the illustrations to the booklet produced by Sylvain Itkine as a programme for the performances of *Ubu Enchaîné* in 1937.

290 Max Ernst: *The Fascinating Cypress*. 1940. Oil on canvas. 29 × 39 1/2". Private collection, Paris.

290 Max Ernst: *Œdipus*. 1934. Plaster. 26" high. Owned by the artist.

290 Max Ernst: Drawing. Reproduced in the catalogue of the Surrealist Exhibition, Amsterdam, 1938.

291 Skull made from Sugar: Mexican popular object.

292 Victor Brauner: *Composition*. 1933.

292 Victor Brauner: *The Inner Life*. 1939. Oil on canvas. Photo Marc Vaux.

293 André Masson: Drawing. Reproduced in the review *Acéphale*, no. 3-4, Paris, July, 1937.

294 Marcel Jean: *Portrait of Mlle L. B.* 1938. Etching. 4 1/8 × 16 1/2".

295 Marcel Duchamp: Cover for the review *View*, Series Five, no. 1, New York, March, 1945.

296 Yves Tanguy: *The Rapidity of Sleep.* 1945. Oil on canvas. 50 × 40". Art Institute of Chicago (Joseph Winterbotham collection).

298 Matta: *The Sun's Anxiety after the Passage of Two Personages.* 1937. Colour crayon.

299 Kay Sage: *No one Heard Thunder.* 1939. Oil on canvas. 35 1/2 × 27 3/4". Owned by the artist. Photo Alex Darrow.

300 Leonora Carrington: Drawing. 1939. Ink. 9 1/8 × 12 1/2". Coll. Max Ernst, Paris.

301 Wifredo Lam: *For the Moon.* Oil on canvas. Coll. Mr. and Mrs. William Copley, Paris, Photo Marc Vaux.

302 Wifredo Lam: *The Jungle.* 1943. Gouache on paper mounted on canvas. 94 1/2 × 90 1/2". Museum of Modern Art, New York.

303 Wifredo Lam in his Havana studio, 1947. On the easel, his painting, *The Eternal Present*, now in the collection Pierre Matisse Gallery, New York.

304 Morris Hirshfield: *Two Women in Front of a Mirror.* 1943. Oil on canvas. Coll. Miss Peggy Guggenheim, Venice.

306 Yves Tanguy: *Real Numbers.* 1946. Gouache. 13 7/8 × 10 7/8". Coll. Countess Pecci-Blunt, Rome.

307 Dorothea Tanning: *Profanation of the Host.* 1943. Oil on canvas.

307 Max Ernst: Sand drawing. September, 1941. Lake Pontchartrain (Louisiana), U.S.A.

308 Max Ernst: *The Eye of Silence.* 1944. Oil on canvas. 42 1/2 × 55". St Louis City Art Museum.

308 Dorothea Tanning and Max Ernst photographed with Max Ernst's cement sculpture *Capricorn*, in the garden of their house in Sedona, Arizona. 1948.

309 Max Ernst: *An Anxious Friend.* 1944. Bronze. 27 5/8" high. Coll. Julien Levy, Bridgewater, Massachusetts.

310 Kay Sage: *Tomorrow is Never.* 1955. Oil on canvas. 53 3/8 × 37 1/2". Metropolitan Museum of Art, New York.

310 Kay Sage: Drawing. Reproduced in the review *VVV*, no. 2-3, New York, 1943.

311 Kay Sage and Yves Tanguy, Bridgewater, Massachusetts, 1954.

311 Dorothea Tanning: *Eine Kleine Nachtmusik.* 1946. Oil on canvas.

312 Marcel Duchamp's studio, on Fourteenth Street in New York (the top floor of the centre building). Photo Pragan.

313 André Breton: *Object.* (Dedicated: 'For Kay, from her friend, December, 1941'). Coll. Kay Sage Tanguy, Woodbury, Connecticut.

314 Joseph Cornell: Object-Box. c. 1950. 12 × 18".

315 International Surrealist Exhibition, New York, 1942. The large hall, with Marcel Duchamp's twine.

315 Four 'compensation-portraits.' Some of a series reproduced in *First Papers of Surrealism*, the catalogue of the International Surrealist Exhibition, New York, 1942.

317 Matta: Cover for *VVV*, no. 4, New York, 1944.

317 Joseph Cornell: *Forgotten Game.* Object-Box. c. 1950. 18 × 12".

319 Alexander Calder's studio, in Roxbury, Connecticut. 1958. Photo Marcel Jean.

320 Isabelle Waldberg: *The Sextant*, 1954. Steel rods. 14" high. Private collection, Paris.

320 David Hare: *Thirsty Man.* 1946. Bronze. 30" high.

321 Enrico Donati: *Bolero.* 1943. Oil on canvas. 40 × 30". Coll. Marquis de Cuevas.

322 André Masson: *La Belle Italienne.* 1943. Oil on canvas. Coll. Sidney Janis Gallery, New York.

323 Leonora Carrington: *The Temptation of Saint Anthony.* 1946. Oil on canvas.

324 Leonora Carrington in her studio in Mexico, 1946. Photograph reproduced in the catalogue of the *Bel Ami* film competition, edited by the American Foundation of Art, Washington, D.C.

325 Matta: *Elminonde.* Oil on canvas. 49 3/8 × 37 1/2". Coll. Pierre Matisse Gallery, New York.

326 Matta: *The Glazer's Achievement.* Drawing. 1947.

327 Matta: *Composition.* 1945.

327 Matta: Drawing for *Le Jour est un Attentat*, by Charles Duits and Leonora Carrington, in the review *VVV*, no. 2-3, New York, 1943.

328 Matta: *The Prophetor.* 1954. Oil on canvas. 118 1/2 × 79". Photo J. Michalon.

329 Arshile Gorky: *The Liver is the Coxcomb.* 1944. Oil on canvas. 72 3/4 × 98". Albright Art Gallery, Buffalo, New York. Photo Sidney Janis Gallery, New York.

330 In Hans Richter's studio in New York, 1953. From left to right: Marcel Duchamp, Max Ernst, Hans Richter.

331 Hans Richter: A scene from his film *8 × 8*, shot on the lawn of Richter's house in Southbury, Connecticut. In the background, sitting in the hollow tree, Marcel Duchamp acts as referee for the game of chess in progress.

332 Max Ernst: *Chemical Nuptials.* 1948. Oil on canvas. 25 3/4 × 59 1/4". Private collection, Paris.

334 Jean Arp: *Mediterranean Relief.* 1941. Marble. 11 1/2 × 8 1/2". Carnegie Institute, Pittsburgh.

LIST OF COLOUR PLATES

Coll. Roland Penrose, London. A 1916 composition (period of the 'Metaphysical Interiors') carries the same title *The Jewish Angel*. It also forms part of the Penrose collection. Photo R. B. Fleming.

61 Francis Picabia: *Amorous Procession*. 1917. Oil on cardboard. 38 1/4 × 29 1/8". Coll. Mr and Mrs Morton G. Neumann, Chicago.

72 Man Ray: *Legend*, 1916. Oil on canvas. 51 3/8 × 35 1/2". Coll. J. B. Urvater, Brussels. Photo Giraudon.

74 Jean Arp: *Torso with Flower Head*. 1924. Oil painted wood relief. 35 × 16 3/4". Owned by the artist. Photo Roger Roche - Éditions du Seuil.

83 Max Ernst: *The Fusible Room Snail and the Heart of the Light Harvester-Woman Racing (Le limaçon de chambre fusible et le cœur de la moissonneuse légère à la course)*. 1921. *Collage*. 10 1/4 × 8". Coll. Mme Simone Collinet, Paris. Roger PhotoRoche - Éditions du Seuil.

110 Marcel Duchamp: *Bride*. 1912. Oil on canvas. 35 1/2 × 21 3/4". Philadelphia Museum of Art (Arensberg collection). Photo Charles P. Mills.

119 Max Ernst: *Relief*. 1927. Moulded and coloured plaster. 8 3/8 × 9 1/8". Coll. Henri Pastoureau, France. Twelve numbered copies of this relief exist, each painted differently. This copy is number 12. Photo Roger Roche - Éditions du Seuil.

129 Max Ernst: *The Orange-Blossom*. 1931. *Collage*. Owned by the artist. Photo J. Lacoste.

140 Francis Picabia: *Hera*. 1928. Tempera on cardboard. 41 1/2 × 29 5/8". Coll. Gaston Kahn, Paris. Photo Roger Roche - Éditions du Seuil.

151 Joan Miró: *Woman Standing*. 1937. Oil on paper. 29 5/8 × 22 1/8". Coll. Pierre Matisse Gallery, New York.

166 Yves Tanguy: *Genesis*. 1926. Oil on canvas. 39 3/8 × 31 7/8". Private collection, Paris. Photo Roger Roche - Éditions du Seuil.

169 Yves Tanguy: *The Ribbon of Extremes*. 1932. Oil on wood. 13 3/4 × 17 3/4". Coll. Roland Penrose, London. Photo R. B. Fleming.

180 René Magritte: *The Rape*. 1934. Oil on canvas. 28 1/2 × 21". Coll. George Melly, London. There are two other versions of this picture: one painted about 1945, during the artist's 'impressionist' period, the other a 1934 gouache made as a cover illustration for André Breton's *Qu'est-ce que le Surréalisme?* (René Henriquez, Brussels, 1934). Photo Wallace Heaton.

182 René Magritte: *The Reckless Sleeper*. c. 1930. Oil on canvas. 43 1/2 × 31 5/8". Coll. Claude Spaak, Paris.

191 Pablo Picasso: *Abstraction, with Cloudy Blue Sky*. 1930. Oil on canvas. 26 1/8 × 19 3/4". Art Institute, Chicago.

201 Salvador Dali: *The Lugubrious Game*. 1929. Oil on panel. 16 1/2 × 10 1/2". Private collection, Paris. Photo Roger Roche - Éditions du Seuil.

212 Salvador Dali: *The Persistence of Memory*. 1931. Oil on canvas. 10 × 14". Museum of Modern Art, New York.

222 Salvador Dali: *Six Apparitions of Lenin on a Piano*. 1933. Oil on canvas. Musée d'Art Moderne, Paris.

239 Victor Brauner: *Composition in Wax*. 1946. Wax and oil on canvas. 11 1/2 × 9 1/8". Coll. Dr A. Acker, Paris. Photo Roger Roche - Éditions du Seuil.

257 Joan Miró: *Person in the Presence of Nature*. 1935. Gouache on cardboard. 29 1/2 × 41 1/2". Philadelphia Museum of Art (Arensberg collection). Photo Charles P. Mills.

268 Oscar Dominguez: *Memory of the Future*. 1939. Oil on canvas. 24 × 19 3/4". Private collection, Paris. Photo Roger Roche - Éditions du Seuil.

277 Paul Delvaux: *The Echo*. 1943. Oil on canvas. 41 1/2 × 51 3/8". Coll. Claude Spaak, Paris. Photo Roger Roche - Éditions du Seuil.

288 Matta: *Here, Sir Fire, Eat*. 1942. Oil on canvas. 55 1/4 × 43 1/2". Coll. James Thrall Soby, New Canaan, Connecticut.

305 Wifredo Lam: *The Caribbean Parade*. 1945. Oil on canvas. 49 3/8 × 43 1/2". Coll. Pierre Matisse Gallery, New York.

316 Yves Tanguy: *Indefinite Divisibility*. 1942. Oil on canvas. 40 × 35". Albright Art Gallery, Buffalo, New York.

337 Matta: *The Angry One*. 1958. Oil on canvas. 28 7/8 × 23 3/4". Coll. Max Clarac-Sérou, Paris. Photo Roger Roche - Éditions du Seuil.

340 Yves Tanguy: *Where Are You?* 1954. Oil on canvas. 10 1/8 × 7 7/8". Coll. Kay Sage Tanguy, Woodbury, Connecticut. Photo Alex Darrow.

345 Marcel Jean and Henri Pastoureau: *Poem-Flottage*. 1956. Oil on paper. 19 3/4 × 25 3/4". Private collection, Paris. Photo Roger Roche - Éditions du Seuil.

351 Jean Arp: *Symmetrical Form with the Flakes of Chance*. 1955. Painted wood relief.

354 Max Ernst: *The Mysteries of Love*. 1955. Oil on canvas. 28 3/4 × 23 3/4". Owned by the artist. Photo J. Lacoste.

360 Joan Miró: *The Ladders in Wheels of Fire Cross the Azure*. 1953. Oil on canvas. 41 1/2 × 35". Coll. Pierre Matisse Gallery, New York.

The book jacket has been designed after a cupboard painted by Marcel Jean in 1942.

GENERAL INDEX

Footnotes ('n' following the page number) are indicated only where the artist's or author's name does not also appear in the text of that page. The abbreviation 'per' indicates that the item is a periodical.

IMPRIMERIE GEORGES LANG - PARIS